The
MUSE
That Soared

TALES OF THE SISKIYOU SMOKEJUMPERS

PAUL FATTIG

HELLGATE PRESS   ASHLAND, OREGON

Hellgate Press
PO Box 3531
Ashland, OR 97520
For Information: *sales@hellgatepress.com*

ISBN: 978-1-954163-47-8

Cover and interior design: L. Redding
Cover photos: Doug Beck

Printed and bound in the United States of America
First edition 10 9 8 7 6 5 4 3 2 1

Praise for Paul Fattig's *The Mouse That Soared*

"The story of Allen Owen, aka Mouse – a 4' 11" combat marine and legendary smokejumper, would be enough to make Paul Fattig's The Mouse that Soared a stirring read. Owen lived an inspired and inspiring life, overcoming seemingly impossible obstacles almost to the end. But the book is chock full of startling characters and high adventure that together make this a welcome addition to the literature by and about those who leap from the sky to take on wildland fire."

—**John N. Maclean**, author of *Fire on the Mountain* and *Home Waters*

"It is my privilege to recommend and endorse Paul Fattig's new book The Mouse that Soared: Tales of the Siskiyou Smokejumpers, a nonfiction account of an elite group of men, now historically remembered, as the ultimate standard of today's forest fire fighters. I have known Paul as a friend and former colleague on two newspapers for nearly 50 years. As a feature writer his research and personal adaptation is among the best in the business, and this collection of personal tales and comradery puts the reader on the fire line."

—**Kenneth Millman**, Former Special Publications Editor
for *The Miami Herald*

"As a boy growing up in the Illinois Valley of Southern Oregon, Paul Fattig often looked up into a deep blue sky as it filled with International Orange and white parachutes. These were the Siskiyou Smokejumpers. Paul and his young cohorts admired these parachuting firefighters for their courage and noble qualities. Sometimes they went to the jump spots and watched as the jumpers laughed and gathered their gear. I doubt that anyone there thought that someday that little boy would write a book detailing the big heart and spirit of the Siskiyou Smokejumper base and some of its' most memorable characters. But The Mouse that Soared *is exactly that. With a keen eye for deeply human stories Paul has produced a work that embodies the best of what we hope for in our fellow man. The German philosopher and playwright, Geothe, once wrote that, 'In Boldness there is Genius and Magic.' This fine piece of writing is a living testament to just how true that can be.*

—**Murry A. Taylor**, Veteran Smokejumper and Author of
Jumping Fire: A Smokejumper's Memoir of Fighting Wildfire.

☞

"To write a book about Mouse Owen, you must describe his universe. Paul Fattig has done that and more. You learn Mouse's path in getting to Cave Junction. And the stories of the people with whom he worked and played are so genuine, you feel a part of the jump base. Or you wish you could have been. I was fortunate enough to meet Mouse and he was bigger than life. You never forget him.

—Abigail Kimbell, US Forest Service Chief Emerita

"In The Mouse That Soared, Paul Fattig has captured the elan, the adventurism, the courage and, yes, the humor of the West's elite smokejumper corps."

—Michael Thoele, Author of Fire Line: Summer Battles of the West

"From 1943 to 1981, the backwoods of southwest Oregon were well protected against wildfires by the Siskiyou Smokejumpers. They were a particularly useful bunch of oddballs. One has to be a bit off in the head to be a smokejumper — someone who dons a parachute and grabs a pulaski, dives out of a plane and lands next to a burning forest and sets to the task of putting the fire out. God bless Paul Fattig for preserving their particularly colorful history. Mr. Fattig's book is history preserved. To read these stories, which are normally only told among their own, is the closest thing to being there as it gets. I strongly recommend reading it while beside a crackling campfire, somewhere deep in a forest, where the only sounds are a distant coyote and you chuckling at the amazing tales of the Siskiyou Smokejumpers. Their reputation as being weird, rowdy and surprisingly useful was true. Paul really showed his interviewing skill with having squeezed so much information from them."

—Brian Ballou, Former USFS firefighter, ODF fire information officer, and the founding editor of Wildland Firefighter magazine

CONTENTS

I am indebted to all the smokejumpers and others who kindly and patiently submitted to oftentimes long interviews for this book. A special thanks to former Siskiyou smokejumper Gary Buck, writer and former smokejumper Murry Taylor and longtime friend and journalistic colleague Damian Mann for poring over the rough draft of this book. Their thoughtful suggestions and observations were much appreciated.

And a big thanks to all firefighters, both wildland and structural, for combating the fires threatening much of the West during recent fire seasons. They are today's superheroes.

Also by Paul Fattig & Hellgate Press:

Up Sterling Creek Without a Paddle:
Confessions of a Recovering Journalist

Madstone: The True Tale of World War I
Conscientious Objectors Alfred and Charlie Fattig
and Their Oregon Wilderness Hideout

INTRODUCTION

A VID BOOK READERS WILL RECOGNIZE the title of this
tome as a tip of the hat to *The Mouse That Roared*, the 1955
novel by the gifted Irish-American writer Leonard Wibberly. His humorous book was a fictitious satire of the Cold War featuring a tiny
but muscular country called the Duchy of Grand Fenwick which didn't
take any guff from the international powers that be. Like the feisty
duchy, the equally spirited Siskiyou smokejumpers also didn't take
crap, especially when it came to bureaucrats.

But this book is nonfiction. Its title is intended to be a double en-
tendre to celebrate both the remarkable man dubbed "Mouse" as well
as the Mighty Mouse in the form of the Siskiyou Smokejumper Base
and all its impressive inhabitants.I have no doubt the late Mr. Wibberly would have been favorably impressed by every jumper dropping
in on the following pages. After all, they demonstrated courage and
humor in abundance.

If you are looking for a person to blame for sparking my interest in
writing a book about the airborne firefighters, look no further than
former smokejumper Bob Wilcox. Although I shoulder the responsibility for going along with the suggestion, he was definitely the idea
man. It all began one day when my wife, Maureen, and I dropped in
one Saturday in September of 2015 at the Siskiyou Smokejumper
Base Museum. Bob, who had jumped out of the smokejumper base
in Redding, California, was serving as the weekend host at the
Siskiyou base. His wife, Lucille, a friend and client of Maureen's,
had invited us to stop by when we were in the vicinity. Located in

southwest Oregon's Illinois Valley some four miles south of Cave Junction, the base was added to the National Register of Historic Places in 2010.

I had never met Bob but knew him by reputation when he was a U. S. Forest Service district ranger in the Rogue River-Siskiyou National Forest. Well respected, he was known for not suffering fools gladly. I was fairly well acquainted with the base, having lived near it as a youngster and later visiting it numerous times as a journalist when Siskiyou smokejumpers were still stationed there and fighting to keep it open. They were also known for not suffering fools, gladly or otherwise.

But I hadn't been to the base since it became a smokejumper museum two decades earlier, long after it closed as an active base at the end of the 1981 fire season. In a herculean effort led by veteran Siskiyou smokejumper Gary Buck and other former smokejumpers, along with local community leaders like Roger Brandt, they have created a wonderful museum which makes visitors feel as though they are stepping back in time. It's easy to imagine jumpers hustling out of the bunkhouse, jumping into a Beechcraft and roaring down the tarmac en route to a wildfire. As a history buff who has spent blissful hours in historical sites from Ireland to Vietnam as well as visiting countless stateside museums, including a wonderful week at the "nation's attic," the incomparable Smithsonian Institution in Washington, D.C., I thoroughly enjoy the authentic smokejumper museum and visit when I am in the area. If you are ever in southwest Oregon, the museum is not to be missed. It is open from March 15 through Nov. 15. Admission is free but donations are gratefully accepted.

As an added bonus, your docent will be a former smokejumper who knows of what he speaks. Like all the veteran jumpers who volunteer their time and knowledge, Bob Wilcox was an excellent guide. After all, he had lived in the world of smokejumping. He also knew I was a recovering print journalist with one book published and another well underway.

"There is a book here if you are interested in taking it on," Bob observed as we walked around the base. "Everything here has a story.

The Siskiyou base was one of the four original bases created in the United States in 1943. And it is unique among all smokejumper bases. It had some truly remarkable people."

Or words to that effect.

The more he talked, the more I realized he was onto something. As a product of the Illinois Valley, I already had a lot of respect for Siskiyou smokejumpers. By the time we got to the parachute loft, I was thinking seriously about the possibilities of a book on the storied Siskiyou parachuting firefighters. Sealing my fate were the jump suits hanging there, each with a name plate all but shouting out personal histories that needed to be retained for posterity.

However, much has been written about the colorful base over the years, including three volumes of the *Book of Gobi* which contains reflective stories written by former Siskiyou jumpers. They were edited by Stan "Clancy" Collins, a former Siskiyou jumper who shepherds words well. If you enjoy a good read, don't forget to pick up copies when you drop by the museum. Like a visit to the base museum, they do not disappoint.

But I needed to follow a different path than the one taken by the *Gobi* books, approaching the Siskiyou base history from the perspective of one who grew up in the shadow of the jumpers, having watched them jump and witnessed their positive impact on the valley as well as the Pacific Northwest. The book would also have to be written for those who had never leaped out of a perfectly good airplane to fight a wildfire.

Indeed, this volume would be redundant if it followed the same route as the *Gobi* books. Besides,with so many stories to tell, this could quickly mushroom into a volume that would make *War and Peace* read like a short story. The jumper tales would be superfluous, causing the most alert reader to start dozing. In the book game, it's bad form for the reader to nod off, you understand.

Harley Patrick, my publisher, suggested loosely focusing on one unique jumper while weaving in the stories of other airborne firefighters who either jumped with him or had a connection with him and the historic base. That jumper would be the thread binding their stories together, he noted. Smart fellow, Harley.

Obviously, I also needed to find a unique individual with a special spirit of adventure, one who not only shrugged at the first hint of danger but whose life experiences were broad enough to carry the weight of a book about a physically small but historically big base which contributed to the national annals of smokejumping. If he were to serve as a strong bond tying the smokejumper tales together, he would also need to have spent the lion's share of his jumping career at the base.

More than half of the 434 men who jumped out of the base have made that final leap into the great beyond. The rest are scattered across the country. Some made a career out of stopping threatening wildfires while others went on to pursue other adventures. Among the latter would be future educators, medical doctors, attorneys, an astronaut and a rocket scientist, a superior court judge and at least one man of the cloth. They were an eclectic bunch capable of reaching high achievements, the Siskiyou smokejumpers.

With so many impressive candidates to pick from those stationed at the base over the years, selecting the central character was a difficult choice. There were the first smokejumpers who helped open the base in 1943, all conscientious objectors, followed by legendary World War II veterans like Jim Allen, Richard J. "Dick" Courson, Cliff Marshall, Robert "Bob" Nolan and Danny On. There were also veterans from the Korean or Vietnam conflicts, impressive folks like Gary Buck, ace pilot Hal Ewing, Tom "Trooper Tom" Emonds and Henry "Buzz" Florip.

Roughly half of the jumpers were military veterans, giving them a bit of a head start over non-veterans since a smokejumper base is run somewhat like a military unit, albeit during idle times a bit like the old *M*A*S*H* television show. But being a veteran was definitely not a prerequisite as demonstrated by the aforementioned conscientious objectors.

Nor can we can't forget folks such as base manager Delos "Dee" Dutton and extraordinary jumpers like Eldo "Mick" Swift and Dave

Laws. Or future astronaut Stuart Russo, rocket scientist Chuck Mansfield and world renowned mountaineer Willi Unsoeld. Then there were the regionally-raised young men who became jumpers in the form of Dave Atkin, brothers Rod and Steve Baumann, George Custer, Rick Dees, Lee Gossett, Mike Mann, Pat McNally, Gary Mills, brothers Bob and Willie Lowden, Wes Nicholson, Rick Oliver, Ray Ospovich, Gary Thornhill, Ron Versteeg and others, including the Sunny Valley boys in the form of brothers Jim, Fred and Don "Mike" Cramer. I came to know many of the jumpers when we were all urchins getting into mischief and other monkey business. By the by, the smokejumpers represented the best among us local yokels.

There were super smokejumpers among those already mentioned. Several of the folks who wore smokejumper gear when they were strapping young men recommended that Swift be the focal point of the book. Others suggested Allen, Buck, Emonds, Mills, Nolan or Thornhill, all outstanding leapers when it came to jumping into smoke. No question they did their band of brothers proud. Their lasting legacies were well earned.

Obviously, my dilemma was I had an embarrassment of riches: there were ample heroic smokejumpers. Everyone I interviewed for this book had interesting tales to tell. Indeed, many warranted a book on his life and times. Sadly, time and space prevented me from interviewing everyone still alive who jumped out of the base. Perhaps they could be in a sequel.

The jumper I decided to weave throughout the book was neither the biggest nor the baddest. Yet, like the base, he was small but lived large. He was also feisty and outspoken, a gung-ho fellow who charged challenges head on. With his big heart and sense of humor, he stood tall among his brethren. His name was Allen Dale "Mouse" Owen, a Marine Corps combat veteran who was 4-foot-11. Although the shortest smokejumper in the nation's history, he stood out among the airborne firefighters. He was also a jumper I knew, albeit only at the journalistic level.

Mouse and the base where he was a rookie in 1970 shared many traits. Both were born in 1943 and died in 1981. Small they both may have been but they were strong, vocal and productive as well as endlessly entertaining. If there is such a thing as destiny, they were made for each other. And both were admired and respected by those fortunate enough to have known them.

To reiterate, this book is not centered on Mouse but on the base and many of the jumpers who lived and worked at the base. As you would expect, smokejumping attracts folks who live life with a certain élan. Again, many other books could be written about the Siskiyou smokejumpers. This book is simply one take on this impressive group.

You undoubtedly noticed no mention of female smokejumpers at the base. There were none, albeit Siskiyou smokejumpers sought to recruit female jumpers near the end of the base's reign but were unsuccessful. However, as you shall see in the following pages, thanks in part to Mouse's active support for allowing women to be given a chance to join the smokejumping ranks, that ceiling was broken, although not at the Siskiyou base.

Since they were created, smokejumpers have prided themselves in the fact you were able to do the hard and often dangerous work or you are out on your posterior. No exceptions. One trait I've always liked about smokejumpers is that they look you in the eye. There is not a whiff of snake oil in the whole bunch. As a former journalist who has sniffed more than his fair share of political snake oil over the years, I very much appreciated not having to suffer from that foul odor while writing this book. There were some unique personalities but I have yet to meet one who was totally barking mad. True, a few may have bayed at the moon a time or two after a hard night of imbibing.

Incidentally, as one who was reared in the Illinois Valley and having always heard the base referred to as the Siskiyou Smokejumper Base, I am sticking to that moniker. Since most bases are referred to by the name of their nearest town, veteran jumpers often refer to the Siskiyou as the Cave Junction base, or CJ for short. I hope they will forgive me that formality. But I have adopted a verb used by seasoned smokejumper who liked to talk about the year they "rookied." I trust Don Orton, our fine English teacher at Kerby Elementary School, would have forgiven me for my continued butchering of the language he loved and cherished.

Nor will some thin-skinned readers be amused by several crude, lewd and rude subjects and incidents that pop up in the following pages. But keep in mind these are smokejumpers, not saints. Still, they have been kept to a minimum. You can avoid those short sections by heeding the "Fair warning" notices strategically placed ahead of the potentially offensive paragraphs.

Please humor me for periodically parachuting in to set the scene or offer an aside to give Oregon-challenged readers a fuller understanding of the remarkable people and unique place that comprised the Siskiyou Smokejumper Base when it was on the front lines of the wildfire battle. I can promise you that once you come to know many of the former Siskiyou smokejumpers, you will not soon forget their indefatigable spirit, audacious humor and contributions to the nation's history of wildland firefighting.

1

FIRE ON THE MOUNTAIN

E ARLY ON THE SWELTERING AFTERNOON of June 29,
1965, a thunderstorm rumbled through the northern end of the
scenic Illinois Valley nestled in Oregon's southwest corner. As
thunderstorms go, it wasn't bristling with firepower. But there were
a few sizzling streaks of bright yellow lightning flashing out of the
dark anvil-shaped clouds, followed seconds later by window-rattling
kabooms and a refreshing but short summer shower. However, unlike a really cranky summer storm, there was no car-denting hail,
no wind gusts flattening trees, no torrential rainfall sending gully-
washers roaring through canyons.

After Mother Nature completed her hissy fit and the storm evapo-
rated into the ether, the sweet fragrance that invariably lingers in the
aftermath of a light summer rain filled the air. A few hours after the
storm, it was as though the relatively small tempest had never happened. The picturesque river valley once again basked under the warm
glow of a cerulean sky. It was turning into another idyllic summer afternoon in southwestern Oregon.

But a thin wisp of smoke could be seen rising from the northern end of Mansfield Mountain just northwest of the sleepy little mill town of Kerby. A lightning bolt had struck earth, igniting a tall pine tree on the rugged mountaintop. Since the storm had not dumped enough rain to quench the dry woods, the down strike hit pay dirt. Although rocky and sparsely covered with vegetation, Mansfield has enough trees and brush to fuel a wildfire. If the blaze took off, it could quickly spread, threatening not only the local forests but rural homes just east of the Illinois River which flows through the belly of the valley. The weather had been hot and dry for weeks. The fire had the potential to take a hike down the mountain and become known as the Mansfield Fire of 1965.

However, the fire never had a chance to make a name for itself. Not long after the sky cleared, the drone of an airplane could be heard overhead. It was a C-45 Twin Beech, an aircraft first introduced in 1937 by Beech Aircraft Corp. of Wichita, Kansas. Although its speed would generally top out at about 190 mph, providing there was no head wind, it was considered a reliable workhorse by the jumpers.

The slow-moving plane circled the mountain as the crew dropped drift streamers to determine the wind conditions below. The twin-engine plane then appeared to be lumbering off, heading away from the small yet growing fire. But its work wasn't done. Far from it.

Banking the lumbering plane in a wide circle over nearby Eight Dollar Mountain, the pilot brought the aircraft around, lining up with Mansfield which lies like a giant loaf of bread on the western edge of the valley. As the aircraft approached the fire, what looked like a bundle could be seen dropping from its belly. Falling like a stone at first, it suddenly appeared to jerk to a halt in midair after a parachute popped open. Resembling a huge orange and white blossom, the parachute descended slowly with the bundle morphing into an airborne firefighter. After a few more passes, the aircraft dropped another bundle which would turn into another humanoid dangling from a parachute.

Descending upon the small blaze were smokejumpers from the

Siskiyou Smokejumper Base, a U.S. Forest Service facility located at the southern end of the Illinois Valley. The smokejumpers landed close to the small fire, quickly put it out and mopped up. Incidentally, smokejumpers never jump on fires because of the inherent danger but also since the convection from the heat would carry them away from the blaze. In any case, they later hiked out, wading across the Illinois River to reach Highway 99 where they were picked up by a Forest Service rig and taken back to their base to await another fire call.

To a 13-year-old like me witnessing the smokejumpers landing on Mansfield that day, they were heroes. The word is too quickly applied these days but it was an apt description for the Siskiyou smokejumpers in that unsettled time and rugged place where positive role models were not overly abundant. In my juvenile mind, they represented the ABC's of champions: Adventurous, Brave and Competent. Few other jobs reached such lofty levels, figuratively and literally. All these years later, smokejumpers still rank mighty high in my estimation.

Our little gray house sat on an area called Sauers Flat which, as the name implies, is a level geographic area in the bottom of the river valley cradled by mountains. Named after the legendary Sauer family who had long farmed the rich river bottom, it lies just north of Kerby and directly east of Mansfield Mountain which juts up west of the Illinois Valley's flat belly. The Sauers arrived in the region around 1870, settling on the flat's fertile farmland in 1919, according to Nick Sauer, a well-liked classmate of mine through Kerby Elementary School and Illinois Valley High School, class of 1969.

From our house, you could see the wisp of smoke rising from the lightning-caused fire. But I probably would not have known about it had not a childhood chum named Russell "Rusty" Earl called to tell me on our dial-up, party-line phone about the fire and the plane dropping the smokejumpers. Rusty's family lived a quarter mile north of our little abode, giving them a better view of the firefight.

Having grown bored of listening in on the party line conversations to pass the time, I ran outside and saw the last firefighting parachutist drifting down. For a kid in Kerby, life did not get more exciting than that. Had James Bond dropped out of the sky, the debonair spy from MI-6 could not have provoked more excitement. I was gobsmacked. You have to understand this was a period and place where the purchase of a new wheelbarrow was news. Indeed, the smokejumper landing was even more exciting than the day my big brother's 4-H pig got loose and we spent a wild afternoon chasing the fat squealer down.

The next morning, Rusty and I literally ran to the top of Mansfield to check out the aftermath of the firefight. One of five children of the widow Gladys Fattig, I had virtually no adult supervision during the summer. I could spend all day and night on the mountain. But Rusty's strict parents required that he be back home by 3 p.m. so we were racing the clock. We figured the smokejumpers would have left their parachutes which we intended to collect as souvenirs and give us bragging rights among our adolescent peers. We did not know the Siskiyou jumpers routinely packed out their parachutes and reused them. While there were no parachutes we did find a drift streamer which had been dropped to gauge the wind. As for the fire, it had burned several pine trees and some brush. Although we ran back down the mountain, Rusty got back a few minutes after his curfew and was immediately grounded. But we both returned to our respective homes forever impressed with smokejumpers and their ability to land on a rugged mountain and quickly extinguish a fire.

At the time, I didn't know a Twin Beech from a turkey vulture. The information about the aircraft and the jump was mined from the year-end reports kept in the logbook at the Siskiyou smokejumper museum. It indicates that was the aircraft flying jumpers out of the Siskiyou Smokejumper Base in 1965.

"Pilot Williams and Sheley dropped Hopkins and Kirkley on the Tennessee Mountain fire, and Cook and Hamilton to Sauers Ridge," according to the report.Ralph Williams was the pilot while Charles "Chuck" Sheley served as spotter, the veteran smokejumper who picks the landing site. The 1965 season summary reports the jumpers were Keith L. Cook of Houston, Texas, and Clifford Hamilton of Oakland, Calif. Hamilton, Kirkley and Sheley will parachute in on later chapters.

By the by,the name Sauers Ridge puzzled me at first since it is a reference to a geographic entity that does not exist in the region. But the other fire was on Tennessee Mountain which is immediately south of Mansfield Mountain. The two geographic features are connected by Free and Easy Pass, the headwaters to Free and Easy Creek. What's more, Sauers Flat is immediately east of Mansfield. As mentioned earlier, Mansfield Mountain rises like a ridge west of Sauers Flat, making it conceivable someone from outside the area referred to it as a ridge and tossed in the Sauers moniker to complete the misnomer. Since the log book reports no other fires in the vicinity during that era, the fire doubtlessly was the one Rusty and I checked out on Mansfield Mountain.

In the small world department, one of the Siskiyou airborne firefighters jumping later that day was the future rocket scientist mentioned in the prologue. Smokejumper Charles "Chuck" Mansfield was the great, great grandson of Moses Mansfield for whom Mansfield Mountain was named. Around 1860, Moses and a brother settled at the north end of what would eventually become known as Sauers Flat. The future NASA scientist was one of four other jumpers the aircraft picked up after returning to the base before returning to the air to deliver the jumpers to two small fires on the Gold Beach District that day. It would have been serendipity to have him jumping on the mountain named after his ancestor but sometimes facts get in the way of a good story. No matter. We will return to the brilliant Chuck Mansfield anon.

During the 38 summers it operated, the Siskiyou base would deploy smokejumpers on 1,445 fires for a total 5,390 fire jumps, according to Forest Service records. That was an average 142 deployments per year jumping on fires. Although the lion's share of their deployments would be in the Pacific Northwest, the Siskiyou smokejumpers fought fires from Alaska to Virginia. How many forests, wildlife, rural homes and human lives were saved by Siskiyou smokejumpers stopping the fires when they were small is incalculable.What is known is the inspiration for the base's creation. But we will need to go back nearly 80 years to a time when the base was a twinkle in Uncle Sam's eye.

2

INCENDIARY ATTACK

H AD IT NOT BEEN FOR World War II and a daring Japanese pilot named Nobuo Fujita, the Siskiyou Smokejumper Base may very well not have been built. After all, the base is barely more than two dozen air miles from the Pacific Ocean whose influence generally kept the coastal mountains damp with rain and misty fog, albeit that climate pattern appears to be changing.However, back in the early years of the 20th Century, coastal wildfires were infrequent and seldom threatening. Most wildfire flare ups during that era were farther inland.

Yet it was the proximity to the coast that made the region potentially vulnerable to fire-bombing attacks by the Japanese during the war. A warrant flying officer in the Imperial Japanese Navy, Fujita came up with the ingenuous idea to employ a submarine-based floatplane – an aircraft equipped with pontoons – to attack the west coast of the United States. His rationale for the attacks is that it would draw American military resources away from the Pacific Theater where they were making life difficult for the Japanese. Historians tell us the Doolittle raid of April 18, 1942, on the Japanese capital of Tokyo and other cities, the first such strike on the Japanese homeland during the war, had shaken the confidence of the Japanese. However, like their football-playing American counterparts, they knew the best defense is often a good offense.

Not only was Fujita's idea approved by his superiors but a Yoko-suka E14Y seaplane known as a *Glen* was attached to the long-range Japanese submarine *I-25*, the vessel to which Fujita was assigned. The *I-25* was a submarine aircraft carrier, a seemingly contradictory term. Yet it had a water-tight plane hangar for the disassembled aircraft and a catapult immediately forward of the conning tower. Although equipped with only one aircraft, it was certainly capable of launching an aerial attack.

By the time the Japanese sub began prowling the waters off the coast of Brookings, Fujita, who became a pilot in 1933, was already a veteran pilot of the little floatplane launched from the *I-25*. Based in the Marshall Islands, its mission was to snoop around enemy bases and sink an occasional enemy ship.

After refueling at its base in January of 1942, the *I-25* with its crew of about 100 was deployed to the east coast of Australia to reconnoiter its major harbors, including Sidney and Melbourne. Early on the morning of Feb. 17, 1942, Fujita flew a reconnaissance mission over Sidney, followed by another sortie over Melbourne on Feb. 26. By mid-March of that year, he was flying similar scouting missions over New Zealand ports.

Returning to its Marshall Island base at the end of March, the sub-marine was refueled and restocked while the crew took a short break. By May, the *I-25* was prowling around the small U. S. military base at Kodiak Island in Alaska in preparation for what would be an inva-sion of the Aleutian Island chain. On the 28th, Fujita was sent aloft once more, this time to fly a reconnaissance mission over Kodiak.

Heading south to Oregon, the *I-25* commander wisely trailed Amer-ican fishing boats to avoid minefields and sailed into the mouth of the Columbia River. It was there late on the night of June 21, 1942, that the submarine surfaced and began shelling the tiny Army base of Fort

Stevens near Astoria. With Fujita standing on deck, the submarine crew fired 17 shells from its 140-millimeter deck gun toward where they believed the fort was located. But the fort commander was just as smart as his counterpart in the submarine. Knowing the chances of hitting the vessel was virtually nil and that the muzzle flashes from the fort's guns would reveal the army installation's exact position, the shrewd Army commander did not return fire. Remember, the coast was blacked out in wartime out of concern for such an attack. As a result, the Japanese bombardment did little more than tear up a baseball field. In essence, you could say the game was a draw, although the Yanks' home field was battered by the visiting team.

However, the *I-25* did make history by launching the only attack on a military installation in the contiguous United States during World War II. Alaska and Hawaii were also attacked but they were territories at the time and would not become states until 1959. In any case, the *I-25* submarine's biggest claim to warfare fame was not its attack on Fort Stevens. That was yet to come.

Indeed, its actions on Sept. 9, 1942, were what directly led to the Siskiyou Smokejumper Base being established in the Illinois Valley. Just as the sun was about to rise over the coastal clouds that morning, the submarine surfaced just west of the town of Brookings off the southwestern Oregon coast. At 6:00 a.m. that day, Fujita, flying with petty officer Okuda Shoji who served as a spotter, launched the little floatplane. This time they were carrying two 168-pound incendiary bombs. Their mission was to ignite forest fires and spark panic.

Fujita dropped one incendiary bomb on Wheeler Ridge near Mount Emily, a mountain some ten miles east of Brookings, starting a small fire. It is unknown where the other bomb fell since it didn't spark a wildfire. Unfortunately for those dropping the incendiary bombs, the local forest had been dampened by a good soaking the night before. It was also on the tail end of fire season that year.

Atop the Mount Emily fire lookout in the Siskiyou Nation Forest, Howard Gardner and Bob Larson spotted Fujita's plane and reported it. Ground based firefighters were deployed to the Mount Emily fire which was reported around noon that day. It was quickly extinguished. Some 60 pounds of bomb fragments were discovered and turned over to Army investigators. Folks in Brookings also saw the plane which flew over the community as it traveled to and from the forest. A U.S. Army Air Corps patrol plane attacked the submarine off the coast of Port Orford but did no major damage although it forced the vessel to hide on the ocean floor some 250 feet below the surface.

But Fujita wasn't done yet. On Sept. 29, he flew for more than an hour east of Cape Blanco, dropping two more incendiary bombs. He reported seeing flames but no wildfires were reported from that sortie.

Although his explosive devices had little physical impact, he was the only enemy pilot to drop bombs on the contiguous United States during World War II. The objective of the incendiary bombs, like the balloon bomb campaign, was to divert attention and military resources from the war in the Pacific.

Back in Japan,Fujita was regarded as a hero. The *Asahi Shimbun*, arguably Japan's most respected newspaper at the time, carried a page one article on Sept. 17, 1942, declaring, "Incendiary Bomb Dropped on Oregon State. First Air Raid on Mainland America. Big Shock to Americans."

The latter, of course, was wishful war-time propaganda. Apart from folks along the West coast, the American public took little notice of the raid. But the U.S. war department – this was before Uncle Sam renamed it the Department of Defense in 1949 to put a peaceful spin on its moniker – was up in arms. It was quickly decided that airborne firefighters in the form of smokejumpers were needed in the West where they could be quickly deployed to battle the blazes set by enemy forces, be they incendiary bombs dropped by airplane or balloon bombs sent from afar.

After his two Oregon bombing raids, Fujita continued flying for the Imperial Japanese Navy, largely as a reconnaissance pilot, although he began training kamikaze pilots late in 1944. Following the war, he owned a hardware store in Japan and later worked for a metal fabrication company.Okuda died in the Philippines during the war. As for I-25, it was destroyed by the destroyer USS *Patterson* near the New Hebrides on Sept. 3, 1943, nearly a year after Fujita dropped his first incendiary bombs on the Siskiyou National Forest.

Before Fujita died of lung cancer in Japan on Sept. 30, 1997, at age 85, he visited Brookings several times as a civilian promoting peace between Japan and the United States. His first visit was in 1962 at the behest of the Brookings Junior Chamber of Commerce as an effort to gin up publicity for the annual Azalea Festival held over Memorial Day weekend. After all, having the pilot visit on the 20th anniversary of his having bombed Wheeler Ridge would definitely draw attraction. But memories of the war were still a little raw on both sides of the Pacific. Some WWII veterans in the region were upset that someone they still considered the enemy was being invited to the area he had bombed. Yet other fellow veterans countered the war was over and it was time to promote peace.President John F. Kennedy and Oregon Governor Mark O. Hatfield, both WWII veterans, wrote in support of his visit. Still, representatives of the Japanese Consulate in Portland visited Brookings to make sure he would not be treated as a war criminal. Those supporting the visit won out. Local businesses and churches raised some $3,000 to pay for his initial trip. He was treated warmly by the townsfolk and served as honorary grand marshal of the festival parade.

In an Oct. 3, 1997, article announcing his death, the *New York Times* wrote of Fujita's quixotic efforts as well as his friendly return to the area he had bombed during the war.

"A quiet, humble man who in his later years was deeply ashamed of his air raids on the United States, Mr. Fujita eventually forged a remarkable bond of friendship with the people of Brookings, the small logging town whose surrounding forests he had bombed," the article stated. "Last week, as he lay dying, the town council of Brookings hailed Mr. Fujita an ambassador of good will and proclaimed him an honorary citizen of the town."

In his first earthly-visit to Brookings, Fujita brought with him his

11

family's 400-year-old samurai sword which had been handed down over the generations, the article noted. He presented the town with the sword which he had carried with him during the war, it added.

In that article, Yoriko Asakura, Fujita's daughter, revealed that her father was initially concerned about how he would be treated when he first returned to the area he had bombed.

"She recalled that her father had been very anxious before that visit, fretting about whether Oregonians would be angry at him for the bombing," the *Times* reported. "He had decided to carry the sword so that if necessary he could appease their fury by committing ritual suicide, disemboweling himself with the sword in the traditional Japanese method known as seppuku."

All told, he would visit Brookings four times and gave $1,000 to the town library to purchase children's books about Japan in hopes the books would plant the seeds of friendship and understanding between the two nations. He also paid for three Brookings-Harbor High School students to visit Japan in 1985. During a 1992 visit to Brookings,he planted a tree at the Mount Emily bomb site as a symbol of growing peace. In 1995, while on his last trip to Oregon, he participated in a ceremony dedicating an historic marker near the bomb site. In October of 1998, his daughter laid to rest some of her father's ashes at the marker on Mount Emily.

And so it was that the man who once fought our country reached across the wide Pacific Ocean to offer peace and friendship.

Fire Balloons
Penned by Pepper Trail on April 13, 2017

This was the Emperor's plan –
To free strange seeds, drifting
On the high western wind
From the burning cities of Japan
Toward the tinderbox of Oregon
There to burst, set America aflame

Thousands were launched
Hundreds reached these shores
A few did, in fact, explode
Enough for the Army to act
Drafting anew force to fight
The balloons, their fires

The nation at war, who
Was spared for this duty
Both tedious and deadly
To leap from the sky
Into the trees, into the flames,
Clinging to sails of silk?

These men, the smokejumpers
Were the disregarded or the unwanted
Either the one or the other
CO's, conscientious objectors
Refusing to kill, or the 555th
Black soldiers, forbidden to fight

And so, enflamed with the need
To be of service, to be seen
They did the only duty
They were permitted to do
In this forgotten battle
They fell into America, burning

3

ESTABLISHING THE SISKIYOU BASE

A LITTLE MORE THAN TWO years before Fujita dropped his incendiary bombs, two U.S. Forest Service firefighters – Earl Cooley and Rufus Robinson – strapped on parachutes and leaped out of an airplane to fight a small fire deep in the Nez Perce National Forest on the Idaho panhandle. The July 12, 1940, jump demonstrated that firefighters could successfully parachute into a rugged location with their gear to battle a blaze, thus dramatically shortening the time it took to reach remote wildfires, principally those sparked by lightning.

The point of creating smokejumpers was to have gung-ho firefighters descend on a remote wildfire and knock it down before it became an inferno too costly to stop. Some would argue that smokejumpers and other wildland firefighters were too successful, creating overstocked forests that now cook when a fire starts. Others point to climate change as a major contributor to hotter and deadlier wildfires, citing as an example the 2020 Almeda fire that swept through southwest Oregon, destroying some 2,500 homes. Yet many note there are areas where a low-intensity fire ignited before fire season begins, one which is carefully controlled as it crawls on the ground and doesn't leap into the forest canopy does more good than harm. But we're focusing now on the Siskiyou jumpers and their efforts to put the blazes out before they had a chance to erupt during the dry season. We'll check in with base veterans later on to get their take on how to best get the jump on wildfires in these changing times.

Initially, national support for airborne firefighters was slow to take off. Yet the U.S. Army began experimenting with paratroopers who took their first test jump on Aug. 16, 1940, a little over a month after the first smokejumpers made history. Paratroopers jumped into the war effort in 1942, including members of the famous 101 stand 82nd Airborne Divisions. With more armed soldiers descending into harm's way from above, their airborne counterparts in the form of smoke-jumpers became more accepted as an effective way to stop a small wildfire in its tracks, particularly during the dry season.

When the U.S. War Department was informed of the incendiary bomb attacks, it decided a swift firefighting response would be needed to counter more attempts to ignite conflagrations during fire seasons. After all, the generals in charge were already concerned about a project by the Japanese called *Fugo* in which incendiary bombs dangling from large hydrogen balloons were carried by the high air stream flowing eastward over the Pacific Ocean to land in the United States where their mission was to ignite forest fires. Although fashioned out of thin paper, many of these ingenious balloons withstood most of what Mother Nature could throw at them.An estimated 9,000 balloon bombs were sent aloft during WWII, of which nearly 300 reached their intended target. Although the intent was to ignite wildfires in forests and inflame panic on the West Coast, some landed as far east as Omaha, Nebraska.

While the balloon bombs had little success in starting wildfires, one killed six people in southern Oregon on May 5, 1945. The tragedy occurred when the Rev. Archie Mitchell and his pregnant wife, Elyse, took five children in a Sunday school class on a picnic about a dozen miles northeast of the small town of Bly east of Klamath Falls. When Archie Mitchell stopped their car, his wife and the students, aged 11 to 14 years old, got out and ran over to check out a strange contraption they spotted among the trees. Having read newspaper stories warning of the large hydrogen balloons carrying both incendiary explosives as well as an antipersonnel bomb, Rev. Mitchell shouted a warning. Unfortunately, the bombs blew up, killing Elyse Mitchell and the children, becoming the only Americans in the contiguous 48 states who died as the direct result of enemy actions during the war. The explosion left a crater about a foot deep and three feet wide. The deaths were just before VE Day – victory in Europe – was declared with the surrender in Germany on May 7, 1945. However, VJ Day – victory in Japan – wouldn't be celebrated until mid-August of that year.

While Fujita's bombs directly triggered the creation of the Siskiyou base, the more widely distributed incendiary bombs carried by the hydrogen balloons prompted Uncle Sam to construct four smokejumper bases in 1943, scattering them throughout the Northwest. In addition to the Siskiyou Smokejumper Base, the other three were in Winthrop, Washington; Missoula, Montana; and McCall, Idaho. Yet the Siskiyou base, at 1,345 feet above sea level, stands alone in being the sole one of the first four bases that still exists in its original location, albeit is now a smokejumper museum and no longer sends smokejumpers aloft in fire season. The property itself now belongs to the county and is used as an airstrip.

By the way, the Siskiyou Smokejumper Base was originally referred to by the U.S. Forest Service as the "Siskiyou Aerial Project." But the acronym "SAP" apparently didn't sit well so it fell by the wayside.

In early 1943, the Illinois Valley landing strip was rudimentary at best, a dirt track scraped out of the extremely rocky terrain by the Civilian Conservation Corps in 1940. The site was without amenities: no structures, no electricity, no water. The smokejumpers were originally housed in platform tents erected at what was then known as the

Redwood Smokejumper Base since it was then located at the Redwood Ranger Station established at the southwestern end of Cave Junction. They were trucked or ran as part of an exercise regimen out to the airstrip which would not be covered with tarmac until 1951.

Indeed, it would take nearly two decades after it opened before the base could truly be considered finished, although it was a functioning facility that first year, albeit rudimentary. While job one for the original Siskiyou jumpers was training and fighting fires, they would also serve as a base construction crew. The war had drawn many young men into uniform, leaving slim pickings in the labor pool. Remember, women were not accepted in construction work, although they were allowed to join the ranks of those building liberty ships. However, there was a ready labor pool of young men in the Civilian Public Service camps around the nation where conscientious objectors to the war were sent after filing formal CO status. The Forest Service asked for CPS volunteers to serve as smokejumpers on the newly-minted bases. The CPS camp inhabitants may have balked at killing other humans but they stepped forward nearly en masse to aid their country to slay wildfires.

Consider a report written by Vic Carter, the Forest Service's smokejumper project leader for Region 1 which includes Idaho, Montana and North Dakota. That region took the lead in recruiting smokejumping COs for the Pacific Northwest.

"Approximately 350 applicants from CPS camps in many states were submitted to the National Service Board in Washington for 'weeding' in accordance with requirements and specifications forwarded there by this office," Carter wrote. "The 118 remaining applications, somewhat evenly divided among the Brethren, Mennonite and Friends groups, were sent here from which the 60 jumper applications were selected, 20 from each religious group. The final selection was based principally upon work and experience background of the man and his health and freedom from previous injury. The educational standards of the group as a whole were so high that this factor was practically eliminated as an influencing element in final selection."

The fellow selected as squad leader was not a CO. Jack G. Heintzelman was a veteran forester, a fire lookout and ground-pounding firefighter working out of the Redwood Ranger Station in Cave Junction.However, unlike the squad leaders at the other three bases, Heintzelman was not a trained smokejumper when he accepted the job. In fact, when Hershel Obye, the Siskiyou National Forest supervisor, offered him the challenging task of organizing the new smokejumper base in the spring of 1943, Heintzelman was a bit taken aback. Telling the supervisor he wanted a day to think about the offer, Heintzelman went to the regional airport in Medford where he asked an Army captain to take him up in a Piper Cub. Having survived his first flight in an airplane, Heintzelman accepted the challenging job.

Obviously, here was a fellow with ample pluck who would have provided one of the most insightful interviews for this book. Consider what he faced back in early 1943. Like his crew, he was untried as a participant in the fledgling smokejumping profession. Yet he remained undaunted.

Although Heintzelman is no longer with us, he left written reports on the formative years of the base, including one compiled at the end of the 1943 fire season and a supplemental one filed for the Forest Service archives on Aug. 17, 1976. Between the two, we get a good perspective on the early-day life as a Siskiyou smokejumper.

"The smokejumper, stripped of all adjectives, is a smokechaser with a faster means of travel," Heintzelman wrote. That description is likely the best you'll find for airborne firefighters, and remains as true today as it was when he wrote it nearly 80 years ago. Here was a writer who didn't take flights of fancy like many of us scribes.

Heintzelman noted he went to Seeley Lake in Montana to train as a squad leader, smokejumper, parachute rigger and spotter.He came back with a crew of 10 men, all trained in the new art of parachuting onto fires. Heintzelman observed the history-making team of COs were mostly Mennonites. They included Walter R. Buller, Kenneth A. Diller, Marvin W. Graeler, Calvin A. Hilty, Charles "Ray" Hudson, Gus I. Jenzen, William S. Laughlin, Gerrit A. Rozeboom, Winton H. Stucky and Floyd F. Yoder. Rounding out the crew was Lillie

White, the base cook who also served as the chef for the 10-man district fire suppression ground crew when it was not in the field.

As noted, the base in 1943 was little more than a dirt airstrip running north and south at what was then known as the Illinois Valley Airport. Heintzelman wrote that the 4,500-foot-long airstrip was 300 feet wide with a 150-foot wide center section which he described as relatively smooth. It being in the middle of what locals often referred to as the rock strewn "Rough and Ready Desert," he was being more than a little euphemistic about its smoothness.

"The only improvements at the airport are a wind sock which functions satisfactorily, and a telephone," he wrote wryly. There were no smart phones back in his day so we're talking one of those now antique crank phones in which our grandparents held the receiver to their ears and spoke loudly into the mouthpiece.

Fence posts had been installed around the airstrip but no wire was stretched between them, Heintzelman added. In other words, a stray cow from the nearby Seats farm, whose pasture future jumpers would later use for training jumps, could wander onto the airstrip periodically.

Clearly, Heintzelman and his crew had their work cut out for them.Fortunately, smokejumper Hudson was an experienced builder and structure designer who took the lead in much of the early building on the base, according to Heintzelman.

As mentioned earlier, for the first few years the smokejumpers lived in platform tents located at the ranger district headquarters in Cave Junction.After first building a hangar for a small observation aircraft at the airstrip, the crew took on bigger structures, including a loft. Some of the building material was salvaged from a Civilian Conservation Corps barracks built along Grayback Creek not far from the Oregon Caves National Monument. By then, the CCC, created by Franklin D. Roosevelt to combat the Great Depression, was defunct.

Parenthetically,if you are the one – thank you – who read my 2018 book, *Madstone*, you may recall that my father, Paul Fattig, Sr. was a member of the CCC who helped build the structures the corps erected in the Illinois Valley, including the Grayback barracks and the chateau at the Oregon Caves. I bring this up simply to brag, you understand.

In his report at the end of the 1943 fire season, Heintzelman indicated he was pleased with the loft.

"At this writing the building is completed with the exception of minor plumbing and several inside finishing jobs which we are saving for wet weather," he wrote. "We have one excellent packing table and can readily improvise another from miscellaneous tables around the ranger station. An early fire season next year will find us prepared in this respect and in a position to rapidly place our equipment back in order."

Still, he lamented that equipment and training only allowed the crew to make minor repairs on damaged parachutes, requiring those with major damage to be sent to Montana to be fixed. Obviously, that was neither an efficient nor economic way to make repairs.

In addition to building the loft, the crew fashioned a device for the smokejumpers to practice letting themselves down from trees they would most assuredly be hung up in at some point.

"The let-down is a pulley device suspended between two trees," he explained. "Using this, we can pull a man in jumping equipment and harness to a height of 60 feet. It then becomes his task to utilize his ropes and lower himself to the ground. This simulates field conditions in getting out of trees should a jumper be left suspended."

They were also constructing a jumping tower to train future rookies and refresh experienced jumpers in the techniques of leaving the plane and absorbing the opening shock, he wrote, adding the tower would be modeled after the tower at Seeley Lake.

"One improvement to be desired should the jumper project remain here is an adequate hangar," he observed. "It is appreciated that building materials are scarce but a hangar could be constructed at a minimum cost with CPS labor and natural materials. Hewn timbers could be used for the structural members and shakes could be made by the crew."

Obviously, the crew had its hands full even when they were not training or responding to fires. Since smokejumpers tend to get down in the dirt when at work or play, they built a bath house where they could scrub down after a long day. As power eaters, they also needed to construct a cook house where they could enjoy the chow provided by the base cook. All the structures intended for smokejumper use were eventually dismantled and moved to the base.

While establishing a fully functioning smokejumper base with all the required amenities was a challenge, Heintzelman had an additional problem literally hanging over his head.

"The most difficult task in establishing a smokejumper project in this region was the obtaining of a suitable airplane," he wrote. "The plane needed to be sufficiently large to handle at least two jumpers, their cargo, a spotter, and a pilot. This calls for a plane of the seven-passenger class. In addition it must be a slow plane or one which can be throttled down to a slow speed."

However, because of the war, there was a scarcity of aircraft that would fit their needs. In fact, there was only one plane in the entire region available for contract to haul a smokejumping crew, according to Heintzelman. Many were assigned to the "Civil Air Patrol Coastal Patrol" or the "Southern Liaison Patrol," he noted, referring to watch-dog groups patrolling the skies for enemy aircraft.

But his dogged persistence in making an aircraft available for the base paid off.

"The S&M Flying Service was awarded a contract calling for use of L.C. Moore's seven passenger Fairchild airplane, and for pilot Larry Moore to fly the plane," he wrote, adding it was the best arrangement available. "Under this arrangement the pilot agreed to have the plane available on two hours notice. In addition, the plane being stationed in Dallesport, Washington, it would take approximately three hours for it to fly to Cave Junction to be available for jumping. This was the theory of it, but in practice the plane's availability was not as spec-ified in the contract."

Although he noted that the pilot was extremely cooperative and made every effort to fulfill the contract, he complained the aircraft was consistently late because of a litany of factors, including difficulties with radio communications and refueling the plane en route.

"This should be borne in mind and should, if possible, be remedied before next fire season," he stressed, adding, ". . . we are losing a great deal of our advantage by not having a plane on tap for quick get-a-way."

A wisenheimer would flippantly suggest he sounded like the leader of a gang of bank robbers but Heintzelman, although his crew only jumped six fires that first season, knew of what he wrote. Getting to a fire while it was small was vital to the success of their mission: knocking down fires before they blew up into unstoppable dragons.

Still, in summing up his report at the end of the 1943 fire season, he saw reason for optimism.

"All fire jumps were made without injury and all smokejumpers save one managed to reach the ground without having to rely on their let-down ropes," he wrote. "Jumps were made everywhere from 200 yards to three-quarters of a mile from the fire. . . Parachutes, unless readily obtainable, were usually left hanging until the fires were controlled. This point calls for emphasis in future planning as considerable time may be lost in collecting a parachute and placing it in it pickup bag. If the chute is on the ground and easily retrievable, it is good business to get it under cover."

But he observed the six fire jumps made that first season should not be considered a fair test of the smokejumper squad's worth.

"This year's Region Six project was somewhat experimental but we conclusively feel that results achieved justify its continuance," he wrote. "CPS men proved to be of good caliber and though new to both parachute jumping and firefighting took to them well."

He also found the Western Air Defense Zone rules implemented because of the war were of little hindrance to the Siskiyou base's mission.

But he was quick to observe that having a jumper plane three hours away from the smokejumper squad was unsatisfactory when considering the smokejumpers' mission was to get to a fire quickly and put it out before it blew up. He also called for additional parachutes.

"Jumpers can jump to fires, control them, return to their base and be ready to go again before their chutes can be repaired and made ready for further jumps," he wrote. Moreover, the 30-foot Eagle back pack parachutes they deployed were problematic because of the abrupt shock to the jumper upon opening. He suggested exchanging them for either 27-foot Eagle or 28-foot Irvin parachutes, both with lesser shock impact.

He also recommended that each two-man jumper team be provided with a radio to provide communications from ground to aircraft. The possibility of dropping a light portable pumper with the jumpers should also be explored, he suggested.

Finally, he called for a larger crew, given the area they initially covered included all the national forests in Region 6 as well as Region 5's Klamath, Trinity and Shasta national forests in far northern California. Although the six fires they jumped in the first season were all in the Siskiyou forest, he rightfully suspected future jumps would be farther afield, requiring more personnel.

"Ten men do not approach satisfactory the need for smokejumping throughout Region 6," he concluded.

Yet, overall, his report indicated he was largely pleased with the conditions at the end of the first fire season, albeit acknowledging there were more improvements to be made.

"The airport is well located in relation to the Siskiyou National Forest and is centrally located in regard to the Siskiyou lightning zone," he wrote, later adding, "All jumpers were extremely enthusiastic and desirous of making more fire jumps."

4

THE FIRST
SISKIYOU JUMP

NO ONE IS STILL AROUND who jumped on a wildfire from the Siskiyou base that first year, at least none I could track down who was still able to talk about the adventurous challenge. Fortunately, the museum has a log book which includes lots of information about base history, including those formative years.

The first official fire jump occurred on July 23, 1943, according to a report written by squad leader Heintzelman. He noted that Siskiyou National Forest supervisor Hershel Obye authorized a "smoke jump" on a fire reported at 9:52 a.m. by York Butte and Serpentine fire lookouts. The fire was between Nome and Labrador creeks, he added, referring to an area a half dozen air miles west of Selma.

"I hurried down to our partially completed parachute loft and gave Marvin Graeler and Winton Stucky, who had been previously chosen for the next jump, instructions as to the fire location, policy on suppression action and equipment to take," he wrote. "The crew swung to and the station truck was loaded with equipment. At 10:32 a.m. we left for the airport, arriving at 10:40 a.m."

Back then, the base was located at what is now the Wild Rivers Ranger District office at the south end of Cave Junction, then a newly fledged town on the east bank of the Illinois River.

"Graeler and Stucky suited up and the remainder of the crew assisted in the loading of the cargo into Larry Moore's seven-passenger Fairchild airplane," Heintzleman wrote. "By 11:30 a.m. we were ready to go and found our first stumbling block. The pilot was unable to obtain permission to leave the ground, due to either communication difficulties or trouble in obtaining clearance from the CAA. By 11:45 a.m. we were cleared, and Moore, (Frank) Derry, Graeler, Stucky and myself took off from the field."

You have to wonder just how much air traffic there could have been over the Illinois Valley in the summer of 1943. Then again, this was wartime and folks would have been very watchful of every airplane flying over the West Coast, particularly after the earlier attempt to firebomb the coastal Oregon forests.

Heintzleman doesn't tell us whether there was any aircraft nearby. Rather, he reported circling the field to gain elevation in the lumbering aircraft before heading northwest to Pearsoll Peak. The newly built lookout was just south of the reported fire.

Incidentally, at the risk of beating a dead horse, I have to mention my father again, even though his name just popped up in the previous chapter. He and Art Cribb, a longtime friend of his, were among those who built the Forest Service lookout atop Pearsoll more than a decade before the base opened. While they were waiting on the mountain for a mule team to bring up the lumber, they made use of their leisure time by carving their names in the rocks a few feet east of the lookout. If they would have built the lookout two dozen years later, dad would have added "Sr." to his name. I am a junior, you understand. I bring this up to let the world know my namesake father was the guilty party, not me.

While we are off the subject at hand, it should be reiterated that Graeler and Stucky were both conscientious objectors to World War

II. The Madstone reader, had he or she not dozed off, will recall the book was about my father's two older brothers, Alfred and Charlie Fattig, hiding out in the rugged mountains southwest of Pearsoll Peak to avoid the military draft during World War I. After three years on the lam, they gave themselves up to Uncle Sam who promptly marched them off to jail.

Of course, that was nearly a quarter of a century before the smoke-jumpers arrived, before any airplane pilots would dare fly over the extremely rugged terrain. Let's get back to Heintzleman and his courageous crew as they approach their drop zone.

"I took the opportunity to point out the country to the jumpers in an endeavor to familiarize them with prominent landmarks and to keep them oriented," Heintzleman wrote. "We passed Pearsoll on the west and turned toward York Butte. This bearing took us toward the location of the fire. Frank Derry was the first to see the fire and pointed it out to me. It was a snag burning on a ridge top between Nome and Labrador creeks."

While circling the fire, the crew saw a small basin just south of the fire and decided it was the landing spot.

"We dropped a test chute which indicated but minor drift," he wrote. "We were ready to go now. The jumpers had been posted on the situation at hand and Moore circled into the jumping line. Graeler, the first jumper, was on his way at 12:18 p.m."

Marvin W. Graeler's plunge out the Fairchild door into thin air a few minutes after noon on July 23, 1943, was the first ever firefighting jump by the fledgling Siskiyou smokejumper crew. But Heintzleman was not of a celebratory nature. This was serious business to him, as well it should have been. After all, he knew full well someone could easily be injured or worse that day. He focused entirely on the job at hand.

"His chute had a good opening and his descent was quite straight," he observed in his report. "He managed to dodge several trees, slipped off the crown of another and landed on the ground and brush about 300 yards from the fire. We circled at 2,500 feet, waiting for Graeler's signal but couldn't locate it in the brush. Finally, we dropped down about 500 feet and saw a yellow cross which indicated he was OK."

After seeing the yellow cloth in the cross configuration, the sign that the jumper was safe and sound, the pilot circled again to gain elevation and dropped Stucky, Heintzleman wrote. The second jumper landed safely near the first landing spot.

"We dropped down and dropped two one-man firefighting outfits on a muslin cargo chute," he noted, referring to tools the firefighters needed to fight the fire. "The last step was to circle and drop a falling saw on a burlap chute. The combination was very hard to get out the door and resembled a flying trapeze bouncing loose. Finally, it straightened out and landed midway between the jumpers and the fire. The entire jumping show had taken 28 minutes."

The saw he referred to was what was referred to as a "misery whip," a long saw with handles at each end which required two people to operate. The nickname comes from the fact it could be a laborious experience, particularly if the saw is dull.

After dropping the saw, the airborne crew flew on down the Illinois River to check for other smokes but found none, he wrote, adding they also found no fire activity over the Labrador fire when they circled over it.

"The OK signal was still out but no other signals were visible," he continued. "We landed at the airport at 1:30 p.m. and I posted Art Cribb who was taking three suppression crew members to the fire."

Heintzleman doesn't indicate how he "posted" fellow Forest Service employee Cribb, although you know it wasn't via email. In talking to older jumpers, it appears he was referring to using radio communications.

In any case, Heintzleman added a post script to his report.

"Two obvious needs were noted on this trip. Better signaling through larger signaling streamers and the use of radio were deemed desirable. Binoculars would have been a great help. As this was my first spotting job for a fire jump, Frank Derry's help and advice was greatly appreciated."

We also get the perspective from the two jumpers who also filed a report on that historic first jump.

"At 9:55 a.m. on the 23rd Jack Heintzleman informed us that there is a good possibility of jumping to a fire and that Stucky and I had been selected to make the jump," Graeler wrote. "We loaded our equipment into a truck and left for the airport at 10:32 a.m. Upon arrival at the airport Stucky and I immediately suited up and the rest of the crew checked out our firefighting equipment and stored it in the plane ready for dropping."

Like Heintzleman, he observed the flight was delayed a few minutes by what was then the 1943 version of bureaucratic red tape. He described the Fairchild as a 7-place aircraft powered by a 450-horsepower engine.

"Jack pointed out the peaks and other landmarks to orient us and familiarize us with the country," Graeler wrote. "We sighted the fire and saw it was a snag burning on a ridge top which ran north and south, dropping down into the Illinois River. The ridge was flanked by Nome Creek on the west and Labrador Creek on the east. These, together with York Butte, which lay directly across the Illinois River and north of the fire, were pointed out to us."

He also noted the basin they would be using as the target zone for the first jump.

"Jack cautioned me to hold to the Nome Creek side as the east side was very steep and the rock slides we saw looked good for anything but jumping. I rode the step as we came in for the jump. With the cut of the motor and the clap of Jack's hand on my shoulder, I stepped off.

"Falling straight with feet down, I received very little shock from my chute, one of the new Derry slotted Irvins blossoming out above me," he added. "It was as easy an opening as I have had. We had been dropped higher than usual and I spent the first few moments experimenting my slipping and getting the feel of my chute. I held into the wind and came nearly straight down. Jack's spotting was so good that I had no difficulty working to the spot we had chosen for the landing."

The ridge was covered with brush and the largest opening between the trees was less than 100 feet, he observed.

"I turned with the wind as I neared trees and used my guidelines to avoid trees to land in the open. But as I came in, the perimeter of the chute caught on the top limb of a tall pine tree and the chute was partially collapsed. The chute slipped off and I dropped 20 feet before it opened again. In landing in a group of madrone trees about 30 feet high my foot caught in the fork of one and tipped me up. I slid down the tree headfirst, giving me full view of the canopy as it settled over the top of the madrones.

"My landing thus broken, I landed easy in some dense brush and unhooked myself from my harness, took off my jumping suit and laid out the yellow cross to tell the plane I was alright," he continued. "The men in the plane had some difficulty seeing my signal as there were no open spaces but I finally saw a streamer showing they had."

Stucky then jumped, landing about 30 feet from him, Graeler added.

"He jumped a 30-foot Eagle (chute) and rode down facing east or exactly opposite from the direction I came down," he noted. "The cargo chute was dropped with our fire packs and landed 200 feet further (he meant "farther") from the fire than we were."

The jumpers were 250 yards from the fire and 100 yards from the ridge top, he observed.

"We took only our canteen and our fire tools as the brush was very dense and we wanted no unnecessary equipment," he wrote. "It took an hour and a half from the time we left the airport until we arrived at the burning snag. Forty-five minutes after I landed we began our attack on the fire."

The burning snag was on the crown of the ridge, leaning toward the north.

"It was burning about 30 feet up and soon after we arrived began to throw sparks. Since the underbrush was still wet we decided to fall the snag before we completed the brushing out. We felled it along the ridge towards the north slope. When it hit it broke at the point it was burning."

Any veteran timber faller will tell you they did the job right by felling the snag the direction it was leaning. A dead snag invariably contains rotting wood, making it extremely challenging to fall with precision. Better to simply fall it with the lean, as they say.

"The spot was hot for awhile but by 3:05 p.m. we had it cooled down and under control," Graeler continued. "Leaving Stucky with the fire, I started back to the packs for food. I miscalculated my direction and missed the chutes and packs in the brush."

After floundering around in the brush and eventually reaching Labrador Creek, he climbed back to the ridgetop and returned to the fire without any food. Graeler doesn't mention the other jumper's reaction but you know he was not a happy camper. After all, the two hadn't eaten since early that morning.

"At 6:00 p.m. Art Cribb and three suppression crew members arrived to help us mop up the fire and pack our jumping equipment," Graeler said. "They had left the ranger station at 1:52 p.m. Two of the crew and I went back and helped Stucky take down the chutes. When we arrived to the fire at 9:00 p.m. Art had nearly completed the mop up job so Stucky and I ate our first meal since six that morning."

The last spark on the fire was out by 1 a.m., he added, noting they hiked out the next morning. They followed the ridge down to the river, then hiked upstream for two miles where they were picked up by a Forest Service crew. After stopping for breakfast at Oak Flat, they were taken back to the ranger station, arriving early that afternoon.

"Several things are apparent to me since making an actual fire jump," he wrote in a postscript. "Our signals were inadequate and a radio would have been helpful. The compass, if carried down by the jumper, would be useful in locating cargo chutes which drift too far."

Sleeping bags were excess bulk, he observed. However, tomato juice, lemons, water and other thirst quenchers would be very helpful and not have to be packed out, he stressed.

The two jumpers also gained essential experience on their first fire, according to Graeler.

"We learned that one can work too hard at the start and it would have been better to have completely brushed out the spot where the snag fell so as to rob the fire of additional fuel," he wrote.

But there was no question he was gung-ho about smokejumping as a quick method to stop small fires before they blew up.

"The saving of time and the fact that a smokejumper is in better condition to work when he gets to a fire outweighs any disadvantages the extra equipment may cause," he concluded.

In his report, Stucky reflected the same facts and echoed similar sentiments.

"I consider this experience as one of the highlights of my life. In my opinion, this is one of the most efficient ways to combat forest fires."

In a post script, although the Heintzleman had high praise for the conscientious objectors who served as Siskiyou smokejumpers in its first two fire seasons, the Forest Service announced early in 1946 that they were no longer needed.

That announcement was made on April 25, 1946, in the *Illinois Valley News*, under the headline, "COs Will Not Jump."

"Conscientious objectors will not be used on the Redwood Smoke-jumper Crew this summer," the article noted. "The jumpers will be recruited from World War II veterans and civilians."

It added that one veteran had already stepped forward.

"Cliff Marshall, who was the first jumper to report for duty, was a master sergeant in the paratroopers," the story continued. "He was active in combat jumps over Normandy and Holland. Cliff was also assigned to ground action in the battle of the Belgian Bulge."

The article concluded by noting that smokejumper recruiting had not yet been completed and that anyone interested should apply at the Redwood Ranger Station in Cave Junction.

5

THE GOBI SALUTE

F AIR WARNING: THIS CHAPTER CONTAINS a potentially
shocking subject that will horrify, mortify and even stupefy hy-
persensitive folks. But it needs to be addressed early on since it was
a form of communicating at the jumper base and provides more
insight into the unique denizens who dwelled there. However, for the
easily offended readers, we'll strive to keep this chapter mercifully
short. Scout's honor.

Presumably a gentleman, Jack Heintzelman didn't mention the subject in his reports that I've read, although he doubtlessly encountered
it during the three years he was stationed at the jumper base. Perhaps
he simply didn't want to give his bosses the finger, so to speak.

Indeed, a Siskiyou smokejumper brandishing the Gobi salute was
proudly extending the middle finger for all the world to see. Yessirree
Bob, the up-yours symbol of western civilization. Flipping one off.
Flying the bird. But before you start gasping and clutching your chest,
understand what is seen as an obscene gesture by most folks today
didn't mean the same to the Gobi inhabitants.

"To us, it meant good luck," observed Chuck Sheley who, in my book, is definitely a gentleman as well as a scholar. After all, the soft-spoken retired teacher and coach is managing editor of *Smokejumper*, an excellent magazine published by the National Smokejumper Association. He is also vice president of the association. Moreover, he knows of what he speaks, having rookied at the Siskiyou base in 1959, jumping through the 1966 fire season. He has witnessed the Gobi salute firsthand countless times.

"When a jumper plane took off, the rest of the crew would all be standing out there with their middle fingers extended," he recalled. "If you didn't get that, you would have felt ignored."

In fact, when you visit the Siskiyou Smokejumper Museum, you will notice several group photographs from the 1960s which, if you look closely, invariably includes a few fellows enthusiastically gesturing with the Gobi salute.

Today, of course, with the f-bomb routinely flouted throughout social media, the sight of an erect middle finger isn't quite as scandalous as it was when smokejumpers populated the base. Still, in Latin, the middle finger has long been known as *digitus impudicus*, meaning it is the "shameless, indecent or offensive" digit. But, like Sheley, most Siskiyou jumpers insist that was never the intention of the Gobi salute.

In any case, the tradition started well before the baby boomers arrived at the base, according to Bob Scofield and Albert "Al" Boucher, both rookies in 1949. Although they were both in their early '90s when interviewed, they couldn't help but chuckle when asked about the sensitive subject.

"They were already using the Gobi salute when we got there," confirmed Bob Scofield. "Nobody seems to know for certain how it started."

However, Scofield, who became a squad leader, believes it may be traced back to the very first jumpers in 1943, the conscientious objectors to WWII. While they may have had strong religious objections to killing, they didn't mind flipping someone off when the mood struck, he added.

Boucher points the finger – not his middle digit – to a jumper named Terry Fieldhouse as the possible originator of the Gobi salute. Fieldhouse who was a rookie in 1947, and jumped through the 1950 fire season.

"Some of us figured Terry was the one who came up with that," said Boucher, also a former squad leader. "Of course, I didn't get into it that much. I figured one of the bosses ought not go around giving everyone the finger. Some people could get the wrong idea, you know."

And he was quick to observe it didn't always mean good luck.

"Sometimes it was because someone was ticked off, at least in the beginning," he said, adding its meaning depended on the circumstances.

Although genesis of the Gobi salute will likely never be nailed down, the fine art of waving the middle finger to project something other than an obscene gesture started before the Siskiyou Smoke-jumper Base was created.

For instance, beginning early in World War II, the 91st Bombard-ment Group in the U.S. Army Air Corps used what its men referred to as the "rigid digit" salute as a light-hearted way to poke fun at a fellow serviceman. According to the January 1977 issue of *The Ragged Irregular*, the 91st Bomb Group Memorial Association newsletter, the renowned WWII unit was proud to adopt a special medal which featured the middle finger standing tall.

"It came into being in the winter months of 1942, an award de-signed by Col. Stanley T. Wray, Group Commander, to boost morale and lighten hearts during some of the darkest days ever faced by the 91st," the newsletter explained.

This was when daylight bombings by B-17s to stop the Nazi threat to mankind were just getting underway. No fighter plane protection existed at that time, resulting in a high loss rate of 10 percent on many missions.

So Col. Wray created the "Order of the Rigid Digit," complete with a small medal of sterling silver displaying the raised middle finger for "assorted goofs, awarded with pomp and circumstance," the newsletter reported. There was also a photo of the grinning full-bird colonel with a middle finger fully erected, so to speak. However, it should be noted he displayed it with palm outward, something that would be considered poor form by the Gobi salute experts. But perhaps he was demonstrating it was intended to be humorous. The medal was awarded, tongue in cheek, to several generals, including Gen. James Doolittle who reportedly cherished it.

The article indicated the Order of the Rigid Digit was inspired by the RAF's "fictional epitome of ineptitude Pilot Officer Percival Algernon Prune" who reputedly destroyed nearly two dozen British aircraft during his training. Ironically, the first recipient of the award was none other than Col. Wray following a landing at Redmond, Oregon, after the brakes on a B-17 bomber malfunctioned. Wray was in the aircraft but not the pilot that day, by the way.

After the hostilities ceased, the 91st association continued awarding the Order of the Rigid Digit in the form of wooden statuettes featuring a fist with the middle finger standing at attention. Perhaps as a nod to those wooden statuettes, the Siskiyou base received a likeness just 12 years after the war ended.

"A guy named Ron Dickey in Redding carved a wooden one in '57 as a gift to the Gobi," observed Lee Gossett, a 1957 Siskiyou base rookie. "This was a treasured item. Then it disappeared. It was rumored some jumpers from another base stole it. I do know one of the Cave Junction airplanes went to the Redmond base and some jumpers borrowed one of its cherished bells. Shit hit the fan."

One of the most famous photographs featuring the Gobi salute is of legendary smokejumper Mick Swift standing high in the top of a pine tree in eastern Washington. Taken by Siskiyou smokejumper Jerry E. Schmidt who jumped during the 1962 and '63 fire seasons, the incredible shot shows Swift's parachute tangled up in the top of the tree he landed in. He is standing on a stout limb, one hand holding onto the trunk and the other waving the middle finger at the passing jumper plane whose crew did a fly by to make sure the jumper was unhurt.

"Dad was never really fond of that photo, I can tell you that," observed his son, Ken Swift, 59. "That was because it [Gobi salute] has a whole different meaning than what most people would think. I think that bothered him."

Gary Buck, a 1966 Siskiyou rookie, recalled being bothered by the famous photograph after seeing it hanging on the wall of the base manager's office not long after he became a jumper. But his reaction wasn't because of the Gobi salute.

"When I glanced at it, the first thing I saw was the chute hanging in the tree and the rope hanging down," Buck recalled. "All of a sudden I realized there is this guy standing out there on a limb. That really shook me up. I said to myself, 'I can't do that. No way I could ever do that.'"

But the former high school athlete who excelled at pole vaulting would eventually make the leap to retrieve his chute after landing in a tall tree. Moreover, during the 17 fire seasons he jumped, Buck became a good friend of Mick Swift who told him about how the photograph came about.

"Mick obviously didn't intend to land in that tree," Buck said. "But the wind blew him into it. He was up about 150 feet. He rappelled down with his let-down rope and went to the fire which he and his jump partners were able to put out fairly quickly."

But smokejumper policy and etiquette required that Swift go back up the tree to retrieve his parachute.

"The other jumpers bet him one hundred bucks he couldn't get it out without tearing the chute," Buck said. "Being Mick Swift, he took the bet. If you look closely at the photograph, you can see it was a difficult tree to climb, let alone get the chute down without tearing it."

Swift couldn't cut the tree down without tearing the chute and cutting any of the chute's 32 lines would be considered tearing the chute, thus causing him to lose the bet, Buck explained.

"So he had to carefully weave that thing out of the tree," he said. "The wind was blowing. There is a dead top just above him which he had to keep an eye on. It was a real challenge."

However, Swift was never one to give up once he began a task, Buck said.

"It took him five hours but he got it down with no tears and they paid him the hundred bucks," he said. "What took him five hours to do would have taken me at least ten hours, and I don't know if I could have done it."

As for the Gobi salute, Buck echoed Sheley's observation.

"For us, it has always meant good luck, but always with a little humor," he said.

Former Siskiyou smokejumper Ron Versteeg, who became an attorney after his jumping days at the Siskiyou base, noted folks not familiar with the base's culture were known to take exception to the Gobi salute. As a case in point, he cited the memorial held at the base after beloved smokejumper pilot Hal Ewing died in 2010 at age 85. Like Mick Swift, Ewing was well respected by his peers.

"There were both jumpers and nonjumpers at the memorial," Versteeg said. "When the plane carrying his ashes took off down the runway to scatter them in the ocean off the Oregon coast, all the jumpers were lined up, doing the double Gobi. That was a normal thing for us because it meant good luck. It was completely appropriate in our culture."

The gesture conveyed their deep appreciation and feeling of loss for a departed companion who held in high esteem, he stressed.

"Of course, the non-jumpers didn't see it the way we did," he said. "As you can imagine, they were very, very shocked that day."

Indeed, horrified, mortified and stupefied. But the smokejumpers knew in their hearts that somewhere, Hal Ewing must have been smiling at all the Gobi salutes in his honor.

Smokejumpers at the Siskiyou base, with Allen "Mouse" Owen second from left, hoist a giant boulder during a rock removal campaign at the site. The Gobi salute was meant as good luck.

6

BAND OF BROTHERS

F EW CAN PUT IT AS brilliantly as 1959 Siskiyou Smokejumper Base rookie Chuck Mansfield, a bright fellow who enjoyed pondering what made things tick, when it came to describing the essence of his fellow parachute-jumping firefighters at the Gobi.

"Here is the thing I appreciate about the former Siskiyou base smokejumpers: to a man, they are a bright, likeable lot," he wrote in an email. "Not only are they smarter than average, but I would wager their education level is far above average, thanks to the fact they had a job that allowed them to further their education during the winter. Sure, they may have allowed one or two jerks into the cadre to make things interesting but I have yet to meet one. What's more, they are all damned interesting. I'm guessing the profession tends to draw folks who like a challenge, be it physical or intellectual."

And this coming from a fellow who was mighty damned interesting. After all, he jumped fires for a dozen summers to pay for his advanced education which culminated in a doctorate's degree in physics en route to becoming a NASA scientist. We will visit him in depth in an upcoming chapter.

The point being, while Allen "Mouse" Owen was a truly remarkable individual, there were many impressive Siskiyou jumpers unique in their own right. We can't visit them all but will touch bases with enough to acquaint you with the impressive caliber of the base's inhabitants over the years.

None know the cast of characters better than Gary Buck, the fellow you met in the previous chapter. The 1966 Siskiyou base rookie would jump for 17 fire seasons, the lion's share at the Gobi. The president of the Siskiyou Smokejumpers Association has given his full measure of devotion to the base and its former inhabitants, including leading the effort to create the impressive smokejumper museum at the former base. Humble, soft spoken with an easy laugh and self-deprecating humor, he is described by his peers as an authority on the base, although he would likely reject that portrayal. Nonetheless, he will serve as our guide throughout this book, dropping in periodically to educate and elucidate us non-smokejumpers on the topic at hand. With that in mind, you need to get acquainted with him.

"The thing about being a smokejumper that I really appreciated was that it brought some wonderful personalities together," Buck observed. "Of course, you can't have the personalities without the job. It's kind of a matched team."

Like moths to a light, there was an attraction which drew adventure seekers to the ever challenging, invariably interesting and sometimes hair-raising job, he noted. Of course, it didn't hurt the Siskiyou base was a bit of an outlier, attracting extraordinary folks who saw the world a little differently than most and weren't timid about expressing their perspective.

It was likely the spirit of adventure, not the $2.20 an hour they were being paid in the mid-1960s, that drove them to give up the safety of airplanes and leap out to land on the edge of a wildfire, he stressed.

"We weren't making much money but it was more than the minimum wage at the time," he said of the $1.25 minimum wage in the 1960s. "I sure liked working with them. They are classy, funny. Real characters. And they would go way beyond the norm to get the job done. Non whiners."

Buck certainly fits Mansfield's studied analysis to the letter: he is both bright and a college graduate, two things which don't necessarily go hand-in-hand. Well-read and well-traveled, he is capable of talking in depth about everything from anthropology to New Zealand. Moreover, he is one who thinks before speaking, a rarity among many of us humanoids.

"When you are out there fighting a fire, you are so dependent on each other," Buck said. "You have to trust each other – their experience, their training, their judgment. Remember, what they do can determine whether you get injured or worse. As a result of that relationship, you become extremely close to the people you are working with.

"When you toss in the humor and crazy things people say to decrease the tension when they are having a tough time, it creates a very unique working relationship," he added. "You form a very tight group."

An Army veteran of the Vietnam war, he likened their bond to that experienced by small military units who band together to survive when advancing into harm's way.

"But this is the only place where it happened to me to this extent," he said of the base and its denizens. "We became so close we called each other brother. It was definitely a brotherhood. You also came close to their families – their kids, their wives, their friends, their mothers, their fathers, even their grandparents. It was a huge family experience. I have never laughed so hard in my life while working or at the parties we had."

That bond remains strong more than half of century after he arrived as a rookie, he noted.

"Sometimes when we get together now we talk about how we were a family," he said. "We still have that close camaraderie factor – our brotherhood."

To see that camaraderie, you need only look at his impressive log home just west of the base where he raised a son and daughter. Perched on a forested knoll, the house was built while the base was still operating. During their time off, fellow smokejumpers came over to lend Buck a hand in erecting the log frame, ala an old-fashioned barn raising. There may have been a few beers hoisted after the day's work was done, of course.

Born in Dayton, Ohio, the son of a U.S. Army Air Corps pilot, Buck attended Granada Hills High School in Los Angeles where he was a standout pole vaulter, graduating in 1965.

"A friend of mine from high school talked me into becoming a jumper," he said. "He was very excited about it. I didn't quite grasp what a smokejumper did. I didn't really know what he was talking about."

At the persistent urging of his friend, he filled out an application form and sent it to the U.S. Forest Service.

"I figured they weren't going to hire us – I was real negative about it," he said. "But he was real positive. He didn't know much more than I did but he thought it would be cool. After all, the 'smokejumper' name sounded cool."

Sure enough, they both received invitations to try out. Buck was summoned to the Siskiyou Smokejumper Base near a town with the unique name of Cave Junction in southern Oregon while his friend was sent to the North Cascades Smokejumper Base in Winthrop, Wash. Neither one had heard of either town, let alone the smokejumper bases.

"When they finally sent me the paper which said I had a job, providing I made the grade, I went straight to the library to read up on smokejumping," Buck said, adding, "I'm serious. I really had no idea what I was about to get into."

If Buck, who stands 6-foot-3, was any taller he would have exceeded the height limit to be a smokejumper. The rationale for the restriction was that a shorter jumper could more easily exit an aircraft. The shorter fellows were also more nimble when it came to landing on uneven ground, so went the thinking of the rule makers.

"We had some who were 6' 4'' – they had to lie to get in," Buck recalled. Of course, most who exceeded the height limit will tell you with a shrug that they were merely compressing the truth a skosh.

Training at the base with nine other rookies, Buck, like most folks contemplating leaping from an airplane for the first time, was a tad apprehensive about looking down at a thousand feet or more of thin air between him and the very hard ground. He knew he would drop like a rock until his parachute caught air, providing it didn't malfunction, of course.

Taking a deep breath, he stepped out into nothingness.

"On my very first jump I nearly landed on a cow," Buck said of what he recalled was just before Independence Day in 1966. "It was on Seats Field. That's where they took us rookies for our first jump. It was a big field – 100 acres – and they figured we were going to screw up.We were supposed to land in a tight group but we were all spread out. I almost landed on the cow and Troop [fellow rookie Tom Emonds] nearly hit a power pole."

Buck can still recall the team leaders shouting at the rookies making their virgin jump that morning.

"They were yelling over the megaphone at me – telling me to not hit the cow," he said. "I wasn't looking down so much as trying to steer."

But he managed to steer away from the steer, so to speak.

"They want to train you to try to make it into a tight spot because that is often what you are facing on a real jump," he explained. "But on the first jump they just want to get you out of an airplane safely and not break a leg when you land."

Landing with a good roll in his initial jump, Buck quickly discovered he had found his niche.

"I loved the job and the people. But there are only a few natural smokejumpers in my book. I'm talking about people who are built for the job, both physically and mentally. I wasn't one. I was not a natural smokejumper. I had to struggle to be a smokejumper. I'm just being real honest. It was hard for me. I got stronger physically but there is a lot to it. There is a shitload of things to learn and remember."

However, other Siskiyou jumpers would disagree about his smokejumping prowess. Gary Thornhill, who jumped for 13 fire seasons at the base beginning in 1968, described Buck as a "stud" when it came to smokejumping. And this coming from a jumper known for being as tough as rawhide and strong as a bull. Like Mansfield, Thornhill, a standout college football player, will be featured in a future chapter.

Buck went to college during the off season, but was drafted into the Army and served a combat tour in Vietnam.

When Buck applied, they were only accepting one person for every 300 applicants, he noted, adding the odds are even more challenging today.

"The reason I got in as easily as I did was because of the war in Vietnam," he said. "They were drafting so many smokejumpers."

In fact, Buck jumped for two fire seasons and was then drafted into the Army and sent to Vietnam for 14 months. However, he noted his smokejumping experience served him well while in harm's way, including everything from the stress of combat to putting wounded buddies on helicopters.

There are similarities between combat and smokejumping, he observed. When battling a wildfire, smokejumpers have to land safely. They may have to help an injured buddy to safety. They need to know when to stay and fight a wildfire and when to retreat.

"In Vietnam, we had to load wounded guys into helicopters," he said. "The smokejumper training helped me prepare for my tour in Vietnam. When I got back from Vietnam, I returned to jumping but took advantage of the GI Bill and went back to school during the winters."

He earned a bachelor's degree from California State University-Northridge, majoring in cartography.

Like many jumpers at the base, Buck was given a nickname. As it turned out, he was a spitting image to Hollywood actor Jon Voight who starred as Joe Buck in *Midnight Cowboy*, a popular 1969 flick. Even today, old jumper friends often greet Gary Buck with a fond "There's Joe Buck!"

"I stayed here because of the people," he said. "We had really good people; a great cadre to work with and good bosses."

He definitely didn't stay because the region was ideal when it came to jumping fires.

"This base was one of the most difficult places to jump," he noted. "That's because there are a lot of trees and rocky terrain. Alaska is the easiest because there aren't very many trees, at least up in the northern part."

His first fire jump was early in the summer of 1966 in what was then the 2-year-old Kalmiopsis Wilderness, a vast mishmash of steep, rocky terrain with numerous snags lying between the base and the coast. The lightning-caused fire was burning in the extremely rugged and remote Illinois River drainage.

"I was a little scared," the veteran smokejumper freely acknowledged of his initial firefighting jump. "When you are out there looking down from 1,000 feet up, the terrain looks rough and scary. There are lots of hazards. Snags. Big rocks."

But the Siskiyou jumpers were well trained. They crew landed safely and made short work of the fire.

"My first fire was actually pretty easy," Buck said. "We got it out. But then we had a 12-mile pack out. We had 140-pound packs. That was a real eye opener. I was 19 and I thought I was in good shape. But that pack out was a killer."

He would drop into the Kalmiopsis several times during his career, including a 1976 rescue jump. Two surveyors were working for the U.S. Forest Service in the remote Tincup Creek drainage when one slipped and fell some 40 feet down a cliff. He survived but suffered a broken hip.

"The other surveyor called her boss on the radio and they contacted us," Buck said, noting the base averaged about one rescue jump a year. "The injured guy was in intense pain. They decided the best thing to do was send a DC-3 down there with 12 jumpers. The plan was to take a litter, hike to where he was and carry him out down the creek to a spot where a helicopter could get in to lift him out to a hospital."

The jumpers all alighted safely in the rugged terrain, gathered their gear and the stretcher, and started hiking down the stream.

"There were places where it was just a sheer wall," Buck recalled. "So you had to walk in the bottom of the creek but it was deep in places. There were waterfalls. It was a heck of a deal to get down there and get him out."

Jumper Mike Hardy, who lived up to his surname, thanks to being a diehard cross country runner, was directed by team leader Mick Swift to scramble ahead of the group until he found a place down the creek where the rescue helicopter could safely land.

"We got the injured surveyor safely out of there but it was a real ordeal," Buck recalled, adding, "The Kalmiopsis was as tough as it gets. The landings were usually hard."

For him, a water landing was preferable, something not likely in the Kalmiopsis since lakes were few and far between.

"Landing in the water was very easy for me – kind of fun, actually," Buck said, noting the jumpers each had one training jump in a lake or pond each year. "When you are out there, if there is a pond or lake near a fire, I'll take the water jump every time. It's easier than it looks. Because of all the buoyancy in your jumpsuit, you only go down a couple of inches. You pop right up, swim to shore, take off your jumpsuit, throw it and your chute over a bush and go fight the fire. It's always dry when you get back."

When it comes to packing your equipment out, it's preferable to have a dry jumpsuit and chute since water weighs heavy on a tired jumper faced with an arduous hike after battling a fire. Hence hanging the jumpsuit and chute out to dry.

"Of course, the clothes you are wearing dry out real fast when you are working on the fire," he observed.

Nationally, smokejumpers at the time of this writing are required to be able to do seven pull-ups, 45 sit ups, 25 push ups and run a mile and a half in under 11 minutes. Back at the Siskiyou base, it was largely the same, although the run had to be 9 1/2 minutes or less, Buck said.

"There are times when you have to run from a fire," he said of a fire blowing up. "It doesn't happen very often but there is a chance you will have to. You have to be prepared for it."

The weight of the packs varied, depending on how many tools were included, but they could weigh from 125 to 160 pounds, Buck said.

"When you were hiking out cross country, the pack outs could be very difficult. If you were walking 20 miles, it was real tough."

Although the record hike-out was roughly 60 miles, it was usually no more than 10 miles, he added.

Smokejumpers never stop training, even the veteran jumpers, he noted.

"I jumped for 17 fire seasons and I trained each season. There are a lot of hazards down there and you can't fight the fire if you are hurt. Fortunately, we didn't have very many injuries, although they did happen."

Rookie smokejumpers generally had 10 training jumps before being placed on the jump list. Each training jump was progressively more challenging.

"They were trying to get the jumpers prepared for what they would face," Buck said. "The Siskiyou base was difficult to jump out of. The easiest place to jump was Alaska. The tundra up there was thick. They called it 'mattress country.' And the trees were normally black spruce that were less than 10 feet tall."

Conversely, old-growth trees in western Oregon and northwestern California were often more than 200 feet tall, he said, adding those trees could be a problem for smokejumpers.

"If you land in a tree, you usually have to repel out. They started with the 150-foot ropes but people came up short. We went to the 200 foot rope."

No smokejumper wanted to repel from a tree only to end up be dangling 40 or 50 feet short of the ground.

"But they trained us very well," he said. "Some guys wash out. Some have a hard time getting out the door of the aircraft. It's one thing to jump into a meadow. But when you look out of the window of an aircraft before jumping to fight a fire, you can see the hazards and you know it's the real deal.

"Jumping in thunderstorm weather is usually difficult because the wind keeps changing direction. One moment, the wind is coming out the west. The next is might be out of the north, then the south."

The goal is to land the jumpers in a tight group, then attack the fire as soon as possible before it has a chance to grow.

"A small fire is easier to fight and costs a lot less to put out," he said.

An experienced jumper serves as a spotter to pick the safest spot to land near a fire, he noted.

"I was a spotter later in my career. Your buddies are depending on you."

After the Siskiyou base closed in 1981, Buck would jump for four more seasons, mainly in Alaska. During the 1985 season he jumped on a fire in western Alaska near the village of Silawik, some 300 miles northeast of Nome.

"It was real windy out there and I was blown backwards," he said, noting jumpers try to turn against the wind when landing to reduce the speed at which they hit the ground.

Unable to turn against the wind, he landed hard, real hard. As he staggered to his feet after the hard landing, he felt a severe neck pain that wouldn't go away. Yet the non-whiner battled the blaze with the rest of the crew.

"I was feeling pretty bad, but I went to work on the fire. When I came out I went to the doctor."

The doctors pronounced Joe Buck healthy enough, apart from suffering from a broken neck. Surgeons operated, reinforcing his fractured vertebrae with a grafted piece of bone taken from a pelvic bone.

"That was the end of jumping for me," he said.

After all, even a rough and ready Siskiyou smokejumper is no match for a broken neck

.

7

MOUSE IS BORN

S CARCELY MORE THAN TWO MONTHS after the fledgling Siskiyou smokejumpers made their first leap into the strange new world of airborne firefighting, a baby boy was born Oct. 4, 1943, in Springfield, Missouri. Christened Allen Dale Owen, the healthy infant was the first of four children born to Lynn M. and Elma L. Owen.

Like the newborn babe, the Siskiyou base was virtually still in diapers early in the fall of 1943, although its first fire season had been already wiped clean, so to speak. Favorably impressed with its first steps in the form of initial fire jumps, Uncle Sam launched plans to guide the young base into an adult smokejumper response center for fires in Oregon and northern California. Like a toddler venturing farther afield upon learning to walk, the base's area of firefighting response expanded exponentially as its expertise and confidence grew.

Back in the Show-Me state, the Owen family was settled down in University City, a pleasant St. Louis suburb. The oldest sibling was followed by brothers Larry and Lane and sister Sandra in that order. Sadly, their sister suffered oxygen deprivation during delivery, resulting in her mental faculties never fully developing.

Allen was bright, confident and an extrovert, all traits he carried throughout his unusually active life, recalled Larry Owen, three years his junior.Like his elder brother, Larry is also a Marine Corps veteran as well as a former Siskiyou smokejumper. Their brother, Lane, who was the tallest sibling at 5-feet-1, is an Air Force veteran.

"Our parents were short like us but they always told us we could do anything we made up our minds to do," said Larry who was an inch taller than his older brother. "Our dad especially encouraged us to not be afraid to do go out and do interesting things with our lives."

The family patriarch, who was also 5 feet tall, had been raised on a Missouri farm. He was accustomed to working hard to accomplish a task, whether it was bucking a field of hay or milking a dozen cows, Larry noted.

"Dad taught us to stand tall among everyone, beginning with our relatives," he said, noting many of their male relatives topped six feet in height. "Dad only had an eighth-grade education and was a farmer. But he had confidence in himself and was over-educated on common sense. He was steeped in that. No one could challenge him on common sense. Knowing we were going to be challenged on our height, he told us we could be anything we wanted to be – within reason.

"Obviously, we were not going to become star basketball players who were always dunking the ball but we knew we could do things that others didn't think we were capable of. So we figured the world was open to us if we applied ourselves."

His older brother took the parental encouragement to heart and led his siblings by example. As soon as he was old enough, Allen had a paper route for the *St. Louis Post Dispatch* and mowed neighborhood lawns to earn spending money. In high school, he became a talented wrestler, one skilled enough to compete at the collegiate level, Larry said.

"Allen was three years older than me – he was a senior when I was a freshman so I kind of tagged along," he said, adding that he also worked as a paper boy, mowed lawns and wrestled.

The point, he stressed, was that the Owen brothers were never sheltered from the world.

"Allen was very gregarious," he said. "I don't think he ever met a stranger. He would go up and talk to anyone."

A 1961 graduate of University City High School, Allen was a good student and a standout wrestler who did well against those in his weight class, his brother noted. Chances are you never heard of the high school but if you appreciate good writing you know of Tennessee Williams. Born Thomas Lanier Williams III, he was a product of University City High. Conceivably, his education there contributed to his becoming one of the nation's top playwrights of the 20th Century, along with the likes of Eugene O'Neill and Arthur Miller.

Although no playwright, Allen Owen could write well, judging from his Vietnam diary which we will peek at in the forthcoming chapter.He received good grades and entered the University of Missouri in Columbia in the fall of 1961. He wrestled his freshman year at "Mizzou," an indicator of his athletic prowess.

While attending the university, his brother regularly worked out with weights to keep in shape, Larry recalled.

"If Allen wasn't challenging somebody or something, he was challenging himself."

Focusing on his major, he studied hard while in school and worked each summer, beginning with a job in the Sequoia National Forest in California during the summer of 1962. The ensuing two summers found him doing more forestry work in Oregon before earning a bachelor's degree in forestry in the spring of 1965.

Whether it was in school or working with his hands, he got on well with others, providing they treated them with decency and respect, Larry stressed.

"Allen was pretty amiable – I don't ever remember him getting in a fight," he said, noting his brother often employed humor to soothe potential conflicts. "I learned that from him and could joke my way out of anything. I'd have them laughing before they could punch my lights out."

Like his brother, Larry was known by his smokejumping peers as being hardworking, yet funny and loquacious.

"It always helps to laugh along with people," he said. "I remember a big guy in a bar telling me, 'I leave little people alone. If I get in a fight with one and win, everybody gets down on me for fighting with a little guy. And if I lose, then they make fun of me for getting beat up by a little guy. So I just stay away from those little guys.' I thought that was really funny."

From using humor to defuse combative situations in civilian life to overcoming obstacles while striving to accomplish goals,his elder brother showed him the way, Larry said.

"There is no question he opened doors for me.both in the Marine Corps and smokejumping, I was able to walk in behind him.I figured if he could do it, then I could do it.I did everything they asked, showing I could do it but I didn't have to fight for it like he did. He went through a lot of battles to fight to be able to do things he wanted to do. He definitely opened doors that would have been closed to me."

Upon completing his formal education, Allen was determined he was going overseas.

"He told me he was either going into the Marine Corps or the Peace Corps," Larry said of the two corps which obviously have decidedly different approaches to life, although it can be argued they do share the end goal of achieving peace. "He wanted to travel and see things."

Allen applied to the Marine Corps first but was told he was too short because of its 5-feet-2 height requirement, three inches over his head.

"The Marine Corps commandant could 'OK' it down two inches to 5 feet but that didn't help Allen," Larry said. "That set him off. He wrote his congressman and other people, told them he was college educated and wanted to serve his country. He asked them to waive the last inch and they did."

While some old clippings refer to the man called Mouse as 4-foot-10 ½", Larry stressed his brother was 4-foot-11. Given the fact he is an authority on his brother, we won't argue over the extra half inch.

"When he was in the Marines, he was the shortest Marine there ever was," Larry said. "I faced some of the same things but it was easier for me because Allen opened the door for me. You could say he was a pioneer in some ways. After he got in, he outshined just about everybody."

It was in basic training where he picked up the nickname of "Mouse." Corps tradition calls for the shortest person in the platoon to be picked by the drill instructors to run errands, hence the name "House Mouse." Both brothers were the "House Mouse" in their respective platoons in basic training.

"They also made Allen a guidon," Larry said, referring to the Marine who proudly carried the flag at the head of the platoon. "They didn't want to stick him in the middle because he would stand out since he was so short."

Short though he was, his brother was not the littlest person to serve in the U.S. military in modern times. Richard J. Flaherty, standing either 4-foot-9 or 4-foot-10, depending on which source one cites, survived two combat tours of Vietnam in the mid-1960s as a member of the Army's Green Berets. Born in Stamford, Conn., he, like Mouse, had to fight to get into the military yet did well, and graduated from officer candidate school. Flaherty was awarded a Silver Star and a Bronze Star for bravery as well as five Purple Hearts, the latter the result of being wounded five times. Both men clearly demonstrated that courage cannot be measured by height.

In basic training, Pvt. Owen did exceedingly well, graduating as the "honor man" in his platoon, meaning he stood the tallest when it came to physical achievement, confidence, knowledge and leadership. Keep in mind that Marine Corps DIs continually attempt to break down a recruit's bearing and composure, in theory to put them under stress in preparation for combat. For his honor man status, he was awarded a coveted set of dress blues which were cut down to fit his diminutive stature. By the by, those very same dress blues can now be seen in the Siskiyou Smokejumper Museum.

"After Allen did well and since he graduated from college, they wanted him to be an officer," Larry said of a recommendation that he be sent to officer candidate school. "But he wasn't interested. He wanted to be in the enlisted ranks and be one of the regular guys. That was really important to him.He was also an adrenalin junkie who wanted to go where the action was. He refused to be stuck behind a desk."

Undoubtedly, Allen Owen wanted to prove that he was capable of accomplishing some of the most difficult physical challenges a Marine could face. He would spend four years in the Corps, including a stint in the highly regarded Force Recon.According to his DD 214 discharge paper, he joined the Corps on Jan. 11, 1966, achieving the rank of sergeant in an impressive 21 months. During his hitch, he spent two years, 11 months and 29 days in the Vietnam War where he witnessed death and destruction firsthand. In addition to citations you would expect for any Marine in combat, including the Combat Action Ribbon, he was awarded the Vietnamese Cross of Gallantry Medal with Bronze Star which was given for valor and gallantry while fighting enemy forces. As with all challenges he faced throughout his life, he clearly showed his mettle in Vietnam.

Early on in his Marine Corps days, he achieved national recognition by being paraded out in the May 6, 1966 issue of *Life* magazine.

"It was a great thing for our family to have Allen in *Life*," Larry Owen said of the popular magazine which could be found on coffee tables throughout the United States. "But, I got to tell you, the Marine Corps wasn't thrilled about *Life* coming out and doing that story. They didn't think it was the best image for the big, bad Marines. I had heard on the sly that they were not happy about it. They thought it was bad for their publicity."

Parenthetically, from the perspective of this former Marine, the article does the Corps proud, demonstrating it was not afraid to let a short but stout Marine show his strength of character.

Moreover, the article demonstrated that American magazine magnate Henry Luce was living up to his publication's promise to its readers. When Luce purchased *Life* magazine in the fall of 1936, it was a largely humor-based publication with a limited following. But Luce had big plans for the weekly magazine founded in 1883.

Consider the mission statement announcing what he intended to share with his readers. As the magazine owner and a fellow considered the most influential private citizen of his time, Luce could wax ad nauseam but we'll go with the abridged version here.

"To see life; to see the world; to eyewitness great events . . . to see strange things . . . to see and be amazed," it reads.

With that, he promptly turned the publication into a major news magazine which was heavy on photographs. During its heyday, *Life* published more than 13 million copies a week, dominating the market. Doubtlessly its most famous photograph was Alfred Eisenstaedt's shot of a sailor in Times Square in the Big Apple who was passionately smooching an attractive nurse in celebration of the victory over Japan on Aug. 14, 1945. Never mind the nurse was a stranger to the sailor who had brought his future wife to the impromptu celebration. It was apparently his way of thanking nurses for helping the wounded, not to mention getting the attention of his intended. On the other hand, she may have been a might miffed when he locked lips with the comely nurse.

The wonderful cover photograph of the May 6, 1966, edition of *Life* showed the former First Lady Jackie Kennedy astride a white horse in Seville, Spain. The headline for the page 78 story was "Jackie Kennedy, Conquistadora." A subhead added, "She captivates Spain with her style." Of course, President Jack Kennedy's widow isn't the one which draws our attention to the old issue of *Life*.

Let's turn to the story beginning on page 113, the one with the headline, "The smallest leatherneck – 4-foot-11 and all Marine." It may have been the last article in the issue but it was one of the best. After all, it focused on Allen Owen and included five photographs of him, all at Camp Pendleton just north of San Diego in sunny southern California.

The *Life* magazine article came out a little over four months after he joined the Corps so it did not include his war experience. A former Marine would quibble with a few items in the short article, including inferring that basic training on the West Coast was at Camp Pendleton. Basic training in the 1960s, just as it is today, was at Marine

Corps Recruiting Depot (MCRD) in San Diego. After completing basic, the recruits were bussed a few miles north to Camp Pendleton where they underwent Infantry Training Regiment (ITR). The Life article incorrectly noted Owen had gone through "Advanced Infantry Training," an apparent reference to an Army requirement on the heels of boot camp. In any case, a *Life* photograph of Allen Owen shows him with an open collar, something a recruit in basic training would not have been allowed back in the day. It was only after basic that we were awarded the luxury of wearing an open collar. Ergo, the *Life* magazine photographs of him were likely taken while he was in ITR at Camp Pendleton.

But, aside from referring to the ITR instructor as a "drill instructor," the writer was spot on. The story noted the training "mainly consisted of running up and down mountains toting enough gear to rupture a pack mule." Most former Marines from that era will recall ITR included running up Machine Gun Hill at Camp Pendleton where the Life photographer captured the images of the short Marine.

"The Drill Instructor reached the last man in the last rank of his raw recruit platoon," the article began."How tall are you, boy?" he drawled in that sneering tone that is as much a part of a Marine D.I.'s equipment as his eagerness to demonstrate hand-to-hand combat.

"Sir!" bellowed Private Allen Owen. "I'm six-foot-two and 200 pounds and the meanest man in the state!"

"Suppressing a grin, the D.I. glared at the smallest Marine that he had ever seen. 'You'll do, Shortround,'" the article continued. "And Shortround, as he has been called ever since, has been doing very nicely, thank you – despite the fact that he stands but 4-feet-11, the tiniest leatherneck in memory."

Indeed, he lived up to the recruiting officer's observation that the 112-pound recruit would be a fine Marine. "He's a mass of muscle and strong as an ox," the recruiter observed in the *Life* article.

The story goes on to report that the Corps had waived the 5-feet-2 minimum height requirement in his case. Out on the rifle range, Mouse fired expert – the highest badge possible in the qualification

Photo from the *Life* magazine article. "Outscaled by everyone around him, Owen...uses the back of a six-foot buddy to fill out a form..."

ranking – with his M-14 rifle and was named honor man in his platoon in boot camp, the article noted.

"This little fellow doesn't ask for anything special; sometimes we have to slow him down," his company commander told the *Life* writer.

More than half a century later, Larry Owen, who followed his brother's footsteps by joining the Corps later in 1966, rightfully looks back at the article with pride.

"Allen showed them he was a good Marine who could do whatever they asked of him," he said. "He was really motivated. All it took was for someone to say, 'Hey, you can't do that because you are too short.' Allen was told too many times that he was too small to do something and it always made him mad. He didn't like anyone telling him or anyone else they couldn't do something because they were too small. That was his hot button issue. He felt everyone should be given a chance to prove they can do the job."

8

GUNG-HO MOUSE

B EFORE JUMPING BACK TO THE subject at hand, namely the Siskiyou Smokejumper Base and its impressive denizens, we are going to parachute down on Mouse when he was stationed in what was then South Vietnam. His three years spent in the war offers insight as to why he would become a gung-ho smokejumper and fit right into the sometimes mad dog world of smokejumping. What's more, his time in the Corps further reveals his ability to stand up to everything life could throw at him, no matter how horrific.

After completing Marine Corps communications school in San Diego where he became a radio operator, Allen Owen was deployed to South Vietnam in 1966 where he reported to the 1st ANGLICO (Air Naval Gunfire Liaison Company) in Quang Ngai. Basically, the ANGLICO teams provided air and naval gunfire along with artillery support to the South Vietnamese forces which had limited military firepower. The naval gunfire could effectively fire roughly 20 kilometers, a distance of about 12.5 miles. Serving as the eyes and ears of the ANGLICOs, the Marines would direct the naval gunfire, and serve as naval gunfire spotters flying in small airplanes to check the effectiveness of the gunfire.

Those who served with Allen Owen will tell you he was a Marine who gave it his all.

"He stood head and shoulders above those physically taller because of the character and leadership qualities he exhibited as a Marine NCO as well as a stellar man," observed retired Marine Corps Lt. Col. Herb De Groft of Smithfield, Va. What's more, Allen Owen was one of the finest Marines he ever met during the 27 years he spent in the Corps, De Groft added.

"Allen joined my air and naval gunfire liaison team in the spring of 1966," De Groft recalled, noting he was a young captain when they were based together in Quang Ngai through May of '67. "When I first saw him, I thought, 'Now there is a squared-away Marine but the smallest I've ever seen.' By God, he proved to be a whole lot more by far than you would have guessed from his small stature.

"He was a terrific fellow Marine who you knew you could depend on, all the way to the gates of hell and back," he stressed. "He was a Marine's Marine: small in stature but mighty in every other human respect."

The lion's share of their ANGLICO work involved riding in the back seat of a 01 Delta Bird Dog, a Cessna spotter plane capable of doing 125 knots, he said. The ANGLICO aerial observer sat directly behind the pilot in the light plane which was capable of doing impressive aeronautic feats, he said. Unfortunately, it was also susceptible to being shot down by small arms fire from the ground as well as being a target for antiaircraft, he added.

A former corporal who became an officer while in the service, De Groft said Allen Owen visited him after smokejumping on fires in Virginia in 1975. During their reunion, they reminisced about their Vietnam days, including one mission which sent their team to Duc Pho about 20 miles south of their base and just off Highway 1. The operation's objective was to retrieve the body of Lloyd Rugge, an Army spotter plane pilot who was shot down on Jan. 26, 1967, De Groft said.

"It cost 20 some Marines their lives in getting his body back but we took out a significant number of Vietcong," he observed.

The ANGLICO base was also the target of rockets fired by the Vietcong, De Groft said, adding they once struck the barracks where Sgt. Owen and his team lived, sending shrapnel through the wall lockers. In another incident, friendly fire from an artillery unit north of Quang Ngai rained 175 mm shells down on their area, he added.

Fortunately, no one was killed in either incident. Through it all, Sgt. Owen was as steady as a rock, he remembered.

"Allen was an absolute gem to work with. He was an original, one who had his own thoughts and wasn't afraid to discuss them, work out the details and make things happen."

And he had a sense of humor that was infectious, one which released tensions among his fellow Marines, he hastened to add.

"I can still see that rascal's big smile," De Groft said. "The time he smiled the broadest was when he beat my rear end in the handball court. He taught me how to play handball and I don't think I ever beat him."

While in Vietnam, Allen Owen kept a diary, beginning Oct. 21, 1966, through Sept. 14, 1969. Neatly printed by hand, it runs for 468 pages, taking the reader through the days he was at war. While the lion's share of the diary needs to be saved for another book, one he has skillfully written, let's peek over his shoulder for a wee bit to better understand his philosophy during those trying times.

Consider Nov. 10, 1966 which, as any Marine can tell you, was the USMC birthday. He and a couple of buddies caught a ride with some other Marines to the nearby village of Binh Son to celebrate the birth of the Corps which goes back to 1775.

"Some of the ugliest aspects of war can be found in places other than combat," he wrote that night. "First, the driver was moving out at speeds of 60 and 65 mph with complete disregard for the Vietnamese. We had so many near accidents. I lost count and stopped watching the road in front of us. Then the guy on the passenger's side scared the hell out of me by opening up on three water buffalo in a rice paddy. It's this kind of stupid disregard for the people that makes me want to crawl into the woodwork. The thing that makes me maddest is the fact that the people assume all Marines are like this."

Incidentally, as a journalist having traveled on Highway 1 from Ho Chi Minh City (formerly Saigon) to Hue, I can tell you that Vietnamese highways, particularly in rural areas, are often packed with slow-moving farm vehicles, pedestrians and even wagons drawn by water buffalo. After all, it is an agrarian culture. Racing along as one routinely does Stateside is not only inconsiderate and rude but dangerous to all.

In his diary, Allen Owen wrote on Dec. 14 that many folks back in the States, presumably family and friends, had asked why he volunteered to serve in Vietnam.

"I'm not really sure I understand why I did but it has something to do with the fact that I had to know what I'd do if I were on the front lines being shot at," he wrote. "I've got to find out if I have enough guts to face death and not run. Combat brings out a lot of truth. . . Life is stripped to the bare bone and you get a small insight as to what it's all about."

In addition to his frankness, the diary also contained the irrepressible Mouse humor that invariably brings a chuckle.

"I'll never forget the statement (Navy) Chief Stoddard made about this being an ugly world for short people because all we see when we look up is a lot of hairy nostrils," he wrote on April Fools Day of 1967. Conceivably, the mischievous Navy chief was not a tall fellow.

Yet the Grim Reaper was never far away.

"Capt. Wallace died today," Mouse wrote on July 20 of that year. "He and Sgt. Smith were in a jeep behind four APC's on their way to Tra Bong when the VC set off a command detonated mine, killing both of them. I didn't know Sgt. Smith very well but Capt. Wallace was always ribbing me about being a Marine and I gave it back to him by cutting down the Army. . .He was talking about cameras and his wife and what he planned to do when he got back to the states."

Allen Owen wrote fondly of connecting with his brother Larry for

Christmas of '67, allowing the two siblings to spend several relaxing days together in the Danang area.

On Jan. 26 of '68, he noted he had ran into an old friend named Cameron and discovered he had been working as a U.S. Forest Service smokejumper before going into the military. This is the diary's sole mention of the profession the Marine would choose after completing his four-year hitch in the Corps. Given the fact he already had a degree in forestry, it is likely he was contemplating taking on that challenge while still in a war on the other side of the planet.

Indeed, he wrote in his diary the following day that he was growing weary of war, having spent more than a year in-country.

"Vietnam is finally getting to me," he penned on Jan. 27. "It not only tears you down physically but it eats away at your mind. I'm tired of people I know and like being killed and wounded and I'll be glad when I can leave this place for good."

But he was more upbeat on Feb. 29, the day he met Lt. Donald R. Saxon who had arrived from Nha Trang to serve as the unit's new commanding officer. "Lt. Saxon seems to be a good head," he wrote, using the vernacular of the day to indicate the officer appeared to be a decent fellow. "Things are looking up," he added.

The two Marines became good friends, both in the Corps and later as civilians when they periodically visited each other.

In an interview early in 2019, Saxon, a retired attorney and college professor living in Salt Lake City, fondly recalled having served with Sgt. Owen in Vietnam. Although they only worked together for some three months, he left a lasting impression, Saxon said.

"I remember getting off the plane at Phan Thiet and he was standing there with some other members of the team," he said, noting the short Marine stood out. "He saluted me."

The officer in charge of the unit after De Groft left for the States and immediately before Saxon arrived had been a naval officer. Owen was glad to see a Marine officer back in charge, according to his diary.

"I thought, 'This guy is pretty sharp,'" Saxon said of first meeting the young sergeant. "Before going to Phan Thiet, I had gone to the

ANGLICO headquarters in Saigon and was briefed about what to expect. At that time, they told me that Sgt. Owen was the smallest Marine ever to serve."

They also mentioned the article in *Life* magazine, he added.

"When I met him, I was surprised to learn he was a college graduate," Saxon said, noting most Marines with college degrees were officers. "He told me he majored in 'pre-tree.' He was really funny, very enjoyable to be around. He kept us all laughing."

Even in wartime, the short-statured Marine did his best to see the humor in life, Saxon noted. At that time, the unit's mission was to support an Army airborne unit, he said. Like De Groft, he recalled going out in small spotter planes when calling in naval gunfire.

"When we called in fire by air, I didn't like being in the plane as much as I liked being on the ground," Saxon said. "It was a very slow-moving aircraft. I felt it was an obvious target."

ANGLICO also sent out a ground team to check on the impact of the naval gunfire, he added.

"Allen and I never went into the field together," he explained. "He was the team chief and I was the OIC [officer in charge] so we went on different teams when we deployed."

A gentleman who retired as a colonel, Saxon recalled a story about Sgt. Owen which he still chuckles over today.

Fair warning: readers who are offended by crude language should skip the next three paragraphs. Still, the coarse anecdote sheds light on our main character, revealing an amusing albeit somewhat embarrassing aspect of human behavior. Then again, he was a young and lonely Marine. I figure we should give him a break or, as we would have said in the Corps during the 1960s, "cut him a huss."You be the judge.

"One day we needed to send everyone out," Saxon recalled, noting the short Marine was nowhere to be found. "I told them they needed to find Sgt. Owen quickly. Well, there was a house of ill repute in the village that he apparently frequented. One of the guys went into the village in our jeep. The story, which I heard second hand, was that the Marine went to the door of the establishment and told them he was looking for Sgt. Owen. The gal there expressed uncertainty about who this might be. The Marine said, 'You know, little guy, about this big,' and held up his hand to show how short Allen was. And she says, 'Oh, petite sergeant, buku dick.'"

With that, the interview temporarily halted while the storyteller and his listener, both laughing uproariously, took time out to restore a little decorum and wipe tears of laughter from their eyes.

"Yes, he brought Sgt. Owen back with him," Saxon said after he sobered up from the laughter.

"I remember he corresponded with a couple of girls while we were there," he continued. "His concern always was, 'How tall is this girl?' I think he always felt he had to prove there was nothing wrong with being 4-foot-11 inches tall."

Saxon, who stands nearly a foot taller, was quick to observe that Sgt. Owen never had to prove anything to those fortunate enough to have served with him.

"Allen was a great guy, a superb Marine and definitely one of a kind," he concluded.

After going on leave in the spring of 1968, Allen Owen noted in his diary on June 24 that he returned to Vietnam where his request to join the 2nd Platoon, 1st Force Reconnaissance Company at Phu Bai had been approved by the powers that be. Although he was initially told he wouldn't have any problem getting parachute qualified, he was informed on July 30 by his first sergeant that a communications man didn't need to be "jump or scuba" qualified. But Owen persisted and accompanied the reconnaissance team to conduct scuba diving exercises on Aug. 1. Chalk one up for the Mouse.

During a reconnaissance mission on Oct. 7, he noted he weighed 110 pounds yet carried 110 pounds of gear, including the radio. Unknown to him, he was preparing for his future smokejumping packouts.

His second victory over his rigid first sergeant came on Oct. 28 when he received orders to go to Okinawa for parachute training which lasted until Dec. 1. "The greatest 35 days I've spent in the Marine Corps: Airborne," he wrote triumphantly.

Then came Dec. 10 when Sgt. Owen met his new platoon commander, Lt. John E. Slater, 24, of Marshalltown, Iowa. Indicating he was favorably impressed by the lieutenant's attitude and intelligence, he noted they went on a reconnaissance patrol on Dec. 13. Led by Slater, it was Sgt. Owen's 14th patrol with the unit.

The mission into the jungle in Quang Nam Province was also fraught with danger. No sooner had the recon team been dropped by helicopter into the green tangle, they immediately heard gunfire from folks who were definitely not "friendlies," according to the diary entry. After evading the larger enemy force for three long days, the recon unit encountered shots being fired on three sides of their position, he noted. Given it was jungle warfare, they were highly dependent on sound since visual confirmation was extremely difficult.

"We knew that we were surrounded and as soon as we moved they would close in and try and wipe us out," he wrote. "We estimated from the sound of the shot to our NW that a group was only 70 meters away. . . It was hairy to say the least. I advised our S-3 (operations) of the situation and convinced them that contact was imminent so they sent choppers to get us.

"We were in thick canopy with trees 60 to 70 feet high so they were going to hoist us out on a jungle penetrator," he continued. "When the birds and the gunships arrived we signaled our position with a pen flare and they lowered the penetrator. The pilot hovered over us for 15 minutes despite the fact he was receiving ground fire from 360 degrees. Everything was going according to plan until there was only Pete, Lt. Slater and myself left."

The diary doesn't fully explain but, as the name suggests, a jungle penetrator employed then was a stout metal device in a conical shape dangling on a cable. Once it penetrated the thick canopy and landed on the jungle floor, three metal bars folded out perpendicularly, serving as primitive seats. Imagine a boat anchor with three foldable metal arms.

Sergeant Owen asked the pilot via radio if they could haul all three Marines up and received an affirmative reply. However, the diary noted the pilot in the "dustoff" helicopter did not know that all three had field packs and web gear on.

With their cumbersome gear, the three Marines had difficulty holding on and were testing the penetrator's 600-pound carrying capacity, despite the fact one of the three weighed in at 120 pounds or less.

"We could barely get on the seat and before we could put the safety line around us the crew chief started the hoist," Owen wrote. "We didn't realize our predicament until we got to the 'hell hole' in the floor of the chopper and they said they couldn't get us in. It wouldn't have been bad except that the lieutenant was just barely hanging on and couldn't last much longer even though Pete and I were trying to hold him on.

"The pilot tried to set down in the first opening he came to but when he got down to 800 (feet) we took fire from every direction and they had to continue on to An Hoad. I was beginning to lose my grip. It finally occurred to me that if we didn't land soon, we would all die. We were only one minute away from landing on a sand bar and had dropped to 300 feet when Lt. Slater lost his hold and fell."

Obviously, it was a horrible moment for everyone involved.

"To the day I die I will never forget the look on his face or the sight of him falling and hitting the ground," Owen wrote. "The helicopter landed immediately but when Pete and I got to his body I knew he was dead."

The dead Marine officer was loaded on the aircraft and taken back to their base.

"When we landed at the medevac pad the whole company was waiting," the sergeant noted. "They were all quiet as the lieutenant was carried away. I went out of my mind a little. I wanted to blame someone and yell and scream at them but it was part of war and nothing I could say or do would ever bring him back. He was a good man and an outstanding leader. Although I'd only known him for a short time I really liked him. I still don't believe he's dead."

On Dec. 17, he noted that he had written a request for a battlefield commendation for the helicopter crew which had rescued his team while under enemy fire. "We owe them our lives," Owen wrote.

His 15th patrol began on Dec. 20, not enough time for him to recover from the previous deadly mission.

"I can't describe my feelings while we were circling the LA, waiting to go in because I've never felt like that before," he observed of the landing area. "Every cell in my body was against my getting off the helicopter but I knew I had no choice. The mental strain I experienced was almost more than I could stand."

Like their last patrol, they quickly ran into the enemy hidden in the jungle but escaped unscathed this time. However, on Jan. 23 he noted that three Marine friends had been killed in combat.

"I will never get used to the swiftness with which death strikes over here," he wrote, reiterating his feeling penned a year earlier. "One day you are shooting the crap with someone and the next day he is dead, and his absence creates a vacuum which can only be filled by time."

But there were also moments when life was good for him in Vietnam, including June 3, 1969 when he made his first training parachute jump in-country, jumping out of a helicopter near Hill 34. That night he took his first night jump. More practice jumps followed in the ensuing days.

"As far as I'm concerned, it's almost impossible to describe what a parachute jump is like to someone who has never done it, but when your chute opens and you look up and see nothing but canopy and clear blue sky, it's one the greatest feelings on earth," he wrote on June 6 after jumping near Red Beach.

His diary does not indicate he ever jumped in combat while in Vietnam. On July 17, he went out on his 17th patrol, the last in his tour. That would be followed by a few more practice jumps in July and August.

"Today is my last day in Vietnam," he wrote Sept. 14. "As I wait for my flight time to get here, I can't help looking back on all the things I've seen and done during my three years in the country. Even now I can't say that my fighting here was totally right or totally wrong and maybe in my lifetime no one will ever be able to answer that question. But I came because I believed I was helping my country and the

Vietnamese, and I still feel the same way. I saw a lot of atrocities committed by both sides in this country, things I would not have believed another person could do. But I also saw acts of courage and bravery never equaled before.

"I would not trade this past three years for anything because I learned a great deal about other people, about myself, about life. I really don't think a person can truly appreciate life unless he's been near death!"

As one who liked to put things into perspective, he closed his diary by reflecting on the passage of time.

"It seems like only yesterday that I was standing in a telephone booth at Kaneohe Bay, Hawaii, telling Mom that I was going to Vietnam in four days and listening to her cry because her son was going to war," he concluded.

Tempus fugit.

THE MOUSE THAT SOARED

9

JUMPING INTO
A NEW CAREER

L IKE ALL SMOKEJUMPER BASES IN 1970, those within the U.S. Forest Service's Region 6 had age and size requirements for all applicants. To be eligible, jumpers had to be 18 to 40 years old, 130 to 190 pounds and at least 5 feet 5 inches tall but not over 6 feet 3 inches. Some were able to fudge a mite by scrunching down when their frames threatened to be too tall or have someone grab them by the back of the belt and pull up while they were weighing in to make sure the poundage wasn't over the limit.

Obviously, the height and weight requirements posed a dilemma for Allen Owen when he applied to become a smokejumper that spring. Never mind he had proven his mettle in war, parachuted in the military, earned a degree in forestry and worked as a ground-pounding wildland firefighter for the Forest Service during the summers while in college. His experience failed to impress the bureaucratic minded: he was half a foot too short and more than 10 pounds too light. Case closed.

Moreover, as a known irritant to government paper pushers following his battle to get into the Corps, he wasn't likely to get away with standing on his tip toes or carrying sandbags when stepping onto the scale. Not that he would have entertained either idea, of course.

"Allen wasn't asking for any favors – he just wanted the opportunity to show them he could do the work," Larry Owen said, echoing what he observed about his brother's battle to become a Marine. "Even though he had all these things going for him, including a lot of experience which could be applied to jumping, they told him he couldn't do the job."

In many ways, it was a replay of his tussle with the military. As he did in his battle against military bureaucrats, Allen Owen took his argument to congress. Once again he was given the chance to prove he was capable of doing the work he sought.

"Of course, the other jumpers at the base also had to be convinced," Larry said. "They were thinking, 'A congressman sent you. What kind of spoiled brat are you? You look like a little wienie. You sure don't look like you could do the job.' And his argument was, 'I've jumped in the Marine Corps. I've been in combat and been shot at. I've worked as a firefighter and I can jump. Just let me show you I can do it.'"

And show them he did.

"Generally speaking, he could outwork just about anyone," Larry said. "He worked very hard to fit in at the base.If someone said he couldn't do something because he was short, he would show them he could do it. That's how he approached life. All you had to do was tell him he couldn't do something and he would prove you wrong. He never gave up."

Mouse nearly got canned shortly after arriving at the base but it wasn't because he couldn't hack the physical challenges, observed Joe Niesen who rookied at the Siskiyou base in 1966. After being drafted by the military in 1968, Niesen returned to the base in 1970 where he came to know the shortest smokejumper in history. Niesen always called his short friend "Al."

Fair warning: folks with weak stomachs may want to avoid the next couple of paragraphs. After all, like Marines, smokejumpers sometimes lack proper decorum. Even readers with cast iron guts will want to suck it in a little before plowing on.

"Al almost got fired when he was a rookie," Niesen said. "What happened is that he went into the bathroom and laid this big turd, one with corn cornels in it. He didn't flush it. Instead, he comes out and puts up a sign that reads, 'See the Iowa corn snake!' Guys went in there and came out laughing. A few may have come out gagging, too."

Base manager Delos "Dee" Dutton was not amused, he said. While he was fully aware that smokejumpers were not delicate creatures, he found the corn snake humor beyond the pale.

"A lot of jumpers could be a little gross but Dee was a little reserved, a little modest," Niesen said. "When he went into the bathroom, he came unglued. As a rookie, Al damned near got fired over that one."

After he stopped laughing at the memory, Niesen stressed that the short jumper overcame that humorous but crude eccentricity and proved he was more than capable of measuring up to the task at hand.

"He was very strong – he could pack as much as anybody else," said Niesen who stands 6-foot-2. "I wish I had half the energy he had. He carried his weight and was very humorous. He was really fun, always the loudest guy in the room. Everyone enjoyed being around him."

Mouse also turned out to be a natural problem solver when it came to overcoming challenges he faced as one who was smaller than other jumpers, observed former Siskiyou jumper Gary Buck.

"Not to sound mean but our chutes were built for somebody who was physically bigger," Buck said. "A person who is 120 pounds or less would likely drift off and you can't be drifting off on this job."

He was referring to the fact a smokejumper under 120 pounds could easily be blown away from the target area by the wind, putting him in potential danger and causing a fire-fighting mission to turn into a rescue effort. Clearly, that scenario was not an acceptable outcome for either jumper or his peers.

"So the problem in this case wasn't his height but his weight," he said. "To solve it, he put extra weight in his PG (personal gear) bag and in his leg pockets. He showed he could get down fine if he had enough weight."

That extra weight was in the form of sandbags at first but, after carrying the sandbags back out, he switched to adding rock ballast which he was able to leave behind at the drop site, Buck said.

The other problem Mouse had to overcome was packing out after the fire was mopped up, he said, although adding that was a challenge to all jumpers.

"One of our worst pack outs was when each one of us had to carry about 160 pounds," he recalled. "For all of us, it was hard. But Mouse was packing out more than he weighed and taking smaller strides than the rest of us. Yet he made it."

Mouse was always working out to make sure he was able to carry his load, Buck recalled.

"He never wanted any help at all," he said, adding there were few things that made Mouse madder than someone trying to lessen his burden.

"After Mouse loaded up his pack, we used to try to steal something heavy out of it when he wasn't looking," he continued. "One guy would distract him while another guy would try to make his pack lighter. When he caught us, he always got real mad and told us off. He wasn't having any of that at all."

The point, he stressed, was that Mouse never shirked his duty, whether it was packing his share out or jumping on a hot spot.

"He was always making us laugh. His humor made the job easier for the rest of us. When you are laughing, the work doesn't seem as hard. We were fortunate to have him."

Tom "Troop" Emonds, who rookied at the Siskiyou base in 1966 and became Mouse's bosom buddy, agreed.

"He was inspiring to everyone," Emonds said. "There were so many times when his humor was just what was needed to decrease the tension. Mouse arrived when we needed him."

But, like Niesen, Emonds said his short friend almost didn't make the cut to become a Siskiyou jumper, albeit for another reason than the aforementioned bathroom incident.Although he wasn't at the base when Mouse arrived, thanks to a detour in the form of a three-year combat tour in Vietnam as a Marine Corps officer, Emonds recalled that base team leader Mick Swift told him years later that he had been dubious shortly after the short rookie arrived to start training.

"Mick told me he was thinking at one point about washing Mouse out during training," Emonds said, noting that Swift was concerned the short jumper wouldn't be able to do everything he would be required to do. "Mick was the nuts and bolts of the base, an unbelievable communicator and a great inspirational leader. Anytime anything went wrong, every eye would turn to Mick because he was the guy who could fix things. He was a legend to all of us smokejumpers. So his word carried a lot of weight."

But Dutton, apparently having recovered from the Iowa corn snake episode, spoke up on behalf of Mouse.

"Mick said that Delos wouldn't hear of washing him out," Emonds said. "Delos said they needed Mouse around because he had already shown even during training that he was an integral part of the organization. And Mick told me that washing Mouse out would have been the biggest mistake he ever made."

Upon completing his rookie training at the base,Allen D. "Mouse" Owen, at 4-feet-11, officially became the shortest professional smokejumper in the history of the United States.

Fortunately, thanks to fellow 1970 rookie Doug Beck, who carved a unique niche within his airborne brethren with his penchant for carrying a camera, much of Mouse's smokejumping career was captured for posterity. Indeed, the lion's share of the photographs in this book were taken by Beck, a Siskiyou smokejumper for nine consecutive fire seasons.

"I always packed a camera in my leg pocket. I enjoyed taking pictures. People got tired of me constantly pulling out my camera but they were always interested in seeing what pictures I got. So it was a double-edged thing."

After developing an interest in cameras as a youngster, he started taking photography classes in college following his rookie year as a smokejumper.

"I liked to record places I've been and, of course, as a smokejumper you see some real unique places and things. When it came to my smoke-jumping pictures, Mick Swift was very supportive. Every time we needed photographic work done, I was elected to do it. I had a decent camera and the interest."

When Beck started shooting smokejumper photos, he often developed black and white negatives in the cooler located in the mess hall.

"Sometimes after dark I'd set up my enlarger and trays and print photographs right in the mess hall," he said.

Between fire seasons, he attended college, graduating from Humboldt State University with a bachelor's degree in fine arts and photography.

"The people I studied with were all art majors but the people I roomed with were all forestry majors," he said.

A fourth generation Los Angeles resident, Beck began his fire-fighting career on a hot shot crew, then joined a helitack team before becoming a smokejumper.

"My first year as a smokejumper was difficult but I made it through. Except for a couple, most of the fires never got big. They were about the size of the mess hall. But that was our job – to keep them small."

Standing 6-foot-1, Beck was a foot taller than Mouse, one of his favorite camera targets.

"Being a rookie with Mouse allowed me to get to know him early on. There was a lot of animosity towards Mouse initially because of the congressional waiver that got him in, being too short and underweight. But he proved himself. He did good, very good.

"I think he could probably do more pushups than just about anybody, other than maybe Dave Laws," he said, then added with a chuckle, "Of course, we always told him that he only had to go down half way."

Like other smokejumpers, Beck observed that Allen Owen was a joy to be around.

"From day one, he was always telling stories. And funny, he was really funny. He had a great sense of humor."

Humor was a necessary survival tool for the smokejumpers, he stressed, although acknowledging some was not for the faint of heart.

"One time we were supposed to land in a meadow near the fire but a ground wind came up and blew us into the trees," he said. "One guy – he wasn't from our base – wasn't able to tie off in a tree and his chute got caught by the wind. He free fell about 60 feet and shattered his ankle."

True, that anecdote is not even remotely funny. But you will chuckle when Beck holds up a photograph he took of the smiling smokejumper relaxing in a hospital bed. Although his lower leg is encased in a large cast, a full bottle of Jack Daniels can be seen on a nearby tray, demonstrating that smokejumper humor has medicinal properties.

In one of Beck's photographs, a small group of smokejumpers holds a large rock aloft. Mouse can be seen helping out by offering an enthusiastic Gobi salute.

"That was the largest stone we found when we cleared the rocks out of what we called the football field," Beck said. "It took us about three weeks to clear the field. I should have been in that picture but I had the camera. That was often the case."

There is a group shot of the Siskiyou jumpers during a break in the infamous 1977 Hog fire with Beck sitting in front of the other smoke-jumpers. "I set it up and handed my camera to guy who wasn't a jumper and told him what to do.'

And the fellow sitting in the driver's seat of the fire rig? That was Mouse.

"I once jumped with Mouse on a little fire up in the Sky Lakes Wilderness," he said, referring to a wilderness in the southern end of the Cascade range. "It took longer to get to the ground and walk over to the fire than it did to put the fire out."

With that, Beck displayed a photograph of a parachute hung up high in a tree in that wilderness.

"That's my parachute," he said, noting it was a bear to remove from the tree. But he agreed the photo was a snap.

10

BROTHER MOUSE

DOUBTLESSLY NO ONE COULD SHARE Mouse's thoughts and feelings of being an extremely gravity-challenged smoke-jumper more than Larry Owen. Indeed, he was only an inch taller than his older brother, had similar life experiences and shared the same gung-ho attitude when it came to facing life's challenges.

"When I was a jumper, I thought I was Superman," Larry recalled. "I really thought I could do anything. Just like my brother, I gave it all I had."

Perhaps that was in part because they both engaged in character-building activities in their youth, including wrestling in high school and working part time to earn spending money, helping them prepare to attack obstacles head on.

"Wrestling is a real confidence builder," Larry said of the sport in which winning or losing depends largely on the individual, not the team. "It gives you a feeling you can take care of yourself."

Like his brother, he also became a sergeant in the Marine Corps after joining in 1966, serving for three years, including a tour in Vietnam. But he is quick to observe his time in country was nothing like the dangers faced by Mouse. After a year stateside on the West Coast,

Larry was sent to Vietnam to a place then known as "Hill 10," a site roughly a dozen miles from of Danang.

"All I did was run the fuel depot there," he said, describing it as two enormous rubber bags and a pump. One bag was filled with 10,000 gallons of diesel, the other 10,000 gallons of gasoline, he noted.

"It was all pretty much self service. We just sat there and looked at it. We didn't have much to do all day except babysit the depot."

However, he concedes that babysitting a 10,000-gallon gasoline balloon in a war zone could be problematic at times, particularly when enemy combatants lobbed shells in the vicinity or saboteurs were intent on blowing up the fuel depot.

Returning stateside and completing his hitch, he moved out west and took up fighting wildfires with a ground crew. After eight years as a Forest Service firefighter, he looked up at the smokejumpers dropping in on fires and felt an adventurous tug. Encouraged by his brother, he applied at the Siskiyou base and was accepted as a rookie in 1976 where he would jump for three fire seasons.

"I don't know if I would have become a smokejumper had it not been for Allen," Larry said. "We were very close. Allen went into things before I did. I just followed him since he was my older brother. He told me to come out to Oregon so I hopped on a Greyhound bus and came out. I ended up working as a firefighter for 14 years. I was a city kid turned loose in the woods – I loved it. And it was all because of Allen."

When Larry Owen arrived at the Siskiyou base, it was easy to make a jump suit for him, observed Wes Nicholson who began jumping out of the Siskiyou base in 1969. When there were no fires to fight, the tall jumper served as a longtime loft foreman where he spent many hours piloting a sewing machine.

"We already had a pattern made for Mouse's jumpsuit so we just made Larry's jumpsuit after the one we built for Mouse," he explained. "The first one for Mouse was a booger bear but it was easy to make one for Larry because of that pattern. We simply made it an inch or so longer."

Like most jumpers, Larry remembers the first time he stepped out of a flying airplane.

"Gary Thornhill was spotting at the door and all I could hear was, 'Shiiiiit! There he goes!'" he recalled, referring to a well-liked veteran jumper who started in 1968.

"In your first jump, you don't really know what is happening – it's kind of a blur," he continued. "You are in a noisy plane. The air is rushing by. You jump out, your chute opens up – it jerks you back. Then you focus. It's kind of quiet and serene. All you hear is the wind."

While floating down, a jumper focuses on where he – or she – is going to land, he said.

"You place your feet like this," he said, putting his feet in a "V" formation. "You look down and can track your direction by the land below. There are two slots in the chutes. When you pull the steering lines, the slots open or close. Depending on whether they are open or closed, you can steer where you are going. And, if you pull both steering lines, you can kind of stall out like an airplane.

"We little guys jumped with the same parachutes as the big guys did. With parachutes, it is one size fits all. If you don't weigh much, you can drift off if you aren't paying attention. The light guys can drift for a while out there while the big guys come down like a bag of rocks. Allen and I would sometimes catch thermals and up we would go. That was kind of fun. But you could guide yourself and it worked out."

Unlike his brother, Larry never added extra weight to give him more pull when it came to dropping down to earth. However, he noted he weighed a bit more, thus giving him a little advantage in their tussle with wind drift.

"You usually jumped about 1,500 feet above the ground so you weren't up there very long. You made a couple of turns and that was it. You don't have a whole lot of time in the air."

The meadow he and the other rookies were aiming for in their first practice jump was about the size of a football field near the rural community of Takilma, a few miles southeast of the base.

"I missed it and landed in a group of small trees," he said. "I wasn't hurt. But when I was getting up off the ground, I hear all these little hands clapping. Well, there was a school teacher on a field trip with her class. They had watched me come down and had run over to where I landed."

All told, he jumped on 43 wildfires, largely in the Pacific Northwest, and suffered no injuries.

"The Siskiyou jumpers jumped in the ugliest jump zone, us and the guys from the North Cascades (Washington) base," Larry said. "We had the steepest land, the worst snags.When we jumped over in Montana we called that 'old guy jump country.' They didn't have the harsh country that we jumped into out of Cave Junction. Between us and the North Cascades' base, we had the worst jump country you could imagine."

Being mischievous, the Siskiyou jumpers invariably laid the bull feces on a bit thick when describing the target areas to jumpers from other bases when they dropped in to lend a hand, he said.

"Every time guys would come over from bases when we needed reinforcements, it was like a combat zone for them. Of course, we would pile it on when we told them about the area where we were going to jump. We'd make it sound as awful as we could."

They didn't need to exaggerate much. In particular, the tall trees in the Umpqua National Forest were dangerously challenging, he said.

"We all had let-down ropes so we would scurry down the tree," he said, noting their let-down ropes were much longer than the ones initially used by the first smokejumpers. "But we then had to go back up to get the parachute down. You didn't leave the chutes. Some of the big guys would pay us littler guys $20 or so to go back up and get their chutes for them."

Still, plunging out of an airplane was the fun part of being a smokejumper, Larry said.

"I thoroughly enjoyed it. Allen and I, when we jumped from a plane, it was like jumping out of a barn door for us, especially the DC-3s. We'd just walk right out. The taller jumpers couldn't do that. They had to duck."

Regardless of whether someone had butterflies when contemplating jumping or looking at a challenging landing spot, they knew hard work was waiting for them on the ground, he said.

After all, they were often called right after a lightning storm had moved through an area, igniting a tree here and there. Moving like whirling dervishes, they would quickly carve out fire lines, cut down the burning tree and make sure the fire was dead out. Of course, if the small fire was already starting to spread, the labor was even more arduous.

"When you hit the ground, that's when the real work began," he said. "Our job was to get in there fast and put the fire out quickly before it blew up. You would work until the job was done. Yeah, it was usually a whole lot of work once you landed."

But there were compensations, he added.

"There were some nice things about it, like sleeping on a mountaintop at night. And you have this padded jumpsuit that is like a mattress and a parachute to cover up with. Then you have the stars to look at in the dark sky. You were out there camping in an area that was quite often very beautiful. You saw sights not many people would ever get to see."

Still, there was plenty of work to be done. Even after a fire was knocked down, more labor awaited, he noted.

"Sometimes you carried out more than 100 pounds and I only weighed a little over 120 pounds at the time," he said of the dreaded pack out. "And it was usually steep and brushy, areas you couldn't drive to. Of course, that's why they put jumpers in there. We dropped into inaccessible areas."

They occasionally cut out a helicopter landing pad but they generally walked miles out to the nearest road, he said.

Because they invariably faced a long pack out, most jumpers were careful about the tools they brought with them. Unless a chainsaw was absolutely necessary and could be used in the area, one was not included in a tool drop, he said. After all, restrictions banning the use of gas-operated equipment such as chainsaws in wilderness areas on public land could only be waived after the powers that be concluded unique circumstances merited their use.

"When you have a real heavy pack, you don't just jump up and start walking," Larry said. "What you would do is put the pack on, grab a tree and pull yourself up. Then you get going, one step at a time until the pack out is done."

But there were a few fires that didn't require a monstrous pack out or even a jump.

"I remember fighting a fire near Takilma not long after the hippies got there," he said of the counter-culture movement which settled in the area in the late 1960s. "We didn't jump on it. They just trucked us out there. Well, here were these hippie gals, some nearly stark naked, fighting these fires with shovels to protect their homes. That was a big shocker in those days."

It also required special concentration on the part of the jumpers, he allowed, noting their training had not prepared them to ignore naked ladies on the fire line.

"There were a lot of hippies out there," he said of the Illinois Valley. "When I first got to Cave Junction, I remember seeing the signs in store windows, 'We do not solicit hippie patronage.' Most local residents were redneck as all get out. A lot of us jumpers looked like hippies back then. I had my share of hair in those days."

Like many wildland firefighters, he spent several winters in the classroom during his smokejumping years. Taking advantage of the GI Bill, he attended the University of Oregon in Eugene for several years but left before acquiring an onion skin.

However, he did acquire something he cherishes as much as any diploma after meeting a charming young lady named Pamela who was working as a cook at the base. The couple celebrated their 43rd wedding anniversary in November of 2020.

"Allen went out with a lot of girls but he never walked down the aisle," Larry said. "He always said, 'I just don't have time for all of that.' He was always busy doing something, always coming up with things to do to keep him busy."

Mirroring his brother, Larry came equipped with a quick wit and a great sense of humor.

"As a jumper, it really helped to have a good sense of humor, particularly when the going got tough," Larry said, noting he and his brother always looked to the funny side of life.

"And there was always a lot of humor to be found out there," he added of the Siskiyou base. "It was all around us. One thing I used to think was really funny was seeing these guys weighing nearly 200 pounds, real muscular guys, sitting around in front of sewing machines. You wouldn't have seen that anywhere else in those days, especially in southern Oregon. That still cracks me up."

Of course, they weren't sewing smoking jackets or hemming blouses for their moms. They were working on parachutes or jump suits. To qualify for the work, they had to know how to use a sewing machine and be approved by the FAA to repair parachutes, Larry said.

"This was life and death stuff," he stressed. "You just don't slap it together and call it good. You had to know what you were doing or you could get someone killed."

He proudly proclaimed that he became quite adept at piloting a sewing machine, a talent he was able to use later in life.

"I made our daughter's wedding dress. Hey, if I know how to use a sewing machine, why am I going to pay someone else to do it? Our daughter liked it. I was proud I could do that for her."

As for the stout fellows hunkered patiently over a whirring sewing machine at the base, Larry sometimes pestered them by dropping a lit firecracker at their feet. The trick was to be able to outrun the startled and invariably angry parachute tailor, he explained.

"At the Gobi, there was always someone playing pranks on someone else. We did a lot of goofy things. Sometimes we did stuff – How should I put this? – that we shouldn't be doing. But it helped us relieve the boredom as well as the stress that we would have from time to time."

Base denizens were also known for periodically bending the rules a little, he allowed.

"There was this one pilot who wanted to try jumping so my brother, who was also a pilot, helped him out. When nobody was looking, they would go up. The pilot would put on a jumpsuit and make a practice jump. Allen would fly the plane back to the base. And no one was the wiser."

After laughing at their aero mischief, Larry noted that some jumpers were aware of the pilot swap but kept mum about it. After all, this was the Siskiyou jumper base where maverick behavior was acceptable. He provided the pilot's name but we'll leave it out, given the pilot-turned-illicit-jumper's sterling standing at the base. No need to besmirch his reputation, particularly since he cannot speak for himself as he has passed away. However, you don't have to be a smokejumping Sherlock to figure out he may very well be the pilot featured in a forthcoming chapter. But, like the jumpers who are in the know, we'll keep mum about his penchant for taking a periodic jump on the side.

"There was also this old guy who had a car dealership in town," Larry said, referring to Grants Pass. "We knew where he had a cabin out in the woods. So we would fly over occasionally and drop him a case of beer. This was in a government plane. Talk about breaking the rules."

However, he reiterated the Siskiyou jumpers worked their posteriors off when they were on a mission to stop a small wildfire before it blew up.

"We worked really hard as smokejumpers," he stressed. "There were no slackers."

In his family's tradition, Larry gave everything one hundred percent, whether he was a ground pounder fighting wildfires, a smokejumper leaping out of an airplane, working in oil fields in southern California, toiling in an Oregon lumber mill, selling insurance or managing restaurants which he was still doing when interviewed.

"Looking back on my life, I did a lot of things until it bored me and moved on," he said. "People will sometimes ask, 'If you could come back in life and be someone else, who would you be?' They think you are going to say someone big and tall. Well, I wouldn't trade my life for that of anyone else. I'm happy with who I am."

Like his brother, Larry Owen lived large in his own way.

11

SMOKEJUMPER DEATHS

L IKE ALL SMOKEJUMPERS, THE OWEN brothers were fully aware anyone leaping out of an airplane to fight a wildfire in remote and rugged terrain amid gusty winds following a thunderstorm faced the potential for serious injury or death. No matter how well prepared and trained smokejumpers are, there is always the potential for a life-threatening accident, hovering like a hawk over a covey of quail. To highlight the danger facing an airborne wildland firefighter, we'll examine the deadliest incidents which have occurred in the profession over the years.

The worst smokejumper tragedy in our nation's history occurred in Mann Gulch in Montana's Helena National Forest on Aug. 5, 1949, exactly 70 years ago today as I write this. As the Mann Gulch fire burned deep in what is now the Gates of the Mountains Wilderness where an energetic Missouri River rushes down out of the Rockies, 15 smokejumpers dropped down to battle the fire. Sadly, high winds fanned the fire, causing what firefighters refer to as a blow up. But it was no ordinary fiery explosion. The blaze virtually erupted, expanding by an astounding 3,000 acres in ten minutes. The firefighters tried to escape by running uphill instead of sprinting into the black – the burned area — as crew foreman Wag Dodge had urged them. Outrunning a fire by racing uphill is chancy at best but running into the black was a new concept in fire survival back then. When the smoke cleared, 13 firefighters were dead, including 12 smokejumpers tragically killed by the fire just two hours after they landed. Dodge was among the two who survived.

The deaths of the young airborne firefighters rocked the nation. Just three years later Hollywood came out with *Red Skies of Montana*, a smokejumper drama starring actor Richard Widmark which was based on the Mann Gulch tragedy. Although the movie was a fictionalized version of the actual events, it inspired young men, including many future Siskiyou smokejumpers, to join the ranks of the aerial firefighters. However, the story is better told in the 1992 book, *Young Men and Fire*, written by Norman Maclean, author of *A River Runs Through It*.

Another historically disastrous wildfire erupted in South Canyon on Colorado's Storm King Mountain, killing 14 wildland firefighters, including three smokejumpers, on July 6, 1994. Their story was superbly told by former journalist John N. Maclean, Norman's son, in the 1999 book, *Fire on the Mountain*. For aficionados of the history of fighting wildfires and its inherent dangers, both books are highly recommended.

Before leaving the family Maclean, where topnotch writing is apparently a genetic trait, let us consider Norman Maclean's observation when contemplating disasters. "Unless we are willing to escape into sentimentality or fantasy, often the best we can do with catastrophes, even our own, is to find out exactly what happened and restore some of the missing parts . . . ," he wrote in *Young Men and Fire*. In other words, study the problems and solve them to avoid future calamites.

Tragic as it was, the first death of an American smokejumper in action doubtlessly pushed the powers that be to fix the problem leading to his demise, namely expanding the length of the let-down ropes that were far too short for the tall conifers in the Northwest. Smokejumper Malvin L. Brown, 24, whose unusual first name was indeed spelled with an "a," died on Aug. 6, 1945, nearly four years to the day before the Mann Gulch tragedy. He met his fate a few miles north of Crater Lake National Park in what was within the province of the Siskiyou Smokejumper Base although its jumpers were not directly involved in the incident.

Brown was a member of the Army's 555th Parachute Infantry Battalion, an all-black unit which is memorialized in a plaque at the Siskiyou base. They were known as the "Triple Nickles," using the spelling favored in the Middle English vernacular. Brown, who hailed from Baltimore, joined the U.S. Army in 1942, working first as a driver for officers.

"That was the kind of job many African American soldiers had during that time frame – the Army was still segregated," observed smokejumper historian Mark Corbet, who jumped for 31 fire seasons before hanging up his jump suit. "President Roosevelt decided early in World War II that they needed to train black soldiers as paratroopers. The word went out that anyone in the Army who met the criteria could volunteer to give it a try. Malvin Brown volunteered and did well."

At the time, Uncle Sam was particularly worried about the Japanese balloon bombs floating east high in the jet stream over the Pacific Ocean and dropping down on the western United States. Often carrying six incendiary bombs and one anti-personnel bomb, they could cause wildfires as well as kill, as the earlier mentioned Mitchell family incident in the spring of 1945 clearly demonstrated. To combat the threat, the military powers decided to train paratroopers as smokejumpers and bomb-disposal experts. Brown became a 555th parachutist at Fort Benning, Georgia, followed by training as an emergency medical technician, otherwise known in military parlance as a "medic."

"It was right after he completed his paratrooper training that he became a medic," Corbet explained. "During the time he was completing his medical training, the other members of the 555th were sent to

Pendleton (Oregon) for smokejumper training. As a result, he arrived a little late for that training."

For those unfamiliar with the Beaver state, Pendleton is in the northeast region. The town is internationally known for its annual Pendleton Roundup where cowboys – and cowgirls – compete in the rodeo first held in 1910. Parenthetically, it's also famous as the home-town of the Pendleton Woolen Mills which started more than 150 years ago, offering long-lasting colorful woolen fabrics which this rustic Oregonian finds he can wear for decades. Although it is now an international business headquartered in Portland, the company was still managed by a 5th generation heir of the founder and continued to operate its woolen mill in Pendleton at the time of this writing. Sorry, but as a native son of the state, I can't help but trot out an Oregon feel-good story now and then.

Sadly, not all Oregon history does one proud. Back when the 555th arrived in May of 1945, minorities, particularly blacks, were generally not warmly greeted in much of rural Oregon, noted Corbet who was born in the spring of 1951 in the tiny town of Diamond which is about 150 miles south of Pendleton as the crow flies. "Two of us were born that year in Diamond – it was considered a population explosion," he quipped.

The son of a ranch hand, he knows eastern Oregon well, having spent his formative years in the region and graduating from Burns High School in 1969. Incidentally, Burns is the only town in Oregon named after a poet, it being the namesake of Scottish bard Robert Burns. The athletes at Burns High School take pride in being known as the "Highlanders," although they stop short of wearing kilts.

"It is easy to imagine Pendleton, Oregon, in 1945," Corbet said. "Most of the young men are away, fighting the war. And 200 to 300 African American young men show up? Their welcome was far from open arms."

Only one Pendleton restaurant, a place offering Chinese cuisine, would serve the black paratroopers, he said.

"Their commander recognized the potential problem and made the soldiers toe the line. If they were given leave, they were sent to Portland. They were provided free bus rides to Portland for that."

Yet there was an effort by the 555th to bond with the community, he added.

"They played baseball games with the locals and they had demonstration jumps. They worked at trying to be accepted but weren't very successful."

Robert Bartlett echoed Corbet's observations. A professor in the Department of Sociology and Justice Studies at Eastern Washington University in Cheney, Bartlett has also studied the history of the 555th in the northwest.

"These men not only fought the enemy but they also fought racism," Bartlett said. "The town of Pendleton was not very friendly to them. But, lo and behold, they found a little secret over in Walla Walla [Washington] 40 miles away. There was a black WAC unit of military nurses."

While the 555th's military mission was allegedly covert, it was a fairly well-known secret in Pendleton, he said.

"It was supposed to be a highly classified mission," he said of what was known in military intelligence as Operation Firefly. "They felt they would be going to Europe but when they finally get their orders they head west. When they arrive in Pendleton, they get off the train to stretch their legs and go into the store. One of the locals sitting on the porch says, 'Well, you got here at last.' One of the Triple Nickle guys says, 'You were expecting us?' 'Oh yeah,' says the local. 'You are the colored paratroopers. You are going to fight forest fires for us.' The Triple Nickle guy asks, 'How did you know?' 'We read it in the New York Times,' replied the local."

Most of the soldiers in the 555th were little more than kids, observed Bartlett, an Army veteran who served in Vietnam.

"But they made history by becoming the first airborne infantry firefighters in the U.S.," he said, noting they were trained to become smokejumpers by veteran smokejumpers from Missoula, Montana. "The smokejumpers provided nine days of training. Nine days. The third week the army taught them how to dismantle the balloon bombs or to blow them up if they had to."

As Army paratroopers, the 555th had been taught to avoid trees because they would be targets in the trees, Bartlett said. Yet, as smokejumpers, they were told by the Forest Service to aim for trees, he stressed.

"They had to unlearn what they had learned," he said.

In addition, they were trained with quick-descent Army parachutes, unlike the slower smokejumper parachutes, Bartlett said. Despite the challenges, they served their country well, he said.

"Their story is unique in military history, in Forest Service history, in the history of the Pacific Northwest. We owe a great deal of gratitude to those who served in the secret war to jump fires under nearly impossible conditions while fighting racism."

At first glance, the 555th appears to have been only tangentially connected to the Siskiyou base since no records reveal a direct link. Yet Neil T. Shier, a World War II veteran who was a Siskiyou smokejumper in the 1946 and '47 fire seasons, told the *Daily Courier* newspaper in Grants Pass in a May 22, 1986 interview that the Siskiyou base had served as a temporary home for some members of the 555th. Given the period he jumped, beginning when the Siskiyou base was only three years old, it is likely he would have known segments of its history lost in time. He was also a former president the Josephine County Historical Society and acutely aware of local history. Moreover, the story was written by Barbara Hahn Delbol, a longtime Oregon journalist and freelancer whose work I trust implicitly. So it is conceivable the Triple Nickles, who were first responders on more than 30 wildfires in the Northwest, did at one point visit the base for a short time as jumpers from other bases had done over the years. Shier, both a Navy and Air Force veteran, passed away on Sept. 25, 2006, taking with him his knowledge of a direct relationship between the all-black unit and the base. He was 79.

What is known for dead certain is that the 555th was responding to a call to fight lightning-sparked fires on the Siskiyou National Forest on the day Brown died, Corbet said.

"Initially, they were going to the Siskiyou. They dispatched from Pendleton and stopped at the Medford airport to pick up a guy who was familiar with the area. They would always pick up a guide when they were jumping in an area they weren't real familiar with. But, by the time they got to Medford, the CPS jumpers from the Cave Junction base were already taking care of the fires on the Siskiyou. So the 555th jumpers were redeployed from Medford to three lightning fires on the Umpqua National Forest."

Malvin Brown had not been scheduled to fly on that fateful day, he noted.

"When the fire call came in for the Siskiyou, the medic for that jump was sick. Malvin volunteered to fill his spot. I don't believe he had all his smokejumper training completed at that point."

Had they not been busy mopping up fires on the Siskiyou National Forest, jumpers from the Siskiyou base would have routinely responded to the Umpqua National Forest fires, he said.

"The Triple Nickles flew north from Medford up by Diamond Lake and put three men out on one fire and three more men on another fire. The remaining nine, including Malvin Brown, were flown over to Lemon Butte on the Umpqua and parachuted down on that fire."

The region is known for its towering conifers which often exceed 200 feet in height, he said.

"It was low elevation with high elevation trees. I hiked in there a couple of weeks ago. There are big, tall trees in those drainages even now. I was trying to imagine those guys landing there back on August 6, 1945."

Based on his studies of historical records, he was able to pinpoint the area where Brown died.

"Where the fire was, right above it was a clearing of about two acres," he said. "On the Umpqua, you don't get openings for no reasons. The opening is an area of loose gravel with only a few boulders. Even today, it would have made an outstanding jump spot."

But he was quick to note that smokejumping today is not the same as it was when Brown was jumping.

"When we jump now, you fly over, drop streamers to see what the wind is doing, then you fly upwind and drop some more. In a spot like that, you might kick out two guys at a time."

Such precautions were not taken in 1945.

"From what we can tell, they jumped five – if not all nine – in one pass from that airplane," he said, noting they were in a DC-6. "In a plane like that, they were flying at least 100 miles per hour. If they dropped that many people in one pass, there would be people hung up all over because you wouldn't be able to get them all in the small jump spot. Some were doomed to land in big trees."

Like Bartlett, Corbet noted the Triple Nickle jumpers were trained to land in trees during their smokejumping training. Two jumpers were injured the day Brown died, including the lieutenant in charge of the unit, he added.

"The jump spot was sloping ground about halfway up Lemon Butte. It wasn't very far from the fire they were going to fight. But they probably didn't throw out any streamers to check the wind. Malvin Brown landed in a very tall tree and his let-down rope was only 50 feet long."

When a smokejumpers today descends a tree with a let-down rope, the firefighter's rope is laced through friction rings sewn into the jumpsuit and tied to the parachute, he explained.

"So you now hang from a rope that is tied to the parachute and you slide down. If you let go, you still wouldn't go down very fast. But back when Malvin Brown jumped, they threaded the rope through a couple of loops on their harness and held on to the rope. The way they had it, if you let go, the rope would come through and you would fall, even if you had plenty of rope."

Corbet stopped talking for a moment as he pictured in his mind what Brown faced in his final moments in a tree estimated to be at least 200 feet tall. You can do the math. If his parachute caught near the top of the tree, with his 50-foot let down rope he was still more than 100 feet above the ground.

"From the records I've read, he slid down to the end of his rope. He knew he was in trouble. But what could you do? You can only hold on so long. Yelling for help wasn't going to do him any good.

Nobody had climbing gear to go up and help him. Two other guys were hurt. He was doomed."

Although single when he joined the Army, Brown had married before becoming a military smokejumper and his wife was pregnant, Corbet said.

"When Malvin fell, he died instantly," he said. "The coroner's report was that he died from a basal skull fracture and other injuries."

Brown's body was later carried by his jumping companions some 15 miles through the rugged country, Corbet said.

"They finally ran into a guy with a mule and his body was placed on the mule. But the mule was having a hard time. It was really steep. The mule got jittery and jumpy, fell down the mountain and rolled and rolled, all the way down into the river. The remains were on the mule during this time. It was horrible.

"One of the saddest things was that they took his remains back to his wife who was pregnant and she had to pay for his burial," he added, then asked, "How could the Army insist that she had to pay for his burial? How could they do that to a soldier's wife?"

After all, Brown was on a mission for the U.S. government when he died, he said. What's more, he had volunteered that day, he reiterated.

"His wife wouldn't have had much money and she just lost her husband. But they did reimburse her the money a couple of months later."

Corbet, who lives in central Oregon near the town of Redmond, figures the reason Malvin Brown volunteered for the dangerous job was the same reason the Oregon native joined the smokejumping ranks. Indeed, soon after graduating from high school, Corbet got a summer job fighting wildfires on a U. S. Bureau of Land Management engine crew. The following summer he was working on a helicopter helitack crew with the U.S. Forest Service.

"A couple of smokejumpers parachuted in to help us with a fire we were on that fire season," he recalled. "For me, watching those guys sold me on smokejumping. One of them crashed into a tree. He was hanging there, then climbed down from the tree. I was mesmerized. Despite the obvious danger they faced, they loved what they were doing. You could see it in their body language and demeanor. I wanted to be a smokejumper.''

He applied the next fire season and was hired as a jumper at the newly-minted smokejumper base in LaGrande in 1974. However, since it had no training facility, he and the other new hires were sent to the North Cascade smokejumper base in Washington to train.

"I didn't get on a fire jump until July. I was raring to go but I had to wait for my turn."

After biding his time, his turn would come in what would be a torrent of jumps.

"By that time, Cave Junction (Siskiyou base) had established a beachhead of jumping in Region 8 – the eastern mountains," Corbet said, noting other jumper bases in the northwest later followed suit. "In my second jump season, I jumped on fires in Virginia, North Carolina, Georgia and Tennessee. The following year I jumped in Arkansas as well as Virginia and Tennessee."

But most of his jumping was in the West, including Alaska. When he wasn't fighting fires in summer, he was in the classroom come winter. He graduated from the University of Oregon in 1973 with a bachelor's degree in environmental studies.

Like most seasoned jumpers, he has landed in trees, sometimes intentionally.

"If I'm jumping into a rocky area or an area that has a lot of dead snags that can skewer me, I'll look for a bunch of small trees. That is often the softest landing you can have. I've landed on trees 25 times or more, probably half of them intentionally."

But there were a few times when landing in a towering tree scared the bejabbers out of him. Consider an incident which occurred in Montana's Bob Marshall Wilderness.

"I got hung up in this big dead snag when I came down. I didn't want to bounce around because dead branches might break. But as I reached down to get my let-down rope, I could see in peripheral vision that some stuff was moving. I look up and the tree I am hung up in was falling over. We are going over and picking up speed. I'm thinking, 'This is really gonna hurt.'

"I get bounced around and all of a sudden I hear this, 'Kaboom!'" he added. "The tree I was in hit the ground but my parachute got hung up in some live trees so here I was hanging in two smaller green trees. I was very, very fortunate."

Indeed, he could have very well suffered the same fate as Malvin Brown.

THE MOUSE THAT SOARED

12

SISKIYOU JUMPER DEATH

WHEN THE WIND PICKS UP at the Siskiyou Smokejumper Base as it frequently does, the gusts invariably rattle the hardware on the flagpole above a plaque honoring Tommy Lee Smith in front of the headquarters building. To those who knew him, the tap-tap on the flagpole is a gentle reminder of Smith's legacy, the only Siskiyou smokejumper to die in the line of duty.

Smith drowned while crossing the Illinois River during a pack out on May 5, 1967. The well-liked jumper and Army veteran was 26. Born in Texas, the 1958 Grants Pass High School graduate who attended what is now Southern Oregon University was the oldest of four siblings.

He jumped for four fire seasons beginning in 1961, was drafted into the U.S. Army for two years, and returned to smokejumping in 1966. He met his fate at the beginning his sixth jumping season.

His death, which occurred on a Friday, was reported in the weekly *Illinois Valley News* in Cave Junction the following week.

"Smitty is dead," the article began. "Tall, lanky, always smiling, Smitty, who had been jumping out of the Siskiyou Aerial Project for five years, drowned while making a river crossing after building helispots in the remote Illinois River Canyon area."

Written by editor Bob Grant who was an avid fan of the Siskiyou jumpers, the article noted that smokejumpers Tommy Lee "Smitty" Smith, along with Rey Zander and Ron McMinimy, both experienced jumpers who had rookied at other bases in the northwest before joining the Siskiyou crew, had parachuted into the rugged area that day. Their mission was to build a landing pad for helicopters, referred to as a "helispot." As it happens, the tragedy occurred just west of York Butte, the site where Siskiyou smokejumpers made their first fire jump in July of 1943. The area is now just inside the northeast corner of the Kalmiopsis Wilderness while that rugged section of the Illinois River is part of the national Wild and Scenic Rivers system.

Upon completing their work upstream near Nome Peak, also in the wilderness, the trio hiked a short distance downstream and attempted to cross the river where they could hike out on the Illinois River Trail on the river's east bank and follow it to a Forest Service road where they would be picked up. Not far below the confluence with Clear Creek, Smith used a bowline knot to tie a 1-inch diameter nylon rope around his waist and started swimming across the river late that morning. Although it was early May, the water, fed by the annual mountain snowmelt, was teeth-chattering cold.

We'll let the *Illinois Valley News*, apparently relying on a report released by then Siskiyou base air officer Delos "Dee" Dutton, continue the sad story.

"Smith entered the calm water with 150 feet of line tied to him, which was used later to bring a rubber raft with their gear across," the paper noted. "He purposely drifted downstream to the chosen landing place, still in calm water but just above the point where the river current gained strength. As he started to climb out on the rocks, the line was caught by the current and pulled him back into the water."

In an attempt to keep him from drifting downstream, Zander and

McMinimy, on the opposite bank, pulled the slack out of the line, the article noted.

"As Smith swung back toward the other shore, he submerged twice," according to the paper. "Feeling the only chance Smith had was to be free, they released the line. Smith started through the rapids and the line caught on an underwater boulder, holding him just below the surface."

Dutton had noted that McMininy and Zander had run downstream while hanging onto the rope but were stopped by a rock wall, causing them to release the rope in hopes Smith would be able to make is safely to shore. A helicopter arrived, picked up the two other jumpers, but an effort to find Smith's body that day was unsuccessful.

Searchers found his body in shallow water on May 13, eight days after he had drowned and roughly 700 yards downstream from where he entered the water. Among the searchers was veteran Siskiyou smokejumper Terry Mewhinney, a longtime friend of Smith and his roommate at the time. It was Mewhinney who pulled his friend's body out of the water, covering him with a blanket.

It was one of the most difficult days he ever had, Mewhinney said in an interview for this book.

"I was his best friend," said Mewhinney, a 1964 rookie who would become the base manager just before it closed. "We were friends before I started jumping. He was the one who called me and talked me into becoming a smokejumper. Everybody liked Tommy. To have that happen to him was so sad."

When Smith drowned, Mewhinney and Siskiyou jumper John Robison, who began jumping at the base in 1965, had been building a helicopter landing pad on York Butte on the east side of the river. Mewhinney had heard a voice report on their radio, "We think we lost a jumper" but he didn't know the details until later.

"It was a horrible, horrible day," he said softly and looked away. Even after more than half a century, the loss of his friend was obviously difficult to contemplate.

In an article in the *Grants Pass Daily Courier* newspaper in 2007 on the 40th anniversary of Smith's death, his mother, Floy Ann Smith, then 88, recalled her eldest with fond memories.

"He was a very good son," she told the paper. "I shed all the tears I ever had the first year or two after he died."

Glenda Marchant, the parachute rigger at the Siskiyou base for more than 20 years, was also quoted, noting he was well-liked and had a pleasant personality.

"It was devastating to have that happen to one of our boys," said Marchant who was living in Coos Bay at the time but has since passed away.

Former smokejumper Gary Buck, who was a 1966 rookie at the Siskiyou base and would jump for 17 fire seasons, wasn't there that day but recalled talking to McMinimy and Zander about the tragedy later that summer.

"Rey was crying," Buck said in 2018. "They had lost a friend. We all did."

Sadly, Zander drowned during a 1986 snorkeling accident in Westport, Wash., while McMinimy, who began jumping at the Siskiyou base in 1966, left the base after 1977, Buck observed.

"Tommy's death hit us all pretty hard," he reiterated.

Charles "Chuck" Mansfield, who rookied in 1959 and later became a NASA scientist, jumped with Tommy Smith for five fire seasons.

"That was so tragic," he said, noting Smith was a good friend. "He was very competent, a great squad leader. Whatever the cause, it was very sad. He was a good guy and an excellent smokejumper. Everyone felt horrible about his death."

Former jumper Tommy Albert, who rookied in 1964 and later became a jumper pilot, echoed his sentiments.

"He was a gung-ho jumper who everyone liked," Albert said. "He was a good friend. It was such a terrible thing to happen to any one of us."

13

HELICOPTER
FIREFIGHTER DEATHS

W ILDLAND FIREFIGHTERS COMPRISE A UNIQUE, tightknit
community, one which rightfully takes great pride in its challenging profession. While they may poke fun at other firefighters
who don't approach a wildfire via the same mode of travel – be it
parachute, helicopter or boots on the ground – they know that when
one is hurt, they all hurt. Indeed, we cannot leave the danger wildland
firefighters face without paying tribute to those who perished in the
Iron 44 Fire helicopter crash in northern California.

The tragic helicopter crash which killed nine, including seven
southwest Oregon firefighters, occurred Aug. 5, 2008 on the 59th anniversary of the Mann Gulch Fire tragedy. Historically, the zenith in
wildfire activity throughout the West occurred during late summer,
obviously increasing the chances of tragedies occurring on the same
dates, albeit different years. Still, it is sobering to contemplate that
back-to-back days in early August brought us the nation's first smokejumper death, its worst smokejumper disaster and its deadliest helicopter crash involving firefighters.

Sadly, the latter involved a former Siskiyou smokejumper.

"It was so horrible for this to happen to these young people and their families," said Mike Wheelock, a 1976-79 Siskiyou jumper, in an interview in 2018 shortly after the 10th anniversary of the tragedy. "Even now, it is very hard to talk about it. But we will never, ever forget them and what happened that day. We will always have a bond with them."

I was reminded of that bond on the morning of Aug. 6, 2008 when I was walking into the federal building in Medford which serves as the headquarters for the Rogue River-Siskiyou National Forest and the Bureau of Land Management's Medford District. At the time, I was writing for the Mail Tribune newspaper in Medford and was en route to an interview with someone about some mundane topic whose subject has long been forgotten. At that point in time, the fatal crash had not yet been made public. Walking across the parking lot towards me was Joel King, a well-respected district ranger who has done his share of firefighting. Normally, he is a friendly fellow who greets you with a warm smile and a firm handshake. Not that morning. Tears streaked his cheeks.

"We've lost some firefighters," he told me quietly, adding he had just learned of the tragedy and knew only that they were from southwestern Oregon. He walked away shaking his head and wiping his eyes.

The terrible crash occurred around 7:30 p.m. the evening before in the Iron 44 wildfire complex deep in the remote Trinity Alps Wilderness of the Shasta-Trinity National Forest in northwest California. With a lightning storm in the forecast, the Sikorsky S-61N helicopter owned by Carson Helicopters had taken out one load of firefighters and had returned to ferry out another load. Witnesses reported the helicopter appeared to struggle when it took off before striking a tree and crashing to the ground, bursting into flames.

All the firefighters on board were working for Grayback Forestry, the company Wheelock started in 1979. He is now the president of the firm which employs more than 400 people, making it one of the largest wildfire suppression companies in the nation.

Known as a tough fellow as well as a good boss, Wheelock said the 2008 tragedy was a pivotal point for him.

"I was going to throw in the towel when it happened," he said. "I had lost firefighters in car wrecks in Colorado. But this was so terrible . . ."

His voice trailed off as he recalled the events that day. On the night of the tragedy, some two hours after it happened, he got a call notifying him there had been a helicopter crash. However, he was told only that three people aboard had been seriously burned and that they have been taken to a burn center in Chico. There was no word on the others in the aircraft, he noted.

At the time, Grayback had a 10-passenger airplane which was used to fly company employees around the West.

"I called the families of the three who were in the burn center," he said, adding he offered to fly them down to see their injured family members. "One wanted to go down to the Chico Burn Center so I flew that family down there. I got there and met with the Forest Service personnel and kept asking them about the other seven, trying to find out if any of those guys were hurt. 'Naw, they are up there and they are fine. There are paramedics up there,' was what they told me. They were under a gag order."

However, the scuttlebutt in the firefighting community was that there may have been fatalities, he observed.

"I started getting a lot of calls. But rumors can get going in these things so I tried to keep calm."

That night after meeting with agency officials, Wheelock went back to his motel room in Chico and tried to get some sleep. That's when he received a call from another Forest Service official informing him that seven firefighters – all Grayback employees – had died in the crash.

"I told myself that was it," he said. "I told myself I'm going to take care of these families, then I'm shutting this thing down. I didn't care. They could come and take everything. I told everybody to stand down until we could sort it all out."

Meanwhile, he was getting repeated calls from the media which had also heard rumors of firefighters killed in the crash.

"I have a chaplain who works for Grayback to provide counseling and he came down," he said, adding they went to the burn center together to see two of the survivors. The third one was in the hospital in Redding.

After walking past the helicopter pilot who was badly burned and unconscious, they visited the conscious firefighter.

"When I get to the firefighter, his face is burned and he is all taped up," Wheelock said. "They told him, 'Here's Mike Wheelock.' I had never met him before. He was a 19-year-old kid. His girlfriend and mom were there."

Wheelock, who had been cautioned not to tell the firefighters about the fate of their friends and workmates, made small talk, asking him how he was being treated.

"He said to me, 'Mr. Wheelock, will you let me go back to work for you?'" he said. "I started sobbing and walked out of there."

But he regrouped to pay his respects to the other firefighter at the burn center.

"His whole face was shattered – all his teeth were broken," he said. "His back was broken. I sat by his bed and was talking to him. And the same thing happened. He said, 'Mr. Wheelock, will you let me come back to work for you?' I was just dumbfounded.

"We took care of the injured and their families and loved on them," he added. "It hit the firefighting community real hard. I went to all the funerals. They were all people of high character who had banded together early on. It was a tight group."

They were all part of the Grayback crew of 20 firefighters working the fire, he explained, adding the first ten had been flown from the Iron 44 site earlier that day.

When memorials were being planned shortly after the crash, there was some ego infighting among agency personnel, Wheelock recalled.

"They were arguing about who was going to be doing the honor guard and all that," he said of a planning meeting he attended. "It was getting out of control. That's when I told them it wasn't about them and their egos but about the people who died and their families."

What's more, he told them to meet him early the next morning in his Medford-area office to iron out the details.

"It got back on track," said Wheelock who, like most former Siskiyou smokejumpers, didn't have a lot of time for suffering fools gladly.

For years, he would periodically meet someone who was an emergency responder at the crash site or who knew one of the victims. That person would invariably pour his or her heart out, he said.

"We had counseling and all the grief education that you need to do. It shaped who we are."

Following an investigation into the crash, the National Transportation Safety Board determined the helicopter was more than 3,000 pounds over its load limit, triggering criminal investigations after witnesses reported other Carson helicopters also appeared sluggish when taking off with a load. Two Carson employees, the vice president and its maintenance director, were sentenced to prison for falsifying records which overstated the company's helicopter safe payload capacity to get Forest Service contracts worth some $20 million. The agency canceled its contracts with the company which also lost its FAA certificate.

The firefighters who died that day, all hailing from southwest Oregon, were Shawn Blazer, 30, of Medford; Scott Charlson, 25, of Phoenix, Or.; Edrik Gomez, 19, of Ashland; Matt Hammer, 23, of Grants Pass; Steven Caleb Renno, 21, of Cave Junction; Bryan Rich, 29, of Medford; and David Steele, 19, of Ashland.

The crash also killed helicopter pilot Roark Schwanenberg, 54, of Lostine, Oregon, and Jim Ramage, 64, a Forest Service flight inspector from Redding, California. In addition to those who died, two other Grayback firefighters and the copilot were seriously injured. None of those killed or injured were aware of the falsified information given to the agency, the investigation determined.

To put a face on one of the firefighters who died that day, Charlson was studying journalism at Southern Oregon University in Ashland. He wrote sports stories for the *Ashland Daily Tidings* and contributed some stories to the *Mail Tribune* which was owned by the same firm as the Tidings. I recall chatting with him once about his firefighting work and came away impressed with both his intelligence and positive attitude. Like the others, he was a fine young man with tons of potential.

May all of those who perished in that unnecessary tragedy rest in peace.

14

BONE BREAKING LEAPS

W HILE ALL WILDLAND FIREFIGHTERS PERIODICALLY face hair-raising moments on the job, smokejumping tends to increase the danger. After all, the airborne firefighters leap out of perfectly good airplanes into what is often remote and rugged mountain terrain.

As a result, injuries are not uncommon. Still, most are not serious, requiring little more than a dozen swear words, a couple of aspirin and a short rest.

For instance, consider an incident involving Bob Wilcox, the fellow you met in the introduction to this book. A rookie at the Redding base in 1963, Wilcox was deployed to the Siskiyou base in July of 1965 as part of a booster crew after a lightning bust ignited 23 fires in western Oregon and far northern California on the 26th. The base logbook indicated the request for booster crews at the Siskiyou base temporarily emptied the Redding base of its jumpers.

Unfortunately, Wilcox was suffering from severe sunburn to his shins, thanks to having spent the previous day baking on the shores of a lake near Redding with his wife, Lucille.

"They dispatched a couple of us to a fire near Oakridge," Bob Wilcox recalled, referring to a hamlet southeast of Eugene. "It was a big tree on fire. I landed fine but the blisters on my shins were really giving me trouble. I had some really big blisters. But I worked on the fire, then walked back to the jump spot where there were some cardboard boxes. I cut some shin guards out of cardboard and taped them to my shins. I went back to work and finished the job that had to be done."

Later, after the crew hiked out to a road and were taken to the nearest ranger station, he inspected his medical handiwork.

"My shins were caked with black soot from the leaking blisters – I was worried it would get infected but it turned out fine," he said, adding jumpers routinely figured out ways to work around such inconveniences.

But no amount of Yankee ingenuity could cure jumpers suffering ghastly wounds. You are about to meet three former Siskiyou smokejumpers whose bone-breaking injuries will give you ample insight regarding the most serious dangers. We'll try to avoid overly gruesome gore but you may experience some grimacing.

Of course, as rugged individualists, smokejumpers aren't known for being touchy feely folks. The Siskiyou crew was certainly no different, taking pride in their ability to withstand a little discomfort. Whining and whimpering was not tolerated. Indeed, they had a reputation of being tougher than rawhide, a legacy forged from the hell of countless wildfires.

But that doesn't mean the Siskiyou jumpers were insensitive. In fact, beneath that rough and ready image were plenty of teddy bears who cared deeply about the welfare of others and the world about them.

Consider Joe Niesen, a military veteran standing barely an inch under the smokejumper height limit. He was as tough as any of his brethren. Yet the former Siskiyou jumper waxes poetic when it comes to talking about the beauty of leaping out of an airplane and having a parachute blossom overhead.

"You know what kept us coming back year after year?" he asked, then answered, "It was because of that wonderful feeling you get when you first jump out. You are up there, drifting in the air, floating freely."

Since Siskiyou smokejumpers employed a static line attached to the plane which yanked the parachute out for them, there were no worries about pulling the parachute cord, he noted.

"So you just step out and everything is absolutely silent – you can see the earth all around you," Niesen continued. "It is just beautiful. There are no motors, no noise. It is just you, your thoughts and that magnificent view. There is nothing like it. Silence and a panoramic view of the world. What an incredibly wonderful feeling. That's what made people come back year after year."

Unless everything goes awry and you get tangled up in a snag, crash to the ground and shatter a few bones, that is.

Born in the summer of 1945, Niesen hadn't given much thought to becoming a smokejumper as a youngster reared in California's Crescent City not far from Oregon's southwest corner. When he turned 18, he started working for the U.S. Forest Service to earn money for college, initially joining a slash crew in the Gasquet area, a hamlet between Crescent City and the Oregon border. The second summer found him working on a fire engine crew in the same region.

"But I started attending the University of Oregon when I wasn't working and I wanted to establish Oregon residency," he said, noting it would reduce his tuition. "So the third summer I got a job on the Willamette National Forest in the McKenzie Bridge District just east of Eugene. I worked the trail crew."

Still, he wanted to be closer to home come summer.

"And the closest place to work in Oregon was the Siskiyou Smokejumper Base just south of Cave Junction," he said. "I applied and was offered a job."

That was in the spring of 1966.

"Like a lot of jumpers, I jumped out of the first airplane I ever rode in. To me, the plane ride was just as strange as the parachuting. We had been jumping off the training tower so I wasn't afraid of jumping. The heights I'm afraid of are maiming heights. I figured jumping from an airplane would not be painful if everything went south."

After jumping for two fire seasons and enjoying the work immensely, Niesen was called up in the military draft. Upon completing a mandatory two-year hitch in the Army, he returned to smokejumping in 1970. The fire season was approaching an end when he was among a group of Siskiyou jumpers deployed to a fire in far northern Washington hard against the Canadian border.

"It was a big fire – about 1,500 acres," he said, noting that was unusual since they were normally deployed to small fires with the goal of snuffing them out before they had a chance to grow. "They had jumped two D-3 loads of jumpers. It was real windy when we were going in."

He and another jumper leaped out of the plane together.

"The wind was clipping along pretty good," he recalled. "Right below me was a great big pine tree which I really didn't want to hit. So I steered around it and dropped down between the taller trees. What I couldn't see was a bunch of snags underneath."

One snagged his parachute.

"I remember looking up to see the snag bent over, arching over with my parachute caught up in it. You are supposed to carefully get your let-down rope rigged up and get down that way. But I gave it a little tug to see how firm it was."

Firm it was not.

"The snag broke – down I went. I fell a couple of stories and remember thinking, 'Oh shit!'"

He landed on a steep hillside, breaking his left hip. Although he was awake and cogent, he could not move.

"One of the other jumpers found me and they cut an opening in the woods for the helicopter to land. They dropped the big first aid kit and Mick Swift gave me a shot of pain killer. It was a lucky thing they had dropped the big first aid kit because another jumper got hit that night by a falling snag. Those snags don't make a sound when they are falling and it struck him in the back. He went into deep shock. Without that kit, he probably would have died."

Siskiyou jumper Gary Mills, who rookied with Niesen, recalled the incident. The Siskiyou jumpers were boosting at the North Cascades Smokejumper Base in Winthrop, Wash., Mills explained.

"It was an intense fire season. You'd jump, then go back to Winthrop but by the end of the day, because there were so many fires, you would be jumping again. And that one fire up by the Canadian border was the fire from hell."

Jumpers would be deployed only to have winds flare up, driving them back from the flames, he said.

"When we jumped, Joe hit the top of a tree which broke when it bent over," Mills said of the tall snag. "He was in bad shape. We had to build a helispot to get him out the next morning. The thing was, we had to protect the helispot from the fire. In the course of doing that, a tree fell and hit the Redding jumper. I was just a few feet away from him when that happened."

The Redding jumper was seriously injured but survived, Mills noted. Obviously, so did Niesen, albeit he was out of commission for an extended period. Within two and a half hours after leaving the site, he was in a hospital in Brewster, Wash. The next day he underwent surgery.

"They put what is called a 'Petersen nail' in my hip," Niesen said of a wicked-looking device with screws and bolts reminiscent of a favorite tool straight out of a medieval torture chamber. He was on crutches until the following spring.

"But I was only 25 and healthy as a horse – I wanted to jump again," he said. "The thing was, if you broke it again with that hardware in your hip, it could really be devastating. So they took it out that spring."

Made of stern stuff, Niesen mended quickly and got a job working in the Siskiyou National Forest's Galice Ranger District in the summer of 1971.

"But I was back jumping for the 1972 fire season," he said, although noting he didn't have the gung-ho feeling about jumping that he had earlier. "I made a few more jumps on fires. I was strictly mercenary. I was jumping for the money at that point."

One day he found himself standing at the door of the plane, hesitating before making the leap.

"I kind of froze," he said. "I was the second guy and they had to make another pass to let me out. That was a no-no on my part. I'm not sure it was a real freeze. We had been in there fighting the fire for a few days and I was feeling really weak."

That was his last jump. With base manager Dutton's help, he got a job as a fire patrolman in the Gasquet area. Niesen would graduate from honor's college at the University of Oregon with a double major in general science and arts and letters.

"Back in college, I had played a couple of years of rugby football," said Niesen who had played football and ran track in high school. "But I realized how much a broken arm playing rugby would cost me. As jumpers, we made pretty good money compared to what most guys were getting during the summer. So I quit the rugby and ended up breaking my hip."

Later, taking advantage of his GI Bill, he earned a master's degree in forestry from Humboldt State University in northern California. He retired from the Siskiyou National Forest in 1998.

"I didn't enjoy crashing into the snag but I really enjoyed smokejumping when I was young," he said. "That feeling of floating in the air was something you never forget."

True story, observed Dale Gardner who arrived at the Siskiyou base a year after Niesen rookied.

"Parachuting is quite an experience, one I'll always remember," Gardner said. "There is nothing like it."

Hailing from near Sacramento, Gardner, born in 1947, wasn't much aware of smokejumping until he went to Humboldt State University in northwestern California where he roomed with jumper Louis "Lou" Wayers who rookied at the Siskiyou base in 1966. Intrigued by Wayers' smokejumping stories, Gardner, who had worked four fire seasons as a ground-pounding fire fighter in California, applied and was accepted in the Siskiyou base's rookie class in 1967.

"There were 14 in my rookie class," he said, noting it was a larger than usual group. "We made up about half the base strength that year."

He fared well in his training as well as the first couple of fire jumps he made. Life as a smokejumper was good. Then came a fire on August 10, 1967.

"It was on the Umpqua," he said of the national forest just north of Crater Lake. "I was trying to get into a jump spot under windy conditions. I hung in a large snag briefly and it broke before I could even get my let-down rope out."

He estimates that he plunged about 60 feet.

"Fortunately, it was steep ground, probably 50 percent slope. Had it been flat ground I'm not sure I would have survived. I hit and slid."

And broke his lower back, although he didn't know how serious it was until after fighting the fire.

"I knew something wasn't right," he said of the intense pain. "There were two of us on the fire and we fought it. After we bedded down and I got up the next morning I realized something was very seriously wrong."

After eight more jumpers were dropped in the next morning, he and two other jumpers hiked out about three miles.

"I was carrying my gear, about 120 pounds worth," he said, adding the pain was nearly unbearable. "It was all I could do to make it out of there. As soon as I got back to the base, I went to see Doc Versteeg."

A former Army surgeon, the medical doctor in Cave Junction checked him out and informed him he needed to see an orthopedic surgeon as soon as possible. Gardner, then 20, was flown to a specialist in Garberville, Calif. by base pilot Hal Ewing. Instead of surgery, the doctor recommended that Gardner immediately go on a high calcium diet but remain largely immobile until the vertebrae fused itself naturally.

"I took it real easy and went back to school that fall," he said.

"Later, when I went back for a check up, I asked the doc when I could get back to jumping. He told me if it happened again that I probably never would walk again. So my jumping career ended the first fire season I jumped."

He graduated from college, taught school for a short time, then returned to the Forest Service where he worked for a little over 30 years, although all of it on the ground.

"When I was a working on the Gold Beach Ranger District, I interacted with the Siskiyou jumpers on a couple of fires," he recalled. "It was great to work with them again. A good bunch of guys."

He also came to know a jumper nicknamed "Mouse" who arrived at the base after Gardner quite jumping.

"He was a larger-than-life character," Gardner said. "He was tougher than a boot, had a super attitude, could outwork darn near anyone and was the life of the party. In the jumper game, everybody knew about Mouse."

As it happens, Mouse was the spotter on the airplane in August of 1980 when Siskiyou smokejumper Mike "Appy" Apicello nearly died in a horrific landing. But first a little background.

Hailing from New York City, Apicello was raised in Manhattan and Spanish Harlem, making him as unlikely as just about anyone in the United States to become a Siskiyou smokejumper.

"I was raised in the shadow of Yankee Stadium," he said. "I saw all the great baseball players on the Yankees from 1960 on. That was the world I knew as a kid."

Yet he had felt a strong yearning as a child to be among trees, not towering buildings. When he was 18, he applied and was accepted in what was then New York State Ranger School in Wanakena on the east branch of the Oswegatchie River in upstate New York. Established in 1912, the school is now under the auspices of the State University of New York College of Environmental Science and Forestry. Today it is called the SUNY-ESF Ranger School.

"It's a small school up in the northern Adirondacks," he explained. "My class size was 86 – 80 males and 6 females. Within a week of graduating, I was offered a job on the Siskiyou National Forest, something I had never heard of. A week later I was moving from the Bronx to Brookings, Oregon."

That was in 1975. Talk about being a stranger in a strange land. He might as well have landed on another planet.

"My first week on the job I am cruising old-growth redwood trees near Brookings and marking trees for cutting. These were the biggest trees I had ever seen."

Parenthetically, while the northern California coastal forests are known for their gigantic redwoods, the redwoods do extend into the southwest corner of the Rogue River-Siskiyou National Forest. The Rogue River and Siskiyou national forests were formally joined after Apicello retired from the U.S. Forest Service.

After cruising timber for a while, he began working on prescribed burns to reduce wildfire threat as well as to improve forest health. These are fires intentionally set in the early spring or late fall to burn underbrush and logging debris as part of an effort to reduce the forest buildup. While it may seem counter intuitive, fire prevention over the years often creates increased fire danger later on because of unnaturally overgrown forests.

"It wasn't uncommon for us to burn more than 10,000 acres a year," he said. "It was a classic way to learn fire behavior."

After he worked his way up to district assistant fire management officer, he was offered the chance to try out at the Siskiyou Smoke-jumper Base. He enthusiastically joined the rookie class in the spring of 1978.

"I remember thinking, 'Wow, this is the greatest job in the world,'" he said of smokejumping. "I really liked the work and the people."

During the next two winters he worked as a commercial crab fisherman off the Oregon coast. For him, life couldn't have been much better, particularly the two summers he spent as a smokejumper.

"It was so removed from my childhood – my parents were second-generation Italians in New York City," he said, noting he had four brothers and sisters. "They were city folk. When I told them I was going out West to the Siskiyou National Forest, they thought I was going to be a forest ranger, my aspiration since I was about five or six. They didn't understand when I told them I was going to become a smokejumper. To this day, I don't think my mother ever knew exactly what a smokejumper did."

Once, when he was 21, he returned to the Big Apple for a visit and went bar hopping with a couple of childhood chums.

"We would go into a bar and they would announce to everyone, 'Hey, here is a forest ranger from Oregon!'" he recalled. "It was free drinks after that."

Back at the Siskiyou base, he would jump on more than two dozen fires.

"We jumped on a fire once outside of Grants Pass when Mouse was the squad leader – there was about eight of us. The fire was going pretty good. All of a sudden we hear this noise out in the woods. It was a county corrections crew that was mostly just kids. Mouse told their supervisor that it was dangerous and they needed to get out of there. He asked us for directions and we told them there was a trail they could take out. 'Get your kids out of here,' Mouse told him. He was adamant about it."

Siskiyou jumpers may have been renowned for their pranks but they were dead serious when on the job, Apicello stressed.

They also looked out for their own. He recalled one afternoon when Mouse was about to sit down to a fried chicken lunch and was called out to be a spotter on a fire. Knowing it was one of Mouse's favorite meals, Apicello quickly boxed the lunch up for him so it would fit into his hip pocket for an in-flight snack.

"Jumpers took care of each other," he said.

They certainly needed to be there for him on Aug. 16, 1980, when they were jumping on the Strickland Butte Fire in what was then the Applegate Ranger District of the Rogue River National Forest. It was shortly after 4:00 p.m. when he made a leap that forever changed his life.

"We were jumping a four-man fire," he said, noting it was in the mountains high in the Applegate River drainage hard against the California state line. "Troop [Tom Emonds] was the squad boss. It was a really nasty jump spot, an old log deck on fire. First guy out was Troop who slammed into a tree and fell into a pile of rocks, injuring his arm. Second man out hit the spot but landed hard. Third man out, Rick Dees, got hung up in a tree. I was the fourth one out and hit some dead air."

Realizing he was not going to make the landing spot, he opted to try for a small nearby meadow. There were several big trees in the area.

"I ran out of running room and hit a tree," he said, noting he intentionally hit the tree in an effort to slow his descent. "Sure enough, it slowed me down. I stopped once, then slid another 16 feet or so. I stopped again, then slid another 20 feet and stopped."

However, dangling high above the ground in a tall tree was not what he had planned.

"I went to reach my arm over a limb so I could lock myself into the tree but before I got my hand over the limb I started free falling. I thought, 'OK, I need to get my knees together and do a roll when I hit the ground.'"

But he doesn't recall slamming into the ground, although he does remember counting up to three on his way down.

"When I regained consciousness, I was laying on a pile of rocks and staring at the base of the tree I had hit. My harness felt like it was too tight. I went to undo my cape wells fasteners (that attach to the jumper's harness) and could only move my left arm. Nothing else worked."

He struggled to keep from blacking out. Intense pain flamed through his shattered body.

"I had broken my back in three places. I shattered my right heel bone and my left knee. And I spit out four teeth."

If that wasn't enough, his diaphragm between his abdominal and thoracic cavities was barely functioning. When your diaphragm contracts, it draws air into the lungs by increasing the volume of the thoracic cavity, allowing you to breathe. Obviously, since the cavity contains the heart and lungs, proper contraction and expansion is essential for respiration.

"My first thought when I came to was, 'Wow. I'm alive,'" said Apicello, then 26. "I remember going through all kinds of emotions – crying, laughing. They said I was as gray as a ghost."

Suddenly, he realized his legs felt abnormally warm.

"I thought, 'Oh, my God! I've broken my legs and am bleeding in my boots,'" he said of his 16-inch high boots. "Well, I figured the only thing that is going to save me is my training and jump partner. I needed to keep calm and keep breathing. About every 20 seconds I'd yell for help."

But it took a little over a half hour before his weak cries, restricted by his breathing difficulties, were heard by other smokejumpers. The first one to reach him was Don Bisson, Emonds' jump partner.

"Don told me later he was telling me jokes to try to get me to stay awake," Apicello said. "All I remember was telling him I was about to go into a grand mal."

Bisson, who had rookied with Apicello, signaled the plane to drop the trauma kit. Unfortunately, the kit landed in top of an old-growth tree. Veteran smokejumper and ace tree climber Willard "Willie" Lowden, who had jumped in 1976-77 and returned in 1980, retrieved the vital trauma kit. Unable to reach the kit by climbing the large tree Apicello had tangled with, Lowden courageously climbed to the top of a nearby smaller tree, then started swaying it back and forth until he could reach out to cut the ropes holding the kit. Talk about a gutsy move.

Ignoring the pain from an elbow severely injured during his hard landing, Emonds opened the trauma kit and gave Apicello a shot of Demerol. After waiting five minutes, Emonds, a former Marine Corps officer whose experience in Vietnam had prepared him for aiding injured combatants, whether the enemy was a snag or a sniper, administered another shot of painkiller to the injured smokejumper.

"Troop took really good care of me," Apicello said. "I was on the ground 55 to 60 minutes before the helicopter arrived. By the time we landed at the Rogue Valley Medical Center in Medford, the helicopter was just about out of gas. We put down right in the parking lot. They got me on a gurney and wheeled me in. I remember looking up and seeing everyone in every window in the hospital looking at me."

But he has no memory of what happened next, having been placed in a morphine-induced coma for several days.

"When I came out of the coma four and a half days later, they had done emergency surgery on my calcaneus," he said of his heel bone, the largest bone in the human foot. "My first thought was that I was hungry, my second was, 'Man, I've got to pee.' Turns out they had never put a catheter in me. And that was the worst pain of all when they put that in. They must have heard me scream throughout the hospital."

It would take several years for him to recover from what would be his last fire jump.

"Going from a smokejumper and really fit to what I was then was difficult to adjust to," he said. "There were tough times. But I told myself I was going to survive and get through it."

Survive he did. Apicello, who would return to the classroom, became the national spokesman for the Forest Service's Fire and Aviation Management Program before retiring from the U.S. Forest Service.

"That tree ended my jumping career but not my career in firefighting. You know, I can still see the tree I hit. When it comes to that day, my eyesight was so clear that I could see every fissure and every chip on the bark of that big sugar pine. Even now, I still see it."

But he has no regrets about moving west to become a Siskiyou smokejumper.

"I had gone full circle from being a green horn in New York City to becoming a smokejumper – that experience changed everything for me," he concluded. "I ended my career on a very good note, working on changing the Forest Service safety policy. We changed it so that every firefighter had the right to say 'No' to an unsafe assignment without any career repercussions. Where that proved itself was on the R&L fire in Arizona where the Granite Hotshots lost 19 firefighters. Two Forest Service hotshot crews had said 'No' to that assignment."

The Siskiyou Smokejumper Base was located at the Illinois Valley Airport a half-dozen miles south of Cave Junction. The historic base is now a museum.

Living quarters for the first Siskiyou smokejumpers in the early 1940s were platform tents erected at the ranger district headquarters in Cave Junction.

By the early 1950s, the smokejumpers were housed in more comfortable wooden barracks built at the base.

An aerial photograph of the Siskiyou Smokejumper Base taken in 1962 reveals a facility fully prepared to fight wildfires. The Rough and Ready Co. sawmill is in the background.

Siskiyou smokejumper Mike Mann takes a plunge in a practice water landing near the base, providing a refreshing dip on a hot day. (*Photo by Doug Beck*)

A Siskiyou smokejumper takes a practice jump over the base, following another jumper whose chute is already beginning to open. (*Photo by Doug Beck*)

A 4-foot-11 Marine to be looked up to

The Drill Instructor reached the last man in the last rank of his raw recruit platoon. "How *tall* are you boy?" he drawled in that sneering tone that is as much a part of a Marine D.I.'s equipment as his eagerness to demonstrate hand-to-hand combat.

"Sir," bellowed Private Allen Owen, "I'm six foot two and 200 pounds and the meanest man in the state!" Suppressing a grin, the D.I. glared at the smallest Marine that he had ever seen. "You'll do, Shortround," he said. And Shortround, as he has been called ever since, has been doing very nicely thank you—despite the fact that he stands but 4-feet-11, the tiniest leatherneck in memory.

Owen bullied his way into the Corps by fast-talking a recruiting officer. That somewhat stunned gentleman urgently recommended that the 5-foot-2 minimum height requirement be waived in Owen's case. "He's a mass of muscle and strong as an ox," the officer reported. Headquarters was duly impressed and Owen, 22, of St. Louis

was on the way to boot camp—all 112 pounds of him. Shortround took boot camp in stride, even though the hazards on the obstacle course were higher, farther and deeper for him than for his fellow recruits. He learned to handle rocket launchers, which are about as tall as he is, picked up an expert's badge on the rifle range and finally was named honor man in his platoon. This award brought him a free set of dress blues—the smallest size in the supply room, cut down to fit him.

After boot camp, Shortround was sent to Camp Pendleton for advanced infantry training, which consists mainly of running up and down mountains toting enough gear to rupture a pack mule. His company commander was amazed. "This little fellow doesn't ask for anything special; sometimes we have to slow him down." Owen's current assignment is communications school, after which he hopes to be posted to Vietnam. He has heard that most of our enemies over there are just about his size.

CONTINUED 113

Top: While training in the Marine Corps at Camp Pendleton, Calif., Pvt. Allen Owen was prominently featured in the May 6, 1966 edition of *Life* magazine.

Bottom: Before the year was out, Pvt. Owen was deployed to South Vietnam where he served for three years. He rose to the rank of sergeant by the time he completed his hitch.

Top: During breaks from his Marine training in southern California, Allen Owen spent a few weekends learning to sports jump in the San Diego area.

Bottom: In 1967, brothers Larry Owen (*left*) and Allen Owen, both Marines stationed in South Vietnam, spent Christmas together near Danang.

Allen Owen, weighing in at a mere 120 pounds at most, was capable of strapping on a 150-pound pack stuffed full of gear and moving out with it. (*Photo by Doug Beck*)

15

LONG-OF-TOOTH JUMPERS

E NOUGH WITH THE FATALITIES AND ghastly injuries in-volving Siskiyou smokejumpers and their brethren. With an apology to the immortal crooner Bing Crosby for butchering one of his popular melodies, we'll henceforth strive to accentuate the positive while dropkicking the negative into the Gobi gorge.

Most of those who jumped out of the Siskiyou Smokejumper Base when it was young are gone now, having made that leap into the great beyond.Let's hope they landed with a good roll in a beautiful place where they could share their stories and reminisce.

But a few are still around, although they are all nonagenarians, folks who are over 90 but short of the century mark. We will meet three in this chapter who were rookies at the base 70 years ago or more. They don't move as quickly as they did when they wore young men's clothes, being a tad more cautious at each step. Yet, as one approaching the sep-tuagenarian milestone which begins at 70, I am in awe of the physical and mental energy of these wise elders of the Siskiyou smokejumping community. When they start talking about their jumping days, there is fire in their eyes and an infectious enthusiasm in their voice. For a moment, they are young men again, eager to relive their jumping days.

Consider the remarkable Roger Newton and the time he stole, er, borrowed a pickup truck while packing out from a fire. When you read the future attorney's rationale for the action, chances are you would also have committed grand theft auto.

But first a little background.

Born in Independence, Oregon, Newton was raised in Ashland in the upper Bear Creek Valley. After completing a hitch in the Army Air Corps, he returned to southern Oregon, applied at the newly-fledged Siskiyou Smokejumper Base and became a member of the 1951 rookie class.

"They trained us so well that I wasn't scared at all on my first training jump," recalled Newton who was 94 when interviewed in 2018. "I only took five training jumps before I was out there fighting fires."

His first fire in 1951 was on what is now the Shasta-Trinity National Forest in northern California.

"Our job was to get the snag down and hold the fire until the ground pounders arrived," he said. "We cut down the burning tree and just about had the fire out before reinforcements got there. Again, we had been trained very well."

He would jump through the 1958 fire seasons, both to pay for his college education, including law school, and because he thoroughly enjoyed the profession.

"There were so many impressive people working there," he said of the Siskiyou base. "You couldn't help but have a great experience."

He quickly became a trainer.

"I trained Stuart Roosa – nice kid," Newton said of the future astronaut who was a 19-year old rookie in 1953. "In Roosa's book, the title was, *Smokejumper, Moon Pilot: The Remarkable Life of Apollo 14 Astronaut Stuart Roosa* – in that order. That showed how much he liked jumping. He was a good jumper who liked fighting fires but, of course, he had to fly rocket ships."

Although the book was written by Willie G. Moseley, the volume authorized by the Roosa family clearly reflects the astronaut's love of smokejumping. Like Newton, Roosa obviously enjoyed his time spent at the Siskiyou base amid the camaraderie of the other jumpers.

Roosa passed away in 1994 but former Siskiyou jumper Lee Gossett, a 1957 rookie, can speak to Newton's training ability.

"Roger trained me as a smokejumper," Gossett said when two were reminiscing during a jumper reunion. "He was one of the mythical gods of smokejumping."

Although smiling, Newton raised his eyebrows at the compliment and protested that many others at the base were more deserving of the praise.

"We had a lot of really good leaders," he said. "Jim Allen was an excellent boss, a rare individual. Everyone liked him. We knew he was there for us. A good man."

Like all smokejumpers, Newton, who made a little over 70 jumps during his career, had several close encounters of the worst kind. The most challenging jump for him was when he and Orville Looper, a 1949 Siskiyou base rookie, were asked to jump out of a Lockheed Lodestar. The powers that be were checking it out to determine whether the aircraft could serve as a jumper plane, Newton explained.

"The plane was big and heavy but fast," he said of the aircraft which served as a troop transporter during WWII. "When you jump, the first thing you always do is check your chute. Well, everything was backwards with my chute when I left the Lodestar because of an inversion. We were going so fast. The wind hit me with such force when we jumped that the chute didn't deploy properly. I managed to get everything straightened out as I was falling and was able to hit the field but it was very scary for a while there."

The incident involving the stolen vehicle may not have been as physically bloodcurdling but it certainly had its moments, he allowed.

"I took that pickup when I and another guy jumped on a fire down in northern California around the mid 1950s," he recalled. "The guy got hurt real bad. He had been severely burned by the fire we had been fighting."

Burning deep in the rugged Castle Crags area, now a wilderness in northern California, the fire had been fanned by swirling winds, entrapping the jumper, he noted.

"He was badly burned – barely conscious," Newton said. "I had to keep him walking because he was going into shock. We walked into the night and finally came to this logging site. No one was around but there was an old pickup with the keys in it."

Concerned his jump partner may not survive much longer, Newton eased him into the truck and drove until they reached a ranger station where he woke up the district ranger. After the injured man received emergency medical attention and was taken to a hospital, Newton, although exhausted, figured he had better return the vehicle and explain what happened.

"When I was taking the pickup back I got stopped by a state trooper," he said of the morning after he took the vehicle. "The logging company had reported the pickup as stolen. The policeman had his gun out and everything when he pulled me over."

After all, the suspicious character driving the stolen vehicle was a rough-looking customer, the kind whose unshaven mug shot used to hang on post office walls. The disheveled suspect was wearing smelly clothes and clearly hadn't had a good night's rest in some time. Little wonder the trooper was a mite edgy. What's more, he had caught the suspect red handed in the stolen vehicle.

"I explained what happened but he didn't believe me," Newton said. "He had no idea of what I was talking about. He had never heard of a smokejumper. He wanted to take me straight to jail. I guess I wasn't making a whole lot of sense at the time."

No doubt the trooper had heard some tall tales spun by suspects trying to weasel out of an arrest but this one was a real doozey. Still, Newton kept a cool head and convinced the officer to at least swing by the Forest Service office before taking him to the hoosegow. Against his better judgment, the trooper placed the suspect in the back of the cruiser and sped off to the forest headquarters. Agency officials not only verified Newton's story but complimented him for taking swift albeit unorthodox action to save the burned jumper's life. Newton was not charged with stealing the vehicle.

"Yes, that was the only time I ever 'stole' a vehicle," chuckled Newton, a dapper-looking gentleman who would practice law in Santa Barbara, California for many years before retiring. "But it was something I had to do to get him help as soon as possible. He wouldn't have made it much longer."

Looking back on his jumping years, he observed it was experience he cherished.

"It was something I felt I had to do as a young man," he concluded. "I never regretted it."

Something there is that draws stalwart young humanoids to become smokejumpers, agreed Robert "Bob" Scofield who was a gung-ho rookie at the Siskiyou base in 1949.

But the former jumper had to ponder the question of what prompted them to volunteer to leap out of a perfectly good plane and attempt to drop as near as possible to a forest fire without being singed or worse.

No, it isn't a peculiar type of insanity, he responded to a wisenheimer suggestion.

"I do know I really enjoyed jumping," he said. "I was on a lot of fires as a ground pounder in the years afterwards but jumping, although tougher, was more adventurous, more exciting. I suppose that was it. We also had great camaraderie. I always liked to think we were the best."

An only child, Scofield was born May 23, 1929, in Centralia, Washington. His father was a carpenter who moved his family periodically as his work demanded. During his younger years, his family lived in a farming hamlet known as Green Acres just southeast of Coos Bay. But the Scofields moved to Portland shortly after World War II erupted.

"My folks worked in the Portland shipyards during the war," he explained.

Meanwhile, because many young men were away fighting in the war, the U.S. Forest Service lowered its minimum hiring age to 16 in hopes of hiring local youth.

"It happened the Forest Service had advertised it had jobs available for the summer," Scofield said. "Since I had grown up pretty much in the country, I figured that might be a good thing to do rather than sit around in Portland. So I started working for the Forest Service."

The summer of 1945 found him on a blister rust crew in the Rogue River National Forest, followed by a similar job on Grayback Creek on the Siskiyou National Forest the following summer. He served as forest fire lookout in the Siskiyou's Galice Ranger District in the summers of 1947 and '48. Late the following spring, he decided to make a leap in his career path. Literally.

"I had become aware of smokejumpers," he said. "I met the pilot of the Siskiyou Smokejumper Base the last summer I was a fire lookout. I was on Serpentine Point on the south end of the Galice District. His Noorduyn [Norseman aircraft] had a problem and the pilot made an emergency landing in a field on the lower Illinois River. I watched him go down and went over there to make sure he was OK."

Fortunately, the pilot and aircraft were unscathed. Scofield was impressed by the stories the pilot told about smokejumpers and their challenging profession.

"So I volunteered in the spring of '49," he said, noting he was just shy of six foot and weighed in at a lean 170 pounds. "I was in good shape. Back then, we did our training at what was then the Redwood Ranger Station in Cave Junction. We had a jump tower and let-down apparatus. We spent part of that summer building facilities out at the airport."

His first training jump was at Castleberry Field, a farmer's field just west of Cave Junction along the Illinois River. Like so many rookies in those days, Scofield jumped out of the very first plane he ever climbed aboard.

"I was a little scared, I have to confess," he said of making his first plunge into 1,000 feet of thin air. "I had just turned 20 years old and it was the first time I had ever ridden in an airplane ride."

Scared or not, there was that strong desire to become an official member of the smokejumping corps.

"When the spotter swatted me on the back, I hopped out," he said of his virgin jump in June of 1949. "After my training, I knew what I had to do."

It all went according to Hoyle, the first of his seven practice jumps his rookie year.

"The only one I had problems with was my third or fourth jump when my chute spun when I came out," he said. "As a consequence, I was hanging there unwinding. My steering slots ended up being pointed in the wrong direction."

A jumper can maneuver his – or her – direction by pulling the steering lines to turn the chute in the direction desired. Air shooting through the slots also gives the jumper the ability to move forward.

"But when you start twirling around, it fouls you up," he said. "On that particular jump, I wound up hanging in a tree."

Fortunately, it was not a tall tree. He was able to disentangle himself easily enough and descend to the ground with his let-down rope.

"My first fire was memorable. Cliff Marshall was the foreman. There were three of us jumping on that fire. Cliff landed on a rock and broke his foot."

A tough airborne paratrooper during WWII, Marshall wasn't going to let a mere broken foot get in the way of completing the mission. Never mind they were in a steep and rugged region of the Six Rivers National Forest in far northern California near the Oregon state line, a region tough enough to hike in without a broken foot.

"He ordered us to go to the fire," Scofield said. "He was our boss yet I couldn't believe we were actually going to walk off and leave him. We knew he was hurt. But we went off to the fire as he had ordered."

And Marshall?

"Why, he crawled down the hill and up the other side of the creek to the trail," Scofield said. "When the ground crew came in, they picked him up. I don't believe he jumped again that summer but he was back the next season. Tough guy."

Like most jumpers, Scofield will tell you it was the fire fighting and hiking out with all the gear that turned smokejumping into hard labor.

"Our packs weighed more than 90 pounds dry," he said. "If it rained, it was much heavier. You'd be surprised how much a chute can weigh when it gets wet. But it was what we had to do. So we did it."

There were a few silk parachutes in 1949 but most of them were nylon, he said.

"Most of ours were military surplus. I was told the landing shock was about the same as jumping off a 10-foot wall. But once you are trained, the jumping itself is not that hazardous."

While many folks may picture a jumper drifting down out of a cerulean blue sky while checking out the beautiful scenery below, that was seldom the case, he said.

"Usually when you are jumping you are so busy steering and trying to get to the jump spot that you don't have time to look around much," he added. "You don't have time to enjoy the ride."

For him, avoiding getting caught up in a tall tree was always paramount.

"Tall trees are always a concern when you are jumping. If you get hung up in a tree and you are OK, then you have to get the damned chute down. That was always a problem."

His toughest jump was in 1950 near Granite Lake in California's Shasta-Trinity National Forest. Although the fire wasn't that difficult to put out, they had to use a misery whip – a long saw pulled back and forth with a jumper at each end – to fall a couple of large pines that were burning, he explained.

"That was a real hassle because the pines were so big. When we finally got that done, the pack out was a real bitch because we had about ten miles to hike to reach the road. It was real tough going. None of it flat."

Scofield broke his right foot in a 1954 jump on the Lost Lake fire in the Rogue River National Forest.

"My chute spun up and I missed hitting the jump spot," he said. "I didn't want to land in the water so I wound up hitting a lava field. It wasn't a severe break so my buddies packed my gear out and I was able to hobble out to a road."

Bone-breaking jumps were not common but they did happen, he noted. Yet he figures jumping itself was not the most dangerous part of the job.

"It's the firefighting that is dangerous," he said. "There is always something that can get you out on a fire."

If it isn't the flames, there are buzzing rattlesnakes, the danger of falling snags or the potential to twist or snap an ankle on loose rocks, he said.

"Most of the fires we had in the early days were in northern California. That was the pattern of the storms. I only jumped four times in Oregon."

The fires he jumped on were largely what he called "fish fries," a term reserved for small fires which could be handled by a few jumpers. The plane they deployed was the single-engine, high-wing Noorduyn Norseman, the one he had seen making an emergency landing.

"It was considered to be an excellent aircraft for that purpose," he said of the aircraft which, in addition to the pilot, carried three jumpers and a spotter.

Scofield jumped for two summers, then was drafted into the army during the Korean conflict. He was sent to Germany where he served in the signal corps. Discharged as a sergeant after two years, he returned to smokejumping in 1953 while attending Oregon State University on the GI Bill during the off season.

Like Newton, he recalled the 1953 rookie who was bound for the Moon.

"Stuart Roosa was a little quiet but he was damned smart," Scofield said of the future NASA astronaut. "You knew he was going places."

Scofield, who served as a squad leader in 1954 and '55, made 51 jumps, enabling him to earn his Gold Wings for having survived the first 50. Of those, 36 were on fires.

"The last fire jump I made was in the Willamette, a fire called the Happy Prairie fire," he said of early September of 1955. "It wasn't doing much. It was only about five acres and we didn't have much trouble putting it out."

After graduating with a bachelor's degree in forest management, he became a timber management assistant on the Siskiyou forest for several years. His next role was serving in fire planning, a job which required him to review all the firefighting reports. One of the reports he recalled studying was the Mount Emily fire ignited by the incendiary bomb in 1942. Scofield retired from the U.S. Forest Service in 1984 after 37 years of working for Uncle Sam.

Scofield and his wife moved from Wyoming to southern Oregon in 2016, settling in historic Jacksonville to be near the old jumper base.

"I liked my years as a smokejumper out in the Illinois Valley," he said. "Good bunch of people. The fellowship with the group was terrific."

That camaraderie sometimes led to a rowdy Saturday night at a lively Cave Junction watering hole called the Owl Tavern, fondly known as the "Hoot," he allowed.

"Yeah, there were several rumbles in the Hoot, mostly with a few loggers who got liquored up a little and wanted to prove their manhood. It was a rough community in those days. But we jumpers could take care of ourselves."

True story, observed Albert "Al" Boucher who rookied with Scofield at the Siskiyou base in 1949. Like his longtime friend and jumping buddy, Boucher – pronounced *bou-shay* – would retire from the U.S. Forest Service.

"Smokejumpers are known for pushing the envelope sometimes, and that was certainly true of the ones from Cave Junction," Boucher said. "But it was the best base of them all. Some of my best times were jumping out of there."

A jumper for a dozen fire seasons, he spent a lot of time at other bases during his smokejumping days.

"Jumpers are obviously a unique firefighting crew," he said. "After jumping, I got into what some people would call the 'real' Forest Service. That's when I discovered how some people in the agency didn't care for smokejumpers and didn't see a place in the Forest Service for them. They figured they were too rowdy."

While he concedes they may have had a point, he believes that boisterous trait made jumpers into very effective and gung-ho firefighters, providing they had strong leaders to keep them in check.

"Of all the bases I had been at through the years, there is no question but that Jim Allen ran the best base of any," he stressed. "He had that quiet way of being in charge. He was fair but firm. I was his assistant and crew foreman for quite a while. He was the best boss ever."

"And there was nothing like steak night on Sunday," he added of the chow hall. "The lady cooking had that big grill to cook on and always told the jumpers, 'Just choose the steak you want.' That was a time for everyone to sit down and talk."

Born in Missouri, Boucher was reared in the Rogue Valley, attending Medford Senior High School in Medford for three years. After serving a hitch in the Navy, he went to the Illinois Valley in 1948 where his parents had opened a small business.

"I tried to become a smokejumper in the summer of '48 but they were full," Boucher recalled. "So I worked that summer in the base cookhouse. I got to know all the jumpers and gave them extra food when I could. We became friends."

In 1948, the base headquarters was located at the ranger station on the southwest end of Cave Junction. Boucher lived in what he described as a tent house behind the ranger station.

"But I knew I was going to get a chance to become a smokejumper the next summer because the boss said, 'Yeah, I'll take you on and see how it works out,'" he said of Allen.

Like Scofield, Boucher made his training jumps at a field on the Castleberry farm. After jumping for two summers, he was called back into the Navy for the Korean War. Upon completing his second military hitch, he returned to smokejumping in 1957, staying at the base through the summer of 1963, jumping a total 115 times.

He also tied the knot.

"I ended up marrying a wonderful gal from Cave Junction – one of the Smith girls," he said of Ruth, his late wife. "She was related to just about every other person in the Illinois Valley. Her family went back to the 1850s in Kerby."

In the mid-1960s, he went to the newly minted Redmond Smoke-jumper Base to serve as foreman, jumping there for three more fire seasons.

"For me, it was fun to jump – a real kick. I was shocked after I found out that some guys were jumping to make money but hated jumping. They called it 'sacrificing themselves.' But I always enjoyed the jumping part."

Like most smokejumpers, he also enjoyed dropping into remote areas of public land few people had ever seen.

"After you stopped a fire in a wilderness area, you have a little time to appreciate the beautiful country. You have a sleeping bag and you have a little camp because you are going to stay there a few days. You have food and water. Of course, we really worked our butts off to stop those fires."

Standing 5' 11" and barely tipping the scales at 160 pounds, Boucher observed that he didn't have the muscle mass typical of many jumpers.

"But I was never injured," he said. "A lot of the guys who were injured were ex-jocks with a lot of muscles. I never had much in the way of muscles. I was always lean. Maybe that's why I never got hurt."

During his 30-year career, Boucher said he worked out of every one of the Forest Service jumper bases.

"I became a spotter and trainer early on. Taking the guys out and spotting for them, that was something I really enjoyed. I suppose that's partly because I would come back to a nice warm meal and a soft bed each night."

Boucher continued to work at the Redmond base after he quit jumping. At one time, there were had 60 jumpers at Redmond, making it one of the larger bases in the West, he said.

"Sometimes you jump some guys in the woods and you think you have enough to handle the fire," he said. "But the weather changes on you. And it becomes obvious that you and four or five other guys aren't going to stop that fire. You know you are not going to get out in front of it. That happened on quite a few fires."

While at the Siskiyou base, he recalled responding to one fire which nearly overcame the crew.

"What we did was grab our gear and walk into the burn," he said of braving the flames and entering the area that had already been burned. "We were all right. It wasn't too intense. We scraped an area so we weren't sitting on hot embers."

There were also plenty of fires which they were able to snuff out before they had a chance to take off, he stressed.

"We usually stopped 'em," he said of his years at the Siskiyou base. "Northern California was where we jumped the most. That was from the state line down to about Redding."

In 1949, his first year at the Siskiyou base, he and fellow Gobi jumpers were deployed to a fire in the tall Sequoias near Porterville, California.

"We flew down in a Ford Trimotor and jumped out of that," he said of one of the three-engine aircrafts built by the Ford Motor Co. from 1925 through 1933.

"We all made down it safely out of that old plane and through the big trees. After we got the fire down, we came out on horseback about 18 miles or so. That was a nice pack out."

In 1950, he was hired early in the season to work on the parachute loft at the Siskiyou base.

"I loved the jumping part but I didn't exactly enjoy the heavy pack outs and the hard work. I was always steering myself to learn everything I could about jumping. I became a master rigger for the FAA and was in charge of the parachute loft."

He trained his wife and several other local women as parachute riggers.

"When we were really busy, they would rig the parachutes for us," he said. "One time the old duffer down at the Redding base requested some riggers and my wife and the other women went down there. They took over until they got the job done."

Like many folks who worked as smokejumpers, Boucher had a side that many of his firefighting buddies never saw. Evidence of that side hangs on the walls of his comfortable home in Redmond in the form of excellent pencil drawings.

"Yeah, I've always done artwork," he said, adding, "In fact, I did the first emblem that is out at the Siskiyou base. I bummed some cedar from old man Krauss out at the Rough & Ready (Lumber Co.) sawmill there across the highway from the base. He told me to take what I needed. Didn't charge me a cent."

Nor did mill owner Lew Krauss Sr. charge Boucher when the smoke-jumper wanted to install a diving board at Seat's Dam on Rough and Ready Creek just west of the base. The dam created a deep swimming hole filled with crystal-clear water, a place popular among jumpers and local youth alike.

"I told old man Krauss we wanted to get a diving board for the dam," Boucher said. "Some guy at the mill came up with the specs and made one, clamps and everything. It was perfect. But within two weeks some jerk stole it."

By the by, Boucher was quick to observe that the Krauss family, which settled in the Illinois Valley around the turn of the 20th Century, donated many materials for other community projects over the years. A quick check indicates he is correct: building a Catholic church, a gymnasium in the Selma Elementary School and restoration of the 1898 Grimmett log schoolhouse when it was relocated to the Kerbyville Museum site in 1960. He also rightly noted that too many local businesses are remembered for their sometimes sharp businesses practices and not for their good deeds. With those good deeds in mind, I now salute the Krauss family, whose lumber business started around 1920 and survived for nearly a century.

Like most former Siskiyou jumpers, Boucher maintained a keen sense of humor, both for rough moments as well as the good times. Consider the time the fellow staffing the fire lookout on Black Butte west of Redmond complained when he was checking in on the radio that he had run out of reading material. No doubt Boucher was grinning when he decided to resolve the problem.

"I went through the barracks and picked up every *Playboy* and other nude magazine laying around that I could find," he said of risqué periodicals. "We bundled them up. I told them, 'Well, it's about time to take a training flight.' We dropped the bundle off over the lookout. All the guy on top of Black Butte said when he checked in again was, 'I got the reading material.' I'm not sure he was amused."

But one of the funniest incidents he recalled occurred out at the Siskiyou base where it wasn't unusual for a lonely smokejumper to ask one of few young women working out on a date.

"Some of the guys would come on to them while the women were working," Boucher said. "There was this guy who decided to flirt with Ruth. He didn't know her status or anything. I was standing there across the room."

A bemused Boucher, then the crew boss, decided to watch it play out.

"The guy told Ruth, 'OK, I'm not going to take 'No' for an answer. Let's go get a beer tonight,'" Boucher said. "Ruth said, 'That sounds like fun but I'd have to ask my husband first.' He said, 'Who's your husband?' She said, 'Your boss – standing right over there.' And she pointed to me."

Boucher stopped talking for a moment to laugh at the memory. "Ruth had such a great sense of humor," he said.

Their son, Don Boucher, was a smokejumper for eight fire seasons out of the North Cascades base in Washington. A forestry graduate at Oregon State University, the younger Boucher worked for the Forest Service for 40 years.

"After he quit jumping, he told me, 'I looked up your record and I talked them into letting me jump one more time than you did,'" Al Boucher said, chuckling. "I guess jumping runs in the family."

As does a great sense of humor.

16

GRAND DAME OF THE SISKIYOU BASE

H ALF A CENTURY AFTER LEAVING the Siskiyou Smoke-jumper Base, Emily Allen's face still lit up with a bright smile when looking out at the place she fondly knew as the Gobi.

"What a history this base has," she marveled while visiting during the 2018 smokejumper reunion at the base. "It drew so many interesting people. They have so many wonderful stories, the smokejumpers."

For the 92-year-old grand dame, they were more than smokejumpers. They were family.

"I called them 'our boys' – still do," she said. "They were such a good group of young men. So many of them went on to great achievements. One became an astronaut. Another was a rocket scientist. Others went on to successful careers in business, in government. There were doctors and lawyers. Some had wonderful careers in the Forest Service. Yes, they were good boys. And they were truly all our boys."

The father figure was her husband, Jim Allen, a legend at the base where he was the manager for 13 years. Arriving in 1953, he stayed through the 1965 fire season, leaving to manage the then newly created Redmond base.

"Jim always said the best years of his career were here," she said. "He loved the base and the people here. So did I."

The feeling was mutual. During the 2018 interview held in a room adjoining the old mess hall, former Siskiyou smokejumper Don Thomas, 82, a 1957 rookie, poked his head in to say hi to the base matriarch. Like Emily Allen, Thomas was attending a smokejumper reunion at the base.

"I just wanted you to know that your husband was the nicest man and the best boss anyone could ever have," he told her. "He was always out there to see us off when we got on that airplane. He gave us a pat on the back and told us we would do well. He was so encouraging. He was making sure we had proper gear. He was a wonderful, wonderful man. And no matter what kind of trouble we would get into in Cave Junction during a night of carousing, he always backed us up."

After thanking him for his kind words and allowing that her "boys" sometimes got a mite rambunctious on a Saturday night, she beamed at the memories.

"Many of the boys have told me they learned a lot from Jim," she said. "During Jim's funeral service, one of them talked about how he always interviewed them after they came back from a fire. He wanted to know if they were getting all the support they needed. He really cared about our boys."

Yet he was also a strict professional who insisted his jumpers to do their jobs well, she added.

"When they were supposed to be ready for work at 7:00 (a.m.), he expected them to be ready to go," she said. "You didn't start getting ready at 7:00. You had to be fully dressed, had already eaten breakfast and everything was ready to go."

The two met in the summer of 1947 when she was a senior at the University of Washington. She had taken a summer job to work at a ranch near Winthrop in eastern Washington.

"It was a working ranch," she said. "I had never been in eastern Washington before. Winthrop still had real boardwalks. But it was a wonderful summer."

The alert reader will recall from an earlier chapter that Winthrop is the home of the North Cascades Smokejumper Base which, along with the Siskiyou base, was among the first four created by Uncle Sam in 1943.

When a dance was held at the town hall, several of the smokejumpers dropped in to kick up their heels. Emily also attended the dance, accompanied by the ranch cook and several other ranch workers.

"At this dance, you danced three dances and stomped your foot when you were through. There was a piano and fiddle playing. Back then, it was so much fun for people to get together like that."

She danced with several young men, including one she found to be very pleasant and mighty easy on her eyes. His name was Jim Allen.

"Jim, the only jumper at the base with a car, asked if he could drive me back to the ranch," she said. "I told him I had to go home with the people I came with. But the cook, a widower who I had ridden to the dance with, wasn't around when it was over. So I ran after Jim and told him he could take me home but he would have to take the rest of the crew, too."

After taking the smokejumpers home first, he raced back to pick up Emily and the other ranch employees.

"That was how it all started for us," she said. "We began dating after that."

Both were from Washington state. She hailed from Longview; he from Camas, although he was born in Montana.

"His mother had divorced and moved to Camas when he was little," she said. "Jim told me that he would like to ask to marry me but he didn't think it would work out because we were from different backgrounds. I said, 'Well, ask me anyway.' And he did."

Her answer was a resounding "Yes!" They were married the following summer after she completed her degree.

"Jim was really intelligent. He could have been anything he wanted to be. But he wanted to stick with jumping. It turned out to be a wonderful life for us."

A paratrooper in the 101st Airborne Division who had been wounded in action during World War II, he knew what it was like to be in harm's way.

"His first combat jump was in Operation Market Garden," she said. "General Montgomery was in charge. It wasn't too successful. Jim said it was because they kept stopping for tea."

Launched in mid-September of 1944 and led by British Field Marshal Bernard Montgomery, the operation's mission was to take out nine bridges in the Netherlands and Germany, including one on the Rhine River at Arnhem. Sadly, the latter proved to be the bridge too far.

"Two of the boys at Winthrop were conscientious objectors," she recalled. "They were still there after the war. One was a Quaker, the other a Mennonite. They were very well liked by everyone, including the war veterans. They did their jobs well."

After tying the knot, the young couple settled down in Winthrop where their two daughters – Kathleen and Mary Beth – were born at home.

"We had a wonderful country doctor who came to our home to deliver them," she said, adding, "I suppose that makes me kind of a novelty these days, having children born at home."

Initially, the young couple intended to stay in Winthrop. Her husband hoped to eventually become the manager of the North Cascades base. But he jumped at the opportunity when he was offered a job as manager of the Siskiyou Smokejumper Base down in southwest Oregon in 1953.

"The girls and I got on the train in Portland and took it down to Grants Pass where Jim met us," she said, adding they moved into the manager's house when it was completed on the south end of the base in 1957. It was the last permanent structure constructed at the base, she noted.

When the Allens arrived, the base was already making a name for itself. But the new manager figured it needed to be expanded a bit to meet the growing demand for its jumpers and aircraft. After President Eisenhower provided funding in 1954 to create a smokejumper base in

Missoula, Mont., Jim Allen decided to call him. After all, he had met Eisenhower during the Market Garden campaign when the former was wounded and recovering at a military hospital and the latter was a four-star general visiting the wounded. At the hospital, Eisenhower had told him to contact him if he ever needed anything. When Allen called the POTUS, he told him about the base and the fact it needed a mess hall, barracks and residence building for the staff. Eisenhower came through with the funding for the three buildings, Emily Allen said.

"The first summer the little girls and I were at the base, Jim and the jumpers had to stay in Medford because they were paving the runway here and they couldn't use it," Emily said of the town some 60 miles away. "My dad had a fit that I was here by myself. He thought I should have a gun."

She laughed at the memory of her father fearing his daughter may have been in peril. Apparently, the name "Cave Junction" triggered images in his mind of Cro-Magnon characters dragging clubs. Actually, he would have observed such a sight had he visited when members of the Grants Pass Caveman Club, all decked out in fur and carrying clubs, participated in the annual Labor Day parade in Cave Junction. But, aside from a few Neanderthals, the Illinois Valley denizens back in the day were not cave dwellers with fearsome habits.

"It was a good place to live – a lot of good people there," she said. "Not many people had telephones back when we arrived at the base but we had one in our house so Jim could keep in close contact with the forest supervisor in Grants Pass and the regional office in Portland.

"The base had a male cook when we arrived," she added. "I don't know whether he quit or was let go. But (team leader) Orville Looper knew a widow lady who was a wonderful cook. Now, some of the boys had been through the Depression and knew what it was to be hungry. She started having steak night on Sunday when they could eat as much as they wanted."

Since fighting wildfires required the smokejumpers to burn a lot of energy, providing good meals was prudent, both for their physical and moral health, she noted.

"But I do remember one jumper who always ate bread and peanut butter and jam, even on steak night. That's what he liked."

As a veteran smokejumper and a fellow who wanted to be a hands-on manager, her husband often served as the spotter when jumpers were dispatched to a fire.

"I used to worry about Jim when he went out on a jumper plane," she said. "But I was always relieved when he was on the Noorduyn. That good old plane was so reliable."

The Allens left for the Redmond base five years before the jumper known as "Mouse" arrived in 1970, but she has no doubt her husband would have been pleased to have him as a Siskiyou jumper.

"Mouse was too short but he made the grade," she said. "Jim would have been fine with that. I do know that if he hadn't been satisfactory Jim would have put him out the door. He was very insistent about that. If you couldn't do your job, Jim didn't want you at the base."

Her husband took the same stance when he began managing the Redmond base, she said.

"We also liked the people there. There was a young doctor in Redmond who had been a kid in the Netherlands during the war. He was so thankful for what Jim and the others had done during Operation Market Garden that he refused to charge Jim for any of his medical visits."

The Allens were married for 68 years when Jim, who was three years her senior, died in August of 2016.

"I was hoping it would have been for at least 70 years," she said.

17

SUPER JUMPERS

THE SISKIYOU SMOKEJUMPER BASE OBVIOUSLY attracted folks who rose above the mundane and searched out a fascinating lifestyle offering experiences that would scare the bejabbers out of most adventure seekers. Nary a mewling crybaby in the cadre. Indeed, like the lion's share of smokejumpers throughout the West, Siskiyou jumpers stood out, no matter their stature or station in life.

That fact creates a challenge when trying to identify the most extraordinary jumper at the base during its nearly four decades of airborne firefighting. After all, it is difficult to select a top gun from so many stout-hearted folks.

Fortunately, several former Siskiyou jumpers, whose combined tenure spanned nearly the breadth of the base's existence, came up with the names of some who made a lasting impression. Keep in mind there are many other extraordinary Siskiyou base denizens but this gives you a good sample of the quality of jumpers.

For instance, Allen "Mouse" Owen stood out, not only for his diminutive height, but also because he didn't back down from anyone or anything, observed Al Boucher, the 1949 rookie that alert readers will recognize from earlier chapters. The two met when Mouse was among several Siskiyou smokejumpers deployed as boosters to the Redmond Smokejumper Base in the early 1970s.

"He was little but one tough nut," said Boucher, referring to a nut that was tough to crack, not someone with a mental deficiency.

"When I saw him, I thought, 'Hell, if he can do the job, leave him alone,'" he added. "He was part of the jumper gang. It didn't matter who was big or who was little. It only mattered that you did the job. Mouse did his job."

Based simply on his ability to overcome obstacles, Mouse was impressive, Boucher reiterated. Yet that is not who he submits was one of the most legendary Siskiyou smokejumper of them all.

"Bob Nolan was really a super man," said Boucher of Robert "Bob" Nolan, a World War II Army airborne veteran who was a Siskiyou rookie in 1947, jumping for three and a half fire season.

"A lot of the bosses wanted all the smokejumpers to look like a Bob Nolan," added Boucher, a former crew boss. "They would get on some jumper during training, badgering him real hard to be more like Bob. I would tell them, 'You are pushing him too hard. Leave him alone. Let's see if he can make the standards.' They forgot we were trying to build stamina. When you are out on a fire, you need to handle an eight to ten-hour shift of digging fireline. Having stamina was more important than looking like a weightlifter."

Not that there was anything wrong with resembling the muscular smokejumper, Boucher stressed.

"But it was unrealistic to expect everyone to look like him," he explained. "Bob was an amazing jumper and an excellent trainer. He taught us everything. From jumping to climbing trees, everything."

The celebrated smokejumper also taught them how to build stamina. Remember, at this point the jumpers were living in house tents on the southwest edge of Cave Junction, nearly half a dozen miles north of the airstrip.

"We needed to do some work out at the airstrip one morning and Bob said, 'Heck, why waste gas? Let's run out there,'" Boucher said. "So we ran out there, did the work and ran back. We ran cross country, across ditches, people's back yards. Bob was one tough nut who wouldn't quit.

"He could have played college football," he continued. "He carried 190 pounds every year. He was really tough. He helped me in training. I told him once that, if it got any tougher, I didn't know if I could hack it. He told me, 'You hack it or I will kick your butt.'"

Boucher wisely opted to hack it.

"Now, Bob could have a quick temper if aroused," he cautioned. "Sometimes he would get into a ruckus in town. I was watching him at a dance one time in Grants Pass and a local lawyer with a sarcastic tongue said a couple of things to him. The next thing I know Bob had him spread over the hood of a car. He told him, 'You open your mouth one more time and I'm going to bust it.'"

No dummy, the young attorney, who later became a well-known district court judge in southwest Oregon, declined not to plead his case before the inebriated court of public opinion that night. Apparently neither looking like a fool nor getting soundly throttled was to his liking. Given the fact he was a decent fellow who became a well-respected judge, we won't trot out his name after all these years.

"Right after Bob got out of the Army, he was an exhibition jumper at fairs and other events," Boucher continued, referring to Nolan's affinity for sport jumping. "He even kept doing that for awhile after becoming a smokejumper."

Consider the *Illinois Valley News* article which ran on the Nov. 19, 1949.

"Bob Nolan, Siskiyou National Forest smokejumper in the summertime, successfully demonstrated a 'batman' stunt in a test in the vicinity of the Redwood Ranger Station," it began. "Decked out with sheets of nylon webbing, Nolan glides 4,000 feet from an airplane, against the wind, before opening his parachute about 2,000 feet from the ground.

"Nolan prepared his own gliding outfit, which consisted of nylon webbing attached between legs and from his wrists to his hips," it added. "By manipulating the webbing plus the impetus generated by the 'batman' body falling through the air, he was able to glide some 4,000 feet against the wind before opening the parachute."

It noted he landed safely, much to the amazement and amusement of those watching from below. Forest Service officials were likely mightily amazed in private but not in public.

"Bob would have stayed in jumping but they gave him an ultimatum," Boucher said. "The Forest Service made up this rule that smokejumpers couldn't do exhibition jumping, even on their own time. They went to Bob, one of the best smokejumpers ever, and told him if he made one more exhibition jump, he was fired. So he quit as squad leader right in the middle of the season and became a logger."

Nolan became a very successful logger who operated his own company for the next four decades or so in southwestern Oregon, a firm which outlasted the base.

"Bob Nolan rightfully figured that was a bunch of bureaucratic crap and he quit smokejumping," Gary Buck observed. "A couple of years later the Forest Service decided it was OK to do sport jumping. And a lot of people did it. Mouse, Mick Swift and a bunch of guys were avid sport jumpers."

Nolan represented the amazing jumpers who emerged from WWII, he concurred.

"There was obviously a big difference between World War II and Vietnam," said Buck, a Vietnam War veteran. "In Vietnam, when you were wounded, you would be medivaced out of there in a half hour or so. But in World War II, you might lay there for a day or so. A lot of guys died from their wounds. It was a miracle that Jim Allen survived and became a smokejumper."

In addition to Allen and Nolan, other WWII combat veterans who became legendary jumpers at the base included Richard "Dick" Courson,Cliff Marshall and Danny On, he said.

A 1946 Siskiyou rookie,Courson was a Marine Corps paratrooper wounded in Iwo Jima in 1945, Buck said. But he overcame his wounds to become a Siskiyou jumper the following year, jumping for five fire seasons while going to college and law school during the winters, he added.

"He became a judge in Oregon – he was an amazing person," Buck said of Courson who was appointed district court judge in northeastern Oregon in 1967 by Oregon Gov. Tom McCall, serving for 25 years.

Danny On, a 1946 Siskiyou base rookie alongside Courson, was a member of the Army's 101st Airborne who was severely wounded while fighting in Italy, he said.

"He is believed to have been the first Asian-American smoke-jumper in the world," Buck said, adding that he jumped for four seasons out of the Illinois Valley base.

Although On was born in Red Bluff, California, his parents had migrated to the states from Mongolia.

"The reason this place was nicknamed 'The Gobi' was because of him," Buck said of the base. "In 1946, they were out here doing some work on the airstrip, digging rocks. The airport is on an old stream bed. So if you do any digging, you dig rocks. And On said, 'Yeah, this reminds me of the Gobi Desert.' After that, they started referring to it as the 'Gobi.'"

While Boucher gives his highest praise to Nolan, he agreed with Buck that other WWII veterans-turned-smokejumpers were also top notch in their field, particularly Marshall. A Silver Star recipient for bravery, Marshall was a first sergeant in the 101st Airborne, Boucher said.

"He was one tough guy who was used to barking out orders. He had been in the 3-Cs (Civilian Conservation Corps) and had also been a boxer. He'd make us run in the morning. Somebody asked him, 'How long is the run going to be?' He'd say, 'Until I make Boucher throw up.'"

With that, Boucher chuckled at the memory.

"So I'd throw up and ask him, 'Can we quit now?'" he said, noting that Marshall seldom stopped the morning run, even when a jumper upchucked. "Yes, he was another tough nut."

Bob Schofield, a 1949 rookie with Boucher, also conceded the

WWII veterans deserved high praise, but suggested yet another superlative when it came to a wildland firefighter dangling from a parachute.

"Willi Unsoeld – we called him 'Bill' – was as athletic as all get out," Schofield said, referring to world-famous mountain climber who was a Siskiyou base rookie in 1950.

"Bill told me the reason he became a smokejumper was because he was hitchhiking north on Highway 99 and saw the Siskiyou Smoke-jumper Base sign," Scofield said. "He came in and talked to the foreman. And he thought, 'You know, I might like to do this.' So he applied and got the job. He was a natural."

This was before Unsoeld gained fame as part of the American climbing team which scaled Mount Everest in May of 1963 via the treacherous west ridge route, the first ever to accomplish the feat. Although Unsoeld paid dearly for the accomplishment, losing nine toes to frostbite, he and his team were awarded National Geographic Society's prestigious Hubbard Medal for its achievement. The medal was presented by President John F. Kennedy in July of 1963, just a little over three months before he was assassinated.

"Bill was a real adventurer and being adventurous is the main thing to being an outstanding smokejumper, I believe," Scofield said. "Adventurous people have more of an open mind. You are interested in doing something that is new as opposed to someone just following along and doing his time. But that's just my opinion."

Unsoeld only jumped one fire season before moving on in his life of adventure. Although 1950 wasn't a very busy fire year with only 21 fires, he did jump on two fires, including the Siskiyou National Forest's Hansen Gulch fire on Sept. 17, a blaze he extinguished by himself, according to the base record book. However, the Siskiyou jumpers trucked to several fires that fire season were not identified and Unsoeld may have also helped suppress those fires as well.

"Bill was a regular guy," Schofield recalled. "I remember when the fire lookout up on Pearsoll Peak was running out of supplies.

Bill and I packed some supplies into the fire lookout. It was quite a hike but he was a hard worker. He was also very outgoing."

Unsoeld later taught philosophy at Oregon State University where he was a charter member at OSU's Mountain Club which Scofield joined when he was studying forestry at the university. Although not at the same level as Unsoeld, Scofield became a skilled climber who scaled most of the high peaks in the Pacific Northwest, including Hood, Jefferson, Mount Shasta, Rainier, St. Helens, Thielsen, Three Fingered Jack and Washington.

"Bill and one of his climbing buddies died in an avalanche on Nisqualli Glacier on Rainier," he said of the climber's death in 1979. "Depending on the time of year, Rainier can be a tough, dangerous climb no matter who you are."

Without taking anything away from the aforementioned jumpers, Gary Buck, after carefully considering the folks he jumped with during his 17 fire seasons, believes the preeminent aerial firefighter at the Siskiyou base was Mick Swift, an impressive fellow who has already popped up several times in these pages.

"Mick was the best – he was just a natural who could do everything," Buck concluded. "And he had that special courage, that ability to keep calm in a dangerous situation. Every jump has a risk in it but Mick never lost his cool."

In addition to being someone others could turn to for jumping advice, particularly before leaping into harm's way, he was also physically imposing, Buck added.

"He was a very formidable character in amazing shape – a physical dynamo," he said. "But he never released that physical monster in anger. You didn't want to argue with him anyway. First of all, he was smart. He knew what he was doing. He was one of those rare people who was able to make the right jumper decisions all the time, whether it was in the plane, parachuting or on the ground.But it was more than that. You wouldn't want to fight with someone who was always fighting for you. People had a lot respect for him."

Eldo "Mick" W. Swift entered the smokejumping world as a Siskiyou rookie in1956, and ended up jumping a dozen intermittent fire seasons out of the base. He would serve as a squad leader and spotter, although he would take a break from smokejumping in the mid-1960s to work for Air America in southeast Asia, a topic that is addressed in an upcoming chapter.

"When Dad was smokejumping, he worked pretty much year round," observed his son, Ken Swift. "If they weren't jumping here yet, he would go back East and jump."

His father loved the work from the outset, said Ken who, like the family patriarch, is an imposing figure, speaking softly but firmly.

"Dad started jumping in late spring of 1956 – when he was still a junior in high school," his said. "He lied about his age to get the job."

However, after "exaggerating" his age and jumping on at least three fires in northern California that fire season which included 77 wild fires for the crew, he returned to high school that fall and graduated with his class the following year.

"When it came to smokejumping, he gave it all he had," his son added.

That give-it-all attitude was the way Mick Swift handled just about everything the airborne firefighting profession could throw at him, inspiring everyone who worked with him, Buck observed.

"When you are up in the plane and looking out at this horrible jump spot down there, you know it is going to be as dangerous as hell," he said. "You know it is going to be a tough jump. But when you have someone like Mick Swift in the door as a spotter, he has the ability to calm guys down. Give them strength, in a sense. He could do that.

"Remember, these guys are already well trained and physically strong," he added. "But even for guys who had been doing it for ten years, when you look out there and see it is going to be dangerous, it gets to you. But he could stand by the door with a jumper and just calm him down. I remember so many times when we got back and somebody would say, 'Did you see the way Mick handled that last jump?' That is a tremendous asset to have in this type of work."

After pausing for a moment to gaze across the now county-owned airstrip that was once the base runway, he recalled what it was like half a century ago to be riding in the old Beechcraft alongside Mick Swift.

"You are up there looking out the windows at some real rough country," Buck said. "It's a very nasty looking spot. There are big trees and hardly any openings. Those things make you a little nervous no matter how many times you have jumped. You are looking at all those hazards down there and say, 'Damn, this is going to be a nasty jump, a really, really nasty jump.' Even after jumping for several years, you are getting real nervous about what you are about to do.

"Then Mick puts his arm around your shoulder like this," he added, holding his right arm up as though it is resting on a jumper's shoulder. "He is talking calmly to you, his head right up against your helmet so you can hear him. He is telling you how it is going to work out, talking to you right through that cage. And it works out."

The point, he said, is that Swift was a reassuring presence in a job where one was sorely needed.

"Mick just exuded confidence," he said. "He could settle guys down at the door. When they weren't looking forward to a jump, he had that magical quality of calming folks down. I've never seen anyone else be able to do that like Mick could. I was a spotter and I never had that ability. He would get them to focus on the basics. He spoke calmly and he had this immense amount of trust. People trusted him. His spotting and management abilities were incredible. He was one of a kind. What a gift."

Whether it jumping on a fire or on a rescue mission, Swift was the one you wanted to be leading your team, Buck said.

"I jumped with him on rescue jumps and he was amazing. There were a few jumpers out there who had to be rescued but there were also members of the public who needed our help at times. The fastest way to get into a remote place was by dropping smokejumpers. We could get in faster than anyone else. With Mick in charge of a mission, you knew it had a good chance of ending well."

When Swift wasn't working hard to complete a physical task, he was building morale, Buck recalled.

"Mick was the king of morale. He worked on our morale all the time. You build up the morale and you have a hell of a crew. Because of him, the crew turned into a brotherhood. You felt like you were with family."

He stopped talking again to remember his boss, smokejumping companion and good friend.

"Mick had this personal way of treating everyone so you wanted to do well for him as a jumper," Buck said, adding, "That is what a great leader brings out in people."

After all, having each other's back in the dangerous profession of jumping fire has to be job one.

18

THE LEATHERMAN

IN ADDITION TO THE SUPER jumpers at the Siskiyou Smoke-jumper Base during its nearly four-decade life span, there were many others who stood out as colorful characters in a profession famous for attracting folks who stood out. Consider Dave Laws, a fellow other jumpers swear was tougher than a logger's boot.

Even today, when former Siskiyou jumpers gather to reminisce, talk often turns to the legendary leaper.

"Everybody called him 'Leatherman' – and that was before the knives," observed 1966 Siskiyou base rookie Wes Brown, referring to the popular Leatherman tools invented shortly after the base closed. "One time I saw him doing one-armed pull-ups. No shirt, and a lit Marlboro in his mouth."

Former Siskiyou jumper Walt Congleton, a member of the 1968 rookie class, recalled watching Laws work rookies into shape by leading them on exhausting runs.

"I've seen him running down the runway ahead of everybody while smoking a cigarette," he said with a chuckle.

"And running backwards," interjected Harold Hartman who rookied at the base in 1965.

"Yep, backwards," Congleton concurred.

Stories about Laws are legendary. Having been unable to nail down a tale about some parched Gobi jumpers being booted out of a watering hole in Missoula where they had gathered to hoist a few brewskis after having stopped a Montana wildfire, I once asked Laws if he could shed any light on the incident. The story was they got a mite rowdy and were asked not to return to that particular drinking establishment.

"That was only because they swung on the chandelier and tore it down – I thought barring us was kind of narrow minded," Laws quipped, adding, "I wasn't with them, by the way."

Sadly, the legendary smokejumper with a great sense of humor succumbed to a stroke in 2017. Fortunately, he was one of the first Siskiyou jumpers interviewed for this book when I started working on it in 2016. What's more, he kindheartedly sat down for each session and didn't make this gimpy scribe run alongside while he trotted backwards, puffing away.

Standing about 5' 9'' and tipping the scales at no more than 150 pounds, Laws didn't have the commanding presence of Bob Nolan or Mick Swift. Yet even in his mid-70s he looked like he could still run down the runway and sprint back.

"I always tried to stay in good shape, working on weights and running a lot," said Laws who, at the time, was living in a small cabin at the base where he kept busy as a volunteer grounds keeper. "You had to be in real good shape for the job. We worked hard, put the fire out, then came back home and started all over again."

He learned to work hard while growing up in Milton-Freewater, Oregon, a farming community east of the Cascade Mountains near the Washington state line.

"I did a lot of farm work as a kid," observed Laws who was born Oct. 22, 1941, in Spokane. "We lived in the pea capital of the world. There were canneries all over the place. So I was always working."

While in high school and college, he also wrestled, a demanding sport which doubtlessly helped boost his extraordinary ability to withstand extreme physical exertion. Incidentally, a significant number of

Siskiyou jumpers wrestled in their youth, perhaps because they gravitated towards tough physical challenges. In Laws' case, we need to
follow the wrestling thread a bit to get a better fix on this remarkable
fellow.

Parenthetically, if you will kindly allow me to jump in yet again to
reinforce a point, I wrestled for four years while attending Illinois
Valley High School where Wayne Thornhill, smokejumper Gary
Thornhill's father, was our coach. As a veteran grappler, I can vouch
for the fact it's a tough sport that takes you to the limit of physical
endurance. Awkwardly reaching around to pat myself on the back, I
was a fairly decent wrestler, twice winning the district title and participating in the 1968 and '69 state tournaments. But there is no doubt
in my mind that Dave Laws, who wrestled in the same weight class,
would have given me a sound thrashing had we grappled with each
other when we were both in our prime.

And it wasn't just the rope-like forearm muscles he still had in his
70s that impressed me. He had that wily gleam in his eyes of one who
would invariably come up with an inventive move, one I couldn't
counter in that swift game of physical chess.

"I've always done things a little differently," he said, adding that
his frequent juvenile pranks combined with a lack of interest in scholarly pursuits prompted high school authorities to urge him to enlist
in the military. "So I joined up and got my GED in the army. That's
what got me into college."

But don't get the idea that he was a poor student in high school.
After all, although he was the youngest in his senior class at 16 years
old, he was also the brightest, according to Dan Lee, his best friend
in high school who later served with him in the army. Dave Laws
dropped out of high school after he was seriously injured as a passenger in a car wreck when a friend fell asleep while driving near Walla
Walla, Wash., Lee wrote in a 2021 email to Dave's son, Dan Laws.

Dave Laws suffered numerous facial bone fractures and had his
face wired back together, resulting in his missing so much school that
he fell behind in his studies, Lee observed.

"His vocabulary was far superior to our teachers and military officers," Lee told Dave's son. "He was very well read."

After serving in the military police – obviously, school officials didn't recognize his potential if properly guided – Laws completed his hitch in 1962 and resumed his scholarly pursuits.

While he had earned the GI Bill for college, he still needed a summer job. Being Dave Laws, he wanted one that was both interesting and tested his mettle. So he applied at the Redmond Smokejumper Base in central Oregon in 1966 and was accepted.

"I got into smokejumping because I wanted to do something that was challenging, that kept me in shape," he said. "While in college, I studied hard and ran nearly every day. I also went out for wrestling. Getting to wrestle with Rick Sanders was quite an experience."

For the collegiate wrestling-challenged, Richard "Rick" Sanders was arguably one of the nation's top college wrestlers in that era.

"Rick was still wrestling there when I was at PSU," he said. "He was a very good wrestler. He took a liking to me and became my mentor. He told me he wanted me to become a national champion. I didn't, but it made me feel good that he told me that."

Born Jan. 20, 1945, in Lakeview, Or., Sanders knew a little about what it takes to become a champion. He was a three-time Oregon state wrestling champion while at Lincoln High School in Portland before attending PSU where he was twice the NCAA 118-pound national champ. He won the silver medal in freestyle wrestling in the 1968 summer Olympics in Mexico City, followed by another silver medal in the 1972 Olympics in Munich. He was a wrestling wunderkind.

Following the 1972 Olympics, Sanders and his girlfriend decided to hitchhike through Europe. While traveling through what was then Yugoslavia, he was killed in a car crash on October 18, 1972 in Skopje.

"I think he was coming to look me up – he knew I was in Yugoslavia," Laws said.

While a PSU student, Laws had gone to Yugoslavia on a two-year scholarship.

"My dad met my mom in Yugoslavia while studying abroad on a Fulbright scholarship when he was a student at Portland State University in '71," Dan Laws explained, noting he was born in Yugoslavia. His mother was living in Oregon at the time of this writing.

As a student studying abroad, Dave Laws focused on learning five languages, including Polish, Czech and Russian. Doubtlessly, he was one of only a few smokejumpers who could quip in multiple languages.

After Yugoslavia, he returned to the Pacific Northwest with his wife and child.

"I could have stayed there longer but I was a smokejumper and I was dying to get back to jumping and fighting fire," he said.

Never mind there was the issue of a fracture he had suffered at the end of his wrestling days.

"It was just a minor neck fracture that happened when I was wrestling at PSU – I was OK," he said of what amounted to a broken neck.

While he acknowledged some jumps can test the strongest spinal column, he was quick to observe his wrestling injury wasn't anywhere near as serious as the fractures suffered by many jumpers in the line of duty.

Like most jumpers, Laws recalled his first jump.

"It was one of the scariest moments of my life. This was at Redmond. I didn't sleep that night. I was really psyched up about jumping but I wasn't sure I could do it."

Yet he was at the base the next morning with the rest of the newbies. They boarded a DC-3 and were quickly over the jump spot.

"I was the last one out. I watched everybody else go. I remember standing there in the door and thinking, 'I don't know if I can do this.' But everybody else had done it. So when the spotter hit me on the leg, I stepped out."

His training served him well. A few minutes later he alighted safe and sound.

While that first jump tested his mettle, there were other jumps that were much more hair raising. Consider the jump he made out of the Redmond base during a very busy firefighting period.

"We had been jumping fire after fire without any breaks," Dave Laws said. "All of us were really tired. One day I got back to base after a hard pack out and got called out on another fire before I could get any rest. The next thing I know I'm up in a plane and getting ready to jump."

At the time, they were jumping two at a time. Laws remembers standing at the door and nodding off.

"I woke up on what I thought for a second was a soft mattress," he said.

It wasn't. He was napping on top of the other jumper's inflated parachute, having somehow landed on top of it. Holy moly. I don't know about you but I would have become incontinent, prompting the fellow dangling below to wonder why it was starting to sprinkle on a clear day.

But the Leatherman was made of sterner stuff.

"I started working my way down the parachute until I slid off," he recalled. "Once clear of it, I pulled my emergency chute and I was fine."

Of course, most of the dangerous incidents he survived were largely routine, such as dropping down among tall trees like those found in Oregon's Willamette or Umpqua national forests.

"Now, I always did everything I could to avoid hanging up in a tree – I never liked tree landings," he stressed.

But sometimes there was no avoiding an encounter with a wooden giant. Take the time he landed in the Umpqua forest.

"I was coming down, trying to get past this big tree," he recalled. "I thought I had it made but all of a sudden I came to a stop."

He looked up to see his chute hung up on a broken branch.

"The limb wasn't very big, but just big enough to hold me up. So I was just hanging there, probably a hundred feet or so above the ground."

Before he could deploy his let-down rope, the chute either broke free or the small branch snapped. Fortunately, the chute caught enough air to slow his descent, allowing him to do a safe tuck and roll.

"In my earlier years, my dad didn't talk about smokejumping very much," recalled his son, Dan Laws. "It wasn't something he really introduced me to or encouraged me to do. By the time I learned more about what he did, I was already pursuing my own interests."

Yet Dan, who produces costume armor that is sold worldwide, would later spend many enjoyable hours talking to his father about his smokejumping career.

"Dad told me about some scary times, including when he fell asleep and woke up on the other guy's parachute," he said, adding, "That had to be his most dangerous jump."

Despite hearing about those close calls, Dan didn't hesitate when he had an opportunity to do some recreational parachuting with his father.

"That was fun – we had some really good times sport jumping," Dan said.

Of course, when his father was jumping fire, it was not for recreational purposes.

"All smokejumpers are adrenalin junkies," Dave Laws observed during an interview. "But we also liked our mission. It was so different. Not only were we doing something different, it was also something that mattered."

Like other jumpers, he felt it was important to stop a small fire before it became a costly conflagration, destroying forests and rural homes. It was a badge of honor that they did their work well.

At Redmond, he became a trainer of young smokejumpers where he acquired a reputation as an exceedingly tough task master.

"I was very physically fit," he said. "But I don't think I was an asshole. I just made sure that the smokejumpers I trained were ready for the challenging job ahead."

In 1973, Laws transferred from the Redmond base to the Siskiyou Smokejumper Base. Gary Buck, a longtime friend and veteran Siskiyou jumper, recalled how Laws became part of the tight cadre.

"The reason Dave came to us was that Mick Swift around May of '73 announced to us, 'Dave Laws is not going back to Redmond this year,'" Buck said. "We all had a blank look on our faces. 'Don't you guys know Dave Laws?' Mick asked us. We all shook our heads. There was about six or seven Gobi jumpers there and none of us knew him."

Swift, who had been sent to Redmond as a member of a backup crew on several occasions and became acquainted with Laws, didn't let the fact none had heard of Laws diminish his enthusiasm for hiring the veteran jumper.

"'Dave Laws is a manager at Redmond – a squad leader – and he isn't going back to Redmond. He would be great for us. We need to hire him!' Mick told us," Buck continued. "We all started laughing because Mick was so intense about it. It was classic Mick Swift, the way he presented it."

While they didn't know Laws, they knew that, when it came to smokejumpers, Swift had a nearly infallible intuition. After all, he was smokejumper's smokejumper.

"Whatever Mick thought, that was good for us – we trusted him," Buck said. "So we said, 'Sure, let's make it happen.' So he went in to his boss and talked him into it in about 30 seconds."

Thus Laws, who was as impressed with the Gobi team as they quickly became with him, arrived at the Siskiyou base in time for the 1973 fire season.

"Mick had gone to Redmond as a member of a backup crew a several of times when I was there," Laws explained, noting the two had become good friends.

"I had been a squad leader in Redmond but when I got to the Siskiyou base, I had to start all over again," he added. "But it didn't bother me. In fact, I liked it. When you become a squad leader and a spotter, you don't get to jump fires that much. So I was happy to be back jumping again."

Like Swift, Laws also garnered respect from his fellow jumpers.

"Dave had the reputation as a physical fitness expert," Buck said. "He was a hard ass, but not in a negative way. He was training you so you had a better chance to survive out there."

Buck recalled meeting three jumpers in Alaska who were trained by Laws back in Redmond.

"These were all upper echelon management types," Buck noted. "One of them asked me, 'You came from the Siskiyou base?' I told him I did. 'Do you know Dave Laws?' he asked. I told him I had jumped with him in '73 and '74.

"He said, 'Man, that guy trained hard,'" Buck added. "Another guy said, 'Laws about ran us to death. That guy is an animal. He is not human.'"

With that, Buck laughed heartily.

"When guys didn't get along in Redmond, they were usually ideal candidates to go to Cave Junction," observed Gary Mills, the last manager of the Siskiyou base. "It was known as a little bit of an outlaw base."

But that fierce independent spirit also created pride in working hard and getting the job done, he stressed, adding that Laws quickly fit in, both on and off the field of battle.

"One time Dave and Mouse, two guys always ready to take on a challenge, got into an argument over who could outrun the other," Mills said. "I don't remember how it started but I remember how it ended."

They held their run-off at the Gobi which had two running circuits known as the "Big Loop" and the "Little Loop," both of which were included in their contest. No doubt Mouse knew he was outgunned since Laws was a trainer known to run younger men into the ground while smoking a cigarette.

"At one point Dave was running backwards while talking to Mouse," Mills said. "They ran about 15 to 18 miles before it finally ended. Leatherman won, something he never let Mouse forget."

But he was quick to note they were good friends who always had each other's back in the rough and tumble smokejumper world.

And so it was that smokejumpers gathered at the Siskiyou base on Sept. 24, 2017, to remember Dave Laws shortly after he made that final leap into the great unknown. One by one, they recalled anecdotes involving their friend and workmate.

When something popped up that caused him a headache at the base-turned-museum, generally because of government red tape, Buck noted he would often go see Laws at his little house at the south end of the facility when the day was over.

"I walked down there one day and I was so pissed off," Buck said. "I started bitching and complaining. He was just sitting there watching me. He was the best listener in the world. I kept bitching for about 10 minutes or so. He was staring at me. I finally stopped for a second. He gets up and goes into the kitchen, opens the refrigerator and takes out a beer and opens it up. He comes back and hands me the beer. This was his way of saying, 'I can't do a damn thing about your complaints but, here, have a beer. It will make you feel better.' I started laughing so hard. That was a classic Dave move. He had a way of impacting things that nobody else could pull off."

Next up was Hartman who had jumped with Laws and later worked alongside him in helping to display an old aircraft alongside the highway on the northeast end of the base, a display intended to attract passersby to the smokejumper museum.

"We need to dedicate that display to Dave," Hartman said, a suggestion which won praise from the crowd.

When someone mentioned there may be a problem with an open cockpit because of birds and other critters gaining entry, Hartman had a proposal that reflected the humor still strong among the former jumpers.

"I think for a six pack of beer, we could get old, retired jumpers to sit up there for four hours at a time," he said.

And they were off and running.

"I'll do it for three beers," one gray-haired fellow yelled.

"Is there anybody who will do it for two?" Hartman shot back, prompting an eager show of hands. Had Laws been present, he would have loved it.

In a more serious moment, Hartman noted that Laws had worked on the pylons which hold the aircraft.

"They were out there, flinging red dirt," he recalled. "I went out to help them finish off and Dave was there, right in the thick of it. I said, 'Dave, shouldn't you be resting?' He looked tired. In the typically Smokejumper Dave fashion, he said, 'No, I'm going to do some work.' He was working his butt off. And it was only two weeks later that he passed on."

Hartman echoed the sentiment made by others that Laws was always quick to help out at the base museum.

"He was a stalwart man," Hartman said. "He wanted to be on top of roofs and everything else."

A well-known cowboy poet and raconteur in the Pacific Northwest, former jumper John Doran said he met his match in Laws. Doran, who rookied in 1972 at the North Cascade Smokejumper Base at Winthrop, Wash., and had jumped out of the Siskiyou base when it needed a backup crew, came to know Laws well when he served as a host at the base museum.

"Now, I'm pretty good on stage and pretty good at come backs," he said. "But that guy, everyday, would get me at least once. He was quiet. He had this way of starting out, 'Well, you know, John, we've got to . . .' And I'd be, 'Oh?' And he'd zing me real good. And I'd say, 'Damn it, Dave, I'm going to get you back.'"

With that, the jumpers gathered around chuckled en masse, recognizing the antics of the man they missed.

"I fell in love with this place a lot because of him," Doran added. "Dave was the one who said, 'OK, John, when you lock up, come on down and we'll have a whiskey and save the world.' We'd sit there and I'd learn so much about this quiet, unimposing person with a dry sense of humor. I found out this man had done more in his lifetime than most people. His gift of language, his artistry, the way he comported himself . . .he was a well read, well versed man."

One former Siskiyou jumper noted that Laws was the most photographed jumper on the base. His reasoning? "When folks came to the museum and asked who a smokejumper was in a photograph in which the jumper's face couldn't be seen, Dave would always say, 'That's me,'" he said, prompting more laughter to fill the void left by Laws.

"I appreciate everyone coming out today to remember my dad," Dan Laws told the group. "You are really a very special group of people. I know he looked back on smokejumping as the best time in his life."

Heeding the suggestion of former Siskiyou smokejumper Tommy Albert, several of Dave Laws' many friends spread his ashes on the large green lawn in front of what was once the base cafeteria. It was a fitting gesture, given the fact Laws, along with other retired smoke-jumpers, volunteered countless hours to make the lawns shine like emeralds on the otherwise rocky terrain of Gobi.

Just remember to step respectfully when you cross the lawn in front of the main museum. After all, you are walking with Dave Laws, Siskiyou smokejumper extraordinaire.

Dave Laws, aka The Letherman (*Photo by Doug Beck*)

19

FIRST FEMALE SMOKEJUMPER

T HERE WERE NO WOMEN SMOKEJUMPING at the Siskiyou base but it wasn't for a lack of trying. In its final years, several smokejumpers, including Gary Buck and Allen "Mouse" Owen, attempted to broaden the base's base by recruiting female rookies.Unfortunately, it closed before they succeeded.

"We tried to hire the first woman smokejumper in 1978," Buck said, noting a female candidate had expressed interest in training to become a Siskiyou smokejumper. "She was a registered nurse at a hospital. I called her up to offer her the job. She went to her boss and tried to get a 3-month sabbatical but they said no. If she would have been given the chance and had qualified, I think the guys here would have encouraged her and treated her well."

But he observed there was resistance to allowing women to become airborne firefighters in the broader smokejumping community in the early years.

"A lot of jumpers didn't think women had what it takes," he said.

Moreover, at the Siskiyou base, no rookies had been trained since the spring of 1979. And there were only two transfers in the spring of 1980, followed by just one in 1981, its final fire season.

"Yet there were still efforts to hire female smokejumpers at the base," recalled Gary Mills, the base's last manager. "We called around but they didn't want us training anybody, men or women. They took all of the parachute repairing and packing equipment away from us. They were doing everything they could do to undercut the base at that point."

They, of course, were U.S. Forest Service officials intent on closing the base, reputedly to cut costs but some observers speculated it was largely because of the base's maverick reputation.

"The mindset was that no woman could carry a 100-pound pack out of the woods," said Wes Brown, a 1966 Siskiyou base rookie who jumped more than a dozen fire season. "That was the bureaucratic mindset back then. It was idiotic."

But it was also true that many male jumpers half a century ago weren't too keen on women joining their ranks, offered veteran smoke-jumper Murry Taylor, a hardy fellow who made 375 jumps in 27 fire seasons and a skilled writer of several books, including the best-selling *Jumping Fire.*

"I was against it when I saw women firefighters for the first time," he admitted. "Then one day I saw a woman who was part of a hotshot crew in Missoula. She looked like the rest of them: rough and tough and dirty. I saw her take out a Copenhagen can, open it and stuff some in her mouth."

Known for being a straight-forward fellow, especially when his curiosity is sparked, Taylor strode over for a chat.

"I said, 'Excuse me for asking but why are you on a fire crew?'" he said. "She looked at me for a moment and then told me she loved the outdoors, loved getting outside, loved the adventure, loved getting in there where it was real tough. She told me she was having a real adventure. It dawned on me that it was the same thing men loved. Her response clicked for me."

The resistance to women joining parachuting firefighter crews waned once Deanne Shulman, the nation's first female smokejumper, proved she had what it takes, he said, noting they simply needed to be given a chance to prove themselves.

"Yeah, women are generally smaller but they showed up with a big heart. Remember, our guys weren't all the same size. We had guys that weighed more than 200 pounds and other guys that weighed barely 130 pounds. Remember, Mouse weighed only 112 pounds or so."

Yet he never shirked his duty, Taylor stressed.

"Mouse was small but he was revered," he said. "Some of our gals weighed 130 pounds or thereabouts. Some guys who weighed 200 pounds or more could carry more but the women worked just as hard."

The point, he stressed, is that anyone who is fit and can do the work ought to be given the chance to prove themselves.

However, when it came to hiring female smokejumpers, Uncle Sam dragged his bureaucratic feet. Federal agencies balked, stalled and backpeddled to avoid even giving them a shot at demonstrating they could do the job.

But the feds were no match for Shulman's tenacity once she set out to prove herself capable. She had already demonstrated she was tougher than rawhide by becoming the first woman firefighter on a hotshot crew. Still, it wasn't about being the first woman anything for her. She simply wanted to become a smokejumper and rightfully felt that gender shouldn't be part of the equation.

When the California native reported to the McCall, Idaho, smoke-jumper base on June 11, 1979, she already had five years of wildland firefighting under her belt, including working on hotshot crews as well as helicopter rappel teams. She had as much or more experience than the other 10 rookies back in the spring of 1979.

To become a rookie at the base back then, would-be jumpers had to make the grade in the physical fitness test which included running 1 ½ miles in less than 11 minutes, 25 pushups, 7 pull-ups and 45 sit-ups. Shulman passed the test. However, she weighed in at 125 pounds, five pounds under the officially required limits from 130 to 190 pounds. The day after passing the physical fitness exam, she was called into the base manager's office and told she did not make the cut because she was five pounds underweight.

Although upset by the decision, Shulman, who noted she had weighed in at 130 pounds when she had left her home in California several days earlier, was encouraged by several veteran smoke-jumpers who spoke *sotto voce* to her as she was getting ready to leave the base. One whispered to her that two jumpers at the base did not make the 130-pound minimum weight yet they were allowed to proceed. Another said it was unfair to terminate her since she had passed the fitness test. And one urged her to contact a veteran jumper named Allen "Mouse" Owen at the Siskiyou Smoke-jumper Base in Oregon, noting that he was both under the height and weight limits but had successfully fought the system.

After getting a job as a firefighter in California that summer, Shulman called Mouse, one of several folks she felt she could trust to ask them for advice. At the time, Mouse was a squad leader at the Siskiyou base.

"Mouse was a unique individual and I loved his perspective on my situation," Shulman told me in an email message on Oct. 27, 2017. "Mouse was absolutely outraged and indignant that right here in America, my inherent rights as a citizen to compete for a job had been denied.From his perspective, gender had nothing to do with the situation.

"In the true spirit of American exceptionalism, he believed everyone has a right to compete and prove they can perform a job," she added. "Pre-screening by height and or weight was completely unnecessary if one could perform all the requirements of the job.Since these abilities were all tested during rookie training, the height and weight requirements were arbitrary and discriminatory."

It was largely on those grounds that Shulman filed a federal Equal Employment Opportunity complaint in September of 1979. She won the case and was offered a smokejumping job at McCall for the 1980 or 1981 fire seasons, although she had to weigh in at least 130 pounds at the outset. However, she had already accepted a job as a member of a helicopter rappel crew in Oregon during the 1980 fire season and elected to wait until the following fire season to give smokejumping another shot.

Meanwhile, Mouse continued to encourage her as well as offer advice on how to prepare for the physical challenge. While she was training to become a jumper, she received a package in the mail from him along with a note dated Feb. 20, 1980.

"Enclosed is my packout bag as promised," he wrote in the same neat print which appeared in his Vietnam diary. "It's made of nylon so water won't bother it, but it should be kept away from heat or nylon-dissolving chemicals. You should shoot for 80 pounds over two miles of level ground at least once a week. Retraining for experienced jumpers begins the last week in April so if you could return it then, I'd appreciate it."

The note was signed, "Good luck and keep the faith, Allen (Mouse) Owen."

Shulman, who followed his training advice and returned the bag as requested, arrived at the McCall base in early June of 1981 where she weighed in at 132 pounds. She successfully completed the grueling rookie physical challenges which included packing 115 pounds over 3 ½ cross-country miles. Overcoming her fear of heights, she also made the required 8 training jumps.

In an article announcing the first woman smokejumper in the nation, the *Spokesman-Review* newspaper in Spokane, Wash., announced, "SHE'S a smokejumper." In the story, Gene Benedict, fire staff officer for the Payette National Forest, was quoted as saying, "There were no special favors, but there were no roadblocks either."

With the arbitrary roadblocks out of the way, Shulman paved the way for other women to become smokejumpers if they, like men, were so inclined and were tough enough to hack it. The 1981 fire season proved to be a busy one for the McCall jumpers, one that allowed Shulman to prove her mettle.

Returning from a fire early in September, she found a handwritten note that had been dropped in her gear bin at the McCall smokejumper base.

Thanks to her moxie and ability, Deanne Shulman
became the nation's first female smokejumper in
1981. She credited Allen Owen for encouraging
her to break the barrier.

"We jumped the West Yellowstone National Park just a few hours
before you landed at McCall so I missed seeing you," it read. "Congratulations on making the grade as a jumper. I hope it was worth
everything you went through to get the job. We leave for Fairbanks
tonight at 1800 so it doesn't look like I'll see you at McCall this year.
A few hard cores still don't like the idea of a woman jumper but most
of the rest had lots of good things to say about you. Guess that's all
for now. Keep up the good work and lots of luck."

Simply signed "Mouse," it was dated Sept. 1, 1981, five days before
he died during a sport jumping accident in Alaska.

"My big regret is that I never met him in person," Shulman told me
in 2017. After jumping five fire seasons at McCall, she worked other

jobs in the Forest Service, including serving as a battalion fire chief in southern California, before retiring in 2011.

Thanks to Shulman's gutsiness and Mouse's encouragement, women are now part of the once machismo world of smokejumping, Taylor observed.

"Women like Deanne Shulman, Sandy Ahlstrom, Paige Taylor and Kacy Rose proved they had big hearts and, quite frankly, were tough as hell," he said of early-day female wildland firefighters. "There are a lot of great women in fire. I worked with some of them and can tell you that many have the heart of true warriors. They were way stronger than I figured they would be on pack-outs. It never harmed the production of jumping to have them in our crews."

Murry Taylor, no relation to Paige Taylor, noted women smokejumpers battling a fire are indistinguishable from their male counterparts, and just as hardy, dirty and stinky on the job.

"They would stand around a campfire at 3:30 in the morning after mopping up, be wet and filthy and ashy, and should be miserable as hell," he recalled. "Yet they would be standing, each with a cup of coffee strong enough to kill a bear, and tell stories and laugh and laugh. When you saw that, you'd tell yourself, 'This is good stuff.' I was proud of all our jumpers who showed they could do it."

At last count, there were 20 female smokejumpers in the little more than 400 smokejumpers in the United States, according to Chuck Sheley, the former Siskiyou smokejumper and retired teacher who is now the editor of "Smokejumper," a popular magazine published by the National Smokejumper Association.

20

KING OF THE
SMOKY SKIES

W HILE BATTLING A REMOTE WILDFIRE in mountainous terrain was job one for the Siskiyou smokejumpers, their lives depended on one special person to get them safely to the work site: the smokejumper pilot.

Harold Thomas "Hal" Ewing was par excellence when it came to delivering the jumpers to the target. He was the king of the smoky skies from 1966 until the base closed.

"Hal Ewing was one of the best people I ever worked with," observed Sheley who began jumping in 1959. "When I was spotting a fire with Hal, we hardly even had to talk. On the way in, he would determine the (wind) drift. I would look for the jump spot. We just did hand signals. Hal was a phenomenal pilot as well as a super guy."

In an interview for the *Grants Pass Daily Courier* on March 2, 1987, the late Ewing talked about the importance of a pilot working with the smokejumpers. At the time, the Siskiyou base having closed, he had been flying out of the Medford Fire Center as the pilot of a small plane – known as a lead plane – whose responsibility was to direct retardant tankers attacking a fire.

"You wanted to make it as easy as possible on the jumpers," he stressed. "The jumpers and the tankers complement each other. You have to have a guy on the ground if nothing more to make sure the fire is out."

As it happens, I was reporting for the *Courier* at the time and wrote the article. The celebrated pilot was approaching mandatory retirement age after flying for more than 11,000 hours for Uncle Sam. That's roughly one year, three months and three days in the air, if my Kerby Elementary School math is in the ballpark.

"They are running me off," he told me with a smile, adding, "If I had my way, I'd start over right now."

A Great Falls, Montana, native where he learned to fly straight out of high school, Ewing joined the U.S. Navy during World War II, becoming a fighter pilot as well as a test pilot for F-4 Phantoms and Phantom II fighter jets. As a fighter pilot, he flew everything from Bearcats to A-6 Intruders, making 92 night landings on carriers in the latter. In short, he was a pilot's pilot.

Retiring from the Navy in 1965 as a commander after 23 years of service, he and his family, which included two sons, moved from a U.S. military base in Japan to rural Cave Junction. Not one to twiddle his thumbs in retirement, he worked for a bit in a local chainsaw shop, then started driving school bus.

In the spring of 1966, smokejumpers Tommy Albert and Garry Peters were working on the Fort Benning shock tower at the base when a school bus pulled up. The tower provided training for rookie parachutists learning how to jump.

"I remember seeing this little guy get out of the bus and walk into the office," Albert said. "We didn't think anything of it. Well, the next thing we know the little guy and John Gowan (pilot) walk out and climb into the twin Beech. Then we saw the little guy get into the left seat. We thought, 'Holy moly!'"

You guessed right: the bus driver climbing into the pilot's seat was none other than Hal Ewing.

"He was an expert pilot," said Albert who became a well-regarded pilot himself after his parachuting days. "He had all of that military flying experience, including a lot of night landings on carriers. He was very, very good."

Veteran Siskiyou smokejumper Gary Buck also recalled the day Ewing dropped by in the school bus.

"We were short of pilots and the next day Hal was out here flying a plane," Buck said. "It was that quick. One day he was a school bus driver and the next day he is a smokejumper pilot. He was a great addition to the base."

Tom Ewing, the pilot's youngest son who followed in his father's aerial footsteps to become a fixed-wing pilot, including dropping off smokejumpers, said his father was enthusiastic about getting back into the air after retiring from the Navy.

"He did not take well to retirement," Tom said. "When he took a bus full of kids out to the base, he liked what he saw."

But his father had already been communicating with the powers that be at the base before he arrived, he explained.

"Back then, that was a pretty tight community," said the 1968 Illinois Valley High School graduate. "Everybody knew everybody. If someone grew tomatoes and someone else grew apples, you just traded. So he got to know Dee Dutton and Jim Allen out at the smokejumper base. And they had talked to him about flying out there."

The rest, as they say, is history. Both Allen and Dutton were enthusiastic about having a pilot of Hal Ewing's caliber and experience at the base and the former Navy pilot was glad to be back in the air.

"They had the old twin Beech out there and that was what he had flown when he was learning how to fly in Great Falls," Tom Ewing said. "He had taken flight lessons in Great Falls and didn't tell his parents. My granddad was upset because that negated my dad's life insurance."

As Albert had observed, Hal Ewing was a mite gravity challenged when it came to height.

"Dad wasn't very tall," Tom acknowledged, noting that his father was 5-foot-6. "And those DC-3s, which he flew a lot when he was carrying smokejumpers, weren't made for short people. They were also tail draggers which meant that, especially for landing or take off, you were working the rudders a lot to keep them on the runway."

It also resulted in a short person having difficulty seeing out the cockpit window while working the pedals, he explained.

"So he could reach the rudder pedals, dad mounted wooden blocks on them," Tom said. "Another problem he had was that the old DC-3s were not hydraulically operated but manually operated. So he got a bicycle and started riding it up and down the runway to strengthen his legs."

In other words, like Mouse, he adapted to overcome every obstacle he faced.

During the 1987 interview for the *Courier*, Hal Ewing said he forfeited a portion of his military retirement pay to return to the air as a Forest Service pilot.

"But it was worth it," he said, noting he relished the atmosphere at the Siskiyou base, particularly the close camaraderie among the jumpers and the rest of the crew. His Siskiyou jumper flights were largely in the Pacific Northwest, but he also dropped them over wildfires from Alaska to Virginia.

While the danger on Siskiyou smokejumper flights may not have been as threatening as that in the military, they had their hairy moments. Take the flight back to the base in the summer of 1970. Everything was going fine and he told the copilot to take over the controls. Shortly afterwards a fire warning light flashed on and a warning bell sounded, only to switch off as suddenly as they had begun. Ewing climbed back into the belly of the aircraft to check it out but could find no problem.

However, Ewing, wisely erring on the side of caution, directed the copilot to land the plane at the nearest runway. Just as the wheels hit the tarmac, the alarms went off again, he recalled.

"When I kicked the door open, I could see molten metal on the wing," he said in the 1987 article. "I yelled to him (copilot) to get the devil out."

No sooner had the two exited the aircraft, flames engulfed it, he said.

In addition to being very safety conscious, his father was also protective of his "boys" at the base, Tom Ewing observed.

"The smokejumpers were family to us," he said, noting his family regularly attended barbecues and other functions at the base. "Dad watched over the jumpers like a mother dog. Whenever there was a hurt jumper down there on the ground, it really frustrated him if he couldn't do anything to help."

Noting he grew up on military bases before they moved to the Illinois Valley, Tom, who was 70 when interviewed in early 2019, said he enjoyed going out to the base as a youngster.

"In fact, Mouse taught me how to jump out of an airplane," he said of sport jumping. "One day he told me, 'I can't get your old man to do it so I am going to take you up in a perfectly good airplane and let you jump out.' It was me and a couple of the wives of some of the jumpers who did sport jumping with Mouse."

He also recalled riding in Mouse's blue Corvette Stingray.

"It leaked like a sieve so when you got into it in the winter – there would be an inch of water on the floor board," he said. "That drove him crazy. But I always thought, 'Hey, this is Oregon and it rains like heck.'"

The jumpers were an innovative bunch, whether it was coming up with inventive pranks or ways to make the base feel like home, he recalled.

"Sometimes when they had a rookie on his first jump, they would load his chute full of talcum powder," he said. "They used talcum powder on pitch that got on a chute so the chute wouldn't stick together. Well, when you put a whole bunch of that powder on a chute, it makes a big 'Poof!' when it opens."

And startled the bejabbers out of the rookie. Then there was Dutton, a hunting enthusiast who built a rifle range near the southern end of the runway in order to get in a little practice for hunting season whenever he got the chance.

"One day dad came home shaking his head," Tom said. "We asked him what was up and he said, 'That Dee. When I was landing and rolling out to the other end of the runway today, Dee told me on the radio to look over at the southeast corner and to tell him if I saw anything. I looked and all I saw what was left of a rabbit was the ears. He had hit the jackrabbit with his rifle.'"

Without question, it was because of his father that he became a pilot, Tom Ewing said.

"I figured learning how to fly would help me learn more about my dad," he said. "I did all the prerequisites to become a smokejumper, but the Forest Service wouldn't let me jump because of nepotism. I felt that was ridiculous but that was the way it was. So I went to work for the contractors who contracted directly with the Forest Service."

Like his father before him, he learned how to fly immediately after high school, although it was at a community college in northeastern Oregon where the former ace sprinter was offered a track scholarship. The school also offered instruction in commercial aviation courses which he eagerly took. After working for a couple of seasons as a contract smokejumper pilot out of the Siskiyou base, he dropped jumpers for a while out of a DC-3 in Alaska, then flew a couple of fire seasons as an air tanker pilot.

"We used to say it was hours and hours of boredom punctuated by a few minutes of stark terror," he quipped.

Interestingly, his father was a lead plane pilot for air tankers at the end of his career while Tom Ewing's professional flying career ended with him in the cockpit of an air tanker. Tom quit flying in the early 1980s to focus on the family business. His wife, Mary Fulk Ewing, a 1969 graduate of IVHS, is an accomplished artist. The couple, who live in Kansas, incorporated her talent with his woodworking skills to create crafts which are sold around the country.

But he has never forgotten the days he and his father spent in the thin air, particularly their last flying missions.

"My dad would fly ahead of the tankers and lay a streamer where he wanted the tanker to drop its load," Tom Ewing said. "Later, when I was a tanker pilot myself, I realized that working with a lead plane was a must. With the heavy aircraft it took to do the job having a traffic pattern established by the lead plane, and a drop zone ready and waiting, saved a lot of airtime, money, and forest. My dad made a difference."

That difference was recalled during the memorial at the base after Hal Ewing died at age 85 in 2010.

"There was no middle ground for Hal," declared a tribute read at his memorial. "He supported those who were on the right track, backed those he felt were unjustly criticized, and gently tried to dissuade those who were going astray. Throughout the years, time and time again, he was always there for the jumpers."

Later, his ashes were dropped by a plane, continuing a Siskiyou Smokejumper Base crew tradition. Veteran Siskiyou jumper turned pilot Lee Gossett spread his ashes on the Pacific Ocean, a fitting end for the famed Navy pilot.

21

SECRET AGENT MAN

A DMITTEDLY, THE ADVENTURES OF FORMER Siskiyou smokejumper Lee Gossett do not measure up to the exciting exploits of the mythical James Bond celebrated in Johnny Rivers' unparalleled rendition of "Secret Agent Man" in the 1960s. But that doesn't mean Gossett and other smokejumpers didn't lead a life of danger when they was working for Air America, a front for the CIA in southeast Asia.

Gossett, along with other former Siskiyou jumpers Louis Banta, Cliff Hamilton, John Manley, John Kirkley, Charley Moseley, Gideon Newton, Mick Swift, Hal Ward and Ed Weissenback, served as air freight specialists for the airline when in fact they were working indirectly for the "company." Nicknamed "kickers," their work largely involved making covert cargo drops out the open doors of airplanes over remote jungles during the turbulent years of the Vietnam War.

"I remember reading a little article in the paper in '63 about Air America," recalled Gossett, a 1957 Siskiyou base rookie. "I was a squad leader in Alaska at the time and remember thinking, 'What in the hell is Air America?' This other squad leader named Gid Newton was being very secretive so me and another squad leader got him in a corner and told him, 'You've got something good going on. We're not going to let you go until you tell us about it.' He said, 'I'm going over to Laos and kick cargo for Air America.'"

Sadly, Newton was only there for about two weeks before he was killed when his low-flying plane struck a mountaintop, Gossett said. A 1955 Siskiyou rookie, Newton jumped five seasons out of the Gobi.

"Then another fellow, Gene DeBruin, a very good friend of mine, left to go over to work for Air America," he said. "I saw him off at the airport. He was over there a month or so and was shot down and captured. He never came out alive."

Although Gossett didn't know it at the time, he had already lost a smokejumping companion to the dangerous work over southeast Asia jungles.

"In 1960, I had jumped with a guy named Dave Bevan," he explained. "The following year, he was one of three smokejumpers killed in Laos. They were among the first 'kickers' over there, working for the CIA. But I didn't realize it at that point."

Despite the obvious dangers, Gossett and fellow former Siskiyou smokejumper Louis A. Banta, a 1951 rookie, decided to apply for a job in southeast Asia.

"So Air America called Louie and I. Well, when you are young, broke and invincible, you answer the call. Louie went over just ahead of me. I followed in January of 1964."

The nearly dozen Siskiyou smokejumpers who worked for Air America were among more than 100 jumpers who dropped cargo that included ammunition over remote areas of Laos from the 1950s into the early 1970s, according to *Smokejumpers and the CIA*, a 2017 book published by the National Smokejumper Association. Since the smokejumpers, who pushed out cargo affixed to wood or steel pallets which were strapped to parachutes, were not active duty personnel, their participation wasn't considered an official act of war, the book noted.

By the by, Gossett has also written a book about his exploits which is called *Smokejumper to Global Pilot – A True Odyssey*. Published in 2020, the book records his life's wondrous journey. Turns out he was not only a very capable smokejumper and pilot, but he proves to be talented storyteller as well, one who could give lessons to most of us who purport to be writers.

Born Jan. 18, 1939, in Simla, Colorado, Gossett was 12 when his family moved to Oregon's Rogue River Valley. Not one to let the grass grow under his feet, he earned his private pilot license while a high school junior. What's more, he would have one smokejumping season under his belt before he graduated from Crater High School in 1958.

"What happened was I had a job pumping gas at the Medford airport when I saw two guys get out of an airplane and they both looked like Indiana Jones," he said. "So I asked them, 'Who are you guys?' They told me they were smokejumpers. I asked them what a smokejumper was. They told me what they did and that they were from the base over by Cave Junction. I thought, 'Wow, that sounds like fun.'"

Being a young man of action, Gossett saw an opportunity.

"I rounded up a couple of friends and we drove over to check it out," he said. "We went in to see Jim Allen. He was a top-notch guy, one we would find out was one of the legends of the base. Anyway, we introduced ourselves and talked to him for a while. He hired us right on the spot. They really needed extra jumpers at the time. That was in 1957."

Although Gossett was just completing his junior year in high school, he was 18, making him eligible for the high-flying summer job.

"Back then, a lot of people only jumped for four years while in college, then they were gone," he explained. "So every spring there were openings. Nowadays there are more career jumpers with fewer openings."

After training at the Siskiyou base, he and two other rookies were sent to the fledgling Redding jumper base where they jumped on six fires that summer.

"Some of the rookies back at the Siskiyou base didn't get any fire jumps that season so it was a good move for us," he said.

The Siskiyou crew made only 50 fire jumps in 1957, making it one of the slowest fire seasons in the base's history, according to its record book. "The summer was cool with only a few thunder storms," the end-of-the-season report noted that year.

The first fire Gossett ever jumped was in northern California's Shasta-Trinity National Forest, a forest known for its steep slopes and rough country.

"It was a four-manner," he said, using a term jumpers employ to describe a fire requiring four people to snuff it out. They landed without any mishaps and quickly put the fire out.

"We built a little helipad for this helicopter to pick us up," he said. "Now, helicopters were a pretty new thing back in '57. This old Bell came in and landed. The pilot was as jumpy as a cat on a hot tin roof. He had every reason to be nervous. He just jumped off that pad and flew screaming down into the canyon. I would have never gotten into that thing if I knew what I know now about flying."

The Shasta-Trinity was also the site of his most horrendous jump, he observed.

"I plowed into one of those big trees and went crashing through the branches upside down. Fortunately, my chute finally hung up and my feet swung out. But I was a little worried for a while there."

As it happens, Gossett liked to land in little trees but tried to avoid the towering ones.

"I once landed on a big ass tree. I couldn't see the ground so I climbed down the tree to where I could see the ground, then used my let-down rope. But you don't leave your chute so I spent half a day with climbers and a saw getting that chute down."

Gossett returned to high school that fall, graduating with his class in the spring of 1958 where he somehow found time to letter in both football and track. He was back at the Redding base the following summer.

Like Laws, Gossett once became entangled with another jumper's chute.

"I got inside the guy's chute," Gossett recalled. "Fortunately, both chutes were inflated and it worked out. But it can happen when you go out too quick after that first guy. It's a little scary."

With Gossett, it occurred after jumping out of a DC-3 over a fire in northern California.

"It was a two-man stick," he said of two jumping nearly simultaneously. "You are pumped up and jump one right after another. If you happen to open up at the same altitude going toward each other – you have maybe a 5 miles per hour forward speed – you can get tangled up. That's what happened to me. I went through his lines into his canopy. But we rode it all the way into the trees and sorted it out when we hit the ground."

Gossett figures he made about 125 jumps, about half of which were smokejumping and the rest sport jumping.

"I liked the camaraderie we had," Gossett said of smokejumping. "You know, you were only in the air a minute or so. We used to jump at 1,000 feet or so above ground."

"We loved jumping 'two manners' because that meant the fire was small," he added. "When we had a snag fire, we always jumped three guys. One guy, all he did was lay on his back and look up at the top, keeping his eyes open for any widow makers breaking at the top. You would never hear them coming, you know. So you had to keep an eye on the tree while the other two jumpers cut it down."

After he was activated in the Army reserves, he wasn't able to jump in the summer of 1959. But he returned to jumping in 1960, retraining in Missoula before going to Alaska where he jumped that fire season and the 1961 season. However, since the Alaskan fire season usually ends by early July, he was able to return to finish out the seasons at the Siskiyou base in both '60 and '61.

In 1962, he was recalled by the Army once again, but was discharged from activity duty in time to return to the Siskiyou base that August. His last year of jumping was in 1963 in Alaska where he was a squad leader.

When Gossett started kicking cargo for the Air America over Laos, he already had a pilot's commercial instrument rating with more than 700 hours and hoped to get work as a pilot.

"When I reported over there, it was like going home because there were so many Alaskan jumpers over there," he said. "I kicked cargo for about a year. I kept trying to work my way into a pilot job but the chief pilot told me, 'Lee, we got a lot more qualified guys than you.' So I left for about 18 months and went to New Zealand to work as a crop duster."

That was where he met his future wife in Mary, a flight attendant. He came back to the states and ended up flying in Alaska in 1966 for the U.S. Bureau of Land Management.

"Air America called me and offered me a job as a pilot," he said. "I went to Saigon and flew for four or five months. But I had a wife and baby then and I wasn't about to bring them to Saigon."

He got a transfer to Laos where his wife and their baby daughter, Lisa, joined him. He was then hired by Continental Airlines and was quickly promoted to captain, a job he held for four years.

"We flew all over Laos," he recalled. "We flew clear up to the Golden Triangle and down to southern Laos. We had three or four bases. Yes, we had CIA contracts. We were doing exactly the same thing as Air America. We were the competition.

"There were CIA guys everywhere and a lot of them were former smokejumpers," he added, naming off several jumpers who turned into company operatives. "In the summer of '63 in Alaska, we got a bumper crew up from Missoula. They came up to give us a hand and we became a real tight unit. From that group, a lot of us fanned out after that summer and went to either Air America, Inter Mountain or CIA. And we all linked up back in Laos."

The Gossett family lived in Vientiane, the capital of Laos, for 5 ½ years.

"Vientiane was a neutral city," he said. "Outside the city was basically war on. But inside the city was the Pathet Laos, the North Vietnamese, the Russians – everybody. You would be over there in the morning shopping with the Pathet Laos in the morning market. You could spot them and the North Vietnamese. But it was all hands off. Life was good. And the money was very good."

The family went to Bangkok or Hongkong about every three months, he said.

One fellow living near them in Vientiane was none other than Mick Swift who had jumped with Gossett out of the Siskiyou and several other bases in the Pacific Northwest.

"Mick was a pistol," Gossett said. "The photograph of him standing in the tree, that was Mick. You couldn't stage that."

As it turned out, Gary Buck had asked Swift about hiring on with Air America.

"But he talked me out of it," Buck said. "He said it was a CIA-run deal that was poorly managed. He said the Gobi here was extremely well managed and Air America was not. If you are going to do a dangerous job – which it was – you want the best management possible. He was not encouraging so I stayed at the Gobi."

Gossett and his young family eventually settled back in the Pacific Northwest where his work included serving as a smokejumper pilot out of Missoula. In his retirement, he still flies, but not to fight wildfires.

"I've spread the ashes of seven smokejumpers so far," said Gossett of taking the remains of former firefighting companions on their last airplane ride. "Unfortunately, there will be more as we grow older."

THE MOUSE THAT SOARED

22

NOT D.B. COOPER

LET'S MAKE THIS PERFECTLY CLEAR: former Siskiyou smokejumper John "Johnny" Kirkley has never, ever hijacked a jet airliner full of passengers for a bundle of cash, although he does own up to having parachuted out of the tail end of a roaring Boeing 727.

By now, you have grown accustomed to fascinating tales told by Siskiyou smokejumpers who have lived exciting lives. But Kirkley's story goes well beyond the merely wild and woolly, plunging over the cliff into the truly astonishing. His will leave you gobsmacked.

As with any story, Kirkley's takes a bit of telling. Hailing from Alabama, Kirkley, now a septuagenarian, was born in 1943, the same year as the base.

"When I was in high school, I was running track," he began. "On rainy days, because we only had clay track, they would take us out to the University of Alabama track in Tuscaloosa. I had met a guy named Charley Moseley who was running track for Alabama and who began jumping out at the Siskiyou base in '62."

While most fans of the Crimson Tide wouldn't know a smokejumper from smoked jerky, they would recognize the name of Charles E. "Charley" Moseley, a legendary star athlete for the University of Alabama.

Intrigued by the tales of smokejumping, Kirkley sought him out when he received a scholarship to run track for Alabama. The two became college roommates in 1963.

"I ran sprints – the 100 and 200," Kirkley explained. "I had the state record and won the Florida Relays as a junior. So I got a lot of scholarship offers. I chose Alabama because they gave me a pair of track shoes."

He was no slouch at running, completing the 100 in a blazing 9.7 seconds.

His roommate was also a track phenomenon.In 1963, Moseley was named the winner of the Hugo Friedman Award as the Crimson Tide's best all-around athlete of the year. His long jump of 25 feet, 10 inches was the seventh best in the university's history.

"Charley had worked as a fire fighter in Brookings before becoming a smokejumper," Kirkley said, noting that Moseley had spent one summer working as a ground-pounding firefighter for the Forest Service's Gold Beach Ranger District before going airborne. "I knew I had to get a little experience before trying to become a smokejumper. I applied at the Galice Ranger District and they hired me."

He was referring to a ranger district in the then Siskiyou National Forest which included portions of the Rogue River.

"I came to the Siskiyou base a rookie smokejumper in '64," he said, adding that he also jumped for the Siskiyou base in the summer of 1965.

All told, he made some 35 jumps. His first fire jump was on the Shasta-Trinity National Forest in far northwestern California.

"We landed right on top of a mountain full of pine straw that was on fire," he said, referring to a thick bed of dry pine needles. "We kept trying to put it out and the wind kept blowing it up. Finally, about 2 in the morning, they got a ground crew in there to relieve us. It was a tough fire."

But some fires were close to the base, like the one he and Doug "Hoppy" Hopkins jumped on a lightning-sparked blaze on Tennessee Mountain just west of Kerby on June 29, 1965.

"It was a big snag on fire – we had a crosscut saw and some pulaskis," Kirkley said, noting no chainsaws were being dropped at that time. "It was a huge tree. We finally got an undercut and got it down, put the fire out."

The two then hiked down to Kerby and caught a ride back to the base.

Periodically, the Siskiyou jumpers found time for a little recreation. In 1964, the year the Kalmiopsis Wilderness was created, Charley Moseley, John Manley and Kirkley decided to go look for an airplane that had crashed earlier that year in those rugged mountains. It had been raining and the smokejumpers had time on their hands.

"Charley had a little MG so we hopped in that thing, figuring we'd be back for dinner," Kirkley said. "It was in the middle of the afternoon. We hiked through all these trees and finally go up there to the airplane that Charley had seen from the air. The plane had already been stripped. Charley, who was leading us, said we needed to go back a different way because the way we had come was too brushy. So off we went."

But they quickly lost their way and spent the night huddled around a little campfire in the drizzling rain. No camping gear or food, of course.

"The next morning we wake up and Charley says, 'Well, boys, I've got bad news. The sun just came up in the West. We're not where we thought we were,'" Kirkley said. Obviously, they were the ones needing to be squared away, not the rising sun.

They resumed hiking and spent another night in the mountains before spotting a jeep road and began trudging out on it.

"We finally found our way out and were about a quarter mile from the car when the twin Beech flew over," he said of a crew from the Siskiyou base which was looking for them. "We were supposed to be back on Saturday. Mick Swift was in the plane and he threw us a note which said, 'We sure enjoyed your steaks on Saturday.'"

A rookie that year, Kirkley had severe blisters on his feet and was sidelined from jumping for a few days while his feet healed. He also suffered endless wisecracks about getting lost in the woods.

"It's rough country, the Kalmiopsis," he said.

Not long afterwards Moseley became a "kicker" for Air America in Southeast Asia. The airline, which had strong ties to Uncle Sam, wanted folks who were not concerned about standing in an open plane door and "kicking" out parachute drops over places like Cambodia and Thailand.

"Charley sent back some applications," Kirkley said. "Me and Mick Swift and John Manley filled them out and sent them back. But they didn't hire me. I had 12 credits to complete my degree and was going to graduate in January of '66. About mid-term I got a telegram which said, 'If you are still interested in working for Air America, come to 815 Connecticut Avenue, Washington. D.C. for an interview.' So I got on an airplane and went up there."

Kirkley, who was majoring in statistics with a minor in accounting, had just turned 22.

"They told me the last guy we hired who was 22 fell out of an airplane without a parachute last week so we are a little reluctant to hire someone that young," he recalled. "My comment was, 'Well, I ain't that stupid. I've been around airplanes a long time. If I'm going to be on an airplane with an open door, I'm going to have a parachute on.'"

He was hired. Following a week's orientation in Taipei, capital of Taiwan, he was sent to join his buddies in Vientiane. They were given gray uniforms with zippers on the pockets. They were also required to sign documents stating they could not talk about their work or would be subject to immediate dismissal.

"You never knew each time you went out what you would be doing," he said. "You didn't know where you were going. They had all these different government entities over there. Basically, we were delivering materials."

They used code names when required, he said, noting that weaponry and ammunition was known as "hard rice."

"There was really never ever any official recognition we were working for the CIA," he said of the Central Intelligence Agency. "It was actually Air Asia Incorporated that we got the letters from. That was what was on the door on Connecticut Avenue in Washington. But after you got over there you realized we were only working for one entity which we called the 'customer.' All the CIA guys on the ground were the customers. We were basically working as contract carriers."

While they were not spies, it was dangerous business. In 1962, three smokejumpers, including two from the same Texas town, were killed while working in southeast Asia for the "customers."

"I didn't know Lee [Gossett] until I got over there," he said. "They only hired special forces or smokejumpers for kickers. You had to be jump qualified and know something about rigging chutes and dropping air cargo."

Swift, who was Kirkley's foreman at the smokejumper base, went to work for Air America three months before Kirkley joined the group.

"They told me if I served three years, then I would get a three-month leave," Kirkley said. "My plan was to work there three years and, if I didn't die, come back and graduate."

He obviously didn't die, although it wasn't for lack of effort.

"In 1967 – might have been '68 – they told us they had a project they wanted us to go to in Takhli, Thailand," he said of a major U.S. air base during the Vietnam War. "It was just north of Bangkok. We didn't know what they wanted us to do."

Turns out the powers that be wanted the smokejumpers to parachute out of a Boeing 727.

"Now, a 727 had a stairwell at the back end of the plane," he explained. "They took that out and cut a hole in the back of the plane. They put a sheet metal sliding board in that hole. They also had roller conveyors in there for the cargo."

They made several test jumps out of the back of the airliner.

"Then they started talking about making some air drops in Tibet. We had already made three or four jumps out of the 727 and had dropped some cargo, proving it could be done. But that was at sea level in Thailand. They had to put all the flaps down so they could slow the thing down to 125 miles an hour so it didn't blow up our chutes when we went out."

The problem was that some of the lowest places they planned to work in Tibet were at 10,000 feet above sea level, he said.

"The 727 became very unstable above 10,000 feet when you were trying to slow it down to 125 with all the flaps down. They decided not to do it. But they had accomplished what they wanted to do, train a few of us to jump from a 727."

Mission accomplished, he went back to school in 1969, graduated, then returned to Laos to return to work for Air America.

"It was getting pretty hot over there by that time," he said. "I felt I had used up my nine lives so I figured I should do something else."

He applied and was hired for a desk job with Air America in Taipei. But he grew tired of being a desk jockey and went back to the states where he got a summer job working as a foreman for a ground crew fighting wildfires in Alaska. When the snow began to fly, he began what turned out to be a 15-year career as a bar owner in the Far North. His first of seven bars was named the "Polar Bar" and located in downtown Anchorage.

It was in that bar one afternoon right after Thanksgiving in 1971 that two well-dressed men strode into the bar.

"I'm sitting there, having a cup of coffee and talking to a customer," Kirkley recalled. "These two guys in coats and ties come in and show me their FBI badges. They said, 'We'd like to ask you a few questions.'"

Although a bit dumbfounded, Kirkley agreed, knowing he had nothing to hide.

"They asked me if I was aware of this fellow who just hijacked a 727 and jumped out of it," he said. "I said, 'Sure, I just saw it on the news.' Then they said, 'We know you have parachuted out of a 727 and we want to know where you were on the night of the 24th.' I told them I was right there tending bar and I had witnesses to prove it."

On the night of Nov. 24, 1971, a man calling himself Dan Cooper, a.k.a. D. B. Cooper, bought a one-way ticket on a Northwest Airline 727 flight from Portland to Seattle. He gave a note to a flight attendant which declared he was carrying a bomb in the attaché case he was carrying. The pilot landed the airliner and the hijacker was given some

$250,000 in $20 bills. After the aircraft took off again, Cooper bailed out, disappearing into the darkness. Although a few rotting $20 bills found years later along the banks of the Columbia River were identified by their serial numbers as being among those given the hijacker, he was never found.

Kirkley laughed at the thought the FBI was checking to see if he was the most famous airline hijacker in U.S. history. Back in 1971, he wasn't laughing.

"I think there were six of us who jumped out of the 727. They came to see me and Charley Moseley and a couple of other guys. They had our records. They wanted to make sure one of us wasn't D.B. Cooper. None of us were, of course."

If you happen to check out the metal name plates in the loft at the Siskiyou Smokejumper Museum, look above Kirkley's name. The metal plate above his reads, "D.B. Cooper Were You? No 1971." The joke is the handiwork of Tom "Tommy" Albert.

"Well, at least the Air America years kept me out of the military," Kirkley said.

THE MOUSE THAT SOARED

23

JUMPERS AND LOGGERS

C LIFF HAMILTON FROWNED WHEN ASKED about the story often told by his smokejumper buddies of the wild night he punched out a logger at a local watering hole.

"Everybody thought I was pretty tough when I beat up that logger but he wasn't much trouble – he was drunk," said Hamilton who was a 1962 rookie at the Siskiyou base, jumping through the 1965 season before jumping two seasons in Alaska and serving as a kicker for Air America. "People said he was 6' 4". But he was shorter than I was, although he was a little stouter.

"Yes, there was a little animosity towards us sometimes – somebody would get drunk and start something," he conceded. "We didn't start the fights but we weren't going to be bullied, either."

It should be no surprise that altercations sometimes erupted between local loggers and the Siskiyou smokejumpers. After all, both professions attracted folks with a high testosterone level. Add a few swigs of alcohol and fisticuffs were inevitable. However, as one hailing from a logging family in the county where the base was located, I would be letting down some relatives if I didn't point out that loggers won their share of the brouhahas.

But John Kirkley, who jumped with Hamilton for two fire seasons, insists there was no doubt who was the victor when it came to the legendary bout involving his smokejumping friend.

"It was basically Cliff and a couple of other guys from the base in a Cave Junction bar one night," he began. "Well, this rookie came in looking for them. He was wearing shorts and checkered ones at that, something you didn't want to wear into a logger's bar in the 1960s."

While Kirkley acknowledged he wasn't there that night, he said the tale's veracity is reflected in the fact those who were present tell the story every time Siskiyou smokejumpers from the 1960s gather to hoist a few brewskis and reminisce.

"What happened was this big logger followed the rookie over to the table and made a snide comment about his shorts," he said. "Cliff said, 'Why don't you pick on somebody your own size?'"

Hamilton was known for his courage, strength and toughness, Kirkley said. The two stepped outside to settle their differences.

"The logger picked up this metal fence post and swung it at Cliff," he said. "But Cliff, who had been a football player and was pretty quick, ducked and popped him. It went back and forth until Cliff knocked him out cold. That is a well known story."

Kirkley had another tale about the well-respected jumper, one the teller wasn't as keen to repeat but figured it would balance things out a bit.

"I had what felt like five gallons of water poured on me one night when I came in the bunkhouse drunk," he said with a laugh. "That was Cliff Hamilton. He doesn't remember it but I sure do."

Whether the loud drunk deserved the sobering bath is another story, although the storyteller did not deny he was a mite obnoxious that night.

Hamilton, now pushing 80 and living in Alabama just outside of Mobile, acknowledged there were plenty of rowdy times during his smokejumping days. Hailing from Oakland, Calif., he became a smokejumper after talking to a friend of his father's who worked for the U.S. Forest Service in Oregon.

"I got a job in the Umpqua National Forest in Oregon, working that first year in the maintenance crew at Diamond Lake and around there," he said. "That was in 1960. The second year I got on fire control. I was there one day and saw a couple of smokejumpers come in from a fire. They were all dirty and it impressed me. I thought, 'I want to do that.'"

On the way back to Oakland, he dropped by the Siskiyou base where he talked to base manager Jim Allen who also happened to be a colleague of his father's friend.

"I got an interview and got hired for the summer of '62," he said, adding he ended up jumping for four fire seasons out of the base, making more than 70 jumps.

When he wasn't working as a Siskiyou smokejumper, Hamilton was a student at the University of California at Berkeley come winter. He majored in physical science, a major which consisted of studying chemistry, physics and math in the field.

"In addition to studying, I did a lot of snow skiing, playing basketball and drinking. I also played football. I wasn't very good at it. I worked my way up to second string on the worst freshman football team in the history in the University of California."

But it was smokejumping with its strong work ethic and bond that left its imprint on him.

"You forget a lot of fires but some stick with you. On one fire on the Snake River, it was so steep that these big pine cones were rolling down the mountain on fire. You had to catch them in your hard hat or they would spread the fire down below you. And you sure didn't want the fire above and below you."

Because the fire had spread, smokejumpers were working alongside ground-based firefighters to stop the blaze.

"That was no fun at all. Normally, smokejumping was like camping out. You had all the fun of jumping down to a burning snag. You put it out and watch it for six or eight hours to make sure it stays out."

Packing out with heavy gear was invariably a challenge in the Lower 48 states, particularly the arduous packouts made after jumping fires in southwest Oregon and northwest California, he said.

"That all changed when I went to Alaska since you didn't usually pack out in Alaska because it was too damned far. They came and got you."

Like most jumpers, Hamilton landed in a few trees.

"First year I was jumping, I hung up two times. Tore up one chute in one. But I got down OK."

He wasn't there when Mike Swift landed on top of the pine tree and a photograph was taken of him giving the plane crew the Gobi salute.

"But I remember when it happened," he said, laughing. "It was the biggest tree around and he landed right on top of it. He was the boss so he got a lot of flak for that."

However, like others who jumped with Swift, he was quick to note that the smokejumper in that tree was a jumper's jumper.

"He was one rugged individual," he said.

Like other former Siskiyou jumpers who would work for Air America, Hamilton found it an interesting period in his life.

"They hired us because they figured we knew something about working around an open door in an airplane. I'm not too fond of heights but it didn't bother me as long as I had a parachute on and something I could hold onto. You could do that over there with Air America.

"You know, we were the most educated workers in Air America," he added, noting most smokejumpers had been to college. "But I don't know if it made any difference."

Hamilton spent most his time in Laos but did make a short visit to what was then South Vietnam.

"When I was with Air America, I found Vietnam a lot safer than Laos, although I was only there two weeks and that was in Saigon," he said. But he allows the feeling of being in a safe area was likely because of the heavy presence of American troops in the area at the time.

Upon graduating from college, he worked for a chemical firm in Mobile for more than a decade, then teamed up with Moseley to work for oil and gas companies in Alabama, Mississippi and Oklahoma.

"After smokejumping and working for Air America, it was kind of hard to come back and sell life insurance or something like that," Hamilton said. "That was a pretty big adventure."

24

WAR BUDDIES

L IKE ANY GROUP SERVING IN harm's way, the Siskiyou
smokejumpers formed a strong bond that is resolute, surviving
as a band of brothers through petty spats, political differences or religious divides over the years. Certainly the small subgroup who
served a stint as Air America "kickers" in southeast Asia have a
special allegiance to each other to this day.

But many former Siskiyou jumpers insist there was no stronger
bond among them than that between Mouse and Tom "Trooper Tom"
Emonds. After all, both were gung-ho jumpers, outspoken and quick
with a joke. What's more, both were college educated with degrees
in forestry. But the strongest link was their southeast Asia experience,
not as Air America employees but as veterans of the Vietnam War.
Both spent three years in country as Marines on the front lines.

"When I returned to the base after the Corps, I wasn't treated very
well at first," said Emonds who was a rookie at the Siskiyou base in
1966 and jumped for two seasons before serving in the Marine Corps.
"A lot of the guys were anti-war. Some were pinning me against the
wall, wanting me to account for why I was in Vietnam. Well, the Ma-

rine Corps never told us why we were there. They just showed us how to be warriors.

"Mouse saw I was having trouble," he continued. "He would come over to me and say, 'Hey Troop, there's them that have been there and them that haven't and they are never going to see eye-to-eye on this.' Mouse was an encourager to me but he also helped the anti-war guys understand what we had been through."

It was through his stories and humor that Mouse was able to connect with people, Emonds observed.

"He could tell so many humorous stories about the Corps and he was so small and so un-Marine like that it was acceptable," he said. "He wasn't bragging or anything like that. He focused on the common people who were in a war together. And talk about funny. He would have all the anti-war people rolling in the aisles, unable to catch their breath, peeing their pants with these stories about what happened to him in the Corps. He made us all laugh with that great sense of humor of his."

But Edmonds wasn't laughing when he first met Mouse in 1970. At the time, he was still in the Corps and Mouse was a rookie at the base. While on leave from the front lines, Emonds and a girlfriend flew into Medford. He was looking forward to reuniting with his jumper pals and showing her the base.

"After we landed, I called the base and asked if they could send someone over to pick us up," he recalled. "They said they had just the guy, a former Marine. An hour or so later this really short guy comes driving up in a blue Corvette with the top down. We all get jammed in there together and take off. Mouse could barely see over the dashboard to drive. And he was just talking away."

Understandably, Emonds, fresh out of a combat zone, was more than a little concerned about whether they would make it intact to the base roughly 60 miles away.

"He was really driving fast and talking about the same speed. I'm thinking to myself, 'Holy Moses! What am I into here?'"

But he also sensed he was getting to know one of the most remarkable characters he would meet in a lifetime of adventures involving fascinating people.

"It was the wonderful beginning of my evolution with Mouse," said Emonds who stood more than a foot taller than his short friend. "You had to be totally impressed with the way he told stories."

No amateur himself as a storyteller, Emonds would make 546 jumps from Alaska to the Appalachian Mountains over 25 years as a jumper. Although he and his twin brother, Ken, were raised in a town called Forestville, they certainly didn't hail from smokejumping country. But his Connecticut childhood changed forever when the two went to a matinee one Saturday.

"It was usually a cowboy movie and I would always bring my cap gun to help Roy Rogers with the bad guys," he said. "I asked my brother what cowboy movie was playing. He said there was no cowboy movie, that it was a nature movie. I was really disappointed."

His disappointment vanished when the *Red Skies of Montana* filled the silver screen. As mentioned earlier, the 1952 flick featuring the memorable Richard Widmark was based on the 1949 Mann Gulch tragedy in which 12 smokejumpers perished while fighting a Montana wildfire. Even with the Hollywood-injected subplot, it remains a classic smokejumper movie today.

"When I came out of the theater, I told my brother I was going to be a smokejumper," Emonds said. "I was about eight at the time."

He would become a smokejumper as he proclaimed but that would happen years later. First, he had to navigate his way through elementary, middle and high school.

"My brother did very well in school and became a doctor," he said of his twin who became an immunologist. "On the other hand, his twin was the kid who couldn't get a decent report card and got yelled and screamed at while getting the living daylights beaten out of him. Dad would always come back and apologize to me later. He always told me he wanted to keep me from having to dig ditches."

When the twin who received the brunt of paternal discipline became a smokejumper, their father figured he had failed, Emonds said.

"As far as he was concerned, I was basically out in the forest digging ditches. He felt like he had failed. He couldn't understand what in the hell he had done wrong."

His father obviously didn't understand the important national role of smokejumpers in wildland firefighting, let alone the fire in his son's belly for becoming a parachuting firefighter. Yet there were palpable signs of the latter. Take the summer young Tom Emonds worked on a local fire crew, known as a "warden crew" in his locale.

"It was illegal as hell. Here I was in the eighth grade and out there fighting fires. Still, it gave me some good experience."

Even in his youth, the future Marine officer who would lead men in combat was showing signs of leadership. After achieving the rank of Eagle Scout, an indication his youthful activities weren't all spank worthy, he often led younger scouts on excursions into the local woods.

"That was on weekends and I would talk about the outings during basketball practice at high school," he said as an aside. "That's when the guys started calling me 'Troop.' Despite what many think, my nickname had nothing to do with the Marines. It started in high school."

After graduating from Nicholas College in Massachusetts with a bachelor's degree in forestry and hitchhiking around the world, he got a job working as a wildlands firefighter in Australia. Meanwhile, he sent letters of inquiry to smokejumper bases back in the states, including the Siskiyou base.

Early in 1966, base foreman Chuck Sheley told manager Jim Allen about the letters from an American expatriate in Australia interested in smokejumping at the base.

"He told Jim, 'Look, we've got this guy who keeps writing us who is over in Australia fighting fires and wants to become a smokejumper,'" Emonds said with a chuckle. "Jim said, 'Hell, if he is that interested, let's give him a try.'"

The base had also received a letter from a Connecticut congressman urging that the young man be hired, recalled Sheley, noting he was a bit dubious at the time.

"Trooper Tom had two strikes against him when he came in," Sheley said. "He was from Connecticut and I was wondering whose congressman's son we were going to have to baby sit. When he arrived, he asked if he could bring his rifle on base. We said, 'What?' He had apparently left his rifle at some tavern down the road."

Emonds was immediately informed the firearm would definitely have to be checked in at the main office, he said.

"When Troop arrived that Sunday, there were ten humble rookies here waiting to start training the next day," recalled Wes Brown, one of those humble rookies. "He looked different. He was dressed different. He had just arrived back from New Zealand where he had been a government hunter hired to shoot deer as pest control. He brought his rifle."

Sheley, who trained the group, agreed he did not fit the usual rookie mold.

"But he turned out to be one hell of a rookie and one hell of a firefighter," he said. "He was a terrific jumper, one of the best. He was also a natural leader who became a real asset to the base."

Ironically, following his rookie fire season, Emonds would join the Marine Corps in order to avoid being drafted into the U.S. Army.

"It was the only way I could get in the second summer as a smokejumper at the base," he said of the 1967 fire season, noting he signed up for the Marines on the delayed-entry program after getting his draft notice.

The following year found him as a young lieutenant on the front lines in Vietnam.

"They sent us into combat straight out of Quantico," he said. "But I had been a smokejumper and had learned to find my way around in the wild. That helped. Of course, compared to combat, smokejumping was nothing."

He also knew how to work with people and listen to their views, particularly those with combat experience.

"The platoon sergeant I had was from Arkansas and had a seventh grade education," he recalled. "But he was the leader of that platoon. He figured his job was to make me into an effective leader. Total unselfishness on his part. So here was an insecure guy who didn't know much about combat with an experienced sergeant totally willing to help him."

Yet Emonds, having traveled through Asia, Europe and the Middle East, brought a unique perspective to the war.

"Nobody wanted to be there, except for me," Emonds said. "We were walking on these trails that had been used for thousands of years. I told my men, 'Look at this. It is the Orient. It has not changed for thousands of years. Look at us. We will be gone shortly and this culture will still be going on here. You should be really glad you are able to see part of humanity not many people get to see.' The troops thought I was nuts about that. But we worked well together. They were so incredible, so bonded. The things people do for each other in combat is truly amazing."

Emonds, who plans to write a book about his Vietnam experience, noted the similarity between the bond among Siskiyou smokejumpers and that shared by Marines in battle.

"They took care of each other, a lot like we did in the Corps back in Vietnam," he said, adding, "I loved being a smokejumper and hanging out with the type of people who were smokejumpers."

Emonds completed his hitch and returned to the Siskiyou base in time for the 1971 fire season, staying until 1980. But the shadow of war hung over many of the Vietnam War veterans. After all, like Mouse, Emonds had been there when fellow Marines, many of them good friends, were killed in Vietnam.

That hit home one evening after spending the day fighting a wildfire in the Smokey Mountain National Park in North Carolina in the spring of 1975, he and Mouse returned to their temporary quarters with other Siskiyou jumpers. Someone flicked on the television to catch up on the news. Leading the news was the fall of Saigon, soon to be renamed Ho Chi Minh City. Although the Paris Peace Accords had been signed two years earlier between the U.S. and North Vietnam, officially ending the war, it wasn't until Saigon fell that hostilities stopped and the U.S. fully withdrew.

"Mouse and I were so mad we were crying – it was real difficult to see it all end like that," Emonds said. "The other jumpers who hadn't been in Vietnam didn't understand what we were upset about. But we had lost good friends over there. That was a very bitter disappointment."

Yet the memories of Mouse he prefers to recall are those of happier days. Take the time when he and Gary Buck would drop in out of the blue at Mouse's house in Cave Junction on a Friday evening.

"We'd walk into his house and say, 'Mouse, you are going with us to town to find some girls," Emonds said, noting "town" referred to Grants Pass, the county seat. "He'd tell us he was staying home and watching TV. We'd turn off the TV, pick him up and carry him out to the truck. He would bitch and moan all the way in but would end up having a great time."

And there was the time they floated down the Illinois River in the spring of 1980 where the river, fed by a melting mountain snowpack, rushed along inside the north end of the Kalmiopis Wilderness. Accompanying them were Buck, Mills and a couple of other Siskiyou jumpers. As they approached a site known as the "Green Wall" which has a reputation for gobbling up white water enthusiasts, they pulled ashore to scout it out before taking the plunge.

"Mouse, who had a helmet on, and I were in the same raft," Emonds recalled. "After we stopped to check out the Green Wall, I got back in the raft. Mouse, who had been asleep, woke up and asked me what was going on. I told him we were going down river."

Emonds paddled the raft out into the river, heading toward the house-size rock in the center of the roaring rapids.

"Mouse, who is wide awake at this point, sits up and yells, 'Trooooop! Baaad!'" Emonds said. "He is pointing toward that big rock. Then he yells, 'Tell my mother I love her.' We got tossed around a little a little but we made it through."

Although it was their first float down through the Kalmiopsis, albeit only in the northern tip, he and Mouse had made numerous jumps deep into the wilderness over the years.

"The Kalmiopsis was always one of the worst places to jump,"

Emonds said. "The brush is horrendous and there are plenty of rat-tlesnakes. Then you always had a long pack out. It was tough on everybody."

The last fire jumps Emonds and Mouse made together were in Alaska after they left the Siskiyou base following the 1980 fire season.

"The Alaskan smokejumpers were doubtful at first of this little guy but Mouse quickly won them over," Emonds said. "He was not only a good firefighter but he always lit up a room when he was in it. He filled up a room with his personality."

Being on the same jump list, Trooper Tom and Mouse often jumped alongside each other in the Far North.

"We were out on the Kobuk River and came up on an enormous bull moose carcass," he said. "Mouse could stand between the antlers."

The smokejumpers smuggled the antlers back to the base at Fort Wainwright where the monstrous rack became a moose mascot of sorts.

Emonds' last flight with Mouse was near the end of the 1981 fire season when their Alaskan crew was fighting fires in the Yellowstone country in western Wyoming. En route to one fire, Mouse became ill in the plane. As a result, Emonds ended up jumping with a smoke-jumper named JJ.

"We were both in the door and JJ says to me, 'It doesn't seem right you aren't jumping with Mouse – he can have my spot if he wants,'" he said. "I looked over at Mouse and he is giving me the Gobi sign with both hands, the double bird."

Obviously the normally gung-ho Mouse wasn't up to jumping that day. But the fire turned out to be in a lone tree in a meadow. Emonds and the other jumper made short work of the fire, although they faced an arduous hike out with heavy packs.

"The first four miles was an absolute nightmare, an area criss-crossed with downed lodge pole pine," Emonds said. "And when we got through that we still had about 17 miles to go."

However, they received a radio message that a horse packer was in the area and could link up with them.

"He had saddle horses for both of us and mules for our packs. But he warned us of a narrow ledge ahead of us. He told us when we got to that spot to just put our hands on the saddle horn and not look down, just let the horses do their thing. Of course, when you tell someone not to look down, the first thing they are going to do is look down."

When they got to the ledge, it was about a foot wide with the abyss on one side.

"The horse's stomach was hanging over the ledge and our feet are against the cliff on the other side," he said. "By the time we got through that, we are both white knuckled. Afterwards, the guide asked us, 'OK, what is scarier: jumping out of an airplane or doing what you just did?' We both said, 'Doing what we just did!'"

During the interview at the base, a handsome chocolate lab named Teddy Roosevelt was sitting nearby, quietly watching as his friend and master talked about his latest challenge. Named after Emonds' favorite president, the pooch keeps a protective eye on him.

"Three years ago I had a stroke – couldn't walk, couldn't talk," Emonds said. "Teddy was a pup who helped me get back on my feet. We now run three miles on the Oregon beach every morning."

Like the bond linking Emonds to his smokejumping brothers, the one between man and dog is resolute.

25

LOCAL JUMPER POOL

W HEN GARY THORNHILL WAS A youngster in the Illinois
Valley, the denizens at the Siskiyou Smokejumper Base and
the close-knit valley residents didn't often mix.

"About the only contact the jumpers had with the community was
softball games, and the smokejumpers really kicked their ass," he recalled. "Of course, there were also a few ruckuses between loggers
and smokejumpers in the bars."

Base manager Delos "Dee" Dutton decided the relationship needed
to be improved, both for the benefit of the base and the broader community.

"He wanted a better rapport with the community so he started recruiting in the local community," Thornhill said. "It was a good move
on his part. Local residents started coming out to watch practice
jumps."

What's more, the base now had a local pool of bright, athletic youth
from which to recruit. And one was Thornhill, a bright, well-respected
young man with an easy-going, engaging personality. Yet he was also
one tough hombre built like a proverbial brick privy.

Born on Sept. 18, 1949, in Alva, Okla., the county seat of Woods County and home to Northwestern Oklahoma State University where his father had played football, he arrived in southern Oregon as a youngster.

"Mom and dad left us kids with an aunt and uncle and came out to Oregon to look for a teaching job," Gary explained, noting the year was 1956. "Dad had a job offer in Forest Grove and one in Cave Junction. He took the Cave Junction job."

To digress for a moment, I am glad he did. As mentioned earlier, Wayne Thornhill was a well-liked teacher as well as wrestling and football coach at Illinois Valley High School. No doubt his job was more challenging than need be, thanks to students like yours truly.

After graduating from high school in 1967, Gary Thornhill worked for the U.S. Forest Service that summer and fall, then started studying in January of 1968 at what is now Southern Oregon University in Ashland, majoring in health and physical education. Like his father, he played college football.

"I was rooming with Pat McNally," he said of a fellow IVHS graduate who had been a Siskiyou smokejumper the previous summer. "He told me some great stories about smokejumping. Then one day, another smokejumper, Bob McCray, who was also a student during the winter, showed up at our dorm room and said, 'Hey, the boss told me to tell you to call him.'"

Although intrigued by McNally's stories, Thornhill had never given much thought to becoming a smokejumper. Still, he had worked for the Forest Service, including serving as a slash burner which, in effect, is fighting fire, albeit a controlled burn.

"But I had never even been in an airplane before," he said. "In fact, I ended going up seven times for practice jumps before I ever landed in an airplane."

Once he started jumping, however, he knew he had found his niche. For the next 12 summers, he was a Siskiyou smokejumper, a job of which he was rightfully proud.

"For one thing, the people at the base were special people," he said.

"The guys were great to work with. And it certainly got exciting at times."

As a rookie, Thornhill joined other wannabe jumpers on the tower in preparation for the real thing.

"The first jump, there wasn't a lot of emotion. You are thinking, 'OK, once he (spotter) hits me on the shoulder, I go out.' It wasn't a big deal. The second time, then I thought about it more. Jumping can be a little spooky at times, depending on the conditions. But you get used to it."

His first fire jump was in the Winema National Forest in the summer of 1968.

"There were four of us jumping on my first fire," he said. "Your training takes over and away you go. Once you get on the ground, then it is just a lot of hard work."

Known as the Wildhorse Ridge Fire, the July 6 blaze he first jumped on was held to five acres, according to the base record book. It was the fourth of five fire calls the base responded to that day, the book noted.

Back in the late 1960s, a jumper averaged a little more than half a dozen fire jumps a year, Thornhill recalled.

"A few years later, it went up because we expanded our jump area to include Region 8," he said, noting the base was in Region 6. "Back in the day, smokejumping was not usually a fulltime job but it could be if you became a squad leader."

Taking a break from college for a few years, Thornhill worked in management at the base before returning to the classroom to graduate. After 25 years in education, he would retire as assistant principal at IVHS where his father taught for many years. His son, Scott Thornhill, is now an administrator at the school. A grandson was an IVHS student at the time of this writing, continuing the Thornhill family tradition.

But Gary Thornhill was the only one who plunged out of an airplane to fight wildfires.

"In addition to Oregon, I jumped in Alaska, Idaho, Montana, Tennessee, Indiana, Arkansas, Oklahoma," he said. "Walt Congleton – he and I were rookies together – and I once jumped an Oklahoma fire. We may have been the only (Siskiyou) smokejumpers to jump in Oklahoma. Whenever I would see Walt, he would say, 'We're famous smokejumpers.'"

Thornhill chuckled, noting the fire was easily extinguished by the two of them. He doesn't recall if it was near his birth town of Alva.

"One thing I do remember about that fire was that the wind was blowing every which way," he said. "I remember we both landed in an old creek bed. It wasn't much of a fire, just a two-manner. We had it out by that evening."

It was early in the spring, a time when hot weather normally hits that region, he added.

"But I really liked working at the base," he said of the Siskiyou. "There was no screaming and yelling during training there. It was all about getting people ready to fight fires. Mick Swift had a lot to do with that."

He paused for a moment as he thought about the well-known smokejumper.

"Mick was one of those rare guys who could fix anything, do anything. He was one you always wanted with you when you were jumping. He was a big guy known all over the smokejumper world. He could care less if someone had long hair or short hair. He only cared about whether someone had the talent to do the job."

He was also someone who liked to keep up with the latest development in the tools of the smokejumper trade, Thornhill said.

"One day he told me about this idea of using fire line explosives to put out fires. And he asked me to go with him to Medford to get certified to use them. I said, 'What?' He told me about how they were using fire line explosives to blow firelines. I told him I didn't know anything about explosives. He told me, 'It'll be good. We can travel around training other jumpers how to use it.'"

So off they went to Medford.

"That's when he said, 'Oh yeah, we do have to pass this written exam,'" Thornhill said. "So he gave me a book. We passed the written exam, then took a practical. He told me to watch him and do the same thing. I did and passed it."

About a year later Swift retired from jumping.

"That's when I became the Region 6 fireline explosive examiner," Thornhill said with a laugh. "Yeah, Mick was quite a character. Good guy."

Like other jumpers, he acknowledged that Swift fooled around with snakes on occasion.

"Unlike Mick, I've never been too crazy about them," he said. "Ray Farinetti, a good friend of mine, and I were practicing water jumps at Seats Dam once. With a water jump, you practice getting out from under your chute if you land in water. You jump off into the water and they would throw the chute over you. The objective was to find a line and start pulling until the chute was off you.

"Well, Ray knew I didn't like snakes," he added of the Siskiyou jumper who rookied in 1964. "So I got the chute off and he says, 'Hey, GT, look what I got.' He was holding up a rattlesnake about a foot and a half long. And he throws it into the pool."

In retrospect, Thornhill, dubbed "GT" since there were already other jumpers named Gary when he arrived at the base, didn't know for certain whether was a buzzworm or not. All he knew for sure was that it looked like the real deal at the time.

"It might as well have been a rattlesnake," he said, noting he was swimming with all his might. "I yelled, 'When I get out of here I'm going to kick your ass.' Ray took off running."

As any sane person would do if an angry Gary Thornhill was on your heels.

In another reptilian practical joke, Thornhill walked out to his pickup truck one summer evening to head home when he noticed something sinister writhing in the back.

"It was a ball of friggin' snakes," he said. "Yeah, it was Farinetti again."

But we can't let Gary Thornhill off the practical joke hook since he pulled a few pranks himself. Consider the time that jumper Stanley

"Clancy" Collins, a transfer who arrived at the base in 1970, built an impressive kite in the parachute loft, a place where various projects were created during downtime.

"Clancy went out and started flying his kite," recalled Wes Brown, a 1966 Siskiyou base rookie. "He was having a great time. GT and some friends were watching him. Pretty soon GT says, 'Watch this.' He gets his shotgun out of his vehicle, sneaks out under the kite and blasts it. That kite just crumpled like a dead bird."

A friend of both jumpers, Brown nearly crumpled with laughter when telling the story.

As a veteran smokejumper when Mouse arrived at the base in 1970, Thornhill helped train the short rookie.

"When I first saw him, I said, 'What is that?'" he recalled. "Mouse turned out great. He was a little stud. He never liked being behind when we were hiking out of a fire. We'd take off and stop to take a break and sit down. Here comes Mouse, walking right past us. He wouldn't stop. He had short legs and didn't want us to have to wait for him. So he just kept going and going."

He remembered the time he and Mouse were among the smokejumpers dropped into the Sky Lakes Wilderness to fight a lightning-caused fire.

"We got the fire out and got packed up and started hiking out. We were following a trail out. At one point, there was a log over a creek. We crossed it and hiked on before taking a break. Well, Mouse didn't come along like he usually did."

So they went back to check on him as they would any jumper missing in action.

"We got to the creek and there was Mouse," he said. "He had slipped off the log and was on his back with his pack jammed between two big rocks. He looked like a turtle that had flipped over on his back."

While Mouse was unscathed and quickly righted, many jumpers were seriously injured over the years, observed Thornhill who made five rescue jumps in his career. He once participated in a rescue jump in the Kalmiopsis Wilderness after a jumper's chute collapsed when he landed in a tall tree. Thornhill and three other jumpers landed nearby and packed the injured jumper to a site where a helicopter could pick him up.

"On that jump, I did the same thing," he said of crashing down onto a big conifer. "I started falling and I thought, 'Oh man!' But right before I hit the ground the edge of my chute caught on a broken limb about an inch thick. When I stopped, I was about four feet off the ground. That could have been real ugly. Things do happen out there."

Yet, when it comes to tough landing spots, sometimes a tree is the best place to land, he noted.

"With knowledge and experience, you learn when and how and where to land. Sometimes the trees are where you want to jump. If there are big boulders below you, you don't want to crash into those. Instead, you jump into that 40-foot 'reprod' over there."

He was referring to a 40-foot young conifer, part of what foresters sometimes refer to as a "reproduction stand." Of course, a jumper would want to avoid tall timber that can be found in the northwest, he cautioned.

"With old timber, the limbs go out and do this," he said, holding his arms down. "You hit those limbs, your chute collapses and down you go. But if you can get your canopy on top of a tree, then you are usually safe."

Thornhill estimates he jumped some 250 times, including fire, practice and rescue jumps. He suffered no major injuries while jumping, although he once cracked an ankle bone.

"What happened was we were jumping into an old logging unit that had turned into a brush field. I came down and hit the edge of a stump that I couldn't see and cracked a bone. No big deal."

Sadly, while was working on the roof of his house late in 2020, Thornhill fell some 20 feet, breaking numerous ribs, puncturing a lung and shattering a pelvis. Most folks, let alone someone in their early 70s, would not have survived but fortunately he recovered. After all, he is Gary Thornhill, one tough hombre.

26

SMOKEJUMPING FOR ROCKET SCIENCE

ILLINOIS VALLEY NEWS **EDITOR AND** publisher Bob Grant wrote a popular "Cabbages and Kings" weekly column which offered readers amusing insights into the goings on in the region in the 1960s and '70s. Like the wise walrus in Lewis Carroll's famous 1872 poem, he talked of many things, of shoes, ships, sealing wax and "cabbages and kings." Grant did not disappoint in June of 1970.

An avid booster of the Siskiyou Smokejumper Base, he wanted local folks to know that former Siskiyou smokejumper Chuck Mansfield, a 1956 graduate of Grants Pass High School, had been usurped, so to speak. In addition to being a Carroll fan, the editor also admired the scientifically-minded jumper and had written about him several times.

"Note to ex-smokejumper Chuck Mansfield: Your crown has been removed," Grant wrote. "The smokejumper base now has a new 'Mighty Mouse.'"

Mansfield, who jumped for 11 fire seasons ending in 1969, was a slight fellow who weighed 130 pounds and encountered problems getting down to earth if there was an updraft, he noted. At 5' 10", the former jumper wasn't exactly gravity challenged, although he was a bit thin in his youth. But we won't quibble with Mr. Grant who was kind enough to hire me as a printer's devil at the then hot-lead weekly when I was a high school sophomore and sorely needed a part-time job. He was a good boss as well as a colorful character with a wickedly funny wit.

Let's get back to his column.

"He's now a NASA man in Houston, working on gadgets he invented himself," Grant added of Mansfield before introducing Allen "Mouse" Owen, the all-time reigning short fellow at the base.

The future scientist jumped during the summer in order to fund his formal education which ended with a doctorate's degree in physics, no small scholarly feat. Although Mansfield never jumped with Mouse, they met when the former came back to visit the base after taking a job with the aforementioned National Aeronautics and Space Administration.

"Mouse was known as a very good jumper," Mansfield said. "When you met him, you could tell he had a lot of drive and let nothing or anyone stand in the way of achieving his goals."

When it came to not letting anything or anyone stopping one from achieving a dream, Mansfield knew of what he spoke.

At first glance, it would seem an improbable transition from being a sweating, smoke-smudged smokejumper working hard to knock down a wildfire to morphing into a white-coated scientist pondering complex physics questions in NASA's Johnson Space Center in Houston, searching for answers to further humankinds' knowledge of outer space.

As improbable as it seems, Mansfield wasn't the only one to make that gigantic leap from the Siskiyou base. The other one was none other than astronaut Stuart Roosa who, at the age of 19, was a rookie at the Siskiyou base in 1953 where he jumped that one fire season.

Think about that for a moment. Out of 434 smokejumpers at the base over the decades, two would work for NASA. What are the odds? Astronomical, of course, pun intended. Yet it reflects the caliber of folks who became Siskiyou smokejumpers.

Much has been written about Roosa who, after smokejumping, became an Air Force pilot, an aeronautical engineer and a NASA astronaut. For an excellent read, check out the 2011 book, *Smokejumper, Moon Pilot: The Remarkable Life of Apollo 14 Astronaut Stuart Roosa.* Written by Willie G. Moseley, it tells the amazing story of Roosa's lofty rise, from his smokejumping days to becoming the Apollo 14 command module pilot. His was a weighty responsibility, piloting the spacecraft to the moon, orbiting for a few earth days and returning the crew safely to the home planet. Lasting 10 days in early 1971, the Apollo 14 mission was the third trip to land astronauts on the lunar surface.

Before the flight, U.S. Forest Service Chief Ed Cliff contacted Roosa and proposed he take along nearly 500 tree seeds, including Douglas fir from the Northwest, to test the impact of space flight on plant seeds. Roosa, who died in 1994, donated a Douglas fir seedling, the progeny of one of the seeds on Apollo 14, to the Siskiyou base and attended its planting in 1975. Sadly, the "Moon tree" didn't survive the harsh Gobi climate, nor did another one planted a decade later. But their legacy lives on in the Moon Tree Run, an annual cross-country race at the base which was first held in 1979. The course follows a portion of the old run the smokejumpers used in training.

Mansfield would run that course countless times. He began jumping out of the Siskiyou base in 1959, and continued jumping until morphing into Dr. Mansfield with a doctorates degree in physics from the University of Idaho in Moscow, Idaho.

"Smokejumpers like a good challenge," he responded with a chuckle when asked about the leap from smokejumper to scientist.

He and his wife, Arlene Hoover Mansfield, who made their home in Los Alamos, N.M., graciously agreed to sit down for a lengthy interview in June of 2017. Unfortunately, he was battling cancer at the time and would pass away on Oct. 6, 2017.

The former Siskiyou jumper had deep roots in southwest Oregon.

His great, great grandfather was Moses Mansfield, the fellow for whom Mansfield Mountain was named. Had you been paying attention, you would have remembered the mountain played a starring role in the opening chapter.

The Mansfield family arrived in southern Oregon during the Civil War, eventually settling in the Illinois Valley. Moses Mansfield and his brother, James, homesteaded on the north end of the flat immediately east of the mountain along the Illinois River. Moses Mansfield also had a gold mine on nearby Reeves Creek at its confluence with the river.

And Chuck'sgreat grandfather, William Riley Mansfield, was a member of the hunting party which included Elijah Davidson, the discoverer of what became known as the Oregon Caves in August of 1874. As it happens, in July of 1966, Chuck Mansfield was flying back to the Siskiyou base from northern California when he spotted a marble outcropping which appeared to have a large opening.A few days later, he and former jumper Doug Hopkins, along with Illinois Valley products Mike Robin and Lee Rosenberg, hiked into what turned out to be a marble outcropping. Inside the outcropping they discovered a small cavern that was dubbed Scorpion Cave.

Back on terra firma, Chuck Mansfield'sinterest in battling wildfires was sparked in his childhood.His father was H. Robert "Bob" Mansfield, an Oregon State University graduate who became the forest botanist in the Siskiyou National Forest in 1948. After studying the unique flora in the region, he actively supported the creation of the Kalmiopsis Wilderness which became a reality when congress passed the 1964 Wilderness Act.

"But when I was little, dad was working in the Bear Valley Ranger District in the Malheur National Forest," Chuck said of the forest in north central Oregon. "This was just before World War II started. At the time, the district only had two guys – my dad and the district ranger."

Obviously, the district was understaffed. As the youngster grew, his father began taking his son along to the "office." Beginning around age six, the boy often accompanied his father, especially during the summer. As you would expect, the youngster looked forward to the forest forays.

Indeed, he couldn't wait to tell his teacher how he had spent his three months off when he returned from summer vacation to enter the third grade.

"When my teacher asked me what I had done that summer, I said I had fought a forest fire – the teacher called me a liar in front of the class," he recalled.

But the youngster was not fibbing.

"The lookouts had been reporting a fire on a ridge but nobody could find it," he explained. "So Dad was going down this jeep road on top of this ridge when I said, 'Hey, Dad, I saw smoke!' He told me he would back up and wanted me to tell him when I saw the most smoke. Well, he backed up about 100 yards or so and I told him to stop."

Lightning had struck a pine tree, igniting it. The fire was still small, less than 50 feet in diameter, he remembered. What's more, the fire was crawling on the forest floor, not exploding across the ridge.

"Dad taught me right there how to be a lead fireman," he said. "He cut a limb off a tree and told me to use it as a broom to sweep the fire back into the burned area. I went around the fire doing that. I also chopped up the smaller pieces to remove the woody fuel. Dad and I lined it without any problem."

That was his first wildfire, and the only one he fought before becoming a smokejumper.

"When I first got on with the Forest Service, I was on survey crews all over southern Oregon," he said. "I saw a lot of country out there but the pay wasn't that good."

After taking a trip to Lakeview east of the Cascades, he returned to the Siskiyou National Forest headquarters in Grants Pass to find everyone responding to a major fire bust. The agency needed someone to drive a truck out to the Siskiyou base. He ended up dropping off loads of cargo at the base and became friends with the jumpers. They encouraged him to try out for the crew.

It didn't take a rocket scientist to figure out that becoming a smoke-jumper would boost his income. After all, this was back when the minimum wage was $1.25 an hour. Since a jumper earned $2.75 an hour at the time, he could more than double his earnings for college.

"Better pay was what initially caused me to decide to start jumping," he said.

As Grant had correctly noted, he was not large for a jumper. When he started, Chuck Mansfield acknowledged he would have been lucky to tip the scales at 150 pounds. But he carried precious little fat.

"I was at the squatty end of the jump list but I was pretty tough at the time," he said. "I could hold my own."

"Whenever Chuck jumped with no wind, he would hang in the air for a while because of his weight," Arlene offered. "But he could carry more than he weighed."

Incidentally, before they met, Arlene's father, a likeable fellow named Charles "Chod" Hoover, found someone he figured would make an ideal son-in-law. Remember, this was an era when some parents were still following the tradition of finding a mate for their offspring. As it happens, the Hoovers lived a couple of hundred yards south of my exceedingly humble childhood home in Kerby. Both Arlene and her younger sister, Darlene, were the belles of our rural community. My siblings and I used to go on some mighty spartan camping trips with their younger brother, Charlie, who answered to the nickname "Shorty." The moniker was apt when he was close to the ground. However, he would outgrow his short status.

"My father met Chuck about two years prior to my meeting him," Arlene explained.

In the late 1950s, the Hoover family patriarch was driving a truck for a company which was laying gravel on the Page Mountain Road, a winding mountain road which wends through a portion of the Siskiyou forest to link Cave Junction to the hamlet of Happy Camp in the Klamath River drainage of far northern California. The truck driver became friends with a young man working for the Forest Service whose responsibilities included tabulating the amount of gravel being hauled in.

"My father would come home in the evening and tell me about this young man sitting up there studying physics while he was waiting for the next load of gravel," she said. "He told me what a wonderful guy he was. He said this was a young man who was really going to go places."

The unlikely friendship between the older gentleman and the young man grew. Soon they were meeting to chat over coffee in a local restaurant. In 1959, her father's young friend became a smokejumper. You guessed it. The young man was Chuck Mansfield.

A 1960 graduate of Illinois Valley High School in Cave Junction, Arlene began working as a clerk typist in the base office, becoming the base dispatcher.

"When I started working at the smokejumper base, Dad asked me if I had met Chuck yet," she said. "I told him I hadn't. But I said there was a young man running around out there who seemed to pop into the office an awful lot. I thought maybe he was the water boy or something. Turns out he was the purchasing agent."

Turns out he was also her future hubby, something she obviously had yet to discover.

"He asked me one day when he was in the office if I was Chod Hoover's daughter. After that, Chuck always made sure he sat next to me in the mess hall. We got to talking."

The mess hall was a popular gathering place, she observed.

"The food was excellent. The cooks didn't put up with any foolishness from any of the jumpers who misbehaved in the mess hall."

Come Saturday night in Cave Junction, the jumpers' behavior often became dramatically more combative, she allowed.

"There was always friction between the loggers and the jumpers down at the Owl tavern. The story was that the jumpers were taking away all the girls in the valley and that really upset the loggers."

Given the fact there were toughs in both camps, there were more than a few brawls which ended with a little bloodletting as noted in Cliff Hamilton's story.

"I recall being on a fairly large fire with about 10 jumpers when, all of a sudden, about 50 loggers showed up," Chuck Mansfield said.

"The loggers always wanted to demonstrate they were tougher than smokejumpers so there were a lot of firelines built that day. But we stayed ahead of them."

It wasn't just loggers who fired up the Siskiyou smokejumpers. There was also competition with jumpers from other bases.

"About five or six of us jumped on a fire over on the Winema where there were about 50 smokejumpers building a fireline," he recalled. "With a bunch of Cave Junction jumpers, we kept working our way to the head of the line because we were working harder than the rest. We could build firelines like no one else."

One of the toughest to ever become a Siskiyou smokejumper was Mick Swift, he said.

"Mick was a close friend of mine and a very special person. He was a year younger than me. A very good smokejumper, very tough. Everybody looked up to him. He was legendary."

He pulled out a photo of his old friend holding a very large and very alive rattlesnake. "I took that photo," he said.

Before Mansfield met the love of his life, he and Swift periodically went out on the town, such as it was in Cave Junction in the early 1960s.

"Mick and I drove up to the Oregon Caves (National Monument) a couple of times, dating the girls up there who worked for the park service. Here was this big brute of a guy and this little guy. That was Mick and me."

But Mansfield wasn't all that interested in the cavewomen, so to speak. After all, there was that young lady back at the base.

"One day when the rookies were having their first jump, (base commander) Jim Allen told me to get the truck and take Arlene Hoover out to the jump field," he recalled, referring to Seats Field about a mile northwest of the base. "That was our first date."

"I didn't know how to operate the seat belt so he had to do it for me," she added. "He was a little nervous."

Unwittingly, Allen was the one who forced their hands when it came to tying the knot.

"What happened was that Jim noticed that we were seeing each other and he told us, 'I'm sorry but one of you will have to go,'" Mansfield said. "Jim was a fantastic person to work for. You knew he always did what was best for the base and the jumpers."

Although he was a tough World War II veteran tested in combat, the base commander didn't want the headache of dealing with a budding romance in a base overflowing with testosterone. Chuck and Arlene heeded his advice. She quit her job and married the love of her life in 1965. The two were married for more than 52 years.

Chuck Mansfield, who made more than 100 jumps, liked smokejumping and flying. Unlike many, he had already been in an airplane before hitting the silk. While in high school, he was a member of an Air Explorer Squadron in the Boy Scouts and had flown several times before graduating. In fact, after winning the regional Soap Box Derby race while in high school, he earned a flight to Akron, Ohio. But he didn't yet have the NASA training to come up with a scientific formula to win the national derby crown.

He also knew several former celebrated jumpers, including Danny On, who had worked with his father, and Willie Unsoeld, his philosophy professor at Oregon State University where Chuck earned his bachelor's degree before transferring to Idaho for his graduate studies. Attentive readers will recall that On was the jumper who came up with the nickname "Gobi" for the base while Unsoeld was the jumper who became a world-renowned mountaineer.

"Amongst ourselves, we smokejumpers often discussed what caused us to jump out of planes and fight fires," Mansfield said. "Nobody could come up with a good reason. But I always thought it was something we could do for the country. Not many people were doing it. We were on the front lines fighting forest fires. If you wanted a forest fire put out before it took off, you called in the smokejumpers."

What's more, it supported his second love back on earth. That would be physics. His first, of course, was Arlene.

While he had the luxury of picking a wife, he didn't have a choice in his first fire. And Mansfield's initial fire jump was as tough as they get.

The lightning-caused blaze was in the Mule Creek drainage in the Rogue River watershed of southwest Oregon just a short flight northwest of the Siskiyou base. The region is known for being steep, rocky and brushy.

"We had a fairly decent place to jump but I ended up on one side of the jump spot, hung my chute up in a tree and was in danger of falling over a cliff," he said. "So I just kind of swung like I was in a swing and swung over to the hillside."

Once he reached the side of the mountain, he used his let-down rope to reach the ground where he could stand upright.

"It wasn't that big of a cliff but it was still about a 20-foot fall onto rocks. And it wasn't a big fire – we got it out real quick. Of course, the whole idea of smokejumping is to get to a fire as quickly as possible and put it out before it blows up. We did that."

Like most smokejumpers, he suffered a few injuries during his career. The worst occurred while jumping a fire in the Willamette National Forest during the 1964 fire season.

"I landed in a big tree and fell about 50 to 75 feet," he recalled. "The parachute was breaking off limbs as I came down, reducing some of the energy I was gaining as I fell. But it didn't slow me enough. All the way down, I kept telling myself, 'You've got to do a landing roll.' I managed to do that but as I rolled over on my back, I hit my head on the ground. That knocked me out."

When he came to a few minutes later, he discovered the impact had split his helmet in half. And he was in severe pain from several cracked ribs and a severely sprained ankle.

"The plane was still circling. I flashed the plane with my mirror but they never saw me."

He passed out again, waking several times only to lapse back into unconsciousness. When he woke later that afternoon, he could hear firefighters working on the fire.

"I knew I needed some first aid. I was able to get on my feet and walk a little. I got partway to the fire but ran into a downed tree that was about five feet in diameter."

Although his path was barred, he was close enough to the other firefighters to yell for help. They quickly came to his aid.

"They carried me back up to the fire and put me in a sleeping bag that night to keep me warm. The next morning at about 5 o'clock six guys from the local district came in with a stretcher. They carried me down the mountain side."

Among the folks meeting them at the nearest road was his parents who had heard through the Forest Service grapevine that their son had been injured in a jump. By noon, he was being treated by a doctor in Springfield.

"I had a couple of cracked ribs and a real bad ankle," he said, then adding with a laugh, "I don't think I had any brain damage."

Judging from his scholastic success and the fact he became a brilliant scientist, probably not.

"The longest hike out I've had after fighting a fire was about 25 miles up in Montana in the Bob Marshal Wilderness just south of Glacier National Park," he said. "They had a pack string which carried all the gear. We jumped out of two DC-3s."

They landed on a meadow near the fire and quickly had it contained. They mopped it up, then hiked down to a camp which had been established. In addition to the smokejumpers, about 200 firefighters had hiked in, bringing pack strings.

"There were two cooks at the camp who made a fantastic breakfast for us. About 9 o'clock that morning, we headed down the trail back to civilization. It was a long hike but we didn't have to carry our gear. That helped a lot."

Even as a smokejumper, his scientific mind was at work. After observing cargo dropped to jumpers being frequently lost in the forest below, he solved the nagging problem.

"Chuck was such a bright guy," Lee Gossett recalled. "We used to lose a lot of climbing spurs when we dropped them with the jumpers. So he decided to invent something to solve that problem. He took a tin can, put a buzzer in it with a flashlight battery, strapped it on with the gear we dropped. You could hear it a long ways away. Problem solved."

Known as the "Mansfield buzzer," the device developed in 1963 has allowed jumpers to easily find lost cargo over the years, from climbing spurs to saws.

"I had wanted to get on as an astronaut but they started cutting back at that point so I went into research," Chuck said of his dream of following Roosa into space. While he never met Roosa, he worked on some of the same NASA projects as did the astronaut, he noted.

"My post-doc appointment to work for NASA was in the space optics branch in the Johnson Space Center in Houston," he explained. "I did all sorts of things while I was there but I mainly worked on optics. I also learned how to do holography."

Webster tells us non-science types that holography involves recording and depicting a three-dimensional image of an object by using a laser and a photographic plate.

"I could look at something and measure the amount of bending," explained the former smokejumper to his baffled listener.

As noted earlier, he was a graduate of Grants Pass High School whose athletes are known as the Cavemen. Let me reassure you the mascot was chosen because of the school's proximity to the Oregon Caves, not for having a knuckle-dragging, one-eyebrowed student body. True, there may be a few knuckle-dragging Neanderthals lumbering around southern Oregon but Chuck Mansfield proves there are also brainiacs.

In any event, he worked at NASA until the end of the Apollo program, leaving in July of 1973 to do contract work for the Los Alamos National Laboratory in New Mexico where he retired in 1993. The Mansfields would frequently see astronauts such as Neal Armstrong, Pete Conrad and Harrison Schmidt. In fact, when their son, Dave, was awarded his Eagle Scout badge, Schmidt was the presenter.

During his science career, Chuck Mansfield worked on everything from the Hubble space telescope to krypton and fluoride laser technology. He also co-authored 18 patents and published 37 scientific papers. After retiring, he wrote a book, *The Biscuit Fire*, focusing on the half-million acre 2002 wildfire which was the largest blaze in the nation that year and the biggest in Oregon history. The lion's share of the fire burned in the Kalmiopsis which his father helped create.Following his retirement, he and his son hiked into the Kalmiopsis every summer for a decade.

"Being a smokejumper was his life," Dave Mansfield said of his father during a memorial at the base in the fall of 2017 shortly after he passed. "And this base was his favorite place in the world."

Charles "Chuck" Mansfield, smokejumper-turned-scientist, was wearing his National Smokejumper Association t-shirt under his suit when he was laid to rest in the Laurel Cemetery in Cave Junction.

THE MOUSE THAT SOARED

27

CAVE JUNCTION JUMPER

A S MENTIONED EARLIER, PLENTY OF local youngsters, after watching a plane from the Siskiyou Smokejumper Base flying over the Illinois Valley, were eager to join the aerial firefighting crew. Some set their sights on becoming a smokejumper while still in their juvenile years. Others donned a jump suit after opportunity knocked. All in all, they are an impressive lot, the local yokels.

You have already met two but there are more locally produced jumpers in the upcoming chapters. Although they spent their formative years in southwest Oregon, they are a diverse lot and represent well the youthful vigor that energized the Siskiyou base. Admittedly, they are also easier for this weary writer to track down than jumpers who, after leaving the base, disappeared into the far-flung places from whence they came.

Geographically, the future jumper born closest to the base was Wes Nicholson. After all, he was born in Cave Junction. With a little Kentucky windage, the newborn infant could have parachuted down on the base.

"Yeah, I was born at home – I was a little early," he said of his Cave Junction roots. "But they put Grants Pass on my birth certificate because my mom had to go in town to get one."

Not long after graduating from Illinois Valley High School in 1964 where he was active in sports, Nicholson was drafted into the Army. The young first lieutenant, a product of officer candidate school, was wounded by mortar shrapnel near Hai Van Pass just north of Danang, Vietnam. He recovered from his leg wound and returned to the Illinois Valley upon completing his hitch.

"After the service, I got a job falling timber," he recalled. "One night I was hanging out in the Sportsmans Bar, having a few beers. There were some people in there I knew from the base – Tommy Albert, Terry Mewhinney and Dee Dutton, the base manager. We sat around bullshitting. Dee asked me if I ever thought about becoming a smokejumper and told me to drop by the base and fill out an application. Well, I stopped by a few days later and he had the application all filled out. So I signed it."

Two weeks later he was notified he was hired. That was in the spring of 1969. Never mind he stood 6' 4" – an inch above the height limit.

"We didn't worry much about that back in those days," he said with a shrug. "So in 1969, they had one rookie – that was me."

Two other jumpers, brothers Claude and Samuel Greiner, were also new to the base that year but they were transfers who already at least one fire season under their belts.

"One reason Dee hired me was that they wanted a couple of jumpers who would be there in the fall after a lot of the guys went back to college," Nicholson explained. "They always needed a few jumpers later in the fall. He knew I would be there."

Like others who hit the silk at the base, he discovered that stepping out of an airplane into thin air was an enjoyable experience, providing nothing went south, of course.

"One thing that amazes everyone the first time out the door of an airplane is the utter silence they experience," Nicholson said. "You don't hear the airplane. You don't hear anything except maybe the flapping of the parachute in the wind a little bit."

His first training jump was in Seats Field just northwest of the base. Joining him were the two transfers and returning jumpers taking their mandatory annual retraining jumps.

"I got hung up in a tree," he said. "Everyone else who jumped that day landed out in the field. I didn't have anywhere else to go but into the trees. But it worked out fine. I got down with no problem."

His first fire jump was on the Klamath National Forest in northern California also went smoothly, he noted.

"It was a two-manner," he said of the fire that only required two jumpers. "It was me and Gary Mills. Wasn't much to it. We got it out pretty quickly."

Nicholson would jump for a dozen fire seasons, ending in 1981 when the base closed. He made more than 250 jumps during his career. As the former longtime loft foreman at the base, he spent many hours manning a sewing machine and working on parachutes.

"A lot of guys jumping at the base were college students or college graduates," said Nicholson who attended El Camino Junior College in the Los Angeles area before transferring to Oregon State University in Corvallis. "So you had a lot of bright people there who were interesting to talk to."

Educated or not, the jumpers were past masters when it came to practical jokes, he observed.

"One time across the runway we had some logs out there to use for rookie training to learn how to use chainsaws," he said. "So I told one rookie to run back to the warehouse to get a battery to start the chainsaw. They sent him back. Then I sent him over to the saw shack where Steve Baumann was working. Steve immediately sent him back to me. And every time they sent him back it was because of something different they needed to know about, like what size battery was needed."

With that, Nicholson laughed heartily. The joke? This was back in the day when chainsaws had no batteries, unlike today when there are many battery-powered chainsaws.

Like other jumpers during that period, Nicholson worked with the man known as Mouse.

"Before he arrived, we had already been conditioned that we were going to get this congressional appointee," he said. "We knew what his size was because we had to build a completely different jumpsuit to fit him. Everything had to be reduced to fit him."

Mouse's jumpsuit was in stark contrast to that of the average Siskiyou jumper at the time, he acknowledged.

"When I came to the base, there were a lot of big boys here. There were tall guys like Mick Swift, Joe Buck, Jerry Katt. And there were other guys who might not have been over six feet tall but were strong, stout guys like Gary Thornhill."

But it turns out that the congressional appointee, although short of stature, was a big man in many respects, Nicholson said.

"Mouse was a shrunken version of Mick Swift. He was a good jumper. He worked as well as the next guy and better than many. He packed his fair share. He did his work load."

And he didn't take any crap from other jumpers, he said.

"He got a lot of static from everybody but he gave it right back. He was really funny. God, there were so many funny things that he said or did that still has jumpers laughing all these years later."

As it happens, Nicholson and Mouse were both the proud owners of 1969 Corvette Stingrays.

"Mine was red; his was blue," Nicholson said. "We had them out at the base. We talked to each other about our 'Vettes' a lot. In addition to jumping, that gave us a bond. Mouse was good guy, a fun guy to be around."

Like many longterm jumpers during that era, Nicholson would fight wildfires from Alaska to Virginia. After the base closed, he continued working in fire management for what was then the Siskiyou National Forest, retired after 28 years with the U.S. Forest Service.

Yet it was the time spent working out of the smokejumper base that stirs a lot of memories.

"One day they were doing some work up at the Pearsoll Lookout and needed some lumber and other things dropped down," he recalled. "So we packed up everything in the warehouse and got it in the DC-3. Flying over Pearsoll, we pushed the lumber out. It went fine, landed right where we wanted it to.

"Well, we came around on the next pass with the next package," he added. "It was really heavy, full of nails, hammers and other tools. We kicked it out and down it dropped, wiping the Pearsoll lookout outhouse right off the mountain."

Fortunately, no one was occupying the facility at the time.

28

THE KERBY KID

A S A YOUNG BOY REARED in Kerby, Gary Mills looked up to Siskiyou smokejumpers. Literally.

"I used to watch them do their training jumps," he recalled of his childhood. "They did some of their training jumps over on the Q-X (pronounced Q bar X) Ranch fields across the river from Kerby. That was just a little ways from our house."

A hamlet on the east side of the Illinois River, Kerby is immediately south of Sauers Flat. It may not get much notice these days but it was once a bustling little burg. Indeed, during the formative days of Josephine County back in the mid-1800s, it was the county seat. That was before the upstart Grants Pass mushroomed up on the banks of the Rogue River, stealing Kerby's political thunder. Kerby is now largely known as the site of the impressive Kerbyville Museum and History Center which, by the way, includes the two-story historic home formerly owned by Lela Ingersoll Cooke, my maternal grandmother. I bring that up simply to crow, you understand.

But let's get back to Gary Mills, a decent fellow not given to crowing.

"One spring day when I was a sophomore, I was watching from my backyard and saw this parachute come down and land in some trees just beyond the big field. I immediately thought someone must have been hurt. I ran from our place over the bridge, across the field and up to the hill."

That was where he found jumper Leroy Cook who was a rookie in 1964. Unhurt and out of the tree, Cook was happily gathering up his parachute when the panting Kerby boy arrived. He explained he had intentionally landed in the tree as part of his training to learn how to navigate his way down from one. The encounter impressed the young lad.

Like most Kerby youngsters, he spent his share of time hunting and fishing when he wasn't in school. Unlike some of us Kerby urchins, he was a good student. He also played sports, focusing on basketball and football, although he was also known to swing a bat in season.

"The smokejumpers had a softball team that played the high school kids," he said. "At that time, the smokejumpers pretty much hired all athletes. So they were always the team to beat."

When Mills was 17, he got a summer job working as a firefighter for the Oregon Department of Forestry in the Illinois Valley. His fire engine crew would respond to several small wildfires that summer, providing him with valuable experience.

The following school year, like most high school seniors, he was mulling over what to do after leaving the hallowed halls. His father, who worked at the now defunct sawmill in Kerby, was an Army veteran who earned the Bronze Star for bravery while fighting in the Philippines during World War II. Like many seniors in rural America at the time, young Mills contemplated joining the military.

"One day some of us were sitting in the school library and talking about what we were going to do after school," he said. "Vietnam was starting to heat up then. I said I might go Army airborne. And Kathleen Allen said, 'If you want to jump out of airplanes, why don't you become a smokejumper?'"

Kathleen Allen knew a bit about smokejumpers. Her father was none other than Jim Allen, the legendary boss at the smokejumper base. Intrigued by the suggestion, Gary Mills applied.

"About three weeks before I graduated from high school I found out I would be a rookie at the base that summer," he said of the 1966 fire season. "For the rest of the school year, I didn't hardly sleep. My biggest concern was that I would freeze up at the door and not be able to jump. But the training was intense enough I didn't even think about it when the time came. They just touched my shoulder and I was gone."

As it turned out, he would be in a notable 12-member rookie class which included folks like of Gary "Joe" Buck, Tom "Trooper Tom" Emonds, Delos "Dee" Dutton and Wes Brown, all of whom left their mark on the base.

Mills, who studied at the University of Oregon for three years between fire seasons, worked at the base from 1966 through 1981. All told, he made about 230 jumps, including training drops.

Like Gary Thornhill and several other Siskiyou jumpers, Mills had never been in an airplane before becoming a smokejumper.

"The first time I ever jumped was also the first time I had ever been in an airplane," he said, repeating a phrase made by many Siskiyou jumpers. "To qualify, you had to have seven training jumps. So it was on my eighth plane ride when we had a dry run that I actually landed in an airplane."

He remained at his childhood home in Kerby the first couple of fire seasons. After all, it was convenient and he appreciated his mom's cooking.

"We all had nicknames and I was known for quite a while as 'Mrs. Mills' Boy' because my mom would call out there to see if I was out on a fire," he said. Later his nickname was shortened to "Millsy," a name that stuck.

Although he fought some tough fires from the Appalachians to Alaska, one of the roughest fire experiences he had was the first one he jumped.

"That was on Indigo Creek in the Kalmiopsis Wilderness," he said of the wilderness due west of Kerby. "Now, the Kalmiopsis had its own reputation. In fact, one of the things that set Cave Junction apart from all the other jump bases was that we had the nastiest jump country."

And Indigo Creek tumbled through the middle of some of the worst country imaginable to land as a smokejumper, he noted. Jumping with him that day was Ron "Mac" McMinimy who would jump for 11 fire seasons out of Gobi. You may recall he popped up in chapter 10.

"There wasn't anything significant about the fire and we landed fine in the jump spot amongst the trees," Mills recalled. "But they hung up the power saw when they dropped it. This was in a tree that must have been 250 feet tall."

Mills and McMinimy linked two climbing ropes together but still lacked sufficient climbing rope to circle the trunk.

"They didn't want us to leave the parachute with the power saw in the tree because they didn't want to keep responding to reports of a parachute in a tree in the Kalmiopsis," he said, referring to the likelihood there would be ample reports from aviation traffic after pilots spotted the parachute.

"What they did was send a guy from the Chetco Ranger District up with a pack horse and a saw," he continued. "He was a real short guy. We had to hike down Indigo Creek to meet him. It was a real tough hike because we were climbing over brush and down rock cliffs. And we had to turn around and climb back up with the saw. We were pretty well beat."

After getting the fire out and felling the tree to retrieve the saw, they then hiked back down the creek with all their gear, including two power saws, to a meadow where the two horses were hobbled.

"Mac was about an inch taller than me," said Mills who stands 6' 2". "But the packer said we could both ride one horse while he rode the other. Well, the horse wouldn't move. The packer got down and whacked the horse. It didn't budge. Mac got off the horse and the packer whacked it again. That's when the horse started bucking. The stirrups were real short because the packer wasn't very tall. My legs started cramping while I was trying to hold on."

Mills, who survived his smokejumping rodeo, recalled jumping fires in the Ozarks where some of the Siskiyou jumpers learned about something called moonshine.

"To test it, you poured some in a Mason jar lid and lit it on fire," he said. "Depending on the color of the flames, you could get a good guess about the amount of impurities in it. If it was white and blue, it tended to be pretty good stuff. If it was a little to the orange, it would have a lot of impurities in it. Yeah, the strange things you learn as a smokejumper."

On the other hand, there were tales of bearded folk living in the mountains west of Kerby who made moonshine, some of which no doubt flamed a bright orange. But we'll leave them for another book.

Early on, Mills jumped in Alaska once as part of a booster team of Siskiyou jumpers sent to the Far North. They were jumping out of Fort Wainwright on a fire in the Tanana River drainage. This would be the hamlet just south of Fairbanks, not the village in the Arctic.

"When I was there, Fort Wainwright didn't have the good reputation it has now. Back then, the crew up there wasn't too impressive and they had all of these old airplanes. We got into two before we had one that ran properly. One was bleeding oil on the tarmac. The other one, a DC-3, we got into and I reached up to steady myself on the horizontal cable and pulled it out of the bulkhead. That didn't leave you with a lot of confidence."

Nor did the spotter. He was wearing an ascot, one of those broad scarves reminiscent of a posh gentleman out on a fox hunt in jolly old England. Siskiyou smokejumpers didn't wear ascots while on the job, you see.

"It was bright white," Mills said. "He seemed more interested in how he looked than what was going on in the airplane and on the ground."

During the jump, they deployed drift streamers to determine how high they were above the ground, he said.

"Drift streamers fell at a certain rate and you timed it," he explained. "If it was 60 seconds, we were probably OK."

Unfortunately, they were marginally OK when they jumped over the Tanana.

"The spotter dropped us so low that Walt Congleton's chute barely opened before he hit the ground," Mills said.

Their troubles were not yet over. The fire they had been deployed to fight had split, creating two columns of smoke.

"That fire came back at us. They sent a helicopter in to pick us up and when we took off, it was so overloaded that it could barely get off the ground. It was shaking real bad. They landed again near a lake and dropped half of us off. We kept looking over our shoulders at the fire coming at us. It was a while before we finally got out of there."

However, when it came to pure weirdness, the training jumps around the Siskiyou base often offered plenty of entertainment, he mused.

"We used to have a jump site out by Takilma," he said of an area southeast of the base which was known throughout the West for its counterculture community during the 1960s.

"Every spring, we would go out there and explain to them the plane was not looking for pot but that we were using the site for jump training," he recalled. "There were some naked women out there, making it difficult for some of us to focus on what we were there for."

Mills was a veteran jumper when a fellow named Allen "Mouse" Owen arrived in late spring of 1970 to join that year's rookie class.

"We had heard about Mouse before he got there. He had been a congressional appointee and nobody had ever heard of that before. They told us he was four feet eleven. He didn't meet the height requirement or the weight requirement. That irritated people because there were a lot of people who wanted the job. It wasn't like everyone was glad he was coming."

Like Nicholson, Mills noted that Mouse's jumpsuit had to be especially fashioned to fit his small stature.

"Mouse had jumped when he was in the Marines and military jumpers also got a bad rap when they rookied as smokejumpers," he said. "They felt it was better to get people who had never jumped before than to get someone who already knew how to jump because they had been trained in a different way. They felt they had to break those habits and retrain them.

"Even the fact he had been in Force Recon in the Marines didn't mean a lot to a most people at the base," he added. "That was really kind of arrogant when you think about it. When you consider the life experiences he had, including three combat tours in Vietnam, he had shown that he should be taken seriously as a smokejumper."

Still, when Mills first saw the man who would later become a good friend, he was a bit taken aback.

"I thought, 'Wow, he is really small,'" he recalled.

But there was also something in the confident way he walked and talked that quickly won people over, he added.

"Remember, you either made it or you didn't – it was all up to you," he said of the training. "Mouse carried his weight. He did the job and more."

What's more, he didn't rattle easily, Mills said. However, he recalled one exception on a fire in the upper Applegate River drainage.

"Mouse and I were up there using fire line explosives," he said of small explosives which, as Gary Thornhill told us, created instant fire lines if laid out properly. "After going through and cleaning the line up afterwards, a bunch of us sat down to grab a quick lunch. I was standing in front of Mouse when I saw a rattlesnake coiled up right by his hip where he was sitting. He could have reached over and grabbed it."

Mills instructed Mouse not to move. Not only was the usually loquacious jumper silent, he sat stone still.

"I grabbed a good-sized rock and killed it with the first throw," Mills said. "Mouse was a little shook up. But that would have bothered anybody."

Indeed, discovering a coiled rattlesnake within striking distance of where you are sitting is enough to give anyone, even the mighty Mouse, a case of the screaming willies.

"There were a lot of things that stood out about Mouse. Maybe it was because he had gone through a lot but he was always worried about safety and his health. You would see him in the day room with these little bags he would set out for his vitamins that he took every day."

The stout little smokejumper with the big voice liked to talk, he said.

"When he was a squad leader, he used to talk a lot during our safety meetings," he said. "It was always hot in there and these meetings would just go on and on. I remember leaving those meetings in the afternoon with my brain just fried. So I came up with an idea. I told him I would tell the guys all the good news and he could tell them the bad news."

Did his plan clam him up?

"Not at all," he replied. "He was quite the talker once he got started."

Yet he was an entertaining storyteller who could transfix an audience once he got going with a good tale, Mills was quick to add.

"Most of the time, we loved to listen to him," he said. "It was just in a hot room during meetings that it got a little tedious."

Mills would work in nearly all facets of smokejumping, from leaping into thin air to serving as spotter and team leader.But he bunged up his right knee in 1979, permanently removing him from the jump list. However, he was the base manager when the Siskiyou base ended its reign. Altogether, he would work for the Forest Service for 36 years.

"Looking back at smokejumping, if I knew then what I know now, I would have enjoyed it even more," he said, adding, "And being at the Siskiyou base with people like Mouse and all the others made it even more special. We had a really good group."

29

20/20 HINDSIGHT

NATURALLY, WHEN CAVE JUNCTION RESIDENT Ron Versteeg needed a physical to become a rookie at the Siskiyou Smokejumper Base in the spring of 1978, he went to the only doctor in town. A strapping 6-foot-3 and a high school athlete, the 1973 Illinois Valley High School graduate was the picture of health. However, he did wear contacts when he wasn't taking an eye exam.

As it happens, the town doctor was Charles N. "Doc" Versteeg Sr., his father. A graduate of what is now Oregon Health Sciences University, Dr. Versteeg was a skilled professional who served as an Army surgeon in World War II. As a war veteran, he could be brusque at times, especially to juveniles who played sports in high school. There were few things we dreaded more than having to go to his office for a physical early each fall and be commanded to turn our heads and cough. We would have rather wrestled naked on the courthouse steps, had there been a courthouse in town and it had steps. But he was a much appreciated medical practitioner who arrived in Cave Junction in 1948. Nearly two decades after his passing, stories are still told of him saving the lives of local folks during the more than 40 years his shingle hung in Cave Junction.

The young Versteeg, of course, wasn't dreading his examination. But there was a tiny hitch.

"Dad lined me up with the eye chart and I couldn't see the small letters," recalled Ron who would become an attorney. "So he told me to move up a little. I moved up and still couldn't see the letters. He had me move up again. Again, I couldn't see them. Then he said, 'OK' and wrote something down. Dad fudged a little for me on the vision test."

Fudged or not, his vision was not an issue during the six years he served as a smokejumper, including three fire seasons in Alaska. "I never had any problems with my eyes as a jumper," he said.

Like Gary Mills, Ron Versteeg, who was born in Grants Pass, grew up looking up to the Siskiyou smokejumpers.

"Sometimes you would see a plane flying from the base to a fire," he recalled. "When I was a kid in the Illinois Valley, the smoke-jumpers were the local heroes. I never saw myself that way when I was a jumper, of course."

Before applying to become a smokejumper, he had worked for the U.S. Forest Service, thanks to a high school friend whose father was an agency employee.

"After my freshman year in college, my friend asked me if I wanted to work in the Siskiyou National Forest," Ron said. "I thought that would be a great summer job."

Reminiscent of Ron's father fudging on the eye exam, the friend's father no doubt nudged open the employment door a bit for his son and his son's friend. Of course, the two had to demonstrate their ability to do the work. They were hired in the Gold Beach Ranger District where their initial task was brush removal along forest roads although they soon morphed into wildland firefighters. After two summers, they worked their way up to become rappellers, firefighters who let themselves down by ropes dangling from a mothership in the form of a helicopter. For Ron, that job opened the door to apply at the Siskiyou base.

His first training jump was on the Q-X Ranch mentioned by Mills.

But Ron landed safely in a field and avoided landing on the back of any nearby bovines. Upon landing, he knew he had found his niche.

"Smokejumping was a lot like playing sports," observed the former high school basketball and football player. "You were on a team and the fire was the game. You spent your time training and getting ready. When you got ready to jump, it was time to play the game. Obviously, you were playing to win. It was serious business.

"Of course, you never knew when there would be a game," he continued. "You could have plans for the night, and then suddenly be gone for a week fighting a fire somewhere. But that was kind of fun, too. You just had to be able to adapt to an ever-changing situation."

So he didn't blink when he was sent to the small town of Ozark in the Arkansas River Valley which has some similarities to Cave Junction, at least when it came to a nearby river, forests and mountains.

"One summer they called me in the middle of the night to let me know we were going to Arkansas," he said. "We first had to pick up some jumpers at Missoula, then flew on to Arkansas."

The Missoula jumpers were sent to the relatively more uptown Fort Smith while the Cave Junction crew was deployed to Ozark.

"But our gear had been stashed in a warehouse at Fort Smith," he said. "So there we are in this little town in Arkansas. A lot of us had long hair and beards back then. Well, in Ozark, Arkansas, that wasn't received too well. Culturally, we couldn't have been more out of place. Some of our guys would be playing hackeysack in the morning. The townspeople just stared at us."

Not knowing what to do with the rough-looking customers from way out west in Oregon who lived in a strange place called Cave Junction, whose denizens were obviously cave people, the Ozarkians put them to work cutting roadside brush until their firefighting tools arrived.

"It was like 'Cool Hand Luke,'" Versteeg said, referring to the 1967 flick starring Paul Newman which depicted jailbirds working as road crews. "But we kicked butt when we did fight the fires so it worked out fine."

No matter the location, humor was always around ready to rear its chortling head, he observed.

"I remember the time when someone – I'm sure it was Gary Thornhill – made the rookies wheel the stairs out to a plane that was coming in," he said, noting stairs were needed for DC-3s. "So they pushed them there. Only it wasn't a DC-3. It was a Beech 99 that didn't need any stairs."

There were also fisticuffs. During his rookie year, a couple of stalwart veteran jumpers decided to go into the lively little burg of Cave Junction.

"They were doing some drinking at the Red Garter," he said of a local watering hole. "Well, someone apparently said something derogatory about jumpers. One thing led to another and a fight started. Someone got thrown through a window. But they came out on the good side of the fight."

Aside from a couple of scratches and bruises as well as slight hangovers, the jumpers were ready for duty the next morning.

"Gary Mills, who was foreman at the time, got the report about the fight and talked to the guys," he said. "He told them they shouldn't be getting into fights but you could detect a certain amount of pride in his tone. He was proud of them for not taking any crap. That smokejumper mentality at the base was pervasive. Gary was the best boss ever. You always knew he was there for you. But we had a lot of good bosses out there."

They also had a good crew, from the strongest in Mick Swift to the smallest in Mouse, he said.

"I was fortunate to have jumped with some really good jumpers. We were young and full of ourselves and bigger than life. It suited me perfectly at the time."

Unlike many young men reared in the Illinois Valley, he came from a middle-class family where a college education was not only encouraged but expected. All of his siblings were college educated. When he wasn't jumping, he attended college, earning a bachelor's degree in chemistry and later graduating from the law school at the University of Oregon.

While he has spent the bulk of his adult life as an attorney, those six summers jumping fire left an indelible impression.

"I always felt it was a privilege to be a smokejumper," he observed. "You had an obligation to measure up. Even in my third year at the Siskiyou base when we knew it was going to close, I gave it everything I had.

"As long as you did your work as a smokejumper, nobody cared what your beliefs were or your lifestyle," he added of Siskiyou base life. "We had guys who didn't fit in at other bases and ended up at the Siskiyou base and were highly valued."

Like all smokejumpers reflecting on the many fires they fought, he has forgotten most of his fiery opponents.

"I remember we saved the Oregon Vortex once," he said, referring to a purported paranormal roadside attraction which includes gravity defying optical illusions near southwest Oregon's Gold Hill. "OK, we didn't really save it but it was near there. A fire there could have reversed the magnetic poles of the earth, of course."

He was joking, but only regarding the reputed vortex, not the wildfire which the smokejumpers stopped in its tracks.

Like other jumpers, he got dinged up a few times but suffered no permanent injuries.

"The worst injury was when I jumped out of Redding and the static line was under my arm," he said of the line attached to the plane which automatically opens the parachute. "It jerked my arm up really hard. I was out of commission for about a month."

While he will tell you the most rugged area he jumped was the Kalmiopsis Wilderness west of the base, noting it was steep, rocky and brushy, one of the worst situations he faced while jumping was near Onion Mountain just east of the wilderness.

"The fire was a couple of acres so they dropped several loads of jumpers," he recalled. "It was surprisingly nice terrain with gentle slopes. But there were these unbelievably hostile colonies of yellow jackets. It was like stepping onto landmines. People would be working and you would hear someone start screaming and yelling. Those yellow jackets were all over the place and they would come at you in a swarm."

And he hasn't forgotten the fire in far northern California where the temperatures were high and the humidity low in rugged, brushy terrain.

"But we finally got it," he said of snuffing out the fire. "The good thing was the bus they sent out to pick us up broke down right in front of a bar. So we spent a few hours at something like 'Hog Waller Flats' waiting to be rescued."

Then there was the fire he and another jumper fought in Montana.

"It was a two-manner. The fire wasn't that bad but we managed to get lost on the pack out. We wandered around for two days before we got picked up."

The biggest challenge wasn't always the fire, he said.

"Sometimes the fire was the least of your worries. Quite often the pack out was far worse. Walking up a mountain side with a heavy pack is no fun."

When it became apparent the base was about to close, he was among the Siskiyou jumpers who went north to Alaska in 1980 where he would jump for three more summers.

Unlike the steep terrain covered with big trees often found in the Lower 48's Pacific Northwest, Alaska was generally a pleasant place to land when you are attached to a parachute, he noted.

"Quite often the ground you land on up there is tundra – it's like landing on a mattress," he said, then offered a moral to the story, "If you want your kids to be smokejumpers, send them to Alaska."

30

WAVY DAVY

A t the risk of sullying his reputation, honesty dictates I divulge that former Siskiyou smokejumper Dave Atkin has been a friend for some 60 years, ever since he arrived at Kerby Elementary School as a fifth grader. Even then, it was apparent he listened to the beat of a different drummer and didn't give a rat's patootie if anyone took exception to it.

Take the day on the playground when we were playing a game called keep away in which, as the name implies, you ran with the ball and kept it away from others until you were tagged. It being Kerby, we tossed tagging aside and tackled when teachers were looking the other way. There was no score kept in the nonsensical game, unless you counted giving the ball carrier a bloody nose during an especially aggressive tackle. Being a fairly fast runner who evaded pursuers by dodging back and forth, I didn't get tackled much but the new kid nailed me that day. Although small, he was surprisingly fast and hit hard.

The future attorney informed me the reason I was caught was that he simply ran straight while I zigzagged. "You were riding on your laurels," he said.

Now there was an idiom I had never heard. Actually, it wasn't until seventh grade English teacher Don Orton explained the term that I discovered an idiom wasn't the first cousin to an idiot. In any case, I didn't have the foggiest what Atkin was talking about. Fortunately, he patiently explained that riding on my laurels meant I was satisfied with my past playground achievements, adding that I wasn't prepared for his style of play. He was spot on. Naturally, I returned the favor with a good revenge tackle a few days later when he was running with the ball.

When we were both on the wrestling team throughout our high school years, I became even more impressed with both his intelligence and tenacity. Despite what some may think, wrestling requires both in abundance. You have to be able to think quickly on your feet to counter your opponent's moves less you get slammed on your back and pinned. On the other hand, it doesn't hurt to be strong, quick and impervious to pain.

Although he was the son of the local pharmacist, Atkin didn't have a cushy childhood. Each evening after wrestling practice was over and the rest of us went home exhausted, the industrious youngster swept and cleaned the pharmacy. In the summer of 1968, between his junior and senior year, he got a coveted job as a firefighter with the Oregon Department of Forestry.

"I was determined to go to college but had to earn money for it," he said. "I loved fighting fires and did that for two summers. So it was natural for me to become a smokejumper."

Although he is 5-foot-6 and weighed only 130 pounds at the time, barely making the minimum weight, he wasn't the smallest in the 1970 rookie class. That would be Mouse, of course.

"There were seven of us that spring," Atkin recalled. "Because of the nature of the training, rookies tend to bond together. Mouse and I were together a lot. I ended up fighting many fires with him."

Since they were both gravity challenged, albeit Mouse more so, they shared similar attitudes and outlooks. Both were also former wrestlers who had taken on their share of tough opponents.

"Any sport like that where you work really hard, you build not only your physical endurance but you learn how to endure," Atkin observed of wrestling. "That's a valuable thing to have to fall back on in something like smokejumping."

The two certainly learned to endure, he noted.

"When we were hiking out, the crew always started stringing out and it always ended up with me and Mouse being in the back. We were taking more steps but smaller steps. Every hour or two, the people in front would stop for a ten-minute rest. Just as Mouse and I would walk up to the group, they would get up and go. They had gotten some rest and were ready to move on."

Following one especially strenuous pack out in which Atkin struggled with a particularly heavy pack, he went straight to the scales when he got back to the base.

"My pack weighed 125 pounds and so did I," he said, although adding that packs were generally bit lighter.

But he figured no one was as tough as Mouse.

"Carrying packs that weighed as much as he did and doing double time, he did great," he said, the latter referring to taking more steps to keep up with the long-striding taller jumpers. "Mouse was such an athlete. He always hung right in there. He took all the hazing in stride. I think his experiences in the Marines taught him how to suffer."

While they were friends, that didn't mean they were lock step in everything. For instance, they were of opposite opinions when it came to the Vietnam War.

"I had long hair and wore an earring – it drove the base manager crazy," said Atkin whose jumper nickname was "Wavy Davy."

You will remember base manager Delos "Dee" Dutton, the same fellow who didn't appreciate unflushed Iowa corn snakes. Yet, like the other jumpers, Atkin was quick to observe that Dutton was well respected by the Siskiyou crew. What's more, long hair was in vogue for many young male adults back in the day, something that did not amuse older folks in rural Oregon.

But there was ample amusement to be found at the base where practical jokes were part of everyday life.

"I heard through the grapevine that someone had put an ad in the *Mother Earth News* for Mouse, unbeknown to him," Atkin said of a counter-culture magazine. "All of a sudden all these gals that he didn't know started contacting him."

True story, Larry Owen confirmed. "Some of them knocked on Allen's door when he was living in Cave Junction," Larry said with a mischievous chuckle reminiscent of his brother's laugh.

Most of the Siskiyou smokejumper humor dealt with the everyday life of a jumper, usually with the veteran jumpers hazing the rookies. But sometimes the rookies turned the tables. Atkin recalled one such anecdote on the heels of the 1970 rookies' last training jump.

"This was up near Bolan Lake," he said of an idyllic mountain lake a dozen or so air miles east of the base. "They told us that, as a reward for our last training jump, they were going to drop in a case of beer. It was a hot day, you see. So we all jump and gathered our gear, waiting for them to drop the last chute which is supposed to be our case of beer before hiking out.

"When it came drifting down, we all ran over," he continued. "Instead of a case of beer, it is this big stump carved as the Gobi. You knew you didn't dare come back without it. We had to pack it out."

To be more specific, the stump had been carved into a fist with the middle finger extended, performing the Gobi salute. As he indicated, they had to pack it out since it was the base's cherished mascot. Weary of being harangued and harassed, Mouse, Atkin and the other rookies came up with a plan as they hiked out, lugging the Gobi.

"After a long hike, we get to the road and go back to the base where we start unloading our gear," he said. "The veteran jumpers gathered around, laughing. Someone asked us how we liked carrying that big stump out. We said, 'What big stump? Do you mean that case of beer that got hung up in a tall tree? It's still up there. You didn't throw any climbing spurs in so we couldn't get it.'"

The rookies were feeling their oats, an idiom that needs no explanation.

"We told them we had a present for them," Atkin said, noting they were near the "Gorge," the nickname for the local irrigation ditch.

"We opened the big pack and told them, 'Here is your damned Gobi.' Then we rookies rushed them and tried to get them all in the Gorge in retribution for them sending that damned stump in. Of course, it didn't go so well for the rookies. Most of us ended up wet and only a few of the veterans did."

But the seasoned jumpers were not through with persecuting the rookies. At the very end of their training, they were solemnly informed they all had to participate in an esteemed ceremony for the chosen few.

"They told us it was a very important ritual," Atkin said. " 'You have finished your last training jump but before we can put you on the jump list, you got to do this little ceremony to join the brotherhood,' they told us. They took us to the loft, one at a time."

There were four big parachutes hanging down, each with a couple of veteran jumpers hiding behind them, he said.

Fair warning: a verbalized acronym that some will find offensive is about to rear its foul face. Anyone acutely sensitive to shocking verbiage should skip the next paragraph.

"The master of ceremonies starts talking in this officious manner, 'As you join this great brotherhood of jumpers in the sky and you look around you will realize that YOU'VE BEEN FUCKED!'" Atkin said, his voice rising at the end of the sentence. "And all these guys jump out of the parachutes, grab us, duct tape us, carry us out to the truck and stack us on top of each other like cord wood.

"After they got us all, they take us out to the woods over by Rough and Ready Creek where they gave each of us a bucket of beer and got us drunk in a hurry," he added. "You had to chug it down and the person who finished first put the bucket on his head. Everybody else had to douse themselves with beer. Then we proceeded to have a free-for-all wrestling match in the creek."

As you would expect for a stream with such a moniker, the creek is notorious for having many boulders, making the wrestling tournament memorably bruising.

"I remember Mac Truck stood up and said, 'Nobody can take me,' causing everyone to tackle him," Atkin said, referring to the earlier mentioned veteran jumper Ron McMinimy. "People the next day had bruises, black eyes and puffy elbows. And we were all saying, 'Yeah, that was a hell of a party.'"

That was on July 12, 1970, according to the base log book which faithfully recorded the brouhaha.

"At first light the next day, when people were still sleeping it off, the fire alarm goes off," Atkin said. "I was on the first five out. They jumped us on Quail Creek down the Rogue River. The fire turned into a conflagration."

According to the base log book on July 13 of that year, the base deployed Atkin and four other jumpers to the fire, then sent an additional five jumpers to try to stop the blaze. But they were unable to halt the Quail Creek fire which spread to some 2,500 acres in that rugged country.

Like all their brethren, the Siskiyou smokejumpers put out many young fires over the decades the base operated. Those fires never warranted names and were quickly forgotten. It was only those who escaped the clutches of the jumpers that became the stuff of legend and the topic of auld lang syne when the jumpers gathered at a watering hole.

He would jump out of the Siskiyou base through the 1979 fire season, one season less than Mouse. After graduating from law school, he started practicing law and now represents the Siskiyou Smokejumper Association pro bono.

"Smokejumpers are a remarkable group of people to work with," Atkin said. "They are capable, competent, strong and smart. You form a bond with them that lasts."

He stopped talking for a moment, thinking back to those distant years when he routinely stepped out of a plane.

"Jumping was over in a couple of minutes. But when the chute pops open, you are almost hanging still. The plane is gone and the sky is quiet. It is such a wonderful feeling, floating there."

After that fleeting moment of calm, the focus is on the landing spot, he continued.

"You instantly get in the zone – it is total concentration. You are observing the wind speed and making adjustments. You have no actual thought but following the training. It is always a challenge to land on the exact spot. I loved it when I landed just right."

He may have been riding on his laurels but we'll give him a break or, to repeat my favorite Marine idiom, we'll cut him a huss.

Standing six-feet-three inches tall, Siskiyou smokejumper Steve Mankle (*center*) towered over the Owen brothers. Allen stands to his right while Larry is to his left. Smokejumpers Gary Thornhill is on the far left and Mick Swift is on the far right. (*Photo by Doug Beck*)

A Siskiyou smokejumper takes a practice jump near the base as part of the annual rite to prepare for a fire season.

Siskiyou smokejumpers enjoyed playing volleyball while waiting for a fire call. *Clockwise from the far left*: Tom Koyoma, Roddy Baumann, Dave Atkin, Rick Oliver and Stan Collins. (*Photo by Doug Beck*)

One of the most famous photographs featuring the Gobi salute is of legendary smokejumper Mick Swift standing high in the top of a pine tree in eastern Washington. Taken by Siskiyou smokejumper Jerry E. Schmidt who jumped during the 1962 and '63 fire seasons, the incredible shot shows Swift's parachute tangled up in the top of the tree he landed in. He is standing on a stout limb, unhurt, with one hand holding onto the trunk and the other waving the middle finger.

Siskiyou smokejumper Wes Brown leaps out of a plane over a fire in August of 1967. A 1966 rookie, Brown jumped more than a dozen fire seasons. (*Photo by Doug Beck*)

The Siskiyou smokejumpers gathered in front of a jumper plane at the beginning of a fire season. During the 38 summers it operated, the Siskiyou base would deploy smokejumpers on 1,445 fires for a total 5,390 fire jumps, according to Forest Service records. (*Photo by Doug Beck*)

After battling the horrific Hog Fire in the Salmon River drainage of northern California in 1977, the Siskiyou smokejumpers gathered for a group shot. Smokejumper Doug Beck, who usually took the photos, can be seen kneeling in the center foreground.

31

MOUSE AND THE PUP

W HEN HE WAS A ROOKIE at the Siskiyou Smokejumper Base in 1973, Steve Baumann didn't much care for the moniker older jumpers hung on him.

"I was 19 and it was my first fire season," he recalled, noting he had been deployed to a small wildfire along with veteran jumpers Gary Thornhill and Pat McNally. "My recollection is that I was doing most of the work and they were sitting around giving me advice. I believe it was Pat who looked over and said, 'You are nothing but a pup.' I told him, 'I don't like that. Don't ever call me that.'"

Naturally, since it irritated him, the senior jumpers immediately bestowed the "Pup" moniker upon the athletic and energetic jumper who bears more than a slight resemblance to the actor Bill Murray and is equally quick with a witty comment. Now, nearly half a century later at smokejumper reunions, Baumann answers to his nickname with pride, knowing it is a sign of respect and lasting friendship.

Of course, back in the day, Mouse gleefully employed the moniker when he knew it annoyed the likeable younger jumper.

"Yeah, we took verbal jabs at each other all the time," Baumann said. "We used to spar just for fun."

His older brother, the equally affable Rod Baumann, and Mouse rookied together in 1970.

"Roddy brought him home for dinner one night," Steve Baumann noted of his family's Triangle 3 Ranch a few miles north of Kerby. "We had steaks. Well, our table was round and the steak plate was being passed along. Being used to eating in the mess hall, Mouse hammers two steaks. The whole family is looking at him. So he puts one steak back."

Baumann couldn't help but chortle at one of his earliest memories of the renowned jumper. "Mouse was one of a kind, a wonderful character," he said.

Parenthetically, in the small world department, the Triangle 3 Ranch site was the area pioneered by former smokejumper Chuck Mansfield's ancestors shortly after they arrived in the Illinois Valley in 1860, according to Arlene Mansfield, Chuck's widow.

Born in Texas in the summer of 1953, Steve Baumann graduated from Illinois Valley High School in 1971, four years after his old brother.

"I don't recall being much aware of smokejumpers until Roddy started jumping," he recalled. "During my senior year in high school, I worked for the Forest Service one day a week. But I wasn't able to fight fires until after August 8 when I turned 18."

The following year found him working in the logging woods, first setting chokers and later chasing on a landing for a veteran logger named Francis Gibney.

"I applied to be a smokejumper and got accepted," Baumann said. "Francis tried his best to talk me out of it. He said, 'Steve, setting chokers is dangerous but smokejumping? Come on. It's more dangerous. You don't need to be doing that.' But I quit two weeks before I started smokejumper training so I could get prepared."

In the interest of full disclosure, after completing my hitch in the Marines in March of 1971, I worked as both a choker setter and a landing chaser for Gibney. He was a good boss, albeit one with a roughhewn sense of humor. Every time he spotted a hitchhiker while driving the crummy along a remote stretch of highway, Gibney turned off the engine for a few seconds as we sped past, causing the engine compression to trigger a loud backfire. The hitchhiker would always jump, yell a bad word and flip us off. I am not proud to admit it but I laughed every time at the logger's prank.

As one accustomed to scrambling around mountainsides, Baumann was in good shape when he started jumper training in 1973.

"But the first couple of weeks were hard," he said. "There were seven of us in our rookie class and two of them didn't make it."

Early one morning they showed up for training and were made to do rolls off what he described as the "elephant fence" in front of the office to prepare for a transformational event. The fence was about three feet high, he noted.

"After we did that, they told us to suit up because we were going to make our first jump. We were pretty excited about that. The jumps were made in the morning because it was less windy, cooler and you would come down a little softer."

Their first training jumps were on a field in the sprawling Q-X Ranch just west of the Illinois River near Kerby, he said.

"I fell in love with smokejumping that day," said Baumann who would make 262 jumps during his 13 fire seasons. He jumped nine fire seasons out of the Siskiyou base, moving on to other bases after it closed at the end of the 1981 season.

"I'm not sure I totally got it but it worked," Baumann said of the uniqueness of the Siskiyou base. "I think it was all the different personalities that made it work and Mouse was certainly one of the most unique."

Like other jumpers, he recalled how the jumpers would "moon" each other when a plane took off down the runway.

"We would line up and moon them, and when you looked at the plane you would see pressed ham in the windows," he said, laughing. "It was all in fun. I suppose it was guy stuff. We didn't have women smokejumpers back then so you could get away with stuff you couldn't do now."

Indeed, the practical jokers among them couldn't stop themselves when they spotted an opportunity to pull a prank. Take the funnel that led to a tube running into the cargo area at the tail end of the DC-3 flying out of the base. The tube led to the outside, allowing jumpers to urinate in an emergency.

"When we had some rookies with us, we would tell them, 'Will you go back there and ask the pilot how much longer it will be before we get there,'" Baumann said. "So they would be back there and talk into this funnel, thinking it was some kind of communications to the cockpit."

They were not amused when a veteran jumper would step up later to use the aerial urinal, he acknowledged after he stopped laughing at the memory.

"No, you never wanted to let your guard down. You either fit in or you didn't."

Like Mouse, the Baumanns fit well in the smokejumping fellowship.

"Mouse and I became very good friends," Steve Baumann said. "I used to run with him frequently. He was incredible. We would run the big loop – about 3 ½ miles – and Mouse would maintain the same pace he started out with.

"What he couldn't do was sprint at the end," he added. "If we started out slow enough to warm me up, I could leap out in front of him when we came back around the other end of the runway. I could always hear him cussing me as I ran away from him."

Although buddies, they were also longtime verbal duelists who chided each other with never-ending friendly banter. Since both were raconteurs of the first order, they kept their fellow jumpers entertained.

"I used to tease Mouse all the time," Baumann said. "He wore a size 6 or 6 ½ shoe. I told him, 'When you wear a pair out, I'd like to have them so I can bronze them and hang them on my rear-view mirror in my car.' I also used to tell him, 'You have a little tiny jump suit, little tiny parachute, little tiny pack-out bag.' I might have also talked about parts of his anatomy being tiny. He would also cuss me up one side and down the other."

He recalled a fire on state-protected land near Grants Pass in northern Josephine County.

"He landed hard and tweaked his knee," Baumann said. "We jumped it in the afternoon so we were digging fire line all night. He was complaining about it. I was the crew boss and so I said, 'You finally hit like a normal-size person and all you are doing is bitching about it all night.' And he started cussing me out, giving it right back to me. We had a lot of fun."

Relaxing in an ice cream parlor in Portland one time after fighting a fire, Baumann and another jumper told a waitress that it was Mouse's birthday.

"He was sitting at another table and we told her, 'See that little guy over there? He is 19 today,'" Baumann said. "So they went over there and beat a drum and slapped a birthday hat on him. You couldn't embarrass him but he sure did not like that. Obviously, we were howling."

While Mouse was small, everything he did was outsize, he said.

"The first car he ever owned was a blue Corvette. It had a big 427 (cubic inch) engine in it. When you saw him coming down the road, about all you could see was his nose sticking up over the dashboard."

Baumann stopped talking about his friend for a moment.

"He was so fun to be around, such a good guy," he said.

Mouse somehow found time to write a column in the local weekly Illinois Valley News, an article under the headline "The Phantom."

"Back then, when he was writing a column for the IV News, we couldn't wait for the paper to come out," Baumann said. "He was very clever, particularly when it came to humor."

"It was a hilarious column, although, unless you were a jumper, it would have went over a lot of reader's heads," interjected Gary Thornhill, citing the inside knowledge.

Although Pup and Mouse were forever bantering, they shared a mutual respect for each other.

"His legs were short so when it came to packing out from a fire those short legs couldn't cover the distance as easy as the rest of us," Baumann said. "And stepping over big logs was always a problem."

Yet he was no shirker when it came to carrying his load, he stressed.

"He was always a hard worker," he said. "He was very, very strong. He could do a gazillion pull ups. He could bench press 250 pounds in free weights even though he weighed maybe 120 pounds."

When he was a young smokejumper, Baumann enjoyed sport jumping with Mouse when he wasn't fighting a wildfire.

"Mouse taught me to sky dive out at Beagle," Baumann said of the popular sky-diving site in southern Oregon. "When he was killed while sky diving in Alaska, I quit. I never did it again."

32

SUBMARINE TO SMOKEJUMPER

S ISKIYOU SMOKEJUMPERS INVARIABLY HAVE stories that are fascinating but the tales told by Don Michael "Mike" Cramer will leave you agape.

Now in his 80s, Cramer earned an associate's degree in forestry from what was Oregon State College before it morphed into Oregon State University. The onion skin led to a series of overseas adventures with the Oregon-based De Long Corporation, including jobs as a timber cruiser and other forestry work for nine years in Indonesia, three years in the Philippines, a year in Malaysia, more than two years in Liberia in West Africa and five years in Siberia.

And there was that short-term forestry contract in South Vietnam in 1968, one which saw Cramer working as a forester smack in the middle of the Vietnam War.

That's when he was shot in the bum from ground fire while riding in a Huey helicopter.

"They took me to Phu Bai where they had a little hospital," he said. "The doctor came in and dug it out. The bullet only went in ¾ of an inch and it didn't bleed much because the cloth was wedged in there."

He figured the bullet's velocity was slowed by the metal shell of the helicopter as well as the seat he was sitting on. Still, he acknowledged it was a pain in the ass.

As the doctor was wrapping up his work, he asked Cramer why he didn't have dog tags or anything indicating his military status.

"I explained to him that I was working on a forestry contract for the Marine Corps," he said of thinning vegetation near a military facility. "Then he asked where I was from. When I told him Oregon, he said he was also from Oregon. We got to talking and he asked who my family doctor was."

It turned out the doctor working on him in Phu Bai was the one who would be taking over the practice of Cramer's doctor in Beaverton at the end of 1968.

"The doctor in Phu Bai was named Chuck Chapman – he became my family doctor in Beaverton for years," Cramer said, adding, "Talk about a small world."

Then there was the letter Cramer received from a fellow in Australia on Dec. 3, 1970.

"Dear Mr. Cramer, On behalf of the Australian Army and the Royal Australian Air Force, and on behalf of the next of kin of those who lost their lives, I express my sincere thanks for your time and effort in identifying one of our wartime aircraft. I would be pleased to offer my thanks and appreciation to your chief pilot Mr. [Harold] Wysong whose skill played an important part in the effort.

"I am also most appreciative of the excellent information, together with photographs, you have provided to our staff in Singapore. This has been of great assistance in planning for recovery of the remains of personnel on the aircraft."

He noted the remains would be buried in a war cemetery in Papua, New Guinea.

"I am grateful to your company, the De Long Corporation, for your services in identifying the aircraft," he added.

The letter was signed, "Yours sincerely, Malcolm Fraser, Minister for Defence." If the name rings a bell, it is because Fraser became the

Australian prime minister in 1975, serving in that capacity for eight years. Hence the un-American way of spelling defense.

Back in the late 1960s, Cramer, after recovering from the posterior wound, was helping the firm set up a logging operation in Indonesia when he was flying in a company aircraft over the remote central highlands near Papua and spotted airplane wreckage. He and coworkers later flew as near the wreckage as possible in a helicopter, landed and hiked to the site where they discovered a DC-3 which had crashed during World War II. Moreover, they discovered skeletal remains of what turned out to have been Australian prisoners of war who had just been released from a Japanese POW camp on the island of Borneo and were on their way home to Brisbane when the plane crashed.

"Everything was remarkably preserved, even the Dunlap tires were still inflated after 25 years," Cramer observed, noting it was very sad the former POWS survived the war only to die in a crash on the way home.

At first glance, it wouldn't seem like Cramer was destined to a life of adventure. Born March 21, 1937, in Eugene, he was reared in the hills outside of Grants Pass.

"Two weeks after I graduated from Grants Pass High School, I opened our mail box and there was a brown envelope in it – my draft notice," he said. "I went to Merlin and visited Debs Potts. He and my dad had served together in the Navy on the [USS] *Missouri*. He owned a sawmill and was also the local Navy recruiter. When I got to his sawmill, I told him about the brown envelope and he said, 'Raise your right hand.' I was sworn right into the Naval Reserve. I didn't want to be a ground pounder on the DMZ in Korea."

By the way, Eugene "Debs" Potts was a mover and shaker in his own right who would become a prominent state senator, rising to senate president and serving nearly 200 days as acting governor.

After working as a forester in Oregon for a couple of months, Cramer decided to join the Navy fulltime and went into submarine service, serving for four years.

"One of my brothers was already a jumper and the other one was starting training," he said of his brothers, Jim and Fred Cramer. "When I got out of the Navy, our folks lived in Cave Junction so I drove up from San Diego and arrived there about 1 o'clock in the morning. About 7:30, my sister woke me up and told me our brother Jim was making his retraining jumps over at Seats Field. So I got up, after driving 16 hours, and went out there with them."

Mike Cramer hadn't seen his brothers in four years so he wanted to be there with the rest of the family to watch the refresher jumps in the spring of 1959.

"After my brother jumped, he introduced me to Jim Allen, the base commander, and to his assistant, Al Boucher," he recalled. "About this time, the secretary from the office came driving up with a telegram. She handed it to Jim Allen and said that two guys who were supposed to report in the following Monday had been in a car wreck in Idaho and were seriously hurt with broken bones. Jim turned to Al and said, 'What are we going to do about that, Al?' My brother spoke up and said, 'My brother here just got out of the Navy and he isn't doing anything. Hire him. You already got two of us. You might as well have all three.'"

So the former submariner, who was accustomed to being under the waves, not soaring in the sky, was among the rookies training at the Siskiyou base in 1959. After jumping that fire season, he transferred to the newly minted U.S .Bureau of Land Management smokejumper base at Fort Wainwright near Fairbanks after being recruited by former Siskiyou base jumper Orville Looper.

Back then, the Alaskan fire season was roughly from mid-April to Independence Day, Cramer noted. When they completed the Alaskan fire season, the BLM flew Mike and his brother, Jim, who had also jumped that season in the Far North, back down to the Siskiyou base where they rejoined their jumping buddies.

"We went back to work at the Siskiyou base on the 4th of July and continued jumping into October," he said. "I did the same thing in 1961."

And that was how he jumped five fire seasons in three years, an impressive feat in a profession known for extraordinary accomplishments.

"Because of that, I got darn near 100 jumps in three years," said Cramer who stands 6' 3".

One fire he recalled was his very first one which he jumped with Richard "Dick" Wessell, a 1956 rookie.

"It was down the Rogue River above Lobster Creek – a lightning strike," he said. "I could see the ocean when I was coming down in my parachute. We jumped fairly early in the morning and had it out by 3 o'clock in the afternoon."

But the toughest challenge was a 1961 fire near the Chena River in Alaska.

"They jumped 16 of us on the fire," he said. "We were trying to hold it but the wind came up. We had 40 mile-per-hour winds. When we finally got us out of there, they came to pick us up in a Grumman Goose on a little lake. When we looked down, we could see everything was black for miles around except by the little lake where we had jumped. We had been fighting that fire on 360 degrees."

Like all former Siskiyou jumpers, Cramer had fond memories of the days he spent at the base when he wore a young man's clothes.

"This place means a whole lot to anyone who has ever worked here," Cramer said during an interview at the Siskiyou base. "The people we had in charge here were some of the best you could ever find. Jim Allen was one of the best guys I ever worked for."

Sitting at the base brought back memories, including one which is a bit risqué so any readers who are squeamish may want to skip over the next few paragraphs.

"There was a jumper here named Dick Light who started in '58 – he started with my younger brother," he said of Richard "Dick" Light who jumped through the 1959 fire season. "Dick, who is no longer with us, was a great big guy. We called him 'Heavy Light.' He was a very well liked, a good guy who liked the night life."

One Saturday night, Cramer and a local young lady were out watching the full moon and other astronomical wonders. They were parked in Cramer's car near a sawdust pile adjacent to the Rough & Ready Sawmill.

"Dick had been dating this girl who worked at a restaurant that used to be over by the highway," he said of a restaurant between the base and the highway. "Her name was Bertha. We called her 'Big Bertha' because she was statuesque."

With that, he held both hands nearly a foot in front of his chest, indicating she was well endowed.

"We used one of her bras as a wind sock when we built an air strip up near Buckhorn Butte," he offered out of the blue.

In any case, the sawdust pile was nearly 100 feet high, Cramer noted.

"We were parked there doing the usual young things when I heard this car come in on the other side of the sawdust pile. The car had a distinctive sound. I knew it was Dick's car because he had these loud exhaust pipes you could recognize anywhere.

"Well, there was a lot of carrying on going on over there on the other side of the sawdust pile – you couldn't help but hear it," he continued. "Pretty soon over the top of the pile in the moonlight comes Bertha without a stitch on. Right behind her is Dick Light in the same state of undress. There they were, silhouetted in the moonlight."

Cramer figured decorum dictated it was time for him to take his date home. After dropping her off, his impish side took over.

"I remembered I had three burlap bags in the trunk of my car," he said. "So I went back to the sawdust pile and filled those bags with sawdust. Then I came back to the base. Back then, we had two barracks. Dick was in one; I was in the other. First, I opened Dick's car and sprinkled sawdust all through. Then I made a trail of sawdust clear to his bunk where Dick was passed out. I filled his pants pockets and his shoes. I liberally sprinkled sawdust all over him, his bed and around him, all very quietly, of course."

The sawdust imp then slipped out into the night and back to his barracks, no doubt giggling all the way.

"When Dick woke up the next morning, he knew darn well somebody had seen him on the sawdust pile," Cramer said. "But I never told anybody I was the culprit until now."

33

SEAL TO
SMOKEJUMPER

W HEN RICK DEES BECAME A Siskiyou smokejumper in the spring of 1975, he heard a lot about Mouse's Marine Corps exploits. As you have read, Mouse, like Trooper Tom, saw more than his fair share of warfare during his three tours of duty in Vietnam.

However, the former Navy Seal, like numerous other jumpers, also served in the Vietnam War.

"Nothing ever against Mouse but everybody always wanted to compare what he did in the Marines with what I did in the Seals," Dees said. "What he went through was tough. No question about that. I would always tell Mouse, 'Be proud of what you did but don't compare.'"

The point, he said, was that he and Mouse were not in competition when it came to war stories.

"Mouse was a good guy who deserved a lot of respect for everything he did," Dees said.

Born in Eugene in 1950, he was largely reared in southwest Oregon, graduating from Rogue River High School in 1968 where, despite his 5' 7'' stature, he was a standout athlete, including playing basketball.

"But my favorite sport was football," he said, noting he received a scholarship to play at the College of the Siskiyous in northern California to play his preferred sport. "I played football that fall, then took off afterwards to visit some relatives."

That's when his Uncle Sam contacted him to let him know he was being drafted. It was April of 1969.

"I was already thinking about going into the Navy and a friend of my dad said, 'If you think you are such a badass, why don't you go into the Seals?'" he recalled. "And I said, 'What the hell is a Seal?' He told me and I thought, 'That sounds like fun.'"

Out of the 80 who tried out for the Seals in his basic training group, he was one of two who made the grade.

"My best friend who I went through training with was a guy named Jim Janos," he said.

That name will not ring a bell but you no doubt recognize his professional wrestling stage name: Jesse Ventura. After years on the mat spent smashing his grunting opponents, Ventura would enter the political ring and became the 38th governor of Minnesota, serving as head of that state from 1999 to 2003.

"Jim contacted us once when he was a professional wrestler," Dees said, noting he and Patricia, his wife of half a century, had dinner with him when he was touring the Pacific Northwest on a professional wrestling exhibition. "We talked about old times and how our lives changed over the years. He was a good friend."

In his squad, he was often the point man carrying a small caliber weapon while Janos followed with an M-60 machine gun, providing heavier firepower, Dees said. However, although confirming he served in Vietnam, he declined to talk about specifics.

"It doesn't matter now," Dees said, adding, "I left Vietnam in early '71. All of that is behind me."

After his discharge, he intended to take a month off to get readjusted to civilian life. However, he was offered a job working on a helitack firefighting team on the second day he arrived back in Oregon. The following year he was training to rappel out of a helicopter to fight wildfires, although he already knew how to rappel, thanks to his Seal training. He was asked to become a Siskiyou smokejumper in 1975 and accepted the challenge.

"In the Seals, we would jump between 5,000 and 10,000 feet above the ground," he said. "As smokejumpers, we jumped 1,000 to 1,500 feet. So those trees were a lot closer a lot sooner. But you get used to it."

His was among nearly two dozen Siskiyou jumpers who jumped on what became the hellacious Hog Fire in far northern California in August of 1977, a fire which exploded, forcing the jumpers to retreat to the Salmon River. He suffered a separated shoulder when jumping the fire, according to the base record book.

"It was real steep and I hit at an angle – slammed into the side of the mountain," he recalled, noting it was the worst fire he ever fought. "We spent hours running away from it. You could hear it roaring. It was big. But I was in good shape so running wasn't a problem."

But most fires were small and relatively easily handled, observed Dees who jumped four fire seasons out of the Siskiyou base.

"I really liked working with Mouse," he said. "He did all his work. He never squelched on his responsibilities as a jumper. When we were on fires, he always carried one of the heaviest packs. And he was very funny."

His wife, Pat Osipovich Dees, who was born in the Big Apple but raised in the Illinois Valley where her brother, Ray Osipovich, was a 1973 Siskiyou base rookie, recalled often seeing Mouse when she worked at a bank in Cave Junction.

"When you work in a bank, people obviously come in all the time to cash checks or whatever," she said. "So one day someone came in and we could hear this voice but we couldn't see anyone. A deep voice. And we are looking around. No one."

That's when Mouse stepped back away from behind the counter so they could see him, she said, noting that prompted all the bank employees to immediately call out a greeting to the well-known customer.

"Everybody liked Mouse," she said. "He was so fun to be around."

Rick Dees enjoyed both the camaraderie and the physical workouts at the Siskiyou base, including running periodically with Mouse.

"There was a lot of pride out at the base," he said. "When the alarm went off, everybody was ready to go after the fire. We weren't going to let it get away. We had a lot of pride in that. The first and foremost thing was to get it out."

Like the Seals, the Siskiyou smokejumpers gave it their all, he concluded.

34

MORE LOCAL TALENT

NOT MANY HISTORIANS ARE AWARE of this but George Custer was a Siskiyou smokejumper during the '73-'74 fire seasons. True story. Of course, we're not talking about George Armstrong Custer but George W. Custer who jumped nearly a century after General Custer met his fate in June of 1876 at Little Bighorn.

The smokejumping Custer, who was reared in Kerby, graduating from Illinois Valley High School in 1971, is among a few more locally grown jumpers we'll visit in this chapter to ensure you have the full flavor.

Like the famous general, he had blonde hair in his younger years and wore a uniform, starting out as enlisted in the Marine Corps before becoming an officer.

"I've never done any research on it but I may be a shirt-tail relative," he said of Gen. Custer.

But his military days came after he climbed into planes and bailed out to fight wildfires.

"I had been working for a pole peeler, a little gypo logging outfit, and was pretty much starving," he recalled. "So I'm sitting in the Dairy Queen in Cave Junction, having fries because that was the only thing I could afford, and Steve Baumann came in and told me they were hiring at the jumper base. He was going to apply. At the time, the smokejumpers were like gods to us kids in the Illinois Valley."

He and Baumann were among the seven rookies in the 1973 class at the Siskiyou base.

"I always told everyone I was a dumb blonde and just went with the flow and wasn't concerned about my first jump," Custer quipped. "In fact, the only time I had been in an aircraft before my first jump was when Mouse took me and a couple of others for a ride in a Piper Cub."

Custer echoed his smokejumping brethren when it came to assessing the abilities of the nation's shortest smokejumper.

"Right when you met Mouse, he became a lot bigger than his physical stature," he said. "He hung with everybody. He worked hard. Us rookies revered him as much as guys like Wes Nicholson, Gary Buck and Gary Thornhill."

During his second season at the base, Custer decided to tie the knot.

"My dad had come over from the coast for the wedding," he recalled. "All of a sudden the siren goes off. I jump in my gear, get on the plane and we're taxing down the runway. Steve Baumann said, 'Hey aren't you getting married tomorrow?' I replied, 'Well, yeah, but you don't think I'm going to miss a jump do you?'"

Fortunately, it was a small fire near the coast which the jumpers quickly extinguished, returning that afternoon.

"After I got back, my dad said, 'If I could have, I would have tackled you,'" Custer said.

The worst fire he recalled was one in the Unita National Forest in north-central Utah in 1974.

"It was early morning and my wife and I were in a little trailer in Cave Junction. The phone rang. It was the base who informed me I was flying out to a fire in Utah. My wife asked me if I was going to be home for dinner. It really hadn't sunk in where I was off to."

The call for what turned out to be the Squaw Basin fire in Utah came in on June 25, according to the base logbook. All told, more than 50 smokejumpers from the Siskiyou, LaGrande, Boise, Redding and Missoula bases jumped on the stubborn blaze, the book noted.

"We were out in front of the fire, building some lines up a canyon," he recalled. "We noticed this helicopter buzzing around. The crew chief got on the line and asked, 'What's going on?' The guy in the helicopter said, 'You guys need to get out of there. Now! The fire has let loose and is heading up the canyon big time.' We went down to this creek that was fed by the snowpack just above us a ways."

They went out into the middle of the stream and sat on some rocks and logs but the local forest was burning hotter by the second with the flames racing toward them.

"The crew chief told us to each get a helmet full of air and go under until this thing blows over. You didn't even notice it was ice cold water. Within a minute or so we all came up and the worse of the fire had passed. But the crew chief took control and saved our bacon."

And, no, he did not make it home for dinner.

Custer joined the Marine Corps in October right after the 1974 fire season drew to a close. He was an enlisted Marine at the outset, then went into the officer corps, rising to the rank of captain. He also completed his college education, earning a master's degree in business administration.

"When Troop found out I was going into the Corps, he was just ecstatic," he said, adding that he became an artillery officer and served a stint as an aerial observer in an OV-10 Bronco aircraft.

One skill Custer learned as a smokejumper came in handy during his military career, albeit during off-duty hours.Like many of the jumpers, he had learned to use the sewing machines in the parachute loft to repair parachutes and other equipment.

"I took that little tidbit of seamstressing and decided to sew my wife's first Marine Corps ball dress when I was a fresh second lieutenant," he said of his wife, Sayre, and the ball on Nov. 10, marking the date of the Corps' annual birthday bash.

"I didn't know that satin was harder to sew," he added. "She had to sit very erect all night because it was a wraparound style and I hadn't put in enough snaps to keep it closed. My enthusiasm often exceeds my capability."

* * * *

As the son of well-liked Cave Junction barber Ken Mann, Mike Mann came to know most of the older smokejumpers while he was still in Illinois Valley High School.

"Mick Swift and a lot of the guys at the base knew my dad," he recalled, noting he started working at what was then the Illinois Valley Ranger District after getting out of the Navy in 1970.

Having a lot of respect for the jumpers and their mission, Mann applied at the Siskiyou base in 1973 and was accepted.

"In all honesty, it was who I knew not what I knew," he said. Yet he proved his mettle to be a smokejumper and continued through the 1977 fire season, jumping 143 times.

One of the worst fires he recalled fighting was an explosive scorcher in the Gold Beach Ranger District.

"It started in a clearcut they were logging. There was another clearcut above that. It spotted into the red slash – dried logging slash. I lost all the hair off the back of my arm on that one. Burned off.

We didn't have anything to pack out because everything burned up. That was a close one."

But he wouldn't have missed his smokejumping days.

"Mouse was my running partner," said Mann who stands 6-foot-1. "We'd run the big loop just about every day, all three and a half miles. We'd start out with him saying, 'OK, Brother Mann, we are not going to race.' 'Oh, no, Brother Mouse, we are not going to race,' I'd say."

They would run a mile or so with Mouse talking all the way, Mann said.

"But I could barely keep up with him until the last quarter mile and that was always a sprint," he said. "We'd get back and he'd say, 'Brother Mann, you said you weren't going to race.' And I'd says, 'Brother Mouse, you started it.'"

In the end, Mann invariably won the race.

"But Mouse was second to none," he said. "He worked hard and always kept you entertained. He'd go see a movie that was good and he could tell you every line in it. I remember once on a fire, waiting for a ride out and Mouse had just seen *Young Frankenstein.* Well, he kept us in stitches for a couple of hours until our ride got there."

Although he enjoyed jumping and his colleagues, Mann wanted to make a career in the Forest Service.

"Mewhinney wanted a full time dispatcher and nobody wanted to do it. I told him if he got me a full time appointment I would do it."

Mann, who would retire from the agency in 1999, looks back on his jumping days as among the most memorable of his career.

"One day when I was dispatching in the last year the base was open, the phone rang," Mann recalled with a chuckle. "This guy said, 'This is Winema dispatch. We have a fire for you.' Well, I reached over and hit the siren. Then I hear this guy on the phone yelling, 'No, Mike, no!' It was Pup in the warehouse. I turned the siren off and got on the PA and said, 'That was Pup. He's playing games with us.' Well, Pup ended up in the Gobi Gorge."

* * * *

Pat McNally, who alert readers will recall gave Steve Baumann his "Pup" nickname, became a member of the Gobi crew weeks after graduating from Illinois Valley High School in 1967.

"When I was in high school, I was working for the state forestry," he said of a summer job. "We were on a fire or two which the smoke-jumpers jumped on. One was in 1966. And I thought as I watched them float down, 'Man, I'd love to do that.' I wondered if I could make it. It looked like a great way to make a living."

In fact, he did make it, jumping 197 times during his eight fire seasons as a smokejumper.

"On my first jump, I was hung over and just fell out," he recalled. "Actually, it went fine. I liked it. I was never injured. A couple of bumps and bruises but no broken bones. I was so skinny. I didn't hit as hard."

He may have been skinny but he was tough.

"Smokejumping stretches you to do more than you ever think you could do," observed McNally who now lives in New Hampshire. "You discover things in yourself you never knew you had in you."

Already a veteran jumper when Allen Owen rookied in 1970, McNally initially wondered how much of the right stuff the short fellow would have in him.

"My first thought was, 'Is he going to make it?'" he said. "Some other people were skeptical at first. Of course, as we all know, he did just fine. But, remember, this was always an encouraging base and we encouraged diversity. It's a mindset as much as anything else. And Mouse really embodied that. He was an achiever, a 'get-'er-done' kind of guy."

Like the other jumpers who knew him, McNally appreciated Mouse's sense of humor.

"He would have us on the floor – we were laughing so hard. Of course, you had to have a good sense of humor as a jumper. You didn't want to show weakness."

When not jumping, McNally attended what is now Southern Oregon University in Ashland, majoring in business.

"I'll be real honest with you – I did not want to go to Vietnam," he said of receiving a college deferment to avoid a military draft. "And smokejumping allowed me to go to college while doing something good for my country."

35

MOTLEY CREW

A S YOU HAVE READ, THE Siskiyou Smokejumper Base drew some mighty interesting characters throughout its existence, arguably warranting a chapter for each jumper about his life and times. But no one is up to reading a 434-chapter tome so we'll stick to the abridged edition.

With that thought in mind, lets meet a couple of former Siskiyou jumpers to give you a flavor of "average" folks who spent part of their lives at the base. None of the Gobi jumpers were average, of course.

Pennsylvania native Don Thomas, who came to the West Coast in the late 1950s to attend college, could have had a career as a stand up comic of the first order.

"I needed a summer job and met this guy at Oregon State (University) who told me I might be able to get hired on as a smokejumper in a place called Cave Junction," recalled Thomas, an Air Force veteran who now resides in southern California. "My response was, 'Where in the hell is that and what in the hell is a smokejumper?' He told me and I applied."

Thomas was hired, arriving at Gobi late in the spring of 1957. He was trained by Orville Looper, a hard-working seasoned jumper who wanted the rookies to be well prepared.

"I remember my second training jump and Orville was on the ground, waiting," Thomas said. "The instructions were, when you are out, check the canopy and make sure there are no problems. Then find the big 'X' on the ground, make a right turn, then a left turn, and then head towards the 'X.'"

They jumped at 2,000 feet above the "X" made of crape paper.

"I remember as I was coming down that I could see people down below. I figured there had to be some 19 and 20-year-old girls in the crowd and I needed to look really good and hit the 'X' dead center."

But as he drifted down, he discovered what he thought were humanoids were in fact bovine in the pasture known as Seats Field.

"Somebody had rounded up every last cow in the state of Oregon and they are all on that 'X' I'm headed toward. There were cows everywhere. So I turn and head for a corner away from the cows. Naturally, the cows started moseying over toward that corner. When I got down to the height of a tall tree, there was nothing but cows under me."

Knowing that he couldn't help but smack a cow, Thomas prepared for what was going to be an udder, er, utter disaster.

"I remember slapping my heels together and hanging onto those risers and slamming into the side of a cow," he said. "I smack into her right side, just below the spine. I bounce off, land flat on my back, the wind knocked out of me."

One of the rookies who landed just before him ran over.

"He told me, 'Don't worry about the bull. I'll take care of him,'" Thomas said. "I remember wondering what bull he was talking about. I look over and there was this bull about the size of a motor home. He was mad, snorting, drooling, pawing the ground. I had apparently just hit his best girlfriend."

The rookie yelled "Shoo bull," then beat feet for safer environs, he said.

"About then, Orville comes running up, kicks me in the ribs, then says, 'Get up, you son of a bitch. You are not hurt,'" he continued. "Well, he was right. I wasn't hurt. Orville then turned and walked off. I'm thinking that bull could smash me into mush but Orville will surely kick my ass if I don't get up. So I got up."

A colorful character who tells a good story, Thomas became a squared-away smokejumper who returned for the 1958 fire season.

"My nickname was 'Black Tom,'" he noted. "I have no idea how that name came about. It was given to me by Gid Newton."

You may recall Gideon Newton was the only Siskiyou smoke-jumper who was killed in Laos while "kicking" cargo for Air America during the Vietnam War.

One of the toughest fires Thomas ever fought was in northern California when he and seven other Siskiyou jumpers were deployed to Redding. They flew down in a Lockheed Lodestar, a big prop plane which rumbled along, he said.

"Redding in the summer was one of the hottest places I've ever been in my life. When we got there, they had us moving 50-pound sacks of fire retardant. Orville was running the show so we didn't get any breaks."

Early the next morning they were deployed to a 5,000-acre fire, jumping about a mile away from the flames. Looking down, Thomas noted the landing area looked flat, much like a lawn from the distance.

"It looked good – no snags or anything to worry about. So I go out the door. But as I get close to landing I realize I am looking at man-zanita brush about 8-feet tall. I went crashing into it."

He survived the crash landing, although he noted he looked like he had been on the losing side of a cat fight. However, since he was unable to quench his thirst before leaving the Redding base, the smoke-jumper desperately needed a drink of water.

"The only water I could find was along a deer trail leading to the fire," he said. "It was black, nasty water with bugs swimming on top. Deer poop was floating in it. And it was the best water I ever drank. I never got sick."

Then there was the time he saw an attractive young lady on the beach at Panama City, Florida, when he was in the military. He and a friend had been looking for female companions and had offered her and another young lady a drink.

"Her first words to me was, 'Get out of here or I'm calling the cops,'" Thomas said. "But we got together and went to a movie. That didn't go as well as I had hoped but I guess it went OK."

Indeed, a few days later the young lady, named Phalva, brought him a birthday cake. Later, when he was an airman stationed in Mississippi, he ran into Phalva again and it went more than OK. At the time of the interview, they had been married some 60 years.

"That just goes to show you that persistence pays off," he said.

* * * *

Tommy Albert, who has made a couple of cameo appearances in earlier chapters, would seem to agree with Thomas.

"I always wanted to be a pilot but it took a while to get there," said the son of an Air Force pilot.

Born 1944 in Greenville, Texas, he was a student at Texas Tech, majoring in business administration, when he learned there were summer jobs to be had as a wildlands firefighter for the U.S. Forest Service. He received a positive reply from the Galice Ranger District in the Siskiyou National Forest.

"Our district ranger considered himself a recruiter for the Siskiyou base," he said of Don Wood. "He was a no-bull guy who ruled his district with an iron fist. But he was fair. Good guy."

Albert was one of three that Wood recommended to then base commander Jim Allen. They were hired in 1964.

"We were trained at the Siskiyou and got one fire jump, then was sent to Redmond which was in its first year and needed jumpers," Albert said. "My first fire was out of Happy Camp on the Klamath National 'Brush' – real brushy. That was a rude awakening. It was the first fire I had been on. Chuck Sheley was our squad leader and Mick Swift our spotter."

In other words, they were in good hands, said Albert who graduated from college.

"They dropped four of us in the morning, then dropped four more. It was a barn burner, a real go-getter. But we eight jumpers got it. We stopped it. They helicoptered us out to Happy Camp where they were gearing up for a big project fire. But we had got it and that was a very proud moment."

Albert only jumped one season at Redmond, then spent the 1965 fire season jumping in Alaska.

"That wasn't fun like it was in Cave Junction," he said, noting he returned to the Gobi in 1966 and stayed through the 1969 fire season. For his final jumping season, he returned to Alaska in 1970.

Like all jumpers, Albert has a harrowing story to tell.

"My most challenging jump was over by Gold Beach. I was jumping with Garry Peters. He and I were on a two-manner. The plane didn't have a jump step and I never could get in position. I jumped out and spun up like a top. I couldn't even pull the guidelines. By the time I got undone I was halfway down."

Like most coastal districts, the Gold Beach Ranger District has some tall timber.

"There was a hole I could see and I aimed for that. But just as I got committed to landing there, I could see a big limb sticking out into that hole. Holy moly. The chute hung up and I looked down and it was a long ways to the ground. That's when I broke free. But the chute didn't collapse. It caught air and I landed OK. But that was the scariest for me. It sure got my attention."

What kept him going was his dream of becoming a pilot.

"At the Gobi, I started the 'Gobi Flying Club' in 1966. The flight operations officer in Grants Pass would fly an airplane down in the morning and three of us would take flying lessons."

They flew a Cessna 150 trainer, eventually soloing at the Gobi. Although Albert started flying airplanes in 1966, he didn't become a government pilot until 1974. He became a jumper pilot flying lead plane in Redding, Calif.

"Being a jumper was the best job a college student could ever have," he said. "But flying for the Forest Service and the Bureau of

Land Management was great. Garry Peters, who had flown combat in Vietnam, told me one day, 'You know, Tom, this is the closest thing to combat flying you can do and yet you don't get shot at.' I told him I preferred flying without getting shot at."

* * * *

Although former Siskiyou jumper Jerry Katt was never shot at while in an aircraft, he recalled one flight which was not for anyone with a weak stomach. It happened the morning after he and some other 1967 rookies at the Siskiyou base visited a tavern in Cave Junction where they consumed a few too many brewskis.

"When we went out the next day for our training jump, Hal Ewing took us on quite a ride, figure eights and everything, and a couple of guys were starting getting sick, really sick," he said, noting the pilot had apparently been tipped off that the rookies were hungover. "I get sick on a boat on the ocean but never had any problem on a plane. And I had no problem jumping then, but some guys were really up-chucking.

"But maybe that was because I never had a fear of heights," he added. "On our farm up at Sandy (Oregon), I used to climb up a 100-foot fir and swing in the breeze. My mom would be petrified."

Born in 1946, Katt was reared on the family farm just east of Portland. After graduating from Central Catholic High School in Portland, he began working on a hotshot firefighting crew, a job he did for three summers.

"The last year I was on the hotshot crew, I saw a friend from Portland State University who was a jumper. And he encouraged me to become a jumper. I knew jumpers were part of an elite crew of firefighters. So I decided to give it a shot."

In 1967, he was among the 12 rookies at the Siskiyou base.

"At the time, they had a 200-pound weight limit and I was playing football at Portland State where they wanted me the other way," said the former defensive end and linebacker. "It was hard for me to get weight off when I came down to the base. I weighed in at 198 or so."

But Katt, who became a fishery biologist, made the team and jumped for three fire seasons out of the Siskiyou base, followed by two years in Alaska and one summer at the Redmond Smokejumper Base.

One of the most memorable jumps he ever had was in the Hells Canyon with three other jumpers, including Gary Mills.

"I had just got my rigger's license," Katt said. "When the first guy jumped, there was an inversion, meaning the chute turned inside out. I had packed his chute. I was second man out and I had an inversion. When the next guy jumped, there was another inversion."

It turned out it was not the rigger's fault but the squirrelly winds that caused the chute inversion, much to Katt's relief.

Down in the Shasta-Trinity National Forest while jumping out of Redmond, Katt hit hard and blew out his left knee.

"After that I threw in the towel. But smokejumping totally changed my life. It was very positive. Particularly, it was working out of the Siskiyou base that did that. It was very sociable, very amicable.

"Anyone of these guys here would have died for you – the base had such a close camaraderie of guys," he added. "We exercised, played volleyball. We did everything together. I don't think there is any doubt it changed all our lives."

THE MOUSE THAT SOARED

36

FAMILY LIFE AT
THE BASE

FEW NON-SMOKEJUMPERS KNEW THE SISKIYOU Smokejumper Base like Nancy Brown. After all, as the wife of jumper
Wes Brown, she and her husband raised their young children at the
base during the 1967 and 1970 fire seasons.

The Browns lived in one of the old cabins on the southeast corner
of the base. Although small, the cabin was snug and comfortable for
the young family.

"Our little kids loved it because all the guys were so nice to them,"
she recalled. "They really seemed to like having the kids there. I imagine it reminded them of their families. The first season I had a little
baby with me. We had two little kids during the second season."

In fact, the couple spent the tail-end of their honeymoon at the base
after getting hitched on June 10, 1967, in Chico. Wes had spent the
previous fire season jumping out of the base.

"We were pulling in just as a thunderstorm hit and there was a fire
bust," he said of their honeymoon. "I wasn't qualified yet because I

didn't have my training jumps but I probably would have gone if I had done them. I told the boss to send me but he said, 'No, no, you are not going on this one.'"

The base manager at the time was Dee Dutton, a fellow well respected and liked by everyone who worked with him, he noted.

"Nancy made some good friends here," he said of the wives of other jumpers. "I called them a 'gang.' The kids would be playing out in the yard. They had a great time together."

Of course, there may have been a few experiences the young couple would rather have avoided. Take the little stove fire in their cabin that first summer.

"We were just married," Wes said. "The first I heard of it was when Debbie, our dispatcher, goes on the PA system and she says, 'Attention everybody. Nancy has a fire in her kitchen!"

As firefighters, everyone at the base dropped what they were doing and raced toward the Brown cabin.

"There were all these guys sprinting to our house," Wes said, noting that Nancy had wisely called the office when the stove fire flared up.

"When Nancy called the office, they turned on the siren," Gary Buck said. "At first, all 28 jumpers were running toward the loft to get ready to get on the plane. The lady in the office ran out and yelled, "Stop! Stop! The fire is down at Wes and Nancy Brown's house.' Everyone turns around and start sprinting towards the Brown's house."

The jumpers arrived at the house en masse.

"Wes, who was running close to me, yelled, 'Turn off the breaker box!'" said Buck who was running near the head of the group. "I turned it off. The guys go pouring into that tiny house. But by the time we got there Nancy almost had the fire out. She was so embarrassed."

"It was just a little fire," she said of the grease fire which was quickly doused.

Naturally, there was a bit of good-natured ribbing afterwards.

The couple would eventually have four children, including a daughter and three sons.

"Dee Dutton was so kind to me and the kids," she said. "We had nothing but good memories of our time there. When the jumpers went out on a fire, the wives would get together. We just hung out a lot because we were all young and some of us had young children."

Reared in Chico, California, she met her future husband while he was going to college in the area.

"Wes was a smokejumper before we got married," she said of her husband who was a rookie at the Siskiyou base in the spring of 1966. "We were both Methodists and met on a church event. We kept running into each other. I think we were meant to be together.

"I worried about Wes every time he went out on a fire," she added, noting the potential danger faced by smokejumpers. "But we also had a lot of confidence on how well trained they were and how good they were at their jobs."

Still, it's natural that a spouse be concerned when a partner goes into harm's way.

"It helped that all of us wives were so close. As soon as the guys were deployed, we would get together and support each other. Our kids would be there, running all around. We took care of each other."

One day in the 1970 fire season a very pregnant Nancy Brown left their little house on the base to let her husband know it was time to go to the hospital in Grants Pass.

"Just as I started down to the office to ask them to take Wes off the jump list, the fire siren went off," she said. "Before I got there, he was up in the air headed to a fire."

Once en route to a fire, a jumper plane didn't return to the base before completing its mission, pregnant wife or not, she noted.

"That was on July 13," Wes said, then added with a chuckle, "It was her fault because she was two weeks early. When I showed up at Josephine General [hospital in Grants Pass], I was covered with charcoal and they told me I couldn't come in. I told them my wife just had a baby and they said, 'You can't come in here like that.'"

Having come straight from the fire to the hospital, he couldn't do anything about his pants and boots but did shed his long-sleeve shirt down to his somewhat clean t-shirt.

"They finally let me in but they weren't happy with me," he said of visiting their newborn son, Geoffrey. Their oldest child is Christopher, followed by Ryan and Alex.

"They all got to ride in the airplane, not legally but they were more flexible in the old days," Wes said. "They have wonderful memories of the base."

At one point, Wes kept another "member" of the family at the base.

"I was doing a research project when I was in California and had an alligator lizard that was about this long," he said, holding his hands a little over a foot apart. "I kept it in a box on the base. Everyone thought it was amazing to see one that size. He ate any bug that wiggled. I let him go out there somewhere."

The Browns eventually settled on land just west of the base not far from Seats Field. The Browns, along with Gary Buck and Tom Emonds, bought 45 acres to build homes on the property.

"We split it up," Wes said. "Mouse bought five acres next to us and we bought those acres from him after he decided not to build a cabin."

The Browns, Buck and Emonds all built impressive homes on their respective parcels. In fact, Browns' daughter, Ryan, was born in Emonds' three-story log home. Sadly, Emonds' impressive three-story log home later burned but the Browns and Buck still reside in their comfortable homes.

While the Brown children liked the crew at the base, one was their favorite.

"All the kids called Mouse 'Uncle Al,'" Wes said. "We taught all the kids here, not just ours, to run up to Mouse and yell, 'Wing me!' He would swing them around and around until he was exhausted."

"Mouse was really good with the kids," Nancy said. "They couldn't really talk yet so they would say to him, 'Wing me!' and he would swing them around. The kids just adored him."

Nancy became a teacher at Evergreen Elementary School in Cave Junction where she would retire as the school principal. To celebrate special events, Mouse would sometimes parachute from an aircraft and land on the school soccer field, she noted.

"He would be wearing his Superman cape – it was a little outrageous," Nancy said. "But the kids just jumped all over him when he landed. And he was so good natured about it."

Wes began teaching at Illinois Valley High School in 1977, a job he held for 25 years. He was also the wrestling coach for 16 years. He taught everything from algebra to biology and chemistry, even physics and forestry.

"When I was teaching at the high school, it was always fun to see a jumper's kid," Brown said, adding, "It was like teaching a member of our extended family."

* * * *

Living near the base was smokejumper Robert "Bob" McCray and his wife, Rhanda, who had a nine-month-old son when he fought his first fire as a smokejumper. A 1967 rookie, Bob McCray had already served on a hotshot crew before arriving at the base.

"When our son Shane was four years old, Bob built him a training harness and dropped him off the training tower," Rhanda McCray said when the couple was attending a jumper reunion at the base. "He showed him how to do a tuck and roll."

We're not talking child abuse here. Their son had grown up in the smokejumping environment and wanted to be part of their world.

"We were here until Shane was almost nine," she said. "Jean, the master rigger at the time, would allow Shane to play in the loft among the parachutes that hadn't been fixed yet. He eventually became an airborne ranger in the Army. When he went to Fort Benning for airborne for training, they took him into the loft and he could smell the rip-stop nylon. He told me, 'Mom, it was like going home again.'"

Like many of his jumping brethren, Bob McCray jumped during the summers and went to college during the winters. After jumping through the 1973 fire season, he worked in the Forest Service's rappelling program until retiring.

"This is family – it always will be," she said of the base. "Many, many families were formed here. We will always love it."

The Browns and McCrays reflect the feelings of other jumper families, Gary Buck observed.

"The jumpers were a band of brothers," Buck said. "So when anyone had kids, those kids were like family to all of us. That made it nice for those of us who didn't grow up here, helping us become part of the community."

37

SMOKEJUMPER BROWN

I N THE SPRING OF 1966, college junior Wesley "Wes" Brown was looking forward to spending the summer of 1966 in Switzerland on a volunteer mission for his church.

Brown, whose parents were both Methodist ministers, was born in tiny Cottonwood, Idaho, on Jan. 3, 1945.

"They moved around a lot," he said. "They left Cottonwood right after I was born, then ministered at two churches in southern Washington before moving to Oregon and finally to northern California."

After graduating from high school in Anderson, California, in 1963, Brown went to what is now Chico State University. In addition to wrestling and playing football, he graduated in 1967 with a bachelor's degree in biology with a minor in chemistry.

Early on in college, Brown worked as a wildland firefighter during the summer in California's Mendocino National Forest. That changed in the spring of 1966.

"My roommate was a football player who was student teaching for

Chuck Sheley. He told me Sheley was a smokejumper up in Oregon during the summers, and that he was looking for a crew. I was interested because I had heard about smokejumpers and knew there was a base in Cave Junction. My roommate suggested I meet Sheley and talk to him about smokejumping.

"I met Chuck over in his coaching office," he added. "My roommate introduced me and Chuck walked over to a file cabinet, pulled out the top drawer, took out an application, sat down at his typewriter and said, 'What was your name again?'"

Sheley quickly filled out the form, asked Brown to sign it and told him he would mail it for him.

"Shortly afterwards I got two postcards," Brown said. "One of them is offering me a trip to Switzerland to spend the summer in the Alps and the other is an offer to go up to Oregon to become a smokejumper. Well, I needed the money."

As soon as classes were over late that spring, Brown arrived at the Siskiyou base to begin training.

"A good percentage of the crew was college students who would go back to school in mid-September," he noted.

While fire season in southwest Oregon now often ends in mid-October, fire season in the 1960s was about two months shorter. That made it ideal for students like Brown to serve as smokejumpers during the summer.

He was among 10 rookies that season, along with Gary Buck, Tom Emonds, Gary Mills and Joe Niesen. After training for two weeks, Brown made his first jump, landing on Seats Field.

"It was a little strange to take off in that Beech," he said. "For one thing, you can't really see out. It's a tail dragger so when the pilot accelerated, we rookies are sliding downhill on the stainless-steel floor. The spotter has anchors so his feet don't slide."

As the rookies slid down the floor, they grabbed the spotter's legs as anchors, he said.

"I was the third guy out. It didn't enter my mind not to jump. The first guy, usually an experienced jumper, goes out, then everybody else followed him because, well, it is so damn much fun."

Noting he has given a lot of thought about what prompts someone to voluntarily leap out of a non-faulty aircraft, he explained it as a non-rational thing to do.

"You do it because everybody else does it. They warned me that the second jump is more stressful because you have more time to think about it. And it was more stressful."

Normally, smokejumpers drop into a fire area from about 1,500 feet above the ground but for his first jump it was 3,000 feet above the ground. That gave the rookies more time to prepare for the landing, he explained.

"In my first jump, I discovered I had almost no depth perception. As I was coming down, this guy comes running over toward me, yelling for me to put my feet together. I had no idea I was about to land. I thought I was still up a couple of hundred feet. Later, I learned to tell when I was getting close to landing."

But he stuck the first landing with no problem.

"It's kind of like the drills when you are on the wrestling team. You practice and go through the moves automatically. Like any good training, it becomes automatic."

After the traditional seven practice jumps, he was deployed the next day on his first fire jump. It was on Store Gulch about 20 miles north of the base in what was then the Siskiyou National Forest.

"I remember it was early in the morning and it was raining," he said of a summer rain which often comes on the heels of a thunderstorm. "It was a big pine tree burning like a big torch. It was really dramatic."

Brown stepped to the door and asked Sheley, the spotter that morning, where the jump spot was.

"He said, 'See that burning tree down there? That's not it.' And he slapped me on the back and out I go," Brown said, chuckling.

If there is no clear landing target, jumpers are sometimes left to their own devices to avoid dangerous areas.

"I landed fine but my jump partner, Davy Ward, hung up about 120 feet above the ground," he said of a fellow rookie. "He was supposed to be in Portland the next day for his brother's wedding. He had thought he would be out on the fire that day, and still be able to make the wedding. Well, two days later he finally gets to Portland to congratulate the newlyweds."

It was so steep Brown had to anchor himself to the base of a manzanita bush to keep from sliding downhill. Unlike most summer rains, the downpour lasted much of the day.

"My sleeping bag got wet – it was really uncomfortable that night," he said.

Brown jumped for 14 fire seasons out of the Siskiyou base, and another season in Region 8 which roughly includes Kentucky, Virginia, North Carolina and Tennessee. All told, he jumped more than 200 times.

"The Appalachians was a different subculture," he said of jumping in Region 8.

He recalled fighting a fire in Arkansas near the small town of Ozark.

"They gave us little shin guard and axes and we had to go trim brush along the road. We didn't jump. We felt like a prison road crew."

They were also warned that the local sheriff was a hardcore fellow who didn't tolerate unruly behavior. After working on the road for about a week, the six-member Gobi crew decided to go into town to have a decent meal.

"There was this winery out of town with a nice restaurant," he said. "But we were a little scruffy. Nobody brought their good dining clothes. We had yellow fire shirts and what not. When we got there, they sent us down below in this kind of banquet room. No one else was there."

In other words, it was as though the poor relatives had arrived and they were shunted off to the basement to be out of sight.

"We drank beer and wine and waited to order our food," he said. "About an hour later we figured out they didn't want to serve us. Finally, we did get dinner but it took a long, long time."

When the jumpers were walking out, they let the manager know in no uncertain terms how unhappy they were with the place.

"We could have been a little drunk," Brown acknowledged. "We got a little obnoxious. Finally, the manager says, 'That's it. I'm calling the sheriff.' We go out, hop in the van and leave. We were long gone before the sheriff arrived."

But his fondest memories are of the Siskiyou base and its crew.

"We had a good bond," Brown said. "A jumper base is not a military organization but it has some of the same undertones. You are in a tight unit. You have a mission to do."

But there are also differences. Consider the chain of command when jumping on a small fire.

"The first guy out the door is the one in charge of the fire," he said. "It doesn't matter if he is a squad leader or not. That has been tradition. But everyone knows what to do and they do it."

However, the squad leader is in charge when the jumpers face a larger fire, he noted.

As in the military, smokejumpers also have to learn to make split-second decisions as facts warrant, he said. For instance, when jumping on a fire, a jumper generally has between 45 seconds and a minute and a half between leaving the aircraft and landing, he added.

"Typically, you make a lot of decisions in a very short time," he explained. "You turn into wind. You are looking for small trees. Sometimes what you think are small trees turn out to be big ones. A rock face you didn't see before may pop up. So you are constantly making decisions. And in that last ten seconds or so as you are coming in to land, you are trying to avoid obstacles like a dead tree or trees that are slippery like an alpine fir. You have to make these turns at the last second. But it is a great feeling when you land safely."

Like any veteran smokejumper, Brown can tell you about close calls when landing.

"If you are in a 'slippery tree' that lets go of your parachute and you are not high enough where it can re-inflate, you can freefall to the ground," he explained of one worst-case scenario. "If there are rocks or something down below, that fall can have severe consequences."

Yet he never suffered a serious injury while jumping.

"I twisted my ankle while playing volleyball at the base," he said. "And I tripped on a rock when I was running across the flats during PT and hit my knee. That took me off the jump list for about a week."

That's not to say he didn't have some hair-raising encounters after leaping from the door of an aircraft.

"We had just flown in from Happy Camp on a small Cessna after putting out a fire down there," he recalled of an incident in August 1968. "Right after we landed the fire siren went off. My gear wasn't on the plane but was coming by truck because there had already been too much gear on the plane and they didn't want to overload it."

He was among the four jumpers exiting the plane and the only jumpers at the base. They were told to get ready to be deployed immediately to a fire on the Rogue River National Forest. But Brown had a problem: no jumping gear.

"So Terry Mewhinney told me to take his gear – we are about the same size. I got his gear on but it felt a little funny. I check everything I could and it seemed OK. But when I jumped out of the plane I realized the harness was not adjusted properly."

And he had the potential to slip out of the harness into a free fall to the earth below.

"I could have slipped out or hung upside down. It could have been one for the record book. I was having trouble steering – I couldn't reach anything. The landing spot was a north slope with tall trees. I figured I was going to hang up somewhere so I might as well try to go into the trees. I hit one tree straight on and hung up. Then I fell about five or six feet, then slipped again, grabbed a branch – the last one – and hung on, about 60 feet above the ground. But I was able to tie up to the tree and repel down."

Like many former smokejumpers, Brown said the work began when you landed on the ground and started building a fire line.

"Mick would always say that all the fun was getting there," Brown said of his former boss and friend.

"He was a natural leader, really smart," he added. "But the lower his voice was, the quieter he was talking, the more you had better be paying attention. He also had this 'rep' for being a great spotter – a calm spotter. And he was. He was really good."

But even the calm and collected legendary spotter had one day that didn't go so smooth.

"I'm standing in the door over a tough jump spot, and he had it all worked out," Brown recalled. "Mick had his hand on my foot, ready to slap me on the calf of the leg as a signal for me to jump. Everything was a go."

That's when Brown, the first one out, noticed the door strap was still hooked, meaning he would not be able to jump.

"So I said, 'Mick, I can't jump – the strap is in the way. He jumped up and said, 'Oh shit!' But he couldn't release it. It was stuck. So he reached over and grabbed the knife I was carrying in a sheath with my reserve and cut the strap real fast. Of course, we passed over the jump spot and had to circle back. So Mick took a little crap on that one."

Brown laughed at the memory of Swift being flustered for even a second since it was a rare occurrence.

"He was one of the best there was," he said.

Gary Thornhill was also one of the many fellow jumpers Brown respected and enjoyed working alongside.

"One time we were on a fire down by Happy Camp. It was about the size of a small building. Well, we got it under control so about 2 o'clock in the morning we decided to get some sleep."

Their sleeping bags may have only been paper but when you are exhausted, a paper sleeping bag is enough to help you into deep REM.

"But I woke up and it is still dark. Gary Thornhill is sleeping next to me and I look over at him and his paper sleeping bag is burning, right between his legs. I yelled, 'Thornhill! You're on fire!'"

Smokejumper Mike Russo, who transferred to the base in 1970, started slapping the burning bag with his bare hands. Unfortunately, the plastic coating on the outside of the bag caught fire and stuck to his Russo's hands, burning them, Brown said.

"I always tell Gary, 'Hey, remember that time I saved your life?'

And he'll say, 'Brown, you are so full of shit.' It's hard to get a rise out of him so I still like to play that one to the max."

Then there was the smokejumper named Mouse.

"Mouse was a charismatic guy," he said. "When he came into a room, you heard the voice and knew it was him. Of course, when someone tried to pick at him, he always gave it right back. Then they would start going back and forth. Pretty soon the whole place would be in a mini-uproar."

The memory brought more laughter from the veteran jumper.

"One time we were at the John Day airport in northeastern Oregon, waiting for a DC-3 to pick us up," he said. "We were all sitting on our gear bags. And Mouse starts going on. I swear he must have talked for an hour. Everyone is laughing and chuckling and making remarks. He could have been standup comedian. He was that funny. But he worked as hard as anyone. No doubt about that."

It came to pass that the jumpers were on a fire on the west side of the Siskiyou forest in the Gold Beach Ranger District. Like the head of a family who doted on his charges, Dutton went out of his way to support his troops, Brown said.

"Dee was a great boss. If you were on a fire that was fairly close, he would send breakfast over the next morning. He would bring the cooks in at around 3 o'clock in the morning. They would cook bacon and eggs and hash browns and toast. There would be orange juice, milk and hot coffee.

"They would take the breakfast over to the loft and put them in five-gallon metal containers and put parachutes on them," he added. "They'd fly the plane over to Gold Beach and drop them. It was a lot of work but that's what he did for us."

There was a big meadow near the fire and Mouse had left his gear in the middle of the meadow, Brown said. It was long the practice of the jumpers to shed their gear where they landed, fight the fire, then return to pack their gear, he noted.

"Well, his gear was still there when they started dropping food. He had a custom-made jump suit that Glenda Marchant – our master rigger –

made especially for him. So he was very careful with that suit. The first few containers landed OK but they were landing near Mouse's gear. He decided to go collect his gear so none of it would be damaged."

With their smaller chutes, cargo containers fall faster than a jumper would, he explained.

"Mouse is out in the middle of this field when they are coming down," he said. "And you aren't supposed to be around when they drop because they can come down hard."

Turns out some containers were literally dropping like bombs.

"Whoever had 'cargoed' the coffee had done it wrong," Brown said. "They had put the straps around the padding instead of taping the padding on after you get the straps on. And this was ten gallons of hot coffee. When these things go out the door 100 miles per hour and the chute opens – boom! The five gallons of coffee falls out of its packaging and is dropping at 100 miles an hour and the chute is just wafting away."

Brown, who started laughing at the memory, stopped to compose himself.

"Mouse – I can still see him – is putting stuff into his bag and looks up at the plane. He sees this coffee coming at him. That is, say, maybe 80 pounds of coffee. Bam! This thing hits about this far from his gear and digs a hole."

He holds his arms wide open to show how close the coffee bomb landed from Mouse who jumped out of the way.

"There is coffee everywhere," Brown continued. "Well, the next one does exactly the same thing and Mouse is out there jumping around to avoid it. It was really funny but dangerous. Fortunately, he survived."

After completing his undergraduate studies in both scholastics and wrestling, Brown spent one school year teaching in Willows, California, then six in Chico before he started teaching and coaching at Illinois Valley High School.

When their daughter was born in 1979, Brown decided to stay home that summer instead of smokejumping. He returned the next summer but 1980 would be his last.

"They were going to close the base after that," he concluded. "I could have gone to Alaska or wherever for the summer but I wanted to be with my wife and our kids."

38

SMOKEJUMPING EDITOR

C HARLES "CHUCK" SHELEY WAS SITTING in a wildfire truck in the Lassen National Forest of northern California in the summer of 1958, waiting to give a radio report at 3:00 p.m.

"All the districts had to call in with a weather report," explained Sheley who was in his second season of firefighting while spending his winters studying at Chico State University. "I started to call in the weather when a fire lookout broke in and told us to break for fire traffic.

"Then he proceeded to describe from the lookout a plane dropping smokejumpers on a fire," he continued. "He did such a good job he could have been on NPR. My heart started beating harder and I told myself, 'I'm not going to be sitting in this tanker next year at this time. I'm going to be jumping out of a plane.'"

A track athlete at college, running hurdles and the 400 meters, Sheley rightfully figured he could handle the physical training although he knew it would not be a walk in the park.

But he wasn't quite prepared for the Siskiyou Smokejumper Base when he arrived for training the following spring.

"When I drove in, I wondered, 'How could they have a place so isolated?'" he recalled asking himself. "It seemed strange. I wondered, 'What am I doing here?' It was a Sunday afternoon and it seemed so quiet, with the exception of the green chain over at the lumber mill."

He was referring to the Rough & Ready Lumber Co. sawmill just east of the highway. "One night the thing (mill) stopped running and everybody woke up because it was suddenly so quiet," he quipped.

While the area was unlike any he had ever known, the 148-pound young man was dead set on becoming a smokejumper. The daily run was no sweat, nor the workouts. He was already well fit for most anything the trainers could throw at him.

But Sheley, now the longtime editor of the national Smokejumper Magazine as well as a retired teacher and coach, didn't know if he was ready when he climbed aboard the airplane for his first jump.

"It was my first airplane ride. I remember we were down at the end of the field and they revved up the engines. I wondered if we were off the ground. They told me they were just warming up the engines."

His penchant for introspection wasn't deterred by the roar of the engines.

"I wondered what the hell I was doing there. I knew if I was back at my old firefighting job on the Lassen forest I'd be sitting on a porch sharpening tools. I thought, 'Wow, I could die in the next ten minutes.'"

He obviously didn't die when he jumped over Seats Field that morning.

"Everything was total rote training," he said, noting he jumped without any hitches and walked away with nary a bruise. "As you get more into it, you start looking at everything – you study the fire, the ground, the wind, the escape routes. Jumping becomes second nature."

Looking at the ground from the air is important in many remote areas because a jumper on land loses that important perspective, he said.

"Once you are on the ground, you can't see much because, especially in the Siskiyous, the trees are so damn big," he said. "You can't see very far."

Perhaps the toughest fire he faced was one burning on Pyramid Peak in the Klamath National Forest just south of the California state line.

"It was a lightning storm one afternoon," he said. "There were four of us in the plane. The fire was crowning. I said to Mick, the spotter, 'Are you kidding me. Send the plane back and get me four more jumpers.' We worked that fire all night. It was a going son of a gun. Every line we built we burned out."

In another words, they burned the area between the fireline and the main body of the fire so the blaze would not make a run and break through the line.

"But that fire blew up at night," he said. "The winds were still squirrelly from the lightning storm."

Despite the fact they had circled the fire with a line, the wind-driven blaze got away from them. Before the fire was stopped, some 200 ground pounders would be called in to help battle it, he said.

Just as he was talking an AT-11 Twin Beech took off from the base runway, drowning out his words. It was a familiar sound to him.

"I could close my eyes and tell you what kind of plane that was," he said.

Sheley would jump for eight fire seasons, making some 80 jumps during his smokejumping career.

"When I was jumping, I always thought I was good at chute manipulation. I did a lot of thinking. I was a good sailor up there. I only hung up in trees three or four times."

While he acknowledged the Triple Nickle jumpers were taught to land in trees during their smokejumping training, he could only shake his head at the thought.

"Whoever told them to do that was nuts. I don't know anyone in the Forest Service who would told them that. I certainly wouldn't have told them that. I could land in a rock pile and come out good. In fact, my second fire jump was in a rock pile down in the Six Rivers country (northern California). By the time the third and fourth man jumped, I had my chute bagged up, my gear in the sack and was walking to the fire."

Anyone hanging up in a tree invariably had more work to do, in addition to the potential of a serious injury, he said.

"And if it rains, you have another hundred pounds on that chute. Hanging in a tree? That's nucking butts, man. Crazy."

After completing his last smokejumping season in 1966, Sheley became a track coach in junior high and high school, a job he held for 53 years. He also taught health and physical education for nearly 40 years. He is the father of three children, all of whom are either in education or law enforcement.

In an email message sent in July of 2018, he reflected on his time at the Siskiyou base.

"You cannot imagine how much affect our time in Cave Junction as smokejumpers had on our lives," he wrote. "When we were hired, most of us had no idea where in the heck CJ was. The eight seasons I spent there established life-long friendships and a love of the area. . . It was an interesting mix – young men from all over and a pretty isolated society in southern Oregon. We all remember and love."

39

JUMPING INTO BUSINESS

A S A YOUNGSTER REARED IN southern California, former Siskiyou smokejumper Mike Wheelock often gazed up at San Gorgonio Mountain, the Spanish heritage name for "Old Grayback," the highest peak in the San Bernardino Mountains at roughly 11,500 feet above sea level.

"I was impressed by it – I stared at Old Grayback a lot during my childhood," he said of daydreaming about his future.

After all, the imposing mountain represented his aspirations to achieve lofty goals in life. The youngster set out to do just that once he got out on his own, making the climb one step at a time.

"When I came to southern Oregon and the tallest mountain in the Siskiyou range was Grayback Mountain, it just made sense," he said of naming Grayback Forestry, a firm he started in 1979 with Greg Schmidt, a smokejumper pilot. Now with roughly 500 employees who work throughout the West, it is one of the largest privately-owned wildland firefighting companies in the nation. Wheelock is the company president.

When it comes to business acumen, it's true that smokejumpers aren't generally the folks who first come to mind. After all, they are known to sweat, stink and swear like loggers working on a brushy mountainside on an August afternoon. Not to put too fine a point on it but, yes, jumpers also do what comes naturally to bears in the woods. Hey, you were wondering so it needed to be trotted out there sans the usual warning.

Yet Wheelock, who popped up in chapter 12 which you may recall focused on the tragic Iron 44 fatalities, has demonstrated that Siskiyou smokejumpers had what it takes to become highly successful in the competitive business world.

His is a success story resulting from dogged fortitude, hard work and, as Wheelock is quick to observe, hiring talented employees, folks like former smokejumpers Ray Osipovich, Bob Wilken, Willie Lowden and Ed Float, all serving as head honchos.

Like all rookies at the Siskiyou Smokejumper Base in 1976, Wheelock was strong and tough. After all, he had played two years of college football and had earned his spurs as a ground-pounding wildland firefighter.

"As a kid in southern California, I always wanted to be a forest ranger. I didn't really know what a forest ranger was but that didn't matter. It sounded really interesting."

A high school football standout, he went to Mount San Jacinto College in California, studying and playing nose guard on the football team.

"The line averaged 250 pounds and I weighed 205 – I got beat up a lot," he recalled, although noting he made honorable mention his first season before being sidelined with an injury his second year.

However, his injury didn't stop him from getting hired as a firefighter on the San Bernardino National Forest that summer.

"I remember putting those boots on and feeling so good about that. I was part of a 10-person helitack crew which was kind of a new thing then. We were making initial attacks. Ultimately though, I still wanted to move north and get a job as a forest ranger."

While he didn't get hired as a forest ranger in 1974 when he made job inquiries in the Northwest, he had ample job offers.

"Back then, they were putting firefighters behind every tree," he said, adding that he took a job in the Galice Ranger District in the Siskiyou National Forest. His main task was to do prescribed burning to improve forest health and reduce the threat of wildfires come summer.

"After two years there, I applied at the Siskiyou jumper base and got hired. I was in awe of all the people there."

It was a large rookie class of more than a dozen, including Larry Owen. Mouse, of course, was already a seasoned smokejumper.

"Mouse was so meticulous, so methodical, with everything he did," Wheelock said. "When he was rigging parachutes, he did everything picture perfect. That's just who he was. He was quite a guy. Mouse – and Troop, too – could tell stories like no one else.

"I don't know where Mouse got his energy but he was always so active in so many things," he added. "The first two years I was a little shy but I became a good jumper and climber. Mouse just took us in. He taught me a lot. And Troop taught me what work was."

But the fear of heights, particularly the thought of clinging to the top of a tall tree, almost grounded his smokejumping career before it started.

"I didn't care for jumping out of a plane but at least that was quick," he said. "But climbing trees really bothered me. In fact, having to climb trees nearly got me washed out of smokejumping."

The game plan for the rookies one day was to land in trees near a meadow to give them experience in using their let-down ropes. Veteran jumper Mick Swift was the trainer, landing in the trees with all but one rookie.

"Well, I landed in the meadow," Wheelock recalled. "Mick was very upset with me. 'You blankety-blank good for nothing, you are going to go up that tree and get my chute,' he yelled at me. So I got my climbing stuff and got up about ten feet. But I'm just shaking. And that was after about a half hour."

He was sawing every limb off as he climbed because he was too afraid to maneuver around a limb. An hour later he had made it to about 20 feet.

"I kept spurring out," he said of disconnecting his spurs from the trunk and losing his grip. "Every time you hug a tree, you tend to spur out. Mick came over and started yelling at me again, 'What the hell are you doing? Get up that tree!'"

Still shaking, Wheelock dropped his hand-held Fanno saw.

"And it missed Mick by about a foot," he said, noting the explosive expletives resumed at full force on the ground below him.

Understand that Mick Swift was not an abusive bully. However, in the role of rookie trainer, he was expected to act like a Marine Corps drill instructor. And Wheelock can vouch for his Academy performance.

"He yelled, 'If you don't get your ass up that tree, I'm going to get my chainsaw and cut it down with you in it!'" Wheelock recalled. "I became more scared of him than I was of climbing the tree. So I climbed up to the top and realized, 'OK, I can do this.'"

When the rookie returned to terra firma, Swift reassured him that he wasn't going to be washed out as a non-hacker. Later, following the fire season, Wheelock and fellow jumper Terry Mewhinney worked on cone retrieval in the Oregon coastal range, requiring daily tree climbing.

"I got really good at climbing trees," Wheelock said.

Like most smokejumpers, Wheelock suffered a few injuries, the lion's share of which were minor. But one incident in northern California could have been very serious.

"I landed in a clearcut that had a lot of debris in it," he said. "A stick jabbed me in the rear end. It missed the padding."

He worked for a while but soon the pain became unbearable. When he checked to see what the problem was, he found blood trickling down his pants.

"So the next day they sent me to Doc Versteeg," he said.

Trained as an Army surgeon, Versteeg was a very good doctor but didn't treat his young male patients with an overabundance of sensitivity. The medical visit smarted a bit, Wheelock acknowledged.

"He made sure I was not going to have an infection – he cleaned it out real good," he said with a grimace as he recalled the procedure.

Wheelock jumped out of the base through 1979, the year he and Schmidt started Grayback Forestry.

"I had bought a portable sawmill in '77 – that's what I did during the winters," Wheelock explained. "In '79, everyone was making money. Twenty bucks an hour was a low wage for builders back then."

But times were tough and Wheelock returned to smokejumping, jumping through the 1980 fire season. The following year, he went to Missoula where he jumped the 1981 fire season.

"To not lose everything, I did whatever work I could find," he said of keeping Grayback afloat. "We had a D-4 cat and did some logging. But we lost a contract and sold everything for pennies on the dollar."

The partnership split up, although Wheelock kept the company afloat, at least in name.

"I finally got a contract picking sugar pine cones for the Forest Service," he said of his company. "We had some old parachutes we sewed together to make the cone bags. We had learned to sew as smokejumpers."

In fact, after he suffered a knee injury while playing basketball, Wheelock continued climbing trees while using only his good leg.

"It was survival," he said, noting that Grayback was still in its infancy. "You did what you had to do to survive."

Sadly, the stress was difficult on his personal life as he juggled two jobs while trying to keep his company afloat.

"I read a lot of books about business," he said. "One of the things I recall was that, after a business failure, something like 80 percent of owners who were married would be getting a divorce."

But Wheelock's business didn't fail. He hung in there, getting contracts from the Forest Service and Bureau of Land Management for small jobs, including everything from picking cones to cutting brush. One day he received a call from a local logging company, asking Grayback to provide cleanup work after timber sales. Other logging firms soon followed.

"Pretty soon we were doing cleanup work for everybody. We did good work and honored our word. We really started growing."

In the early 1980s, the BLM also approached Grayback, asking the company to do full-service prescribed burning like that being done on national forests in the Northwest, including the Mount Hood and Olympic forests.

"They told us they had a backlog that needed to be done in Oregon and wanted to get it done," he said. "We started bidding on prescribed burning contracts. It was a natural for us. I started hiring former smokejumpers. We started doing it all over the West. We'd start down in northern California and southern Oregon in the winter and spring, and move north as it warmed up."

Although much of it was burning logging slash, there were also contracts for prescribed burning aimed at ecological improvement. The company turned to innovative approaches, including using helicopters to torch debris.

"We burned thousands and thousands of acres," he said. "We opened up offices in Montana, Idaho and a couple of places in Oregon."

In 1986, the Forest Service as well as the state of Oregon began hiring more private firms to fight wildfires, dropping their earlier practice of hiring folks off the street to do the job, Wheelock observed.

"We used to do 80 percent fuels work and reforestation with 10 to 20 percent fires," he said. "Now it is the other way around."

The 1987 wildfire season was a busy one which included the lightning-sparked 90,000-acre Silver fire in southwest Oregon. "That's when we really started getting big," Wheelock said.

In 1992, Grayback bought a helicopter, using it mainly to "helitorch" large areas of logging slash. Basically, that involves a helicopter carrying a drum of gelled gasoline which is attached to the aircraft or carried in a sling. A giant drip torch dangling down from the drum is employed to ignite the slash.

"Back then, I thought I was a pretty important dog," he recalled with a laugh. "I'd have them take me to a burn site and go around looking it over."

While former smokejumpers took the lead in running large parts of the company, he concentrated on bidding for contracts.

"We pioneered a lot of the contract work with the government in terms of making them work. Eventually, in 2001, we talked the government into five-year contracts for initial attack crews. We sat down and told them, 'Hey, you see the need for us. But for me to go to a banker, I have to have some kind of guarantee.' They understood that."

Unfortunately, the company ran into rocky times again in the mid-1990s.

"We almost lost it. We expanded too much. We thought the government was going to really embrace this firefighting. I remember turning in vehicles ten cents on the dollar to the bank. Before that, they would roll out the red carpet. We had one bad year and they were calling in all my notes. It was another lesson in life."

THE MOUSE THAT SOARED

40

A BLOWN JUG

C ONTRARY TO WHAT YOU MAY suppose, a blown jug is not a jug of moonshine that went bad and blew up in the Oregon hills. Nor is it a jug you blow on to make mountain music in those hills. Not that such things didn't occur, mind you.

But we'll let Gary Buck explain how the term became part of Siskiyou smokejumper parlance:

"It happened when Walt [Congleton] and I did a two-man'er on the Fremont [National Forest] in 1972," he began, referring to a fellow Siskiyou smokejumper who began jumping at the base in 1968.

"We jumped in there and had to cut a huge tree, the biggest tree I've ever cut down," he said. "There were some guys from a ground crew on it and they had a big saw. But they were very nervous about cutting this tree. It was so big it looked like a redwood. It was burning at the top so they made a trench out there for it. The idea was to fall it in the trench so it doesn't spread the fire when it falls."

No big deal to the two Siskiyou jumpers. They stepped up to the task, landing it perfectly in the trench.

"That's all they wanted jumpers for was to fall the tree," Buck said. "So they were really happy to have that done. They brought in a rig to take us to the Redmond Smokejumper Base so we could catch a flight back to Cave Junction."

When they arrived at the Redmond base, all of its jumpers were deployed on other fires.

"The foreman came out and said, 'Why don't you guys grab a bite to eat and get some rest. You are one and two on the jump list and all we've got right now,'" Buck recalled. "So we got a bite to eat and relaxed a bit. But Walt isn't the kind of guy that likes to sit for long so he decided to walk around the base a bit to check things out. After we got our gear together, we walked around, checking out the loft and everything. Finally, we go out on the apron and look at the twin Beech, the only aircraft they had at that moment."

After giving the aircraft a once over, Congleton pursed his lips and shook his head.

"Walt says, 'The left engine has a blown jug,'" Buck said. "And I said, 'What the heck is a blown jug?' He told me the engine had oil leaking out of a cylinder on the left side. He said that is a blown jug, meaning the cylinder is blown and the plane is not safe to fly."

Yet they both knew that if a fire call came in, they would be asked to fly on that very plane.

"Walt insisted we go in and tell them they can't fly that plane," Buck said. "Well, I've got to tell you I was a little nervous about that. I was only a GS-6 at the time. Walt was, too. And we are going to go in and tell the foreman who is a GS-11 that his plane is no good? And we're not even from the base?"

But Congleton was adamant. Buck reluctantly accompanied him into the office.

"The foreman looked at us and almost started laughing when Walt told him," he recalled. "He said, 'Well, if we have a plane here, it is ready to go. That is what you have to remember. If we want your opinion, we'll ask you. And we don't want your opinion.' Walt told him again that it was dangerous to fly the plane."

But the foreman refused to accept Congleton's on-the-spot diagnosis.

"The foreman said, 'We will determine if we fly the plane. You are a smokejumper. If the siren goes off, you will get in the plane, take off and jump the fire. That is all you need to know,'" Buck continued. "Walt shot back, 'Nobody should get in that plane. It is dangerous to fly.' They went back and forth like that for about ten minutes. The foreman is getting pissed but Walt doesn't back down at all."

At this point, the foreman began yelling. Congleton still didn't back down. He yelled back at the foreman.

"Walt repeated, 'We are not getting on the plane,'" Buck said. "I'm thinking, 'Uh, really, are you sure, Walt?' But I didn't say anything. I trusted Walt's conclusion. The foreman threatened to call our boss at Gobi. Walt told him to go ahead. The foreman finally said he would go get the pilot and we would all walk out there. 'When the pilot tells you that plane is OK, you are going to get on that goddamn plane when we tell you to!' the foreman told us."

The jumpers agreed.

"When Walt showed the pilot the problem, the pilot didn't say a thing. He went back in and called an aircraft mechanic. The mechanic came out there. And they immediately shut down the plane. It wasn't going anywhere."

Shortly after that, a Cessna 182 arrived at the base.

"Over the speaker we hear, 'Walt Congleton and Gary Buck, get your gear. You are going home,'" Buck said. "The foreman wanted us out of there. But it took a lot of balls for Walt to stand up to him like that."

The point, Buck noted, that it was his and Congleton's lives that would have been on the line if the plane had malfunctioned while deploying to a fire.

Congleton, who has an engineering degree from Oregon State University, hails from the remote hamlet of Paulina in northcentral Oregon where his family had a ranch.

"Being a ranch kid, I always had a burning curiosity for airplanes and how they flew," Congleton explained during a visit to the former Siskiyou base. "I inspected airplanes whenever I could. When I saw the dirty grease streak along the cowling, I knew it could be a blown jug. I had worked on a lot of machinery on the ranch."

When Buck and Congleton returned to Gobi and related the story to their bosses Dee Dutton and Mick Swift, both concurred they had done the right thing.

"About three years later, Walt was looking for a promotion and there were no vacancies at the Gobi because nobody was leaving – everybody liked working there," Buck said. "But there was an opening at Redmond for a squad leader. Guess who was hiring? The same foreman. And guess what? He hired Walt. He must have figured that if he could spot a mechanical problem by just looking at a plane that he would be a good man to have. That was pretty cool for him to hire Walt. "

In addition to doing the usual ranch work and learning to spot machinery with a blown jug during his formative years, Congleton felt a certain longing when he saw a plane fly overhead.

"I hauled a lot of bales and punched a lot of cows," Congleton said. "But a cousin and a good friend got hired on as smokejumpers in Redmond. When I heard about their jobs, I wanted to try it. For a 20-year-old working on a ranch, smokejumping seemed real exciting. After all those years on the ranch and watching planes go over, I wanted to get into one."

In the spring of 1968, he applied at the Redmond base but was told by manager Jim Allen, the legendary former Siskiyou base manager, that all the jumpers they needed had been hired for the fire season.

"But Jim told me about the Cave Junction base where he had just been," Congleton said. "Back then, I didn't know where Cave Junction was but I applied. Out on the ranch we had just got a telephone and one of the first calls I got was from Cave Junction and a guy named Dee Dutton."

Delos "Dee" Dutton, of course, was the Siskiyou Smokejumper Base manager at the time.

"I think he figured because I had been raised on a cattle ranch that I knew how to work so he hired me," Congleton said.

He jumped for 13 years, including a decade out of the Siskiyou base.

"When I first saw Mouse, I naturally thought he was pretty short,"

Congleton recalled. "But it didn't bother me at all, especially after seeing him do the physical training on the first day. Besides, I knew he had been in the Marine Corps and had seen a lot. I knew he would be good. And he was very good."

What's more, Mouse's personality was far larger than most, he added.

"He was a joy to have around, was what he was. Sometimes when we were having a pack out, it could get really hard. And I'm talking really hard. I had done a lot of ranch work but those pack outs with a 110-pound pack is about one of the meanest things you'll ever do. Sometimes you wonder if you will ever get where you are going. Yet Mouse always got there."

Occasionally, jumpers would step in to help each other, Congleton said, noting that help sometimes extended to Mouse.

"But I also remember seeing Mouse on his hands and knees when he was going up a hill," he said. "He would not quit. He would always get there. It was a treat to have Mouse on a fire. He made you laugh. He was special. But there were a lot of special people out at the base. "

Congleton would make about 240 jumps, of which roughly 200 were on fires. While he remains fond of the Siskiyou base after all these years, he was never too keen on jumping into the mountains immediately to the west.

"When the fire siren went off, you always hoped it wasn't that way," he said, pointing west toward the Kalmiopsis Wilderness. "It is rugged, rocky and steep. And it is a hell of a long ways out of there when you had to hike out with a heavy pack."

Like many other jumpers during his era, Congleton fought fires throughout the West and east as far as Virginia.

"My first airplane ride was right here at this base," he said. "I don't think I ever got over that excitement. I've always enjoyed jumping out of a plane."

But he wisely refused to fly in one with a blown jug.

41

TOO TALL
JUMPERS

H ERE IS THE SCENARIO: THREE tall roughnecks from Texas walk into a bar in West Yellowstone one night in 1959 when they run into some smokejumpers hoisting a few. Guess what happens between the young oil rig workers, all brothers, and the gung-ho airborne firefighters when you toss in some alcohol?

Nope, they had an amiable chat and shared a few laughs.

"Like a lot of other future jumpers, we saw that movie, 'Red Skies over Montana,' and wanted to jump out of planes and fight fires," said Larry Welch, one of the brothers. "We got some jumper base application information from them."

Gary Welch, the older brother, rookied at the Siskiyou base in 1960, followed by Bernie and Larry Welch in1961. While Gary would jump for three fire seasons out of the Siskiyou and Bernie for two, Larry made more than 200 jumps in his 17 fire seasons as a smokejumper, including six jumping out the Siskiyou base. The tallest of the brothers, he was also based in Alaska and at the Redmond base.

But standing 6' 4" and weighing in at 225 pounds when he first checked in as a Siskiyou rookie nearly grounded his dreams of becoming a smokejumper. Like Wes Nicholson in chapter 27, he was forced to shorten his height a mite.

"I had to scrunch down a little," Larry Welch said of losing an inch to make the grade. "That part was easy. Now, when it came to making weight, that was really hard. They wanted you to weigh no more than 200 pounds so I had to lose 25 pounds."

That meant going on a crash diet and drastically cutting back on liquids.

"One time when I knew I wasn't going to make weight, I didn't drink water for 24 hours and lost 12 pounds," he recalled. "That was a real challenge."

Another challenge was taking that first training jump over Seats Field west of the Siskiyou base.

"For people who had never seen a parachute up close before, we didn't know if the chute worked half the time or a fourth of the time," he observed. "Of course, after a couple of jumps you realize it is hard to get that much cloth up in the air without it slowing you down a whole lot. We got used to it."

Like many jumpers, the Welch brothers spent their winters in class.

"Back then, we were working our way through college," Larry said. "I didn't know what I wanted to be at the time so I'd jump and go back to college."

After meeting a jumper who taught during the winters, he figured he had found the right combination. He would retire from a career of teaching and coaching, both in middle and high school.

Like most smokejumpers, he never forgot his first fire jump. It was in the big tree country near Winthrop, Washington, northeast of Seattle near the Canadian border.

"We had a 5-foot crosscut saw and had a 7-foot diameter tree to fall," he recalled. "We notched both sides with an ax and started sawing. After a while they dropped us a chainsaw but they didn't drop any gas. So we had to finish sawing with the crosscut, then pack the chainsaw out that we never got to use. It was a tough fire."

But it didn't faze his enthusiasm for smokejumping.

"You know, after I graduated from high school, I worked in oil fields. I made a lot of contacts and could have gotten on with a freighter carrying oil through the Panama Canal. But after I started jumping, I knew this was what I wanted to do. I really enjoyed the camaraderie among the jumpers."

Like the other jumpers, he also appreciated the food at the Siskiyou base.

"When you have good food, good friends and an exciting job, that's pretty hard to beat."

Working with competent individuals like Jim Allen also made a huge difference.

"Jim was a very good boss," said Larry who had Allen as a boss at the Siskiyou base and later in Redmond. "He ran the ship and you knew it. There wasn't any guessing about it. Everybody respected him greatly."

And Larry, one of the tallest smokejumpers ever, thoroughly enjoyed working with the shortest.

"When I first saw Mouse, I told him I was going to put him in my leg pocket for a reserve so I'd have a reserve firefighter as well as a reserve parachute," he said. "We got along great."

No slouch when it came to telling stories and wisecracking, Larry Welch always enjoyed chatting with the loquacious smokejumper.

"He could go to an hour-long movie and come back and talk to you about it for three hours," he said. "He had a gift for gab and some interesting colloquial sayings. People liked him."

But there was no question his shorter friend faced tough times as a smokejumper, he noted.

"There are definitely drawbacks," he said of being less than five-feet tall. "During pack outs, when you are 6' 4" and come to a 3-foot high log, you just step over it. He had to walk all the way around or take his pack off, throw it on the other side and climb over."

But Mouse would balk at someone offering him a little assistance, he said.

"I remember one time that I offered to pack more out if he would climb a tree for me. Mouse said he didn't mind climbing the tree but didn't want any help packing out. He had a lot of pride."

Welch broke his pelvis during a practice jump during a windy day in Washington state while he was stationed in Redmond.

"That was my last jump," he said. "I figured I had been lucky thus far. I was also getting to an age when I needed to focus on teaching. But I had no regrets."

Interviewed during a reunion at the Siskiyou base, he stressed the importance of it to all three brothers as well as all the others who jumped out of the base.

"This place is our legacy," Larry Welch stressed. "We need to preserve it, all the buildings and everything. This is a very special place with special memories. It has to be preserved for all of us."

* * * *

Like Larry Welch, former smokejumper Mike Hardy is 6-foot-4, a smidgen too tall to pass muster when it came to qualifying as a smokejumper. So he also crouched a skosh to be accepted as a rookie in 1975 at the McCall base in Idaho.

"But they had a jerk, the second in command, who was a real stickler for bureaucratic rules," he recalled. "If a guy was an ounce overweight, he couldn't jump. And he kept telling me he was going to kick me out because I was too tall."

But Hardy kept his head down, so to speak, and weathered the storm, completing his first smokejumping season without being given the boot. But he knew he had to find another home if he intended to continue smokejumping.

"They had all sizes down in Cave Junction," he observed. "Guys that were too little and guys that were too tall. And they had a great mess hall and that was an important factor for me. So I applied in 1976 and was hired."

Despite his height, Hardy jumped through the 1999 fire season, stopping when he turned 51. He made 297 jumps, including on 150 fires. In addition to McCall, he made a tour of smokejumper bases in the West, including Fort Wainwright, Redmond, Redding and the Siskiyou base.

Although he did a two-year hitch in the Marine Corps immediately after graduating from high school in southern California, he had been interested in fighting wildfires since he was a youngster.

"When I was 13 and lived near the San Gabriel Mountains, a young guy from Maine got hired on as a firefighter and died in a fire," Hardy recalled. "Our class sent a letter back to his family in Maine. I never forgot about that firefighter."

Upon completing his military commitment, he worked on several fire crews in California, including serving on a hotshot crew in the Los Angeles National Forest.

"I read a *Day in the Life of Ivan Denisovich* by Alexander Solzhenitsyn and *Papillon* by Henri Charrière – two books about prison," said the well-read Hardy. "I guess I started seeing the romance of a hot, miserable job. Somehow it all started making sense to me. Before that, I didn't like fighting fires that much."

When he became a smokejumper, that took the romance to a higher level, he figured.

"All of us would be telling ourselves, over and over, 'We're living the dream,'" he said. "And we'd be sweating, breathing in the fumes from the plane, then smoke from the fire. It was quite a dream, to be sure."

But he knew that dream could be turned into a nightmare if a jumper had a bad landing.

"Down in Oregon, that was the toughest jump country. The trees were bigger and I was always nervous about big trees. I was proactive, steering away from them. But in the Alaskan interior, the trees were no taller than we were so it wasn't so bad. I never really got hurt. A couple of close calls, though."

He jumped with Mouse in 1976 and '79, then again in 1981.

"Just about everybody was shorter than me so Mouse wasn't that much of a surprise when I first saw him. But I remember he would be in a practice jump and everyone else would be down and he'd still be floating up there because he was so light.

"But he was a good worker," he added. "He did way more work than he should have. And what a character. He was such a good storyteller."

The two were based together in Alaska in 1981, he noted.

"But I had been sent down south to the lower '48 when Mouse died," he said. "He didn't get the down south detail. I wish he had, maybe he would still be with us."

In retrospect, of all the bases where he was stationed over the years, Hardy appreciated the Siskiyou base the most.

"It was the most fun. They were gung-ho but they also had fun. They made it interesting. We would do things like play volleyball. Every time you lost a point, you had to do five pushups. You'd do a hundred pushups or so. We worked hard and played hard. Everybody was in good shape. It was a good place to be."

42

SPORT JUMPING MOUSE

W HEN MOUSE WASN'T JUMPING ON wildfires, he invariably sought out challenging activities, including skydiving at the Beagle Sky Ranch, a private airport roughly a dozen air miles north of Medford. The site has long drawn sport jumpers from miles around.

One skydiver who came to know Mouse at the Beagle Ranch facility was Abigail "Gail" Kimbell. If the name rings a bell, it's because she was the first female chief of the U.S. Forest Service when appointed the 16th head of the vast agency in 2007.

Mouse and fellow smokejumper Rick Oliver, an Illinois Valley High School graduate who rookied in 1968, often went to the Beagle Sky Ranch when they weren't jumping fire, Kimbell said.

"Mouse and Rick were very experienced so they went with more experienced people because they were going higher and doing freefalls longer," she said, although adding she once jumped with Oliver.

"But I only made 13 jumps," she added. "I certainly had no claim to fame there. Unlike people like Mouse and Rick, I was just a beginner. The two of them were real gentlemen and real fun to be around. To the rest of us, they were icons because they were smokejumpers. People revered the two of them."

For smokejumpers, the skydiving was largely done without the knowledge of their bosses, she stressed.

"If I recall, it was a bit on the sly because smokejumpers weren't encouraged to do skydiving," said the future Forest Service chief with a chuckle. "We weren't to acknowledge they were there."

Boston-born Kimbell, 65 at the time of the interview in the fall of 2018, was reared in New England where she earned a bachelor's degree in forestry from the University of Vermont, followed by a master's degree in forest management from Oregon State University.

"I was one of eight kids and one way to tire us all out was for our dad and mom to take us hiking," she said, noting the hikes created in her a love for all things forest related. "We would go on these wonderful hikes into the White Mountains in the summers. I became aware of forests and the concept of public lands being lands that people could go hiking on without getting permission. I learned then that we are so fortunate as a society to have all these public lands."

One of her first jobs on public lands was with the U.S. Bureau of Land Management's Medford District in southwest Oregon. She worked in the district for three years.

"When I worked for the BLM I was in the field almost all the time, working with a forestry crew. I remember one afternoon watching a red-tailed hawk gliding overhead in the breeze. I remember saying out loud, 'That would be a real magical thing to do.' Turns out one of the fellows I was working with was a skydiving instructor and a jump master. I wound up starting skydiving training."

That was in the fall of 1974.

While Kimbell described herself as just another person at the popular skydiving site, she said the diminutive smokejumper drew attention.

"Given his stature, he got extra looks," she said. "But he was also an amazing human being. He was a powerful individual. His presence was bigger than he was. He was personable, thoughtful and respectful of differences. He worked hard and expected everyone around him to give it all they had."

Moreover, he had a quick sense of humor, she observed.

"He was very funny," she said, adding, "He was just a very pleasant guy to be around."

Kimbell left skydiving behind when she moved to Alaska in 1977 to take another federal agency job.

"Mouse was someone who, after you met him, you never forgot him," she said. "All through my early career I would hear stories about Mouse. They always made me smile because you knew anything was possible with that guy. He was a unique individual. The world was a sadder place when he passed."

When Mick Swift's son, Ken, was teenager, he also learned to skydive at the Beagle site, thanks to Mouse.

"Mouse was my sport jumping instructor back when I was 15," Ken Swift said, adding that he also did some recreational jumping with both his father and Mouse. "Mouse was very meticulous about everything. Nothing was left to chance. Everything had to be perfect."

Steve "Armo" Armitage also did sport jumping with both Mouse and Mick Swift in the 1970s.

"Mick had this weird parachute called a 'pterodactyl' – when anyone was jumping with one we always ran out to watch because it was always a 50/50 chance if it was going to work," Armitage said, describing the parachute as having two wings.

Armitage and his wife, Deb Kalmakav, became good friends with both Mouse and Mick Swift while skydiving with them at the Beagle Sky Ranch. He began jumping there in 1973; she early in 1976.

He originally started skydiving in Kalispell, Montana in 1971, chalking up nearly 20 jumps in the Big Sky country. All told, he made more than 1,200 skydives, mostly at the Beagle ranch, totaling more than 12 hours of free-fall time.

"My first skydive with Mouse was at 12,500 feet – it was my 50th jump," he said of Dec. 8, 1973. "We had 60 seconds of free fall time together. We fell down to 2,500 feet. I made hundreds of jumps with him."

A teacher by training, Kalmakav, a native of Canada with a teaching degree from the University of Alberta, logged 1,028 jumps.

When Armitage, a forester, took a job with the U.S. Bureau of Land Management in southwest Oregon in 1971, he heard about the skydivers at Beagle. The popular skydiving site was owned by veteran pilot and skydiver George Holberton.

"That was where I met Mouse," said Armitage who stands 5' 5". "Mouse always made me feel tall. He was the only guy I ever called 'Shorty.' But he was built like a brick shithouse. He was very strong."

When they first met in 1973, Mouse was a rigger at the Siskiyou base.

"I was working in the Illinois Valley at the time and sometimes I'd take my jumping gear out there to jump with Mouse," Armitage said. "He had a Cessna 170 then."

Both husband and wife jumped for different reasons.

"I've never been an adventure person," Kalmakav said, noting she has always been apprehensive of heights. "I don't even climb ladders. But I was living in a very boring town in Canada. But I met a jumper who was jumping down in Kalispell and I went with another friend down to see that."

At point she was a hardcore WFUFFO – *what for you want to jump out of airplanes?* or words to that effect. After watching friends jump, she eventually was talked into jumping. Yet it would take her 50 jumps before she started enjoying sport jumping.

"It drained all my brave cells to learn how to jump," she said.

"Me, I was totally opposite," Armitage said of his Michigan childhood. "As a kid, I was scaring my mom because I was climbing to the tops of trees. I always wanted to fly."

"When my parents would come down from Canada to visit us and they knew that if they wanted to spend any time with us they had to go out to the drop zone," she observed.

Like his many other friends, they note Mouse made life interesting and fun in so many ways.

Armitage recalled the night in 1974 when a flock of skydivers was spending the night at Holberton's house. Mouse brought a girlfriend.

"We were all sleeping on the floor in the living room," he said, noting that Mouse and his lady friend became amorous that night, judging from the noise. "So the next morning, Mouse sits up before anyone else said anything and says, 'I just want you all to know that I had an epileptic fit in the middle of the night. If you guys heard me, I'm sorry.' And poor girl was just covering her face. That was the kind of humor he had. Oh my God, the things that would come out of his mouth."

And there was the time when Mouse was piloting the plane and had just got off the radio after reporting he had a load of jumpers.

"For some reason, he started telling us about having his hemorrhoids surgically repaired," Kalmakav said. "He told us all about it as we were going to altitude. Finally, at the end of the story, the tower came on and said, 'Mouse, great story but you can turn your radio off now.'"

When it came to jumping, Mouse was totally focused at the task at hand. For instance, he was looking forward to earning a sky crest recipient (SCR) rating which requires a formation of eight people, Armitage said.

"And we had a night-time SCR planned which, obviously, is at night," he said. "This was during a full moon."

However, one of the jumpers decided to bow out, leaving one less than needed.

"But we didn't tell Mouse because we knew he would be upset," Armitage said. "We were flying in a twin Beech. So he is walking up and down the Beech, pissed off that there were only seven. By now it had clouded over and you couldn't see anything. Me and three other guys were hanging out the door of the Beech, trying to figure out where the hell we were. It was pitch black."

Finally, Armitage decided it was time to jump. They all took the plunge, including Mouse. But the planned formation never occurred because they couldn't see each other. It was parachuting pandemonium.

"Mouse and I were close together and he was screaming bloody murder," Armitage recalled. "He was yelling, 'Where the hell are we? I can't see a damned thing.' He was really bitching."

"He was livid," Kalmakav said. "When the moon went behind the clouds, he said, 'God damn it. This is ridiculous. Something is going to happen to somebody.' He was furious."

Remember, this was before GPS was at your fingertips. As it turns out, they were near the Dodge Bridge which spans the Rogue River some 10 miles north of Medford. All the jumpers landed safely, although no one made a landing that gave them bragging rights.

"Mouse used to wear big goggles," Armitage said. "When he landed, his goggles were twisted up on his face. I told him, 'Great jump, Mouse.' He said something like, 'Oh, bull. Damn it to hell' He was still cussing up a blue streak."

"He had gravel up his nose," she interjected. "He just ploughed right into the ground headfirst. He looked like he had been in a car wreck."

In fact, Larry Owen, who described his brother as an adrenalin junkie, has a photograph of his brother apparently taken shortly after that jump. It shows Mouse with a bandage on his nose.

"You can't see his hand but it is all jammed up, too," Larry said. "They had been doing night jumps over at the Beagle ranch. It was during a bright full moon. They were out there in a light plane, thinking this was really cool. Well, just when they started jumping, a cloud came over the moon. They couldn't see the ground and hit it a little harder than they had expected."

Fortunately, they all walked away, albeit a little bruised and scrapped, thanks to the earth coming up sooner than expected.

Steve Armitage estimated that Mouse jumped more than 800 times, much of it skydiving. In his records on Sept. 8, 1979, he made a note that Mouse was making his 775th jump.

"That was my 1,000th jump and I recorded the jumps made by other people, including Mouse," he said, adding. "I don't know if that was just sport jumps."

What he does know is that their friend was extremely careful when jumping.

"He was always very safety conscious, very careful with his equipment and with jumping," Armitage said. "We would take our main parachute and just sort of throw them together when we were folding them. He would lay his out on a table and be very precise, very methodical.

"Mouse called us from Alaska after Joan died in May," he said of a skydiving friend who fell to her death in the spring of 1981. "He said, 'Well, at least she died doing what she loved doing.' But when Mouse died, that was the final straw."

Armitage took skydive number 1,252 – his last – on Oct. 18, 1981. It was a somber moment because he, his wife and two other skydivers were carrying a portion of Mouse's ashes which they intended to release over the drop zone at the Beagle facility the jumper had loved.

"We were in George's [Holberton] 185," he said of a Cessna the Beagle owner purchased new in 1975. "Mouse had flown that plane a lot. He always wanted a 185. We made the mistake of opening the bag before we made the jump. We were going to throw the ashes and follow. But when we opened the bag, most of Mouse's ashes blew back into the plane. Bone chips and dust all over the place. We cracked up because we figured he wanted to stay in the 185. If that plane is in existence today, I guarantee you there is still part of Mouse in there somewhere."

"Yes, there was a cloud of Mouse in the plane," his wife recalled.

In Mouse's honor, the skydivers jumped in a circle but did not close it as they normally would because that was the slot he would have jumped, Armitage said.

"Mouse was the third friend in a nine-month period to die while skydiving," he said. "That is part of the reason Deb and I quit."

THE MOUSE THAT SOARED

43

SMOKEJUMPER WITH PATIENTS

G REG GONZALEZ WAS ONE OF the least likely of any jumper in the history of the Siskiyou Smokejumper Base to end up at the Gobi.

After all, the son of foreign service officer Raymond Gonzalez, former U.S. ambassador to Ecuador, had spent much of his formative years in Europe and Central America.

Yet, like so many future Siskiyou jumpers, he became interested in smokejumping when he was a ground-pounding wildland firefighter. In his case, it was during the early 1970s in the upper Rogue River region, including Crater Lake National Park and the northern portion of the Rogue River National Forest. He attended college in California during the winters.

"We would see these jumpers dropping down and the idea of smokejumping really intrigued me," he said. "So when I heard about the smokejumper base out at Cave Junction, I applied."

All told, the 1976 Siskiyou rookie made about 75 jumps during four fire seasons at the Gobi and one in Alaska.

It was while working in the upper Rogue River region in 1973 that Gonzalez met a young lady named Cheryl when he visited a vegetable market called Jim's Produce in Medford. The following year when he returned to his summer job he made a point of dropping in at Jim's Produce.

"My dad owned it – I was working there," she explained, adding, "We got married six months later."

Greg Gonzalez would later make the big leap from smokejumper to medical doctor, graduating from the Oregon University School of Medicine medical school in 1984. The pediatric specialist, who retired after nearly 40 years in practice, and his wife now live in Colorado.

Although he had already indicated an interest in medical work, coming to the aid of a fellow smokejumper who broke an ankle helped seal the deal.

"We had flown out of Redmond and, as a certified paramedic on that same plane, I jumped next with the sole purpose of tending to him," Gonzalez explained. "They would have dropped the first aid kit which at that time had injectable Demerol for pain control but, as I recall, he was very stoic and refused any. We removed his boot and stabilized his ankle and were then evacuated by helicopter."

They were flown to the St. Charles Medical Center in Bend, the hub of central Oregon.

"I accompanied him to the hospital, hanging with him in the ER until his x-rays revealed a fracture and then we got a ride back to the base once he was splinted," he said. "I remember talking to the doctors and thinking it would be cool to do that type of work. And, lo and behold, it was."

As a young man, Gonzalez also found the work of a smokejumper very cool.

"Back then, I don't think my father had any concept of what a smokejumper was," he recalled. After all, the ambassador, who served as ambassador to Ecuador during the Carter administration, had never seen a smokejumper dropping out of the sky.

"But my parents came out to visit the base one summer and I

showed them around, including the plane we were using at the time," Greg said. "They were impressed by what we were doing."

Incidentally, Ambassador Gonzalez received a thoughtful note from former President Carter on Dec. 24, 2019. The Carters had visited the Gonzalez family when the family patriarch was in the state department, Greg noted.

"Congratulations on your 95th birthday!" it read. "What a great milestone, not only for you, but also for your family and all those who have been able to enjoy your friendship. I will always be grateful for your fine service as Ambassador to Ecuador during my administration." It was signed, "Sincerely, Jimmy Carter."

Regardless of your politics, you have to acknowledge it was a class act by the former POTUS.

In its own way, the Siskiyou base was also a class act, Greg Gonzalez will tell you.

"The base retained its people because there was such a tight bond," he said. "So the level of experience was such you had the best of the best. I felt very confident in the people who trained us. And because they were so good at what they did, they were able to chart their own course."

There may have been a few practical jokes, he allowed.

"It was tradition to hide Gobi stones in the rookies' packs during their simulated pack outs," he said, adding, "Always good for a few laughs at the end when they unpacked their gear."

His wife also had a positive experience during the time they spent in and around the Siskiyou base.

"We lived there in the summers and in Eugene during the winters where we went to school," she said, noting they lived on Siskiyou smokejumper Dave Atkin's beautiful property on the east bank of the Illinois River for three summers, camping out and enjoying life when wildfires were not rearing their fiery heads.

"For us, even those who were not smokejumpers, all the people at the base were family," she said. "The Browns had children. It was a super special place, a special community. We have lifelong friends from the Gobi."

With Mouse's tutelage, she and her good friend Nancy Brown took to the sky as skydivers at the Beagle ranch. It all began one morning at the Siskiyou base in 1978 when Cheryl Gonzalez ran up, bursting with news, Brown said.

"Cheryl came up to me and said, 'Nancy, guess what? We are going to skydive!'" Brown said. " I had never seen Cheryl so excited. I told her, 'I'm so glad for you.' And she said, 'No, we – all of us, including you – are going to skydive. And Mouse is going to teach us."

Although married to smokejumper Wes Brown, she never, ever intended to jump out of an airplane for any reason.

"I didn't want to do it. But Cheryl said I had to because Mouse was going to be our teacher. So I told her I would go."

Besides, four of their good friends who were also married to airborne firefighters planned to give skydiving a whirl.

"Mouse named us 'Owen's Angels,'" Brown said, noting that one jump satisfied her curiosity about how it felt to leap from a plane. "He was very funny but he was so serious when he was training us. We were well trained. He was so safety conscious."

Cheryl Gonzalez echoed her sentiments.

"I only did three jumps before I became pregnant with our first child," she said. "Owen's Angels was a group of wives or girlfriends of the jumpers. We had a lot of fun. We even had underwear with a heart on them with wings off to the side. Mouse was pretty flattered."

Her husband became a good friend of Mouse shortly after arriving at the base.

"When I was a rookie, I got a ride with Mouse in his Corvette over to see Cheryl one weekend," Greg Gonzalez said, noting Mouse could barely see over the dashboard. "That was quite an experience."

He recalled Mouse often deployed self-deprecating humor, especially when it came to the blue sports car.

"I told him once that I thought I saw him driving downtown in his Corvette and I said, 'That was you, right?' Mouse replied, 'You mean the Corvette going down the road and nobody driving? Yeah, that was me.'"

Pete Hawley, who rookied with Gonzalez, compared Mouse's humor to that of actor/comedian Robin Williams.

"I first saw him in 1973 when I was training at Redmond to become a rappeller," he said. "This bunch of jumpers came in that night to boost and there was this short guy who was real loud. He seemed to be the center of entertainment for 40 or 50 guys, just kept cracking jokes. I didn't know his name and had no idea where he was from. He could do the work and be funny, too."

Hawley, who joined longtime friends Greg and Cheryl in the interview in a local coffee shop, recalled when Mouse was a squad leader at the Siskiyou base. About that time the powers that be decided jumpers had to carry a shovel along with a chainsaw while working, he said.

"You couldn't get a lot of work done if you were carrying both but Mouse had to implement the order," Hawley said. "He chewed me out for about five minutes when he saw I wasn't carrying a shovel with my chainsaw. And I was thinking, 'Thank God for my ear plugs.'"

Raised in Salem, home of Oregon's capitol, Hawley initially worked on a hot shot crew after graduating from high school in 1971 but became a rappeller when his hotshot crew was selected to be trained as helicopter rappellers.

"Rappeller crews are a good compliment to smokejumpers but my dream was to become a smokejumper," he said. "When I was 11 or 12, I saw the movie, *Red Skies over Montana*. I really wanted to become a smokejumper."

As it happened, Warren "Poncho" Villa, who had fought wildfires with Gonzalez in the upper Rogue River region, broke his ankle in his first training jump as a rookie in 1976. Hawley filled his slot while Villa became the dispatcher that fire season but would come back the following summer as a jumper.

"What I had heard about the base was it was the coolest base and least military-like of any of them," Hawley said, adding that proved to be true. "My first day at the base was July 4, 1976. It was one of the best things to happen to me."

Hawley jumped out of the base until it closed in 1981, then jumped for another two fire seasons at the McCall base in Idaho.

"But there was nothing like the Gobi," he stressed. "I would have stayed there if it had stayed open."

He and Gonzalez recalled the time they jumped on a fire in northeastern Washington hard against the Idaho state line. Unfortunately, the parachute carrying their tools hung up in a tall tree.

"The plane flew off before we could let them know we needed some climbing gear," Hawley said. "It was about 40 or 50 feet up to where the tools were hanging. Fortunately, the fire was small. It wasn't really doing anything. So we used our boots to make a fireline."

Made by boots or not, the fireline held that night. Of course, when another fire crew arrived the next day, the two acted nonchalantly, as though stopping a fire with just their boots was routine. But Gonzalez did use tools in the form of climbing gear to retrieve the firefighting tools hanging high in the tree, thanks to gear brought in by the reinforcements.

The worst fire he ever fought was the infamous Hog Fire in August of 1977 in the rugged Salmon River drainage of northern California.

"We landed in what we thought was tall brush from the air," Gonzalez said. "But it was actually madrone and oak."

Most of the jumpers got hung up in the trees, many of which were 40 feet tall, he recalled. The jumpers left their chutes hung up in the trees to go fight the fire, planning to retrieve them when their work was done.

"But when the fire heated up, the wind lifted some of the chutes off the trees and you could see them floating across the sky above us," he said. "I have a vivid memory of that. It was really spooky."

Because the fire blew up, the jumpers weren't able to build much fire line but spent two days fighting their way through dense vegetation on the steep slopes to escape the flames, he observed.

"We had to run for it," confirmed Gary Buck who also jumped the Hog Fire. "We had 23 guys jumping on it – two DC-3 loads. And we couldn't stop it. But we didn't jump it until 24 hours after it started."

The lightning bust ignited numerous fires in the Klamath National Forest, largely in the Salmon River Ranger District, all of which combined to become the Hog Fire, according to the record book.

But the writer back at the base may have employed a wee bit of hyperbole.

"This date would stand along with such days as Pearl Harbor Day, the sinking of the Maine and the fall of the Alamo in the history books," the logbook reported on Aug. 11, 1977. "It would scar the hearts and minds of the Gobi forever with the horrid memories of that day. The battle of Armageddon was poking its ugly head over the horizon.

"Upon return to the base of our 23 jumpers, we found out our people had to abandon the fires due to rolling material and terrain and fall back to the Salmon River," it added.

It noted total acres burned exceeded 50,000 and manpower topped 5,000 people, including more than 120 smokejumpers.

"We got off relatively light in the way of casualties to jumpers considering the terrain and the fire behavior," the report noted. "(Rick) Dees suffered a separated shoulder and there were a few cases of poison oak. Equipment losses included 6 sets of jump gear, 15 mains (parachutes), 15 reserves, 2 chainsaws and numerous letdown ropes. Two of the mains were seen floating off in a convection column."

It was one fire a future medical doctor would never, ever forget.

"I wasn't sure we were going to make it out," Gonzalez said. "There was so much brush. You could hear the roar of the fire getting closer. They had to evacuate us by helicopter."

THE MOUSE THAT SOARED

44

THE SOCIALITE MOUSE

MARY ORTON DIDN'T KNOW ALLEN D. "Mouse" Owen when he was floating in the air or battling a wildfire on a mountain side. Now a retired elementary school teacher, she knew him as a gentle person when he was enjoying a pleasant night out on the town.

"He was always quite a gentleman," she said, noting she first met him in 1977 and remained friends with him until he left the base. "I knew him out of his smokejumper realm. He was a gentleman who treated women nicely. He was always so funny and entertaining. He had a wonderful personality."

A native of Phoenix, Or., she is a graduate of what is now Southern Oregon University, majoring in education.

"My first teaching job was at Evergreen Elementary," she said of the school in Cave Junction. "That was the end of summer in 1976. When I first moved to Cave Junction, the place was vibrant. The base was in full force. There was an influx of young people. Everything was really hopping. I planned to stay only one year. I ended up teaching 30 years at Evergreen. I loved it there."

In fact, she retired the same year as Nancy Brown, the school principal to whom former Siskiyou smokejumper Wes Brown is happily married.

However, back in '76, Orton had a good friend who also started teaching at Everygreen that year. Moreover, her friend had dated Mouse and remained a good friend of his.

"When Mouse wanted to go out on the town, to a movie or dinner, he would call Molly and me," Orton said, referring to her friend. "We would go with him. He always insisted on paying for the movies and dinner. It was pure entertainment. So much fun."

The trio would often travel to Medford, a town with several theaters some 60 miles northeast of Cave Junction.

"It was a long drive and he would talk nonstop, both ways," she said. "We would be laughing so hard all the way. If one of us was driving, we could hardly stay on the road because we were laughing so hard."

She will never forget the time they went to a restaurant dubbed the Mon Desire in Central Point, a posh eating establishment back in the day.

"Very good food," she recalled. "Molly, Mouse and I were having a nice dinner in one of the little rooms. You were in a little room but it was open enough so you could still see into the other rooms. Of course, Mouse was doing his monologue. Molly and I were just laughing our heads off."

That's when a young couple came in and sat at the table next to them.

"The girl was scantily dressed in shorts and a halter top so her back was bare," Orton said. "They ordered champagne and the young waiter brought in a bucket of ice and set it in a tripod next to her chair. As he walked away, the tripod collapsed and the ice dumped down her back. There was a crash of ice, a shriek from the girl and Mouse stopped talking. When he stopped talking, that's when the entire restaurant fell silent. I told him to keep talking but he was speechless for a moment, something very unusual for him."

The point, she noted, was that it was the absence of his voice which captured everyone's attention.

"It wasn't the crashing ice bucket but the silence of not hearing him," she said. "He had a voice that carried and he was so entertaining. People couldn't help but listen to his conversation. When he stopped talking, everyone around him would stop and look to see what happened."

But there were occasions when even Mouse was stymied by events, as was the case of a meal that the fellow from St. Louis found a little too strange for even his adventurous tastes. It had to do with chicken feet. We'll let Mary Orton tell the tale.

"He told Molly and me about going into this small village in Vietnam with his unit and he was really hungry. They were invited into this home and served soup with chicken feet in it. Mouse loved to eat but, as hungry as he was, he couldn't eat the chicken feet. He took a couple of spoonfuls of broth, then convinced them he was full. Of course, the way he told it made us howl with laughter. He was so hilarious."

Mouse's monologues were something all his friends looked forward to hearing, she said.

"He would keep you in stitches. Did Mouse embellish his stories? Probably, like most people do. But it was the way he told them that was so entertaining. He was a remarkable orator. He was fun to be around."

He was also someone who was kind and giving, offering assistance to anyone who needed it, she noted.

"One time he offered his Corvette to Nancy Brown to drive it into Grants Pass," Orton said of the 1969 Stingray. "She and another smokejumper wife needed to get into town for some reason."

By the way, we Kerby residents in those days referred to going to Grants Pass was "going into town." If you were merely popping into Cave Junction, it was "going uptown." Kerbyites were very particular, you see.

Back to her story. The problem was that Nancy Brown had no experience driving a Corvette equipped with a stick shift, Orton observed.

"Nancy had never driven a car like that and didn't have a lot of experience with the gears," she said, noting the sports car lacked its usual fluid mobility that day. "I suspect she was pretty hard on the clutch. Mouse didn't know if he would see his beloved Corvette again. But she brought it back with no scratches or anything. However, Nancy did say she never wanted to drive that car again."

Ken Swift, Mick's son, recalled riding home in the Corvette after wrestling practice at Illinois Valley High School

"When I was in high school, Gary Thornhill and Mouse would come down to wrestling practice and work us over," he said, noting that Mouse would drive his Corvette to the school. "Mouse worked the smaller kids over and GT would work the bigger kids over."

Ken Swift, who graduated in 1976 and took second in the state wrestling tournament that year, always looked forward to the ride home after practice.

"As kids, we loved it," he said. "There would be about four of us squeezed in there. Getting to ride in a Corvette back then was very cool."

Orton recalled when she and Molly were talking to their young students at Evergreen Elementary School about careers in the late 1970s. To demonstrate one high-flying profession, Mouse dropped in out of the blue. Literally.

"We got all the 4th graders out on the soccer field," she recalled. "I think it was Gary Buck who told the kids that if they were quiet they could hear Mouse yell. They were very quiet and they heard him. He landed right where the kids were."

The smokejumpers then went into the school and talked about their work and what it entailed, she said, adding that dropping in on the class doubtlessly attracted their attention and interest.

Not long after she met him, Mouse bought a small house in Cave Junction about two blocks from where she lived.

"This was when the hot-air popcorn poppers were popular," she said. "Occasionally, he would call me up and all I could hear was the popcorn popping. He didn't talk. That was the invitation to stroll down the street and visit Mouse, have some popcorn and listen to one of his monologues. It was so pleasant."

Back in the day, the young teacher drove a 1966 Dodge Monaco. This was when Detroit was building what were called "sleds." They came with big engines and plenty of room to pack people in, including half a dozen smokejumpers out for a night on the town.

"One night, there was Molly and me and about six smokejumpers – I was driving," she said, noting it was winter and the jumpers were among the few who over wintered in the Illinois Valley. "Mouse was in the front seat when we were coming home from Medford. And, of course, he was doing his monologue and everyone was laughing."

But they fell silent when they were crossing the Applegate River where they were suddenly enveloped by fog. The headlights were useless.

"The fog line disappeared when we came to a stretch where another road intersected with the highway," she said. "You couldn't see anything. Mouse just clammed up. He stopped talking until we could see the fog line again. He told me that his life passed before him in that moment."

She recalled one macabre story told by Mouse when he and another smokejumper had a small plane and started an aerial delivery service during the off season. They were asked to take the corpse of a young woman from California to Texas.

"The only place they could put the body was in between the seats," she said, noting that gas in the corpse caused it to move. "The young woman sat up and emitted a big sigh, then lay back down. That really spooked them. But it was funny the way Mouse told it."

Orton got married in 1981, the same year the base closed.

"So I lost contact with Mouse after that," she said. "Of course, it was also the year he died. That was very sad."

She stopped talking for a moment to remember her good friend.

"Mouse was such a beloved man," she said quietly. "What a legacy he left behind. Mouse was 'Uncle Al' to all the kids. No one could meet him and not be impressed."

.

45

MOUSE ROOMMATE

Standing 6' 3," Steven Mankle would seem to be an odd roommate for the shortest smokejumper ever. But Mankle, who rookied with Larry Owen in 1976, got on very well with both brothers.

"When I came back the year after I rookied, Mouse needed a roommate for his house in Cave Junction and that worked out good for me," Mankle said. "He took all the lower cabinets and I took all the upper ones. It worked out perfectly for us. Of course, Mouse being Mouse, he kept life very interesting,"

Born and reared in Albuquerque, Mankle, now in his early 70s, was going to Linn Benton Community College in Albany, Ore., when he decided to visit Dorcey Wingo, a friend in Alaska in 1974. Formerly a helicopter pilot in Vietnam, Wingo was flying helitack firefighters out of Fairbanks to wildfires.

"I had done helitack firefighting there in Fairbanks for two summers," Mankle explained. "But I kept watching the smokejumpers across the runway from us. They kept doing the initial attacks and coming back while we were doing all the mop up. And I figured it would be a much better job to go in there and do the initial attack and come back."

As fate would have it, Wingo would fly rappel crews out of the Siskiyou Smokejumper Base in the spring of 1975. We'll let Wingo hover for the time being, returning to him in the next chapter.

Mankle dropped in after his friend arrived at the Siskiyou base. He was impressed by the jumpers, applied the following spring and became a rookie.

"I barely made it under the height limit," he acknowledged, noting he had faced a similar height limit when serving in the submarine service in the Navy. He shares that seemingly contradictory military background with Mike Cramer, another former submariner and a well-respected former Siskiyou jumper you've already read about.

For Mankle, a fellow with a way with words as well as a talented musician, parachuting out of a plane seemed to come naturally.

"During our very first rookie training jump, I was the first one out the door. I loved it. For me, it was a magic moment. When you jump out of a plane, time distorts. Time no longer runs in a chromatic scale you are used to. Each time I jumped, that magic moment got bigger and bigger. It was more fun than the last time I did it."

He was impressed with fellow Siskiyou jumpers, including the shortest one ever to wear a jump suit.

"Mouse was small in stature but he didn't put out small stature energy. He was someone to be reckoned with. I was in awe of the guy. I tried to learn everything I could from him. He was a fountain of wisdom when it came to smokejumping and parachuting."

Mouse was also a natural leader, he added.

"Everything to him was a challenge which he faced head on. One of the things I got from Mouse was not to look at something as insurmountable or not. From his standpoint, it was, 'Ok, this is what we got in front of us. We need to deal with this situation now. It is the challenge we need to overcome now. Let's do it.'"

Although he was short, Mouse was not opposed to running for exercise, he said.

"I hated running," he said. "Not Mouse. And he would talk nearly all the time when he was running. I would be gasping for breath and trying to keep up. And there he was, 'talk, talk, talk.' It was hilarious."

He chuckled when recalling how a Mouse tale would often begin. "He would usually start out with, 'There I was. . .' and you knew it was going to be good," he said. "Mouse was fun to be around. He was a great roommate."

Wingo, who had moved on from the Siskiyou base after the Forest Service relocated the rappel helicopter following the 1975 fire season, came back for a visit with his girlfriend and a dog. They stayed at a cabin Mankle and Wingo had earlier built in nearby O'Brien. But the dog refused to come out from under the cabin when it was time for them to leave. So Mankle adopted the pooch.

"She was a springer spaniel who liked to dig in flower gardens. I took her over to Mouse's house. He liked his flower gardens nice and neat so we had an issue developing there. As it happens, I knew a gold miner who fell in love with the dog. They ended up prospecting together so the problem was solved."

Mankle and Mouse went to Medford to see the movie *Star Wars* when it came out in 1977.

"We had a great time," he said. "Mouse definitely had that Yoda aura about him. He was always making me laugh. He always came up with the right comment when it was needed to cause levity. His timing was impeccable."

With Mouse's encouragement and instruction, Mankle learned to sport jump, something he enjoyed. But it isn't for everyone, he said, noting his daughter, when she became old enough to try sport jumping with him, took one jump and was done.

"That sudden altitude change when you are skydiving can be hard on your sinuses," he said.

Unfortunately, Mankle broke his ankle on a fire jump later in the '77 season, grounding him.

"That was over by Redmond. It wasn't big timber or big mountains. Mainly, it was a lot of reprod."

He was referring to young trees, using a forester's shorthand for young reproduction.

"The spotter saw this patch of young trees and that was our spot. I nailed the spot but what we couldn't see was a boulder under the trees that were about six feet tall. I broke my right ankle when I hit it. I had to crawl out of there."

He spent the rest of the year as a dispatcher. Later, he worked in the Grand Canyon on a helicopter construction crew, a challenging job given the lay of the land.

All told, Mankle made about 35 jumps, all in the Pacific Northwest.

"I loved jumping but I also liked the job and the guys I worked with," he said. "It was a job where you had to watch each other's back. Things could always go wrong in a hurry if you weren't careful. We had a lot of camaraderie."

And his former roommate helped build that important esprit de corps at the Siskiyou base, he stressed.

"Mouse not only did his work but he inspired me to push a little harder when the going got tough. He lived by example. I really appreciated that about him."

46

WHIRLYBIRD OPERATOR

WHEN DORCEY WINGO ARRIVED AT the Siskiyou Smoke-jumper Base in the spring of 1975, he wasn't exactly met with open arms.

"They called us 'rope sliders,'" recalled the helicopter pilot for a squad of rappelling firefighters who descended from the aircraft by rope. "We were excess baggage as far as a lot of the jumpers were concerned. They figured they could handle all the fires."

But Wingo figured there is a need for both airborne firefighters, depending on the fire's location.

"If the fire is close, we can get there real quick," he said. "But if the fire is 40 miles or farther away, they are going to beat us there. So we could do a lot of good things if we worked together."

Still, looking back on his one season at the base, Wingo was glad he spent time in what he says was a truly unique place.

"It was a riot. There was a great group of people here and good food in the mess hall. You couldn't beat it. I made some good friends at the Gobi."

Hailing from Duncan, Oklahoma, Wingo, now approaching his mid-70s, learned to fly helicopters after being drafted into the U.S. Army. Arriving in South Vietnam in March of 1969, the warrant officer flew out of the Pleiku air base in the central highlands, serving as a helicopter gunship pilot during the midst of the war. Returning to the states, he began working as a contract pilot, arriving at the Siskiyou base as a helicopter pilot for a squad of rappelling firefighters who descended on ropes from the hovering craft.

"We were part of a three-year contract but we only did the 1975 season at the Siskiyou base," he said, noting the contract crew and aircraft was relocated the following year to the Josephine County airport at Merlin, a small town about 35 miles north.

"Initially, there was some apprehension at high levels that jumpers and rappellers would not mix well, but the 18-man rappelling crew blended right in and each group called on the other for reinforcement frequently," according to the 1975 base log book. "They made a total of 100 rappels on 21 fires."

Overall, the fire season was relatively mild, it noted.

"I spent a lot of my time sitting in my hippie van drawing cartoon sketches while waiting for fires," Wingo recalled. "A few jumpers told me they didn't care for some of my sketches."

Like everyone who spent time at the base during that period, he became a friend of a fellow nicknamed Mouse.

"He was one of the guys who threw me into the gorge," he said of the irrigation ditch which once flowed across the rocky ground. "I had an engine lose oil pressure. I was operating a twin but the 212 doesn't fly very well on one engine so I had to get the boys back and do a running landing. It wouldn't hover very well with that kind of load on one engine. Of course, that was a first for me. And anytime you have a first on the base into the gorge you go."

Like all bound for the gorge, he was bound by tape and pitched into the water.

"You lay there and shiver. Your reproductive organ shrivels so it wouldn't be recognized by a medical doctor. Finally, Mouse, the safety officer of the gorge dumping operation, came along to make sure you were not intent on shooting anyone before cutting your bonds."

The log book noted that Dutton and Swift also received baths in the Gorge that year.

"In 1975, Dutton left to take the job of equipment specialist in Region 6's office in Portland," it reported. "Before leaving the Siskiyou base, he became the first Forest Service employee to make 300 jumps. He was promptly thrown into the 'Gobi Gorge' to make it official. He was followed by Mick Swift, chief instigator," it added.

Wingo only flew 35 hours while at the base, most of them as training exercises.

"The Siskiyou Smokejumper Base and its people were incredible," he said, adding, "It was really very special."

So was pilot Wingo, observed Ron Versteeg, a former rappeller before becoming a smokejumper.

"Dorcey was a really good pilot," Versteeg said. "When you rappelled when Dorcey was the pilot, it was like rappelling from a rock. He held the helicopter so steady, making rappelling safe for us. He was very, very good."

Wingo is the author of *The Rise and Fall of Captain Methane*, a powerful book published in 2010 about his 40 years of piloting helicopters, chalking up some 15,000 flying hours. Well told in a witty style, it tells of his flying adventures from Vietnam to Peru, Mexico to Alaska.

But it also includes a dead-serious in-depth chapter on the night of July 23, 1982, when he was piloting a Bell UH-1 helicopter hovering over the movie set in *Twilight Zone: The Movie* at the Indian Dunes ranch on the Santa Clara River in southern California. A blast from a pyrotechnic device intended to mimic a large mortar explosion tore off the tail-rotor, causing the low-flying aircraft to spin out of control. The crash killed actor Vic Morrow and two child actors, Myca Dinh Le and Renee Shin-Yi Chen, who were on the ground.

The incident, which was followed by a nine-month court case in which the filmmakers were acquitted, shook Wingo to the core.

"When things go horribly wrong and your flying machine cuts down three people on camera, there's no making it go away," Wingo wrote, adding, "It never goes away."

47

JUMPER FRIENDS
DROP IN

C ENTURIES AGO, LONG BEFORE FOLKS started plunging out of airplanes to fight wildfires, a Greek philosopher named Aristotle cautioned, "The guest will judge better of a feast than the cook." Despite his peculiar way of talking and the fact our subject at hand is not about food, you get his gist. To get a largely unbiased assessment of the Siskiyou Jumper Base and its former denizens, perhaps we ought to get the perspective of a couple of outsiders, preferably smokejumpers who trained elsewhere and never served as permanent denizens of the Gobi.

Ideally, these would be veteran smokejumpers proud to have jumped fire and lived to tell fire tales in retirement. In other words, we require gray-haired folks with gravitas in that courageous community of firefighters.

Fortunately, there are some who fit the bill.

Cowboy poet John Doran, who hangs his Stetson in his ranch house in a remote hamlet called Twisp in the northcentral outback of Washington state, has high praise for the Siskiyou base. The former smoke-jumper rookied in 1972 at the North Cascade Smokejumper Base at Winthrop, Wash.

"We were boosted down there around Labor Day when there was a fire bust in southern Oregon and northern California," he recalled of dropping in on the Siskiyou base during his first fire season. "After the fires were stopped, they sent most of the North Cascade guys home. But, because it was still dry and hunting season was coming up, they had me stay for about a month because they were a little short of jumpers."

That was fine with him since he enjoyed living at the Gobi and working with the Siskiyou jumpers.

"The North Cascade boys and the Cave Junction boys liked work-ing at each other's bases," he said. "Our bases were like brothers. They were both historically significant as among the first bases in the nation. So we considered ourselves brothers."

In fact, several of the towering figures at the Siskiyou base were linked to the North Cascade facility, he noted.

"Jim Allen was very instrumental at this [Siskiyou] base but he got his start at North Cascades," Doran said. "There were a lot of simi-larities between the two bases. Others bases, like Missoula and Mc-Call, they were fine but they weren't the same kind of bases. They didn't have the heart and soul this place had."

Both the Siskiyou and North Cascade bases had fewer than 50 jumpers when he was jumping, he said.

"The North Cascades had the first practice jumps and the second fire jumps in the history of smokejumping," Doran said. "When I jumped in the '70s, that was when these two bases were at their peak. In the early '70s, these two bases were primo. They had great jumpers."

Doran, who stands 6' 2", although he will tell you he is actually 5' 14," knew Mouse.

"I loved the man. Mouse and Mick were always investing in some-thing and they were up at the North Cascades in '73. They tried to con-vince me to invest in Scotch whiskey. They would buy a cask that was in a warehouse. It would later be sold and they would make their profit from that. Well, I was 20 years old and I couldn't even buy whiskey.

"But I went out drinking with Mouse a couple of times," he added. "He was one entertaining character."

Doran, who jumped for three fire seasons, broke his right leg on his 82nd jump.

"That was my last jump. It was my fault. I hit a tree wrong. I swung into the tree and put my foot up to try to take some of the shock."

He would recover and eventually retire as a structure firefighter, a career he enjoyed despite not being able to drop down from a parachute.

"I always liked working with jumpers because they have a certain mentality about getting the job done. It was a hazardous, intense job that they did well. And this base did it very well."

Murry Taylor couldn't agree more. And after 375 jumps over 27 fire seasons, including 205 fire jumps and 170 practice jumps, he certainly has gravitas in the annals of smokejumping.

"All the jumper bases had their best years and their best times," Taylor observed. "But when the Siskiyou base was at its best, it was the best of them all. It had a heart and a spirit. Those guys had such a great bond. They worked hard together and played hard together."

Taylor knows of what he speaks. Not only is he a veteran wildlands firefighter, he is also a forester and a wildland fire consultant who has taught "fire school," rudimentary lessons in fighting wildfires to his forested neighbors in northern California. In addition, he is a prolific author who has written three books, including *Jumping Fire*, a highly-regarded memoir of his smokejumping adventures in Alaska.

In the beginning of *Jumping Fire*," he quoted Joseph Campbell who noted, "What we are all really seeking is an experience where we can feel the rapture of being alive."

"I think smokejumping had moments where the rapture of being alive was so completely clear," Taylor said. "I remember many times as a smokejumper having that sudden realization that this is where I'm supposed to be, exactly with the people I'm supposed to be with, doing exactly what I'm supposed to be doing. That happened many times."

Having boosted out of the Siskiyou base on several occasions, he is a student of the Gobi crew.

"Its success had a lot to do with Dee Dutton but more than any other single individual it had to do with Mick," he said. "Mick Swift was the leader unofficially. And Dee was a strong enough guy to recognize that. He and Mick got along really well. They were two really tough guys who worked well with others."

To digress for a moment, both Delos Dutton and Eldo Swift were christened with unusual first names which conceivably helped toughen them up during their formative years, ala "A Boy Named Sue" song of Johnny Cash fame.

Back to Taylor's perspective on what made the Siskiyou base special.

"At a lot of bases, the leadership was straight out of the military," he said. "We would have military-type PT. When you asked someone why we were going to do something, it was 'Because I said so.' They made us do 'busy' work."

At the Siskiyou base, although it may have had a more militaristic air before the Dutton and Swift era which Taylor saw as Gobi's best years, jumpers were largely free to their own devices once all the work like base and equipment maintenance was done, he said.

"They did not make you do 'busy work' when there wasn't a fire bust. They had the most progressive base. They had esprit de corps. They were a happy, happy family."

What's more, they were an inclusive bunch, he stressed.

"Other bases would work to exclude people who were marginal, maybe not that strong, but the Siskiyou base worked to include people. When Redmond couldn't get along with Dave Laws and thought he was a rebel, treated him punitively, that was the kind of guy that Mick wanted. He had an eye for the 'Dirty Dozen.'"

The point, he stressed, was what mattered was whether the jumper was good at the very tough job at hand of leaping into a rugged area and fighting a fire before it could ignite into a costly and devastating explosion.

"There was great heart at the Siskiyou. Those guys came back year after year. They had the sweetest get-along of any base."

Again, he cited Swift as the fatherly figure who reached out to befriend folks, including visiting jumpers.

"When we would go over there and land, turn around right in front of the jump shack and shut the motors off, by the time the door opened, Mick Swift was right there at the bottom of the steps, greeting us and shaking hands," he said. "He shook hands with everyone coming off that plane like you were the King of England. The lowest rookie received the same greeting. It made people feel good. Mick loved people."

Born in 1941, Taylor was reared on a farm west of Fresno, California. Perhaps the fact his great grandmother was a Choctaw Indian influenced his love of the outdoors, he observed.

"I don't know if your love for nature comes through your DNA or not," he mused. "But when I was a little kid, I used to stand out in the field and stare at the mountains in the distance. My folks liked to camp in the mountains, something I really loved. On one of our trips home, we passed this little cabin with a jeep out front, a wood pile and a chimney with smoke coming out. I thought, 'There is the luckiest guy in the world.' As soon as I got old enough I went to mountains and got a job working for the Forest Service."

While working for the agency, he began fighting wildfires as a ground pounder.

"That to me was the most exciting part of the job. There was rushing to the scene, the urgency of getting important work done, the helicopters and air tankers roaring overhead. In the mornings I'd be flying in a helicopter back toward the John Muir Wilderness and watch the sun come up over the Sierras. I thought it was wonderful.

"Then one day I was responding to a fire up near Jackass Meadows and heard on the [agency] radio there were smokejumpers jumping the fire," he added. "There was a DC-3 on final up against the deep blue Sierra sky. Out they came, orange and white parachutes. I thought, 'That's got to be the most fun way to go to a fire.'"

The spring of 1965 found him training at the Redding Smokejumper Base in northern California to prepare for leaping out of airplanes to land near a remote fire and put it out before it blew up into a conflagration.

"I've always thought about what made smokejumping so great for so many of us," Taylor said. "First of all, it was a journey back to nature. We had to deal with nature on her terms. Back when I started, we never got much support from airtankers. We were put into a lot of situations where everyone had to dig deep. There was a tremendous bonding that took place."

When he wasn't jumping to fight wildfires, Taylor earned a degree in forestry from Humboldt State University in Arcata, Calif. He would jump throughout the West, including Alaska.

Taylor is also the only smokejumper – I'd bet my first born male son on this if I had one – who has been kicked in the gonads by a U.S. senator. While many will swear they have been figuratively booted in that sensitive spot by a member of Congress, he quite literally was by the late Alaska U.S. Sen. Ted Stevens, then the senior senator from Alaska and a fellow known for being brash.

"Senator Stevens came to our jump shack," Taylor said of the smokejumper base at Fort Wainwright. "One of our bosses had me suit up and explain how everything worked to the senator. He asked me what that cross strap was."

Stevens was referring to the thick strap protecting the crotch of the jump suit.

"My boss told him that the strap goes down into the boots and prevents a jumper from getting hurt if he lands on a branch," Taylor said. "Then he said, 'Show him how it works, Murry. Spread your legs.' Then the senator – wham! – kicked me right in the crotch."

True story, one reported as a humorous blurb in the national Bureau of Land Management newsletter at the time. Thanks to the strap, Taylor didn't double over, although he was more than a little surprised. While the senator was known for verbally kicking folks in the crotch, it is likely the only recorded time he actually kicked anyone in the nuts as a senator.

But the lion's share of Taylor's smokejumping adventures were more pleasant.

"I remember jumping with Mouse up on a fire near the Devil's Punch Bowl in the Siskiyous," he said of a mountain range along the Oregon-California state line. "On the pack out, he walked in front of me. From the back, it looked like the fire pack box was only about a foot or so off the ground. You could only see the top of his helmet and the flick of his boot heel. It was like a walking, talking fire pack box."

Taylor chuckled at the memory of a jumper that everyone liked and respected.

"He was a talker," he said. "When Mouse was up, he was hilariously funny. But he always did his job."

People like Mouse and other colorful characters at the Siskiyou base was what made it unique, he reiterated.

"The Siskiyou had great influence on the history of smokejumping and the direction it took in a real important time," Taylor said. "It was a tragedy when it was sold down the river and closed."

THE MOUSE THAT SOARED

48

UPHILL BATTLE

WHEN THEY WEREN'T JUMPING FIRES, the Siskiyou smokejumpers were often kept busy sprucing up the base. In 1977, jumpers Gary Thornhill and Gary Mills were told by base manager Terry Mewhinney to cover the interior pine boards in the headquarters with paneling.

"I really didn't want to cover this fine wood but Mewhinney made me," reads the tongue-in-cheek graffiti signed by both jumpers and uncovered when the paneling was removed years later as part of a restoration effort.

While in jest, the note could have been hung on the proverbial horns of a dilemma that Mewhinney was caught on at the time. He was the head of the base the Forest Service was soon bent on closing.

"We all felt bad about it," Mewhinney said of the pending base closure. "I had to do a balancing act. By then, I was well advanced in my career. If I came out too damn strong against it, they would can my ass."

So Mewhinney attempted to thread the needle, causing him to be squeezed by both sides. The bottom line was that he had what was arguably the toughest job at the base.

Born in Grants Pass, he moved down to California as a youngster with his parents where he completed high school.

"I moved back up to Oregon as soon as I was out on my own," he said, noting he missed the great outdoors of his native state. "I had some friends who lived up Galice Creek and they had some friends who worked on the Galice Ranger District. I got a job on the fire suppression crew."

That was in 1961. For three fire seasons, he gained valuable experience as a ground-pounding firefighter responding to lightning or human-caused wildfires.

"In 1964, I got a call from my friend Tommy Smith, a jumper at the smokejumper base," Mewhinney said, referring to the well-liked jumper who died while crossing the lower Illinois River during a packout in May of 1967. "He said, 'Hey, we had three rookies who washed out. You should come down here and try out.' So I tried out and got a job."

Like so many rookies, he had never been in an airplane before he jumped out of one with a parachute. And, like many before him, turns out he was a natural.

"With every jump you are a little nervous but I loved jumping," said Mewhinney who jumped for five fire seasons. All told, he made 125 jumps. Aside from getting slightly dinged up a couple of times, he emerged from his jumping career largely unscathed.

"Like everybody, I sometimes landed in trees. You usually tried to land in a reprod [reproduction] patch if you could. But I never really had any problems with trees. You always had your let-down rope. Of course, you had to go back and get your parachute."

But he relished the time he served as a smokejumper at the base.

"Smokejumping, I loved it," Mewhinney said. "Every time I flew over the country and saw a lake, I always thought we could be down there in a few minutes.

"I loved to go fishing and hunting as a kid," he added. "I suppose the love of the outdoors was one reason I wanted to become a jumper. That, and the adventure. I liked the challenge of it. Fighting fire just fascinated the heck out of me. And it was a good living."

While he enjoyed smokejumping, he also wanted to further his career. In 1970, he took a Forest Service job in Klamath Falls east of the Cascade Range. When the manager's job became available at the Siskiyou Smokejumper Base, he applied and was hired. He held the post from 1976 until 1980 when he was succeeded by Gary Mills, ironically one of the wooden note signers.

"Terry Mewhinney had been the base manager before me and he had been trying to upgrade the place," Mills said. "But that was an uphill battle."

"I struggled when I was there as the manager," Mewhinney acknowledged. "The time I was managing the base, the Vietnam war was just over. So we had a whole bunch of Vietnam vets who were not happy with the government at all. Many were college graduates – very smart – and me not having a college degree. So I struggled."

It was a far different world than that faced by legendary base manager Jim Allen, he observed.

"Jim had his act together – he was a good thinker," he said of the fellow who hired him as a smokejumper.

In retrospect, Mewhinney figures he would have done some things differently.

"One of my mistakes, and one shared by other managers before me, was that we weren't active enough in the community," he said of the greater Illinois Valley. "We had one boss who made us jumpers dig up rocks and then bury the damn things for exercise. But if we had gone out and done things like cut wood to give to elderly people, we would have gotten our exercise as well as made a better rapport with local people."

Moreover, they should have reached out repeatedly to local residents beyond baseball games and the like, he said.

"Why I didn't do that is beyond me," he said.

The point, he said, is that the local residents would have gone to bat to keep the base open. Instead, the focus was too often on the negative.

"There used to be a tavern down by the state line," he said of a bar just south of the California line. "Well, the jumpers were drinking there, then went outside and mooned the traffic going by."

Even in the rough-edged region in the late 1970s, full grown men exposing their posteriors to passersby raised more than a few eyebrows, he noted.

"God, did I hear about that – I was the manager at the time," he said. "For weeks I got complaints."

Other issues took their toll on the morale, he said. For instance, when rappellers arrived in the region, it didn't go well, he recalled.

"The smokejumpers didn't care for them because they took fires away from jumpers. They were getting the fires that were closer to the base, taking work away from us."

Meanwhile, the food at the cookhouse was very good but there was a problem, he said.

"A lot of the guys didn't like to eat there because we took the food out of their pay. If you ate morning, noon and night, there was a hell of a lot coming out of your pay. They hated that and I don't blame them."

But when the agency announced it was closing the base, that was the death knell for smokejumper esprit de corps, he observed.

"Mouse was really outspoken against it," he said. "He talked to anyone who would listen about how he felt it was a wrong decision. But he wasn't the only one. Just about everyone was upset."

But Mewhinney preferred to accentuate the positive when reflecting on the base he once called home.

"It was a lot of the little things you took for granted, things like volleyball," he said. "It was one of the best ways to keep in shape we had. It kept everyone agile and limber and strengthened their bones. And you had to do pushups every time someone made a point."

Then there were the people, folks like Glenda Marchant who taught him how to repair parachutes.

"That was such a cool thing to learn," he said. "She was a real asset out there."

Many others also made a difference, he said.

"Mouse was a really, really nice guy," Mewhinney said. "He was all for jumpers, but not so much for management."

Although noting he didn't hang out with Mouse very much, he stressed the short jumper was a friend to all.

"He was definitely one of the best-liked smokejumpers on the base. You would see him driving his blue Corvette around. He would stop and talk to the pilots and everyone. Everybody liked him. And he was busy all the time, doing stuff."

Like many other jumpers, he said Mick Swift was the most talented jumper he ever met.

"And Chuck Mansfield was so interesting to talk to," he said. "Chuck was always going out and looking for caves. He found holes in the ground where air was blowing out. I liked stuff like that. I wish I had gone out with him when he was doing that."

He stopped talking for a moment as he thought about the base where he spent part of his life.

"It had a lot of good things going for it," he said, adding, "We had a lot of really good people there."

One of the two new smokejumpers to arrive at the Siskiyou base in 1980 agreed. He was Tom Hunnicutt, a transfer from the Redding Smokejumper Base where he had been a rookie in 1978.

"I was one of the very last new guys to go to the Cave Junction base," Hunnicutt said. "After the '78 fire season, I got married and we had a baby so I didn't come back and jump in '79. But I had that itch so I applied in '80 and Cave Junction picked me up."

He and fellow transfer Patrick Withen, who also jumped at the Siskiyou base in '81, were the only new jumpers at the base in 1980. There were no rookies that year. In 1981, there was only one transfer in Jerry J. Hunter and, again, no rookies.

"It was only five months out of my life, but my experience at the base really touched my life," Hunnicutt said. "The smokejumpers there were an impressive group of guys with some good leaders. And everyone had a great sense of humor."

Although new to the base, Hunnicutt, a Navy veteran, was no neophyte at fighting wildfires.

"I had the desire when I was younger to fight fires," said the Butte,

Mont., native who later lived in New Jersey and the Bay Area. "After I graduated from Sonoma State (University) in '74, I started hitchhiking with the intention of getting a job as a firefighter."

He found work at the Six Rivers National Forest in northern California. "They hired me on as a temporary," he said. "But I came back and worked for two more years on a tanker truck. The next year I applied with the Mendicino Hotshots and was hired. Then I met the woman who would become my wife."

After he received a post card from the Redding base, asking him to apply, he talked it over with his wife.

"She said go for it," he said. "Becoming a smokejumper takes it another step. They have a lot of good qualities."

Hunnicutt, who has a degree in psychology, noted that he was barely tall enough and heavy enough to qualify as a smokejumper.

"But when I first started out, I looked at guys training me and these were people I felt I could trust. They jumped all the time. If they could do it, I could do it. I had respect for what we were doing but no fear. If you have fear, you aren't going to be a good jumper."

Mouse excelled at smokejumping in part because he had conquered any fear he had of leaping into thin air to battle a fire below, he said.

"Mouse was an incredible person," he recalled. "He and Troop were best friends. I was fortunate to have been there when they were at their peak."

He recalled jumping with Mouse in early August of 1980 on a fire just north of Grants Pass.

"I had just jumped a fire the day before so when the siren went off, I'm thinking I'm not going to go on this one. The first plane load took off and they dropped them. Mouse was in that group. Then they wanted more jumpers. I went but I still didn't have my head in it. First two guys went out, then the second two and it dawned on me that I'm going to jump this fire."

Unfortunately, the static line caught his right arm, yanking it up against his helmet.

"Bam! My arm hit my helmet really hard," he said. "But I look up and saw that I got a good chute. With my left arm, I managed to steer to the spot. My right arm was hanging limp. I couldn't swing a tool when I landed."

Unfortunately, Mouse had slammed into a boulder, bunging up a knee.

"Troop was the fire boss and the first jumpers had gotten a line on one side of the fire," Hunnicutt said, noting he and Mouse, unable to dig fire line, were instructed to burn out the vegetation between the fire line and the fire.

"We started burning out – there was fire everywhere. I'm looking at Mouse. He remained cool. We continued burning out. The two fires came together and just settled down. By that time, ground crews started to come in and they asked us to stick around because there was an incredible amount of snags. Willie Lowden, he could put trees down anywhere you needed them to go. We jumpers stopped that fire. And Troop had put the plan together."

The fire was Aug. 4 just north of Grants Pass, according to the entry in the 1980 logbook. Two planes dropping eight jumpers each were deployed, it noted.

"Tom Hunnicutt had a close encounter of the static line and got a beautiful bruise on his upper arm," the log reported. "He finished out the time on the fire but then took a couple of days off to recuperate a bit. Mouse caught a downdraft just before impact on this fire and bounced down a hillside. We thought he'd be out for the season with a messed up knee. But he heals faster than we gave him credit for. In a couple of weeks he was back on the jump list."

Out of the 30 jumps he made in his two seasons as a smokejumper, that was the only time when he was injured, Hunnicutt said.

"Mouse taught me to rig parachutes towards the end of the season," he said of learning how to inspect, repair and pack parachutes. "That's standard for second year jumpers to learn how to rig parachutes. When we had fires going, we were in the parachute loft, rigging chutes. When it came time for us to be qualified, he made the arrangements and drove us to Medford to the FAA office."

While he and the other jumper took a written test and demonstrated physically that they were capable of rigging parachutes, Mouse sat patiently in his blue Corvette.

"We both passed," Hunnicutt said. "Afterwards, we went out and had dinner to celebrate. It was a good memory to end the season."

49

SISKIYOU BASE CLOSES

A FTER THE REDMOND AND REDDING bases were established in 1964 and 1957 respectively, they overshadowed the older Siskiyou Smokejumper Base, observed 1949 rookie Al Boucher.

"Both the Redmond and Redding bases overlapped Cave Junction," he said. "So their calls for fires were really going down. It wasn't busy like it used to be in the early days. They were also known for speaking their mind, something that didn't set too well with the big bosses."

All things considered, he figured it was a needed facility.

"Sometimes someone would tell me they should have closed that base earlier because there were no real fires in the area while the base was there," he said. "And I would tell them, 'You just said it. There were no big fires because we put them out.' After the base was closed, there were a lot of big fires."

During the Siskiyou base's final year, Gary Mills served as manager.

"I was basically sitting on the place while they were shutting it down," he said of 1981. "It wasn't a lot of fun."

With the powers that be bent on closing the base, serving as the base manager in the waning years would have obviously been a thankless job. After all, the manager was caught between bureaucrat pressure and smokejumpers not afraid to voice their opposition to closing the historic base.

"They made the decision to close it but they didn't take any action for a long time because there was so much resistance, both on the base and outside of the base," Mills said. "Some in the Forest Service were opposed to closing it and there were quite a few in the public sector who were also upset it was going to close."

Several factors entered into the decision, including the cost of upgrading the site with a new loft and other improvements, he said.

"And they didn't place a lot of value on the Kalmiopsis," he said of the wilderness. "Most of the high-priced timber was in the Umpqua and Willamette forests."

Yet Mills recalls many holding out hope the base would survive the cut.

"Towards the end we jumped a lot of fires and had a lot of outside jumpers come in. We supported overhead teams out of the base. We had a lot of activity. We were very proud of what we accomplished. But the Region 6 office in Portland didn't want to hear good stories out of the base. And it was tough to get people to write letters in support of the operation."

Several jumpers were blackballed by the Forest Service as a result of their outspoken opposition to closing the base, Mills said.

"There is no question they did not want Mouse or Troop – too vocal. I had to tell them that the bottom line is 'They don't want you at the base anymore'"

Actually, by 1981, Mills was also under pressure to leave the base.

"They wanted to get rid of me, too," he said. "I was pretty much sidelined. By then, I had also messed up my knee."

Mills, then a GS 9, was able to land a job as a GS 8 at Detroit Lake west of Eugene, a job he enjoyed.

"When I was at the base, I didn't think I could work anyplace else for the Forest Service," said Mills who would retire from the agency. "But I had a great time at Detroit. My boss was kind of a hard-nosed guy but he and I got along very well."

Emonds recalled the day when Mills told him and Mouse that they were being blackballed by the Forest Service because of their outspoken efforts to save the base.

"Mouse and I knew what we were: loudmouth agitators speaking out against closing the base," Emonds said. "That's why we got blackballed from the Forest Service."

The problem with smokejumpers is that they were independent minded, he said, noting that was particularly true with the Siskiyou crew.

"If you are in a fire somewhere and the person in charge doesn't have a plan that works, smokejumpers are apt to say, 'To hell with that,' and do what needs to be done," he said. "Well, that doesn't set too well with someone back in an office. That was one of the reasons the base was closed."

He recalled a meeting between smokejumpers and decision makers from the Region 6 office in Portland.

"When some smokejumpers started yelling and screaming at them, I didn't do that, even though I probably had a reputation for just that," he said. "But I really think it wasn't so much to cut costs as to cut out a base that was considered hard to control because the smokejumpers weren't afraid to say what they thought."

Larry Owen echoed similar sentiments.

"My brother and Troop and some others got riled up and took on the heavies in the Forest Service to try to keep that base open," he recalled. "Not only did the base mean a lot to them but they also knew it was a money saver in terms of stopping fires before they got big and really expensive to fight."

Like his smokejumping brethren, Ron Versteeg felt it was a bad move when the Forest Service decided to close the base.

"I felt it was a real mistake," he said. "It was also sad to see it happening."

Not surprisingly, he supported reopening the base.

"I'm an old guy out of touch who hasn't been on a fire for more than 30 years," Versteeg said. "But the best time to stop a fire is when it is little. Once it gets big, it becomes a force of nature. When that happens, the only thing that is going to put it out is nature. You can run bulldozers and airtankers and all kinds of fire crews but you really need to get there early. With smokejumpers, you can do that. Every minute counts."

When the Siskiyou base was in operation, smokejumpers were expected to be in the air within five minutes of a fire siren screaming, he noted.

"A strong initial attack is necessary if you are serious about stopping a fire when it starts. You get six guys jumping and six more on the way. You can do a lot of good. I don't get the mindset that we were somehow saving money by closing the base"

Logging may help in some instances but it is not the solution to reduce wildfires, he offered.

"If you want to see a fire burn hot, watch a fire go through logging slash," he said. "Or watch it go through a tree plantation where all the trees are five feet tall – all the same height. The fire will just explode."

Old growth trees withstand a wildfire better than young thickets, he noted. What's more, smokejumpers bailing out of a fixed wing aircraft are better able to get to a remote wildfire quicker than anyone else, he added.

"I'll always believe this base could do a lot of good if it is reopened," he said.

To a man, former Siskiyou jumpers will tell you that closing the base was shortsighted.

"It's common sense," Gary Thornhill observed at the tail end of the summer of 2017 which was a horrendous fire season. "Take the fires we had. If they had a Beech 99 that could load six guys, they could have had six guys on any of those fires in southern Oregon within half an hour. They could have put those fires out.

"They used to call the Siskiyou the asbestos forest because when there was a fire, we launched," he added, then reiterated, "Just common sense."

50

JUMPING IN THE
FAR NORTH

I N THE 30 FIRE SEASONS that John Dube spent smokejumping, he met countless colorful characters who thrived at living on the edge. But there was one who stood head and shoulders above the rest.

"Al Owen – he was one of a kind," Dube said."My first impression of him was one that stayed with me all these years. He was quite a talker. You see, I'm kind of a quiet guy and Mouse was not quiet. When I wanted quiet I sure didn't get it when Mouse was around."

But he was smiling as he recalled his loquacious friend.

"All the while I knew Mouse, it was that way," he added. "On the other hand, I didn't need a lot of attention. So that made it perfect for me and Mouse to work together. He was always very entertaining."

The two first met as rookies in 1970 when Dube, a rookie at the Redmond Smokejumper Base, served as a booster at the Siskiyou base where Mouse was also in his rookie season. They also spent Mouse's last fire season together as fellow jumpers in Alaska.

"We were interchangeable," Dube said of the Redmond and Siskiyou bases. "When Redmond was built, the idea was it was going to be 'THE' base for Region 6. They were going to consolidate the Cave Junction base and the North Cascade base, centering it all on the new Redmond base. But there was quite a lobby not to close those two bases."

Born in Corvallis in 1949, Dube graduated from Phoenix High School in the Rogue Valley in 1967. After working as a ground-pounding firefighter for the U.S. Forest Service and a stint as a structural firefighter for the Corvallis Fire Department, he applied as a smokejumper at the Siskiyou base.

"Back then, you listed your first and second choices," he recalled. "Well, they didn't have any openings in Cave Junction or McCall, my second choice. But McCall told me they had forwarded my application to Redmond which had some openings."

As it happened, in addition to Jim Allen, Redmond also had former Siskiyou jumper Al Boucher as foreman and future Siskiyou jumper Dave Laws as trainer of the rookies.

"Dave really intimidated us," Dube said of his rookie training. "He used to take us on runs out into the high desert out there when it would be 110 degrees in the sun. We'd be dropping. He was like a rabbit running out through the sage brush. And then he would stop and have a cigarette."

After four fire seasons at Redmond, Dube decided to head north to jump in Alaska for the U.S. Bureau of Land Management's jumper base at Fort Wainwright near Fairbanks.

"I didn't fit well with the Forest Service – it was too regimented and very good old boy. I was done with them and they were done with me. I found my home with Alaska smokejumpers. It was where I needed to be."

What's more, Dube, who jumped 26 fire seasons in Alaska, saw in base foreman Al Dutton an excellent boss whose gut instinct invariably landed right on the drop zone when it came to hiring new jumpers.

"In my mind, he had a certain amount of genius to pick up a lot of 'rejects' from the Forest Service," Dube said. "These were guys, mainly from the Cave Junction base, who didn't quite fit in the Forest Service model. But their independence and willingness to speak their mind was what made the Alaskan smokejumpers."

When Mouse arrived in Alaska with Gary Buck and Tom "Trooper Tom" Emonds, Dube was already a veteran Alaskan jumper, having jumped in the Far North for half a dozen years.

Incidentally, Emonds recalled that Dutton had contacted him to see if he and Buck wanted to jump for the BLM in Alaska.

"I got a call from Al Dutton up in Alaska who offered us jobs as smokejumpers," Emonds said, adding that Mouse wanted to stay and fight the agency. "Me and some other guys drove up to Alaska without Mouse. We were devastated he wasn't with us. When we walked into Al's office he said he just got clearance to offer Mouse a job. But he said the job may not be there tomorrow. So Gary Buck and I went to a phone booth – they still had phone booths in those days – and called Mouse. We told him to take the job or we were going to tape him up and haul him up there. He took the job."

For a moment, Dube pondered how to describe the Siskiyou smokejumpers.

"They were strong-minded individuals which made for a very unique group dynamic. They had a very tight group. They were a bit socially isolated from the rest of the smokejumper bases. Maybe that was because the base was a little smaller than the other bases. Whatever the reason, they were definitely an independent bunch."

That brought to mind an incident following a fire jump he made in the Ochoco National Forest in Oregon.

"Afterwards, we got a ride back with the district ranger who was taking us to the Redmond base," Dube said. "We started talking and he brought up smokejumpers and other firefighters he had worked with. He told me, 'Smokejumpers are OK, as long as you use them in their place of putting out small fires. But, I have a big fire that is cooking, I want a hotshot crew. That way I get 20 firefighters. If I order up 20 smokejumpers, I just get 20 opinions.'

"I didn't take that badly," Dube added. "Independence was our biggest asset. We were a cast of characters."

And he freely acknowledged he fit into that category.

"Hey, I'm a true dinosaur," said the avid reader. "I've never had a TV or telephone. I've never had a credit card. I've never eaten a McDonald's hamburger. And I've never been in a Walmart store."

While not suggesting other jumpers he knew were of the same mindset, he reiterated that they were all independent minded.

"We needed to be different – I think that set us apart," he said, adding, "As I got older, I realized that a lot of people look back on their life's work and don't feel good about it. I felt good about doing work that suited me. I think a lot of jumpers feel that way. Certainly Mouse liked what he was doing."

Like others who jumped with Mouse, Dube noted that short stature did not hinder his work ethic.

"The weight that guy could pack for his size was amazing. We were in awe of that. He was very strong. I don't think I ever heard anyone complaining that he didn't carry his share of the work load.

"In jumping, you either contribute or you don't last," he added. "It may be that one person's weakness is another person's strength. Mouse would not have been around if he wasn't carrying his weight. I remember we had some difficult jobs and we would ask for Mouse because of his size. I remember hoisting him up in a tree that we couldn't climb but one he could. I can see him now standing up there on a limb and remember thinking, 'I'm glad he's up there and not me.'"

In Alaska, the trees were not as large as those in Oregon or northern California, he noted.

"For the most part, we didn't have the 200-foot trees to deal with or a lot of rocks to land on," he said. "But we had more water landings in Alaska and we also had more hypothermia to deal with because of exposure to the elements. And we went without food and (potable) water for longer periods of time. So it all evened out."

Although Dube never jumped east of the Rockies, he jumped a few fires in western Canada.

"The Siskiyou base had some of the roughest jump country in the Lower 48," he said. "It was always a challenge."

In the summer of 1977, Dube had only one day off, thanks to a ferocious firefighting year.

"Of course, it isn't the season that determines how hard it is but the fire and the terrain it is in. But I liked the grab bag nature of smokejumping. It was totally grab bag who you were thrown in with and where you were going. And fires were all different from season to season."

By the by, Dube is only the second person I've ever met who has been to the remote village of Lower Kalskag in Alaska, a place I visited as a journalist in the mid-1980s. The first was a dentist from Alaska who I happened to meet in 1999 in Danang, Vietnam, of all places.

"Well, since I jumped for 26 seasons in Alaska, I got to see more of that state than most people," Dube was quick to observe. "Most of it was in the interior but we even jumped down on Afognak Island."

For the Alaska challenged, Afognak is immediately north of Kodiak Island.

After Dube quit fighting fires, he continued working for the U.S. Department of Interior in its cultural studies section in the Alaskan outback. His work included archaeological surveys on public lands.

"I don't remember the last time I jumped with Mouse," he said of 1981. "But it seems to me we had gone down from Alaska to backup just before Mouse died early that September."

By then, most of the Alaskan jumpers had already stood down since nearly all the firefighting they were still doing would be boosting bases down in the Lower 48, he explained.

"But I remember the very day Mouse died," he said. "Louie Reister, who was a former North Cascades jumper, was the one who told me about Mouse's accident. I was out at a little night spot we used to go to after work. Louie came in and said, 'I've got some real bad news.' It was unbelievable to even think that Mouse was gone.

"And I remember one of the first things I asked, 'Is Troop OK,'" he said of one of Mouse's best friends. "We couldn't do anything about Mouse but we were worried about his friends. And he had a lot of them."

51

MOUSE MAKES
HIS FINAL JUMP

W HEN LARRY OWEN CONTEMPLATES HIS big brother's death, he tries to accentuate the positive.

"We had a lot of discussions about him sport jumping," he said. "He told me once, 'Someday I may jump out of a plane and not make it. But remember that I was having fun.' I suppose that made his death a little easier for me to accept. But it was still hard. He was only 38 when he died. He is dearly missed.

"He was so helpful to a lot of people," he added. "He was so fun to be around. He had a great sense of humor. I'll always miss him."

He paused for a moment to remember the man many fondly knew as Mouse.

"He was like a shooting star, not some dim thing up there in the sky that lasts forever. That's how he looked at life. He lived on the edge, that's for sure."

Allen "Mouse" Dale Owen was born in 1943, the same year as the upstart Siskiyou Smokejumper Base. Tragically, he died in a jumping accident in Alaska on Sept. 6, 1981, just as the base was completing its final jumping season. Coincidence? Surely, but it does give one pause.

When he died, the Alaska Smokejumpers based at Fort Wainwright released a statement about the incident leading to his death that Sunday afternoon at the North Pole Skydiving Club about 20 mile south of Fairbanks. He had been participating in a contest in which four-person teams attempt to form various hook-up patterns while in freefall from 8,000 feet, it noted.

"On his fatal jump, Allen's team successfully formed five separate patterns, capturing the weekend record," it stated. "At 3,000 feet, immediately after their parachutes had opened, Allen and another jumper collided with each other. They both were using square ram-air canopies which have considerable forward speed."

After the collision, Mouse's canopy malfunctioned, causing a strong spin, according to the statement.

"Apparently, his lines were entangled with his body, preventing him from jettisoning his main canopy which would allow a safe, clean path for his reserve deployment," it read. "At 500 feet, his canopy collapsed completely. Observers saw his reserve chute flash out and entangle into his main parachute lines. His reserve parachute never did deploy."

A registered nurse at the scene attempted resuscitation without success, it added.

"None of us here at the Alaska Smokejumpers can really comprehend that Mouse is gone," the statement concluded. "He was our cheerful friend and one of the toughest, most careful and skilled smokejumpers. Mouse has become a legend with the whole smokejumper world, not only because of his small size and powerful strength, but because of his vivacious spirit. Mouse lived more fully, did more things, was more active than any one of us. We will miss him."

At the time, Allen, who had become an airplane pilot in Oregon, had just been hired to serve as a co-pilot delivering supplies to the oil fields on Alaska's North Slope, his brother said.

"He was going to work as a commercial pilot," Larry said. "He had just stopped at Fort Wainwright to do some sport jumping. But the minute you put other people in the sky it becomes dangerous, especially if you are sport jumping with people who aren't as experienced. It was so devastating to lose him like that."

On the day Mouse died, Don Bell, his roommate during the 1981 Alaskan fire season, was working as a deckhand on a tug boat on the Yukon River.

"I found out what happened to Mouse when we got into port in Nanana, 50 miles south of Fairbanks," recalled Bell who was 33 at the time. "I drove up to Fairbanks and got very drunk. I know getting drunk didn't help but I felt so bad about his death.

"Mouse was a wonderful person who went the extra mile. He was a hard worker. You could find no better person to work with. But he was also a good man, a good friend."

The author of *Barge Notes*, a book based on a journal he kept as a deckhand on the Yukon River tugboat, Bell jumped for 12 fire seasons, making about 100 fire jumps. He lives on the northern Oregon coast.

Hailing from North Carolina, Bell was about 12 years old when he met a smokejumper and decided that was the job for him. After high school, he was accepted as a rookie in 1969 at the smokejumper base in McCall, Idaho. But he took a break from smokejumping the following year to serve as a wilderness ranger in the Wind River Mountains of Wyoming.

He traveled north to Alaska in 1971 to return to smokejumping at the Wainright base, staying through the 1981 fire season which ended for the Alaskan smokejumpers in early August that year. When Mouse arrived at the base in the spring of '81, he chose Bell as his roommate in the barracks.

"Mouse jumped his very first fire that year with me. We got a call to a fire on the banks of the middle fork of the Koyukuk River. It was a small fire, one we figured was started by a survey crew who had built a warming fire which they didn't put out and it started spreading.

"I landed on a gravel bar and Mouse landed in a tree," he added. "The trees up there aren't very tall but Mouse was trained to do a let down and started to let his rope down. I don't think he could see over the top of his helmet to see how high he was. That's when I told him that he was only about three feet off the ground."

After they both had a good laugh, Bell, who stands 6' 2", reached up to help his friend down sans the letdown rope

"We put that fire out pretty quickly. While we were working on it we hear this helicopter which landed on the gravel bar. And this tall Texan gets out and asks, 'Are you boys smokejumpers?' We said, 'Yeah.' And he says, 'What time do you want dinner?' He told us he was from a pipeline camp that was fairly close."

Since all they had to eat were boring C-rations, the two smoke-jumpers were ecstatic at the prospect of a hot meal. The pipeline camp cook did not disappoint.

"When the guy came back, he had two plates with two steaks in each one along with a baked potato and corn on the cob. Not only that but there was also a tall, cold Budweiser for each of us. Mouse couldn't believe it. We were both so tickled."

Before leaving, their newfound friend gave them a radio to enable them to contact the camp should they need any help.

"He told us there was a grizzly bear coming down the river. He said, 'If he bothers you, we'll come over in the helicopter and chase him off.'"

The bruin was a no show and the two made short work of the fire, Bell recalled.

"We slept on the banks of that beautiful river that night. In the morning, the guy returned with two plates filled ham and eggs, hash browns and doughnuts. He also brought us a big thermos of coffee. We had a really great time on that fire."

As for Mouse's height, Bell never gave it much thought.

"Of course, you couldn't help but notice his size when you first met him. But he did his work really well. He was very strong. And what a sense of humor!"

Back at the smokejumper base, Mouse had a .44 Magnum handgun, apparently to ward off bears.

"It was about as big as he was. He polished it every night in the room."

Fortunately, Mouse never had to confront a grizzly with the weapon which was a mite light when it came to stopping those large bruins inhabiting the Far North.

Bell jumped on another Alaskan fire with Mouse, one burning in tussock grass.

"It's real hard to walk on – you got to keep stepping real high to get over those big humps of grass. If you walk a 100 yards in them you get tired. Well, Mouse was ahead of me carrying a big firepack box. I could see this firepack box moving over the tussocks but I couldn't see any head or legs. It looked like a firepack box moving by itself."

He laughed at the memory.

"I really liked Mouse," he said. "He had a great sense of humor. One night a mosquito kept buzzing my head. When he landed on the wall beside me, I let him have it and put my fist through the sheet rock. Mouse said, 'Did you get him?' And he started laughing real hard."

He stopped talking, noting it had been nearly four decades since his friend died.

"I wish he was still here," he said. "Everyone who knew him was very sad when they found out he had passed."

Indeed, he left many friends behind but none as close as Tom "Trooper Tom" Emonds who had gone to Portland that Labor Day weekend to visit a lady friend and pick up his pickup truck.

"I went to see my friend and a little before 2 o'clock that afternoon I closed my eyes and envisioned Mouse on my watch face, laughing," Emonds recalled. "Here I am with this girl and I'm being dominated by this thing with Mouse. She asked me, 'Troop, what are you doing?' I said I had to leave and headed back to Cave Junction. Driving south, I couldn't help but think about all the funny things Mouse had said and done."

The next day he attended the annual Labor Day parade in Cave Junction.

"I was there with my little boy in my arms," he said. "Gary Mills sees me and comes running over. He grabs my hand and he says, 'Troop, Mouse is dead.' It was like I had been hit with a hammer.

"I could not eat," he added. "I could not sleep. I had been through a war where many people were killed. I had been responsible for getting people killed, people who had saved my life in the war. But I never totally lost it until Mouse died. When I finally fell asleep, I would wake up hoping Mouse's death was all a bad dream. He was such an important person in my life. I literally reeked with grief."

Emonds later met with Larry Owen who showed him Mouse's death certificate.

"I looked at the time of death and saw he had died a little before 1 o'clock," he said. "Well, that was in Alaska. Down here, it was a little before 2 o'clock. That sent a chill up my back. I don't have a religious thing. I don't know what goes on after death. But it is remarkable that I envisioned him in the face of my watch to the minute when he was pronounced dead."

After Mouse was cremated, most of his ashes were dropped from the Beech aircraft over the Green Wall on the Illinois River. It was in the aircraft where John Denver's song, "Country Road" had been played ever since the Siskiyou jumpers had jumped back east. It was their theme song. Former Siskiyou jumper Garry Peters was the pilot.

"When I die, I want my ashes dumped with Mouse's ashes at the Green Wall," Emonds said, adding quietly. "He had such an impact on my life. Mouse was an incredibly good friend."

Tears flowed when he later read the eulogy he wrote for Mouse during the 1981 memorial at the Siskiyou base where an estimated 400 people gathered. Indeed, even all these years later, reading Larry's copy of Emonds' handwritten eulogy is enough to make your eyes glisten. It is heartfelt and powerful.

"The most famous legend, the most beloved of all smokejumpers is gone!" Emonds told the crowd. "Mouse touched jumpers throughout Alaska, the Siskiyous, the Cascades, the Sierra Nevadas, the Rockies, even the Ozarks and the Appalachians."

In a dozen fire seasons beginning in 1970, Mouse had made more than 260 fire jumps, Emonds noted.

"Wherever smokejumpers gathered – around cooking fires, under storm shelters in the Alaskan wilderness, at bars or kegger parties – the song of Mouse would be sung," he said, noting his good friend who weighed in at 120 pounds carried a gear bag weighing 145 pounds.

"Beneath this giant load two small but mighty legs pumped twice as fast as everyone else's," he told the crowd. "Two small but mighty lungs bellowed an endless stream of wise cracks no matter how hard, no matter how long the trail. A commercial pilot, a graduate forester, he understood and loved the water, the land, the animals, the sky. He was a national treasure."

In his journey through life, Mouse gravitated towards people of value, Emonds continued.

"People were his hobby – his greatest investment in life," he said.

As a former Marine who, like Mouse, spent three years in combat in Vietnam, Emonds was one of the few who had shared the dangerous path his friend had taken in war.

"He was the smallest ever to wear the eagle, globe and anchor," he said of the Corps' emblem. "He brought his humanity to the battlefield. His ordeals in fields of fire were seldom spoken of except to fellow Marines. For them, he shared a special loyalty, an unexplainable pride and kinship.

"To the battered people of a battered land the tiniest Marine was always 'Nho To Miang San' which translates 'Little Big Mouse Honorable Sir,'" he continued. "For it was he who had the biggest smile, the greatest heart and always 'C rats' for the children. He spoke their language, honored their customs."

He was referring to C rations which were given to troops in the 1960s.

Mouse was in Vietnam during the year of the sheep in 1967, the year of the monkey in 1968 and the year of the rooster in 1969, Emonds noted, adding, "All in combat, all in the most dangerous places in Vietnam."

Emonds observed that Mouse never married, never had children, but adopted the families of his friends.

"Hence the children of his friends became his flock," he said. "He was Uncle Al, the guy who wore a little light blue, skintight suit. He had a cape and a big 'S' on his chest. We once heard a little voice say, 'Mommy, is Uncle Al really Superman?'"

Noting that when Siskiyou jumpers gathered, Mouse was the master of ceremonies, he said.

"A fountain of wit and humor," he said. "A brilliant leader, our most dynamic teacher. Oh, Mouse! Oh, Uncle Al, you shared with us so much. How can we ever honor you the way we were so honored to be with you in life? Thank you for the laughter, dear man. For your kindness, dear, dear Mouse. We are all better for having mingled with you. We are so proud of you. You were so terribly, terribly special – so dear."

As only a former Marine and fellow smokejumper could, the man known as Trooper Tom bid his friend farewell.

"*Semper Fi* and keep your feet together, brother Mouse," he concluded, adding, "We'll be with you before very long."

Donald Saxon, Mouse's former ANGILCO commanding officer in Vietnam, wrote a letter of condolence on Sept. 16, 1981, to Allen's parents after learning of his friend's death. The former officer wrote of their friendship forged in war, creating one of the most poignant condolence letters ever penned.

"Allen was a very special person," he wrote, noting he first met him at Phan Thiet in Vietnam. "As a young Marine lieutenant, I was the officer in charge of an ANGLICO team. Sergeant Owen was the team chief. Allen and I had occasion to work together for the next several months and were involved in many operations and combat patrols.

"I think the combat environment tends to create an urgency in interpersonal relationships which might not otherwise exist," he added.

"Mommy, is Uncle Al really Superman?"

"As a result, Allen and I became very close friends in a short period of time. I am sure that by now you have heard many tales of Allen's bravery under fire and aggressiveness in battle. I personally observed Allen's performance in combat and can assure you that the descriptions of his bravery and courage are understatements. He was always ready to perform and always willing to assume the most difficult, arduous and dangerous tasks. My difficulty, if any with Allen, was in placing a mild damper on his aggressive enthusiasm."

But he noted his friend was more than enthusiastic.

"Within the same 24 hour period, I have seen Allen expose himself to hostile fire while bringing friendly artillery within 25 meters of his own location in order to effectively assault and eliminate an enemy position, and visit and provide candy for the children in the orphanage in Phan Thiet," he wrote. "The children loved Sergeant Owen."

Saxon indicated in the letter that Allen and he saw each other only a few times after completing their military hitches but made the most of each visit.

"Allen died as he lived," he wrote. "Adventure was his lifestyle. I suppose his pursuit of adventure was somewhat related to his diminutive physical stature. But Allen had nothing to prove to those of us who knew him. We knew the character of the man and loved him for it."

52

CLOSING BASE WAS SHORTSIGHTED

OBVIOUSLY, IT WILL NEVER BE known what impact the Siskiyou Smokejumper Base and its airborne firefighters would have had on the wildfires in the region if it had not closed down in the fall of 1981. We will never know how many wildfires would have been put out before they erupted into conflagrations. Nor will taxpayers ever know how much they would have saved in the long run.

But those who have studied wildfire patterns in the nearly four decades since it closed conclude there is no question vast amounts of resources and money would have been saved had the base remained open. In fact, if Siskiyou smokejumpers had been deployed to Biscuit Hill on the edge of the Kalmiopsis Wilderness less than a dozen air miles from the base on July 12, 2002, they say they would have made short work of the lightning-caused fire burning in an area of brush and scrubby pine trees. Instead, the fire gathered steam, becoming the Biscuit Fire which burned nearly half a million acres. At a suppression cost of hundreds of millions of dollars, it is the most expensive wildfire in the nation to date, they note.

There is no doubt in most former Siskiyou Smokejumper Base denizens that they saved countless taxpayer dollars when they dropped in to stop wildfires in their infant stage.

"Statistics prove this – it's not just my opinion," Gary Buck stressed. "From 1910 to 1942, the base wasn't open. They had over 20,000 acres burned a year on the Siskiyou on average. From 1943 when the base opened to 1981 [when it closed] it went down to an average 2,000 acres per year. From 1982 until now, after the base was closed, the average is more than 28,000 acres average burned a year. "

He argues the base should be reopened to save both forests and dollars.

"Smokejumping is the most efficient, remote initial attack system you can have," he said, noting that is still true some 80 years after the profession was launched. "Fixed wing aircraft can get to remote places faster than a helicopter and it is so much cheaper."

Most of the wildfires they fought were small, he said.

"But that was the beauty of the job. You put the fire out when it was small and prevent a lot of destruction while saving taxpayers a lot of money."

As a case in point, he is quick to point to the 2002 Biscuit Fire, the largest in the nation that year.

"If this base had been active, we could have easily put it out. It was started by two lightning strikes. The suppression cost for that fire was $480 million. And that's just suppression, not resources."

Although there were only about 28 smokejumpers at the base on most summer days, there were also jumpers from other bases in the northwest ready to back them up if need be, he said.

"And we were always ready to go to other regions – Alaska, Virginia or wherever – if they needed us. The idea was to get the fires out before they got big, becoming harder and more costly to put out.The standard definition of a smokejumper's mission is to parachute into inaccessible areas to suppress fires.

"The goal is to get in there quick and put fires out while they are small. That saves taxpayers a huge amount of money because it costs so much more to fight fires once they get big and more dangerous. It also saves natural resources and helps to protect rural communities." During the nearly four decades the base was open, about 700 acres on average burned each fire season on the Siskiyou National Forest, Buck observed, noting that amount has increased dramatically in the past 40 years.

"More than one million acres has burned on the Siskiyou forest alone since the base closed," he said. "With inflation, putting out what became the Biscuit fire would have paid for the base being open at least 700 years."

Even before the climate began to get hotter and drier, Siskiyou smokejumpers more than paid their way, he said.

"When we were here during fire season, we would often work 100 days at a time with no time off. We didn't get days off. The only way to get a day off was to call in sick and no one ever wanted to do that. You didn't want to let any of the other guys down."

There are currently nine smokejumping bases in the U.S., seven of which are operated by the U.S. Forest Service and two by the U.S. Bureau of Land Management, according to editor Sheley of the *Smokejumper Magazine*.

"Those smokejumpers are still doing what smokejumpers do," observed Wes Brown. "But you never hear about them because they are doing what they are supposed to do: put fires out before they get big. Nobody ever hears about those fires since they never grow big enough to get a name. There are 450 smokejumpers still out there, doing the job. They are the stealth firefighters."

Former Siskiyou jumper Mike Wheelock agreed with Buck that the base could have easily put the Biscuit Fire out had it still been in operation.

"When the Biscuit Fire hit, I told them if they didn't get on it, it would burn half a million acres," he said. "It was real dry and it was July. Sure enough, it got to 496,000 acres or so."

He believes there is plenty of blame to share, from the environmental community to forestry practices. The problem was an unnatural buildup of vegetation, he concluded.

"You have all these trees per acre, and then throw climate change and budget cuts in there, something has to give," he said. "I'm a firm believer that fires are part of the ecosystem. I do prescribed burning. But you can't just start lighting the forests on fire. There is too much smoke, too much burnable material."

There are also too many homes in and around forested areas, resulting in some folks balking at the smoke caused by prescribed burning to reduce the threat of a summer wildfire, he noted.

"I'm not saying any side is all right or all wrong but we need to come together. Our forests are becoming the victim of our politics. This country has to put aside politics if we are going to save what is still out there – old growth, owls, watersheds. These fires are going to keep happening, denuding more than the logging did."

In areas that are not commercially viable to log, thinning can both improve forest health and reduce the threat of a calamitous wildfire, said Wheelock who describes himself as a supporter of collaborative efforts to address the burning issue.

"We need a balance, to start looking at the big picture," he stressed.

Former Siskiyou jumper Mike Mann suggested a simple solution which he believes would save money and resources.

"If they would preposition jumpers here now when there is a thunderstorm, they could take care of fires relatively easy before they blow up," he observed of the Siskiyou base. "It would save taxpayers a lot as well as forests and probably some structures."

Former Siskiyou smokejumper Tom "Trooper Tom" Emonds, who went to Russia as part of a UN project in 1996 as part of an international effort to improve wildfire suppression efforts, echoed similar sentiments.

"In 2017, we lost more than 12,000 houses to wildfires," he said. "That is evidence we're not doing the right thing in fighting wildfires now. We need to work together to figure this thing out."

And he raised the concern that enemy saboteurs could attempt to ignite wildfires, reiterating that was the very reason the Siskiyou base was created in 1943.

"It doesn't take much of an imagination to do something like that," he said. "Using fire as a weapon was one of the things that Sun Tzu wrote about 2,500 years ago in the *Art of War*. Fire was the 12th principle of war."

Fortunately, when the Japanese attempted such an endeavor during World War II with a pilot using incendiary bombs, they chose a period when summer was waning and cool, wet weather had already set in on Oregon's coastal mountains, he observed.

"But with climate change, the forests in the West are much drier and fires much more dangerous," he said, adding he worries about the future of people living in fire-prone areas, particularly in the West.

"And I see people who should know something about adapting to this changing climate doing very little," he said. "I fear the country is in big trouble."

The problem, noted Emonds who has been developing firefighting tools since his smokejumping days, is that many fires start in light fuel such as dry grasses.

"Most people don't understand that the most dangerous fuels are these light fuels," he said. "When you have brown grass, low relative humidity and wind, you have a scenario that can be deadly."

He noted the infamous Mann Gulch fire was burning largely in light fuel, enabling it to race along, overcoming the escaping firefighters.

"This theory that you have to put the forest into intensive management doesn't cut it," he said. "With climate change, the problem is the fast and deep drying that is going on."

Deploying smokejumpers as first responders to remote wildfires, snuffing them out before they have a chance to become a threat, is one proven solution, he said.

"If they hadn't closed this base, jumpers from here could have stopped the Biscuit Fire when it was just a couple of trees burning," he said, echoing the concerns of his smokejumping brethren. "It would have been like so many fires we put out over the years. Nobody ever heard about them because they never got big enough to have a name."

THE MOUSE THAT SOARED

53

SMOKEJUMPER HISTORY LIVES ON

I F YOU ARE A MUSEUM buff who enjoys stepping into history, drop in on the Siskiyou Smokejumper Base Museum in southwest Oregon. As one of four bases built in 1943, the Siskiyou base was on the national ground floor of American smokejumping.

Restored and maintained largely by smokejumpers who worked out of the base until it closed at the end of the 1981 fire season, the facility retains much of its originality.

Indeed, the moment you pull into the parking area, you expect to hear the fire siren blare and see smokejumpers streaming out of the bunkhouse and beating feet to the twin-engine 1940-era Beechcraft jumper plane parked on the runway in front of the base headquarters. Any minute, you just know that old tail dragger will roar to life.

"This museum is incredible," said Ken Swift, son of legendary Siskiyou smokejumper Mick Swift. "I'm so glad the guys got together and did this. My dad would have loved it."

Smokejumper Base Museum entrance

The younger Swift helped move the antique Beechcraft airplane that jumpers once leaped out of when deployed to a fire. That aircraft will stay where it is in front of the base headquarters while another will be placed on a pedestal near the entrance to the airport.The twin-engine Beechcraft would only carry four jumpers while the larger DC-3 carried 12 to 16 airborne firefighters.

Among the visitors dropping in during one summer weekend was Grants Pass resident Kathryn Read and Nick and Holly Miller, both teachers from Fremont, Nebraska.

"I had no idea this museum was here," Read, then 52, said of the museum. "I grew up here in Josephine County but have been away until a year and a half ago. I was wondering what happened to the base and all the jumpers. This is wonderful."

The Millers had known little about smokejumpers until stopping by the base museum.

"Smokejumping isn't something that happens in Nebraska – we don't have a lot of trees," Holly Miller said. "So I had heard very little about smokejumpers or what they do."

But she saw something about the Siskiyou Smokejumper Museum on the internet while planning their trip and included it into their travels through the West.

"We decided to check it out," said Holly, then 27 and a music teacher. "It is an interesting place. For instance, I didn't know there was a bombing on the mainland during World War II until I found out about the incendiary bombs."

They were led through the museum by renown smokejumper Tom "Trooper Tom" Emonds.

"It was very interesting," observed Nick, also 27 at the time and a science teacher. "I was definitely not expecting to hear a firsthand account from someone who had actually jumped. I thought there would just be some pictures and a few informational signs.

"I teach chemistry and physics," he added. "When we talk about heat transfer, fire and firefighting would be an interesting way to talk about that. It also helps to keep students interested if you aren't just talking about the periodic table. This museum is about real life. Very impressive."

If you are at the museum on a weekend between March 15 and Nov. 15, your host will be a former Siskiyou smokejumper like Emonds. Each knows of what he speaks.

To close out this chapter, we'll turn to the smokejumper who has guided us thus far to take us on a tour through the base as it is today.

"I was here 12 years as a jumper and more than 15 years with the base museum," Gary Buck said of the museum which opened in 2004. "Smokejumping and this base has been a big part of my life."

The museum's mission is to preserve the unique history of the Siskiyou base while increasing public awareness and its contribution to the history of American smokejumping. There is no admission fee, although donations are welcome.

"We want to keep it free to the public. Some have suggested we charge five dollars or so per person. But we would rather not do that. We've had vans pull up with four or five kids and their parents. You can tell the kids are excited but the parents always ask how much the fee is to see the museum. When we tell them there is no charge, everyone piles out. We want to keep it that way so everyone will have the opportunity to know the history of this base. This museum is so unique. All the buildings are original. And we have the jumpsuits, parachutes, old sewing machines we used to repair gear – every tool we used."

When you step inside the parachute loft, built in 1948, making it the oldest still standing on any smokejumper base on the continent, you will see the original paraphernalia smokejumpers needed to complete their mission, including parachutes, climbing gear, fire packs and jump suits. What's more, each suit has the name of the jumper who wore it, just as it did 40 years ago.

"We were firefighters quickly responding to a fire," Buck said of the need for the name tags. "You only had so much time to run up and grab your suit and get on that plane so you had to know instantly which one was yours."

While giving me a tour when I first started working on this book, he stopped for a moment to look at the jumper suit which looked like it was made for a boy.

"This one belonged to Mouse," he said as he reached up to affectionately tug on a sleeve of the suit once worn by the shortest ever smokejumper in the nation as well as a good friend to all who jumped with him.

Buck stepped into the old headquarters building, circa 1936. It was originally at the district ranger headquarters in nearby Cave Junction until it was moved to its present site in 1961.

"The jumpers used this building down there in 1943," he said. "They were trucked out here to jump fires. During World War II, the jumpers were conscientious objectors who lived in tents at the ranger station in Cave Junction."

Buck recalled when the parachute loft bustled with the noise of sewing machines repairing torn chutes.

"We had big sewing machines when I got here. Smokejumpers did the packing, repairing and all the sewing."

Jump gear, harness, cargo bags and other items were all made in the loft, he added.

The sewing machines lined up in the loft are industrial strength machines, mind you, the kind that is capable of mending a tough jump suit or leather harnesses.

In the middle of the loft is a repair table about 30 feet long which was used to repair parachutes. It was not uncommon to walk in and see a muscular smokejumper with calloused hands gently sewing a parachute or even mending a torn shirt, Buck said.

"A lot of guys became very good at using these machines," he said of the jumpers-temporarily-turned-tailors. No doubt they weren't made fun of since it could have resulted in the joker having his nostrils stitched together.

When using the repair table, a jumper would first spread the torn chute on it.

"We would take a thread picker and take out the thread in the seam all the way around," Buck said. "Then we would take the new material, lay it down and pin and tack it, then sew it in."

At one point, the base had 17 industrial sewing machines, all of which were used by the smokejumpers, Buck recalled.

"I never met a smokejumper who knew how to sew before becoming a smokejumper," he said. "But many learned to sew after learning to jump. You had to repair your chute and jump gear."

Of course, there was an occasional accident when an energetic young man running a sewing machine tried to get the job done a little faster than was prudent, he said, noting one friend drove a needle through his thumb.

"But he was fine – smokejumpers are tough," he said.

Still, he allowed the scream from a normal humanoid would have been heard a mile away.

"They didn't use sewing machines as much when the materials started changing," he said. "With jump suits, they went from canvas to cotton to nylon to Nomex material which was more fire resistant. Now they are using Kevlar."

A jumper wearing Kevlar has a better chance of not being harpooned by a sharp limb, he noted.

He picked up two signal streamers which were kept in a leg pocket in case of emergencies.

"Each one has a code on it," Buck explained. "You could pull one out if your radio didn't work and signal the aircraft."

The code is quite specific. For instance, you would fashion a "6" out of the streamer if someone had a broken back.

"Every jumper had two of these so you could make a big '6' out of these streamers if you needed to," he said.

In addition to the tools, there is also an impressive array of historic photographs on display, giving visitors a view of everything from looking out the airplane door to smokejumpers on the ground battling fires. Beware: you may also see a couple of shots of jumpers flying the Gobi salute but remember it meant good luck to the Siskiyou crew back in the day.

"Normally, we had 28 smokejumpers here," Buck said of fire season. "But we've had up to 150 jumpers here at times when we had a big fire bust."

The Siskiyou base was among the four original smokejumper bases in the United States, along with one in Missoula, Montana; McCall, Idaho; and Winthrop, Wash.

"This base is the only one of the original four that has the original buildings still standing. You look at this architecture here. You can't find it anywhere else now because the rest of the original lofts built like this are all gone."

The first jumpers at the base, conscientious objectors followed by World War II veterans, all used silk parachutes, Buck said.

"The silk chutes had a very dramatic shock to them when they opened up. They just about knocked your head off. The conscientious objectors were here in '43, '44 and '45. In 1946, we started getting a whole bunch of 101st Airborne, 82nd Airborne and Marine airborne jumpers who basically took over this base."

The silk chutes were replaced with nylon ones which opened less abruptly, he said.

"When it comes out slowly, it doesn't jerk you around so much," he explained.

He picked up a bag which contained a parachute, noting it allowed the chute to emerge slowly, thus reducing the jerk.

"Everything here had an important purpose," he said, adding that changes were made as better gear was developed.

"For instance, now they use the square chutes," he said. "Mick Swift was the one who really started the square program even though he wasn't jumping in Alaska where they started it. It was the Bureau of Land Management that started using square chutes in Alaska. Mick went to the boss up there and told him about the square chutes, how they would work better for the jumpers. That was just another story about the way Mick got involved in things. He got things done."

He noted that it is about 40 feet from the top of the chute to the jumper.

"You are going to be landing in trees about 25 percent of the time. It doesn't matter how good a jumper you are, how good the pilot is, how good the spotter is. If you land in a 40-foot tree, you will likely have your feet on the ground. If might mean you just have extra work getting your chute out. Of course, you go to the fire first."

If you are caught in a taller tree, a jumper deploys what is known as the let-down rope which, as the name suggests, is intended to be used to drop safely to the ground.

"We started with a 150-foot rope but we ended up with a 250-footer because people caught in trees were coming down and discovering the ropes were too short," Buck said, adding, "You sure don't want that."

He picked up a drift streamer. In the early days of smokejumping, radio communication was not readily available, he observed.

"We didn't have a lot of radios at first," Buck said of the early years of smokejumping. "What we did have was the drift streamers to check the wind, then the signal streamers when we hit the ground.

"The spotter in the plane will be working with the first jumper out," he said, noting the spotter is always a veteran jumper. "He is also working with the pilot, trying to coordinate getting these guys in. They throw out the drift streamers first and pick out the best spot closest to the fire for them to land."

With the colored signal streamers, a smokejumper could signal the aircraft if there were any injuries or other information that required action on their part. A code written on a signal streamer told the smokejumper what sign he needed to spell out on the ground to send the correct message to the aircraft crew.

"You could signal the aircraft if there was an injury or if you needed food, water, chainsaw – things like that," Buck said.

He stopped talking for a moment as he surveyed the gear he and the more than 400 smokejumpers once used in their mission to stop wildfires in their fiery tracks.

"This is a special place for us," he concluded. "Everything here was used by smokejumpers. We all feel like we made a difference."

54

SISKIYOU JUMPERS
OWN IT

THE WORD THAT CAME TO mind upon receiving the news was petrichor, that pleasant smell arising upon the first rainfall following a long dry spell. Indeed, that must have been the feeling of former Siskiyou smokejumpers at the tail end of 2018.

But it wasn't rain that put them in good spirits. Nearly 40 years after Mouse died and the Siskiyou Smokejumper Base closed, the former smokejumpers became the proud owners of the historic place they once called home. In addition to purchasing the nine historic structures, the Siskiyou Smokejumper Museum Board signed what amounts to a 100-year lease with Josephine County for the 3 ½-acre parcel containing the historic structures.

The official agreement with the Josephine County Board of Commissioners, unanimously approved by the board, means the history of the nation's smokejumping legacy in southern Oregon will live on long after the jumpers, now all in their 60s or older, have leaped into the great beyond.

"The acquisition gives us more security in terms of getting grants and similar support," explained Gary Buck, the museum board president. "If people know that the old base is safe and will be cared for over a long period, they are much more willing to support it. They know it will be here for a very long time."

The building acquisitions and the long-term lease demonstrate that the smokejumpers' tenacity and willingness to take on a challenge should never be underestimated, he added.

"When we started working on trying to save the base, a lot of people never thought we would be able to do it. They figured it was a lost cause. Well, they underestimated us."

Yet he allowed that, shortly after the turn of the century, the fate looked bleak for the former base named to the National Register of Historic Places in 2010.

"Back around 2000 or so, the county was going to bulldoze it all because they didn't have enough money, people and time to take care of it. But, in addition to our relationship with the place, we felt it was an important part of local history as well as national history."

Still, the county was serious. In fact, the original barracks, built out of lumber salvaged from the Civilian Conservation Corps barracks along Grayback Creek near the Oregon Caves National Monument, were torn down at the county's behest around 2000, he said.

"That has all changed now," Buck said. "We are going to be able to preserve the smokejumper base."

There was a sigh of relief within the former smokejumper community.

"It's wonderful to know the jumpers now have the ability to preserve the base," observed former jumper Larry Owen, Mouse's brother. "The first thing that crossed my mind when I found out about it was that Allen would have been really happy to see that happen. The base meant so much to him."

A former Siskiyou jumper whose name was not made public donated the money to purchase the property. Total cost was $281,000, including $181,000 for the structures and the rest for the leases and a deposit for making critical repairs. Two consecutive 50-year leases will ensure the acreage containing the buildings will be controlled for a century by the smokejumpers and those who follow in their footsteps, Buck said.

The agreement came just in the nick of time because a 10-year lease for the museum between the smokejumper board and the county was ending at the end of 2018.

"We talked to Simon Hare who grew up here in the valley and has been a supporter of the museum," Buck said of a county commissioner at the time. "We were thankful for all his help."

In a Dec. 22, 2018, article in the *Grants Pass Daily Courier* newspaper, Hare, whose term was coming to an end and he was not running for re-election, discussed how he became involved in preserving the historic site.

"I have a long-standing family connection to the smokejumpers, so they really wanted to work with me on this," Hare told the *Courier*. "I just put the package together . . . It was important to them to get this done before I was out of office.

"We're trying to add an element of security, sustainability and the idea that they're not going anywhere," he added, referring to the base structures. "It's a great deal for all parties concerned."

The nine buildings include the warehouse, parachute loft, headquarters office, saw shack, cook house, barracks, bath house, small residence and garage. Most were built during the 1940s or shortly thereafter.

"A lot of them were paid for by Dwight Eisenhower," Buck said, reiterating that base commander Jim Allen had contacted the president to request the funding for building the structures. "Eisenhower really liked the smokejumper program."

The headquarters building was previously the Redwood Ranger District station in Cave Junction. It was dismantled and moved to its present site shortly after the base was established.

"The base was originally called the Redwood Smokejumper Base," he explained, noting it quickly adopted the Siskiyou moniker to clarify its area of operation.

"They didn't get power out here until the late 1940s," he added. "That's when they really started building here."

The rustic parachute loft built in Cave Junction was torn down and the current loft erected in 1949. The remaining barracks building was built in 1954.

"Preserving the base is still a challenge," he said. "These buildings are old. The headquarters building is about 80 years old and the loft is around 70. But we are ones who saved the old buildings after the base closed. When they needed repair, we paid for all of that. We will continue that, of course."

The bottom line, he stressed, is that owning the structures makes repairing them much easier.

"The fate of the buildings is now secure because we own them. Owning the buildings is a great step for us in terms of preserving the smokejumper legacy."

After the base closed following the 1981 fire season, the Forest Service bequeathed the property to the county.

"The county will continue to use the airstrip – there is no change there," Buck noted.

Nor is there a change in the enthusiastic support by former smoke-jumpers to protect the base, he indicated.

"We've still got roughly 200 guys who jumped out of here who are still alive," Buck said. "Some of these guys are 90 years old or more. Others are in their 70s and 80s. They aren't as mobile as they used to be but they are durable and they support what we are doing here. This base means a lot to them."

Noting that several adult children of former Siskiyou smokejumpers are now on the board, Buck said the goal is to have the next generation step in to preserve the base and its history when the former jumpers have sprung from this mortal coil.

"There is a lot of history here, both on a local and national level," he said. "We intend to preserve it for posterity. This place has an incredible story to tell."

T HE FOLLOWING IS THE LIST of the 434 smokejumpers who served at the Siskiyou base from 1943 through 1981. Those who transferred from another smokejumper base to the Siskiyou but did not rookie there have a "T" following their name.

1943

Walter R. Buller	43, 44
Kenneth A. Diller	43, 44
Marvin W. Graeler	43, 44
Jack G. Heintzelman	43-45
Calvin A. Hilty	43, 44
Charles R. Hudson	43, 44
Gus I. Jansen	43, 44
William S. Laughlin	43, 44
Gerrit A. Rozeboom	43, 44
Winton H. Stucky	43
Floyd F. Yoder	43, 44

1944

Elmer W. Neufeld	44
Robert H. Painter	44
Arthur C. Penner	44

1945

Elon H. Eash	45
Roger L. Frantz	45
Chalmer C. Gillin	45
Albert L. Gray	45
Millard W. Green	45-50
John L. Harnish	45
Donald F. Hostetler	45
Arthur S. Hoylman	45
Daniel N. Kauffman	45
Willard S. Krabill	45
Clarence Leasenbury	45
Ray J. Mast	45
Emerson Miller	45
Leonard Pauls	45
Dale R. Yoder (T)	45

1946

Ed Adams	46-47
Ralph Clark	46
Tommy Cornell	46
Richard J. Courson	46-50
Bob Gerling	46
Millard W. Green (T)	46-50
Paul Hankins	46
Andrew Henry	46-47
Herbert Krissie	46-49
Fred Logan	46
Merle Lundrigan (T)	46
Cliff Marshall	46-53
James Middleton	46
Len Miguel	46
Danny On	46-47, 52-53
Daniel J. O'Rourke	46
Ray Phillips	46

Clem L. Pope	46		John Meyers	48
Neil T. Shier	46-47		Bill Padden	48-53
Paul P. Siler	46		Bob Richardson	48
Ken Smith	46		Armand O. Riza	48-49
Tom Steel	46		Robert A. Snyder	48-51
John O. Thach	46		Ward V. Speaker	48
Calvin Thompson	46		Robert E. Sweet	48-49
Wilber Wasson	46		K.J. Westphall	48
Francis Webb	46		Roger D. Wolfertz	48-49

1947

1949

Leroy Barnes	47		Dick Bethel	49
William Beaird	47		Hobbie W. Bonnett	49
Harry L. Cummings (T)	47		Albert N. Boucher	49-54
Albert H. Devoe	47			57-63
Terry Fieldhouse	47-50		Bud Falk	49
Charles Foster	47-48		Bert Foster	49
Lyle J. Hoffman	47-48		Delmar E. Jaquish	49, 51
Harold Lahr	47		Larry Looper	49
Walter McNally	47		Orville C. Looper	49-56
Robert L. Nolan	47-50		Fred Michelotti	49-50
Alfred Rosin	47		Lowell Scalf	49-50
			Robert J. Scofield	49-50
1948				53-55
Jack Barrett	48		Donald E. Wallace	49-50
Paul Block	48-50			
Charles Clemensen	48-49		**1950**	
Richard B. Cole	48-50		Andre Brunette	50, 53
Robert N. Cummings	48-49		Bob Butler	50
Arthur T. Honey	48		Henry "Buzz" G. Florip	50-51
Starr Jenkins	48		Joe Gardner	50
Gudmond Kaarhus	48		John Harns	50
Paul G. Kovaleff	48-49		Edgar Hinkle	50-51
Robert A. Moffitt	48-49			53

John Lovejoy	50	Glen Sheppard	51	
William O. Lovejoy	50	George Wilson	51	
Hallie E. Norton	50	Bill Wright	51	
Wilford L. Olsen	50	**1952**		
R.H. Proctor	50			
Maurice Robertson	50	Donald L. Basey	52	
Willi Unsoel	50	Jay T. Brazie	52	
1951		Bill Clarke	52	
		Gordon Cook	52	
Richard Allewett	51	Leroy Crippen	52-53	
Louis A. Banta	51-52	Jimmie F. Dollard	52-54	
Roy L. Belli	51	Thomas A. Elwood	52,	
Paul M. Bryce	51-52		54-55	
	56, 58	Axel A. Johnson (T)	52	
Philip E. Clarke	51-53	William E. Kester	52-53	
55-56		John R. Lindlan	52-54	
Gilbert L. Coody	51	Paul Lukens	52	
Gordon C. Cross	51-52	Delano Lund	52	
54		Harold W. Meili	52	
Paul L. Dominick	51	Dick Merrill	52	
Steve Downer	51	Bob Ramsey	52	
David Goblirish	51	Phil Smith	52	
Dick Gregory	51	**1953**		
Don Hansen	51			
Charles Harter	51	James A. Allen (T)	53-65	
	54-58	Bill Arrington	53	
Bobby G. Johnston	51	Calvin Austin	53	
Lamar Lecompte	51, 54	Bill. B. Buck	53	
Eddie Ledbetter	51	Don Chapman	53	
Darwin T. Miller	51	Robert G. Crick	53-56	
Bob Newberry	51-54	Mel Greenup	53-55	
Roger E. Newton	51-58	Richard Harris (T)	53	
Clarence Rowley	51-54	Art Jacobs	53	
John Shallenberger	51	H. James Oleson	53-56	

Mel M. Palmquist	53	Harold L. Werner (T)	55
Stuart A. Roosa	53	Jim C. Yandell	55-56
Ernie Showers	53		58
Robert E. Wood	53-55		
James L. Wright	53-55	**1956**	
		David E. Arnold	56-57
1954		Richard L. Board	56,
Glen A. Botkin	54		61-62
Jim Ferrell	54-55	William B. Brophy	56
Jack D. Heiden	54	Murray Brunt	56
Phillip M. Hodge	54-56	Jim Edison	56-57
Robert G. Lewis	54	Jim Eggers	56
James R. Moore	54-54	Joe Emory	56-57
Joe Spalinger	54	Jimmie H. Hardisty	56
Douglas P. Stinson	54-55	George Koehler	56
Thomas F. Tincoff	54	Keith Morrill	56
Warren L. Webb	54-56	Ronald Price	56-59
		Linwood Reed	56
1955		Floyd G. Rogers	56
Robert G. Berry	55-57	Doug Sutherland	56
Charles Buckner	55-56	Eldo "Mick" W. Swift	56,
Bob Calverley	55		62-65
Jim Dail	55		69-77
Milan Ferry	55-58	Richard L. Wessell	56-61
Dan Hayes	55		66-72
Robert L. Kester	55-56	Kenneth R. Wicks	56
Jim Kesterson	55	Lawrence J. Wright	56-57
John T. Koester	55-56		59-62
Jack Long	55		
William E. Long	55	**1957**	
Leonard W. Macatee	55-56	Harvey Allen	57
Harold J. Maxwell	55-56	Ralph Bryant	57-58
Gideon Newton	55-58	Michael J. Byrne	57-59
	60	Ron Cherry	57

Lee Gossett	57, 62	Fred L. Cramer	59-65
Robert A. Harrison	57	James L. Fritz	59-64
Ray Hull	57	Richard L. Groom	59-60
Gordon L. Kellogg	57, 61	Charles R. Mansfield	59-69
John R. McDaniel	57-59	Glen W. McBride	59-60
Ronald B. Nelson	57	Gary L. Meredith	59
Ernie Nicholson	57	Gerhard H. Mortensen	59, 63
Norman E. Pawlowski	57-61	Michael E. Mulligan	59
	64	Hugh G. Rosenberg	59
Ken Rosenburg	57-61	Chuck Sheley	59-66
Wayne G. Shrunk	57	David H. Slagle	59
Donald O. Thomas	57-58	Gardner P. Smith	59
Robert D. Tyson	57-58	Benny R. Tucker	59-60
Jack Vines	57-58		
Carroll Zachary	57	**1960**	

1958

		Alvin F. Baker	60-61
		Phillip G. Beardslee	60-62
William G. Byrne	58	Charles A. Crowley	60
Ted. E. Cook	58-59	Ronald L. Donaca	60
James L. Cramer	58-59	John C. Helmer (T)	60
Phil Harvey	58	William M. Knight	60-63
Michael A. Lehman	58-59	Ronald L. Lufkin	60-62
	61	Michael H. McCracken	60-61
Richard E. Light	58-59	William L. Olesen	60-62
Clifford E. McKeen	58-59	Jim Page	60
John P. Murchison	58	Bill Peay	60
John S. Murray	58	Jack J. Ridgway	60-61
Jerry R. Reid	58-59	Cecil O. Riffe	60-61
Bill Roberts	58	Michael B. Simon	60-62
William R. Ruskin	58	Ron Thoreson	60-61
		Roger D. Towers	60
1959			62-64
		Jan Vanwagtendunk	60-61
Russell R. Beem	59	Gary E. Welch	60-62
Don M. Cramer	59		

Dennis W. Wheeler	60-61	**1963**	
1961		George R. Bliss	63
		James B. Grubs	63-64
Paul P. Boyer	61-64	Allen B. Hill	63-64
Truman L. Sandelin	61-62	Larry C. Lufkin	63-67
	64		69-71
Tommy L. Smith	61-64	Bill Moseley	63
	66-67	Garry R. Peters	63-66
Bernie R. Welch	61	Larry J. Peters	63-64
	64	James F. Schmidt	63
Larry D. Welch	61-62	George M. Straw	63-64
	69,		66
	73-75		
1962		**1964**	
		Tom Albert	64
Gilbert H. Boundy	62-63		66-69
William J. Denton	62-63	Leroy Cook	64-66,
Ronald E. Garner	62-63		70-71
Clifford W. Hamilton	62-65	Ray Farinetti	64, 66
Jere A. Hancock	62		70-73
Doug Hopkins	62-65	Michael V. Johnson	64-65
Jerry P. John	62-63	Edgar R. Jones	64-65
	65	John P. Kirkley	64-65
Steven T. Johnson	62-63	J. Keith Lockwood	64, 66
	65	Patrick McMahon	64
Peter R. Landis	62-64	Terry M. Mewhinney	64,
John L. Manley	62-63		66-69
	65		75-77
Charles E. Moseley	62-63	Warren Pierce	64
Tom A. Pettigrew	62	Eric T. Schoenfield	64-66
James S. Roberts	62-63		72
Jerry E. Schmidt	62-63	Ed Weissenback	64
Hal K. Ward	62-65	Dick Zedicker	64

1965

Terry Cowart	65
Terry Egan	65-68
Harold Hartman	65-66, 70-72
Jerry W. Howe	65-66
Jon T. Klingel	65
Myron B. Kreidler	65
Leon Oswalt	65-68, 70-72
Thomas Reeves	65
Douglas Robinson	65
John E. Robison	65-67 70-73
Alex A. Theios	65-66 69

1966

Wesley A. Brown	66-78 60
Jerry L. Brownwood	66
Gary J. Buck	66-67 71-80
Delos Dutton (T)	66-74
Tom "Troop" Emonds	66-67 71-80
Emett C. Grijalva	66 74-78
Ronald D. McMinimy (T)	66-77
Gary L. Mills	66-80
Joe. A. Niesen	66-67 70-72
James C. Tomasini	66
David B. Ward	66-68

Louis H. Wayers	66-71

1967

Doug J. Bucklew	67-68 72-75
Robert E. Bunn	67
Daniel A. Casey	67
Dale D. Gardner	67
Robert B. Hooper	67 70-76 78
Jerry A. Katt	67-69
Robert G. Lowden	67 70-72
Robert H. McCray	67-73
Patrick T. McNally	67-74
Stephen W. O'Dell	67-70
John T. Remley	67
Jay D. Scott	67
Gary E. Sharp	67
Lee W. Smith	67-69
Ray Zander	67

1968

Gregory W. Barnes	68
Allen J. Bersaglier	68-69
John S. Casad	68-69
Walter S. Congleton	68-81
Thomas H. Greiner (T)	68-69
Chris R. Hartman	68
James A. Miller	68-69
Lawrence Oliver	68-76
David P. Oswalt	68-80
Gary W. Thornhill	68-79

James Vroman 68-70
Alex A. Wold 68
74-77

1969

Claude A. Greiner (T) 69
Samuel L. Greiner (T) 69
Wes R. Nicholson 69-81

1970

David E. Atkin 70-72
74-79
Roddy K. Baumann 70-75
Douglas C. Beck 70-78
Ernest Carlson 70
Stan Collins (T) 70-72
74-76
Michael W. Leclercq 70
Allen D. Owen 70-80
Ralph E. Rhodes 70-72
Michael Russo (T) 70-71
David S. Warren 70

1971

Fernando J. Abeita 71

1973

Steve A. Baumann 73-81
Francisco C. Cablayan 73-77
George W. Custer 73-74
W. Roy Floch 73-76
David G. Laws (T) 73-74
Michael L. Mann 73-77
Raymond Osipovich 73-81

Dain M. Smith 73-76

1974

Gary A. Cote 74-76
Thomas Koyama 74-77

1975

Pat Armijo 75
Dean Cernick (T) 75-79
Rick Dees 75-77
80
Edwin D. Floate (T) 75-79
Daniel A. Marsh (T) 75

1976

Richard Dehart 76-78
Greg Gonzalez 76-79
Michael J. Hardy (T) 76, 79
Peter D. Hawley 76-81
John K. Hughes 76-77
Willard Lowden (T) 76-77
80
Steve Mankle 76-78
Robert J. McCann 76-78
Larry Owen 76-77
Robert Terrell 76-78
Loy Tucker 76
Warren D. Villa 76-77
Eric Ward 76
Mike D. Wheelock 76-78
80

1977

Howard T. Clark 77-78

1978

Michael G. Apicello	78, 80
Art N. Benefiel (T)	78-79
Donald G. Bisson	78-81
Joe E. Budenholzer	78
Theo Collins	78-79
Robert Lightly (T)	78-81
Mark Miller (T)	78-79
Ron Versteeg	78-80
Robert G. Wilken 7	8-79

1979

Richard Blackwood	79, 81
Don Campbell (T)	79
Pat Davis	79-80
Ralph Dickenson	79
Jamie W. Floyd	79-80
Jeff Neal	79-80
Donald Rees	79
Tom K. Smit	79
Paul L. Williams (T)	79

1980

Tom Hunnicutt (T)	80
Patrick Withen (T)	80-81

1981

Jerry J. Hunter (T)	81

THE MOUSE THAT SOARED

ABOUT THE AUTHOR

Contrary to what he sometimes tell folks with tongue held firmly in cheek, the author wasn't actually raised by wolves in the wild. But it is true his grandparents homesteaded in Southern Oregon, and that he and his siblings, like their father and his siblings, were born and reared in the region where they all ran rampant in the mountains, making wolves exceedingly nervous. After an uneventful hitch in the Marine Corps and what he describes as a less than stellar scholastic performance at the University of Oregon, he managed to obtain a degree in journalism. Over the subsequent decades, he was able to convince more than a dozen newspaper editors from Alaska to California to hire him, decisions which he hopes did not leave a permanent blemish on their careers. Upon retiring to become a recovering journalist at the end of 2013, he immediately fell off the wagon and started writing books. *Up Sterling Creek Without a Paddle* was his first non-fiction book, followed by *Madstone* and *The Mouse That Soared.* He lives happily with his wife, Maureen, in rural Oregon.

www.hellgatepress.com

Made in the USA
Las Vegas, NV
13 July 2022

51528968R00252